JOYCE

The Return of the Repressed

JOYCE

The Return of the Repressed

Edited by Susan Stanford Friedman

CORNELL UNIVERSITY PRESS, ITHACA AND LONDON

First published 1993 by Cornell University Press.

International Standard Book Number 0-8014-2799-1 (cloth)
International Standard Book Number 0-8014-8073-6 (paper)
Library of Congress Catalog Card Number 92-54966

PRINTED IN THE UNITED STATES OF AMERICA

*Librarians: Library of Congress cataloging information appears
on the last page of the book.*

⊗ The paper in this book meets the minimum requirements of
the American National Standard for Information Sciences—
Permanence of Paper for Printed Library Materials, ANSI
Z39.48-1984.

For my mother, who loved butterflies
Anne Thompson Stanford
1917–1992

Contents

Acknowledgments

This volume on Joyce began in my desire to travel, which led first to the 1986 Joyce Symposium in Copenhagen and then to the 1988 Joyce Symposium in Venice. I would not have been able to edit a book on Joyce without the generous support and encouragement of many Joyceans at these conferences who welcomed a new voice in their community. I particularly thank Jane Marcus (for getting me to Copenhagen), Marilyn L. Brownstein (for helping me formulate the topic for my panels in Venice), Phillip Herring (for sharing his great knowledge of Joyce and his library of Joyce criticism), Robert Spoo (for helpful orientations to the Joyce world), and the Women's Caucus of the Joyce Society (for supporting the work of scholars like me on Joyce and modernism). I also thank Bernhard Kendler of Cornell University Press for his support and guidance and the anonymous readers of this volume for their insightful critiques and encouragement. And I appreciate the efforts of the organizers of the 1988 Joyce Symposium in Venice: Rosa Maria Bolletieri Bosinelli, Carla Marengo, and Christine van Boheemen. I must also acknowledge the permission of Rosa Maria Bolletieri Bosinelli, Carla Marengo, Christine van Boheemen, and John Benjamins Press for allowing me and Joseph A. Boone to include in this volume expanded versions of our conference papers, which they have included in their conference volume, *The Languages of Joyce* (Amsterdam and Philadelphia: John Benjamins, 1992). Finally, I thank the contributors to this volume for so graciously accepting my suggestions; they were a dream to work with.

S. S. F.

Abbreviations for Texts by James Joyce

CP	*Collected Poems*
CW	*The Critical Writings of James Joyce*
D	*Dubliners*
E	*Exiles*
FW	*Finnegans Wake,* cited by page and line number
Letters	*Letters of James Joyce*
P	*A Portrait of the Artist as a Young Man*
	A Portrait of the Artist as a Young Man: Text, Criticism, and Notes
SH	*Stephen Hero*
SL	*Selected Letters of James Joyce*
U	*Ulysses,* 1961 Random House edition cited by page number; 1984 and 1986 Hans Walter Gabler editions cited by episode and line number

Introduction

Susan Stanford Friedman

Joyce: The Return of the Repressed is a collection of essays on James Joyce's work which probes the various ways his texts can be read as sites of repression and insistent return. Working broadly and differently under the umbrella of psychoanalysis and poststructuralism, the authors of the essays read Joyce's texts as scenes of writing and reading in which the psychodynamics of repression, disguised expression, and fragmentary return can be interpreted or at least scrutinized. The central questions explored are founded on the concepts of the textual and political unconscious developed by such theorists and critics as Julia Kristeva, Jacques Lacan, Jacques Derrida, Shoshana Felman, Jonathan Culler, Fredric Jameson, Peter Brooks, and Michael Riffaterre. With varying emphasis the contributors examine the interconnections between and among the psychic and the political, the textual and the historical, the erotic and the linguistic. Adapting different methodologies to a common project, the authors incorporate concepts and interpretive strategies from psychoanalytic criticism, feminist criticism, new historicism, African-American criticism, deconstruction, narrative theory, Marxist criticism, cultural studies, and textual criticism. Finally, the collection includes essays on substantial portions of Joyce's oeuvre, including *Stephen Hero, Dubliners, A Portrait of the Artist as a Young Man, Ulysses,* and *Finnegans Wake.*

Poststructuralists—both within and outside the Joycean fold— have accelerated in recent years the project of rereading Joyce within the framework of recent developments in literary theory

loosely conjoined with the poststructuralist emphasis on the materiality and significance of language in inscriptions of desire, subjectivity, the social order, and history. Margot Norris's *Decentered
Universe of "Finnegans Wake"* (1976), Colin MacCabe's *James Joyce
and the Revolution of the Word* (1979), and the collection edited by
Derek Attridge and Daniel Ferrer, *Post-Structuralist Joyce: Essays
from the French* (1984) pioneered the rich possibilities of reading
Joyce in conjunction with poststructuralist theory and, conversely,
of reading theory in the light of Joyce's modernist and postmodernist projects. Beginning with Bernard Benstock's *James Joyce: The
Augmented Ninth,* a collection based on the 1984 Joyce Symposium, the volumes based on the annual Joyce symposia have increasingly represented a strong contingent of Joyceans who are
adapting various poststructuralist strategies to the reading of Joyce.
The 1989 special issue on feminist readings of Joyce of *Modern
Fiction Studies,* edited by Ellen Carol Jones, systematically combines feminist inquiry with poststructuralist theory, and *Joyce between Genders: Lacanian Views,* the Fall 1991 special issue of the
James Joyce Quarterly, edited by Sheldon Brivic, grounds psychoanalytic readings of Joyce in Lacan. And since the early 1980s many
individual studies have used poststructuralist theory to probe the
textuality, sexuality, and intertextuality of Joyce's oeuvre.[1]

1. See for example, Margot Norris, *The Decentered Universe of "Finnegans Wake"*
(Baltimore: Johns Hopkins University Press, 1976); Colin MacCabe, *James Joyce and the
Revolution of the Word* (London: Macmillan, 1979); Derek Attridge and Daniel Ferrer,
eds., *Post-Structuralist Joyce: Essays from the French* (Cambridge: Cambridge University
Press, 1984); Morris Beja, Phillip Herring, Maurice Harmon, and David Norris, eds., *James
Joyce: The Centennial Symposium* (Urbana: University of Illinois Press, 1986); Bernard
Benstock, ed., *James Joyce: The Augmented Ninth* (Syracuse: Syracuse University Press,
1988); Bonnie Kime Scott, ed., *New Alliances in Joyce Studies: "When It's Aped to Foul
a Delfian"* (Newark: University of Delaware Press, 1988); Morris Beja and Shari Benstock,
eds., *Coping with Joyce: The Copenhagen Symposium* (Columbus: Ohio State University
Press, 1989); Christine van Boheemen, ed., *Joyce, Modernity and Its Mediation: European
Joyce Studies, I* (Amsterdam: Rodopi, 1989); Derek Attridge, ed., *The Cambridge Compan-
ion to James Joyce* (Cambridge: Cambridge University Press, 1990); Ellen Carol Jones, ed.,
Feminist Readings of Joyce, special issue of *Modern Fiction Studies* 35 (Autumn 1989);
Sheldon Brivic, ed., *Joyce between Genders: Lacanian Views,* special issue of *James Joyce
Quarterly* 29 (Fall 1991); Christine van Boheemen, Rosa Maria Bollettieri Bosinelli, and
Carla Marengo, eds., *The Languages of Joyce* (Amsterdam: John Benjamins, 1992). For
recent individual studies using poststructuralism, see, for example, Patrick McGee, *Pa-
perspace: Style as Ideology in Joyce's Ulysses* (Lincoln: University of Nebraska Press,
1988); Frances L. Restuccia, *Joyce and the Law of the Father* (New Haven: Yale University
Press, 1989); Vicki Mahaffey, *Reauthorizing Joyce* (Cambridge: Cambridge University
Press, 1989); Suzette Henke, *James Joyce and the Politics of Desire* (London: Routledge,
1990); Jean-Michel Rabaté, *James Joyce: Authorized Reader* (Baltimore: Johns Hopkins
University Press, 1991); Kimberly J. Devlin, *Wandering and Return in Finnegans Wake*

Joyce seems ideally suited to such poststructuralist readings for two main reasons. First, as Sigmund Freud frequently stated, poets often "discover" what philosophers and others come to theorize many years later. Poststructuralist theory is, in the eyes of many, an extension into philosophy, psychoanalysis, and linguistics of what writers such as Gertrude Stein and Joyce forged in literary discourse. As Patrick McGee writes in *Paperspace*, Joyce has functioned "as a symbolic bridge between the modern and the postmodern" in the development of such theorists as Lacan, Derrida, and Kristeva.[2] Joyce's texts, particularly *Ulysses* and *Finnegans Wake*, anticipate and perform with an increasingly dazzling display many basic tenets of recent critical theory—most specifically the deconstruction of the Cartesian subject and the linguistic reconstitution of the subject as forever in process and unknown to itself; the materiality of language in all its thickness, density, opaqueness, undecidability, and ephemerality; the endless play of words in chains of reference that signify not "meaning" but indeterminate processes of meaning; and the binary of masculine/feminine as the master plot of phallo(go)-centrism in Western culture.

At their best, readings of Joyce as the prototypical poststructuralist engage theory in a mutual dialogue with literature that avoids what Shoshana Felman calls the "subordination" of the literary text to the higher authority of theory and fosters new insights into both theory and text produced by their juxtaposition and interpenetration.[3] At their best, they also probe deeply, often playfully, into the intricate pathways and tracings of linguistic webs and textualized desires. At their weakest, such readings remain caught in a hermeneutic circle: Joyce becomes the ideal terrain upon which to prove the theories that his texts themselves anticipate. The poststructuralist reading thus becomes its own confirmation. The theory that privileges unpredictability produces a repetition of readings in which Joyce (always) signifies the truth of Derrida or Lacan. At their weakest, too, such readings also often "forget" the "real" of history and experience toward which language gestures, even if the refer-

---

(Princeton: Princeton University Press, 1991); Sheldon Brivic, *The Veil of Signs: Joyce, Lacan, and Perception* (Urbana: University of Illinois Press, 1991).

2. McGee, *Paperspace*, 2.

3. See Shoshana Felman, "To Open the Question," in *Literature and Psychoanalysis: The Question of Reading: Otherwise*, ed. Shoshana Felman (Baltimore: Johns Hopkins University Press, 1980), 5–10.

ence of Joyce's texts can never be fully manifest outside language.[4] Whether strong or weak, however, poststructuralist readings of Joyce retain a certain explanatory power based on the paradox of how Joycean texts seem to *repeat* the very theory they *anticipate*.

The second compelling reason for Joyce's association with poststructuralism is that Joyce has become within the academy, as well as in the culture at large, something of an icon of and for modernity—and this in complex ways, for contradictory reasons. For some, Joyce is *the* canonical writer of the twentieth century: *the* Chaucer, Shakespeare, Milton of his time. His placement on the pinnacle of modernity's pedestal repeats the double gesture evident in the canonization of his predecessors. As Shakespeare is often said both to epitomize and to stand apart from his age in sheer genius, Joyce is for some the supreme avatar of modernity and its most brilliant practitioner.

But for others, Joyce serves as metonym for modernity, a fragment of the whole that stands in for the deconstruction of the very notion of icons and canons. For these, Joyce contributes supremely to the concepts of the death of the author and the disintegration of the Cartesian subject by his inscriptions of a modern consciousness forever split from certain knowledge of itself. For these, Joyce writes not in the language of the high priests of Western culture but rather speaks the problematic of these discourses—parodying, exaggerating, mimicking, decentering their logocentrism on behalf of *Otherness*. Woven in and among the strands of the canonical in his texts are the discourses of the noncanonical, of the marginalized and repressed. His texts, for some, speak what has been unspeakable, represent what has been unrepresentable in the phallogocentirc discourses of Western culture: the feminine, the unconscious, the racial Other.

For a third group of readers, Joyce is neither idol of nor metonym for modernity, neither universal genius nor the Other's champion. Rather, he is read dialogically as a voice containing many competing discourses—some in league with ideology, some subversive to it; some reproducing the dominant religious, sexual, political, and literary traditions, some resistant to them. Within this framework

---

4. In a related critique of poststructuralism from within its boundaries, see Thomas M. Kavanagh, who writes in his introduction to *The Limits of Theory* (Stanford: Stanford University Press, 1989), 5: "What we had introduced as a discourse of the radically Other seems to have produced only the most resolute sameness and orthodoxy."

Joyce remains one voice, however multilayered and conflicted, among many other voices. His play with Otherness ambivalently attests to the power of these other voices emergent on the scene of a modern world split open: the voices of women, the voices of racial, ethnic, sexual, and regional Others, insistently testifying to the breakup of empire and the disruptions of gender, race, ethnic, and class systems.

As *the* elite of the elite, Joyce is read as the supremely modern writer, the inventor and technologist of modernist and postmodern- ist poetics. As the champion of alterity, Joyce is read as the inscrip- tion of modernity's fragmentations. As the site of contestation between authoritative and marginalized discourses, Joyce is read as the textualization of modernity's discontents. And for many critics, aspects of all three approaches interweave into dialogic representa- tions of Joyce wherein different strands of his modernity compete with and often undermine one another, in part accounting for the controversies that swirl continuously about his work. Common to all these approaches, however, is an association of Joyce's moder- nity with rupture, a radical break from the epistemologies, ontolo- gies, psychologies, and formalisms of the Victorian past. The disorientations and displacements of this break are variously associ- ated with exhilaration or alienation, joy or despair, and utopian desire or nostalgia for the past. But the assumption of modernity's break with the past structures these different responses.

The essays in this volume tacitly acknowledge the significance of rupture, but they are premised on the psychoanalytic notion that nothing is completely lost, only "forgotten." The consciousness of rupture may well be a defining characteristic of modernity, but this psychic reality could itself represent the repression rather than the abandonment of what came before. This view, common to all the volume's essays, goes further than an insistence on some forms of continuity between modernity and its precursors. Consistent with the poststructuralist critique of "origin," the essays presume that the already written and already read are contained within the texts that proclaim to "make it new." The task becomes not so much to identify strands of continuity between modernity and its past but to interpret the psychodynamic processes of repression and return as they are enacted within the defining texts of modernity.

Psychoanalytic theory—particularly that first formulated in *Stud- ies in Hysteria, The Interpretation of Dreams*, Freud's papers on technique collected in *Therapy and Technique*, and *Beyond the Pleasure Principle*—is essential to the project of the essays in this volume. Freud's notion that dreams and symptoms are disguised expressions of repressed desires posits a hermeneutic for decoding the linguistic and hieroglyphic transformations accomplished by the dream-work. Interpretation of the repressed depends on reading the traces of its insistent return. Paradoxically, however, Freud's theory of the unconscious splits the known from the unknown in the human psyche so profoundly that the hermeneutic that begins in an affirmation of interpretability ends in an awareness of undecidability. We can untangle the process of repression only so far before we come up against what Freud calls "the unplumbable mystery" at the core of every symptomatic expression and up against our own entanglement in what we would untangle.

The authors of the essays in this volume adapt Freud's concepts of repression, return, and interpretation to the project of reading Joyce's texts. Lacan's notion that the unconscious is structured like a language facilitates this adaptation, and his integration of Freudian psychoanalysis with Saussurean linguistics foregrounds the analogy already present in Freud's work between the linguistic workings of the psyche and the psychodynamics of a text. In turn, Kristeva's adaptation of Lacan in relation to semiotics fosters this analogy. In *Revolution in Poetic Language* she reverses Lacan's famous axiom to suggest that not only is the psyche structured like a text but also that the text is a "signifying process" that functions like a psyche. The dialectical play in all texts between the pre-oedipal semiotic and the oedipal symbolic modalities of language is the linguistic process that is constitutive of the subject.[5] This notion of the text-as-psyche implicitly posits a textual unconscious. Like the psyche, the text is split, psychodynamically engaged in a perpetual process of repression and return. Kristeva's view of the text as a site of ongoing psycholinguistic process underlies the various interpretive strategies developed in this volume for reading the textual unconscious.

For Kristeva, particularly in her early essays collected in *Desire in Language*, a focus on textuality—conscious and unconscious—

---

5. See especially Jacques Lacan, "The Agency of the Letter in the Unconscious, or Reason since Freud," in *Ecrits*, trans. Alan Sheridan (New York: W. W. Norton, 1977), 146–78; Julia Kristeva, *Revolution in Poetic Language*, trans. Margaret Waller (New York: Columbia University Press, 1984), 13–106.

includes an analysis of context: the text's intertextuality, its dialogic intersections with "the historical and social text."[6] Similarly,
the psychoanalytic, text-centered readings in this volume include
an analysis of history and the politics of repression and return in
Joyce's oeuvre. As Jameson argues in *The Political Unconscious*,
the textual unconscious is also a political unconscious: history's
insistent return marks the text as a site where forbidden narratives
have been repressed and disguised.[7] Cultural narratives not only
of class but also of gender, religion, ethnicity, race, and sexuality
circulate through Joyce's texts, reworked and renegotiated as part
of his modernity. The growing anonymity and mechanization of
modern life, the spiritual and material violence of human relations,
the epistemological crises of disintegrating empire and nation con-
stellate in Joyce's texts as part of a political unconscious of modernity. In McGee's words, Joyce writes "as the symptom of a historical
process."[8] Stephen's cry in *Ulysses* that "history is a nightmare
from which I am trying to awake" has served, like Joyce himself,
as modernity's characteristic lament and metonym for rupture. For
Hayden White in "The Burden of History," Stephen's statement
signifies the modernists' "hostility toward history," rejection of
"historical consciousness," and "belief that the past was *only* a
burden."[9] In contrast, the essays in this volume share an assumption that it is not the erasure of history but its insistent return as
nightmare and desire which marks modernity's stance toward the
stories of the past.

A final dimension of the textual and political unconscious resides
in the intersubjective space between Joyce's texts and their readers.
In such essays as "Turning the Screw of Interpretation" and "The
Case of Poe," Shoshana Felman has positioned the textual unconscious in the transferential scene of reading, in the inevitability
of the reader's entrapment in the complexes inscribed in the text.
Adapting Lacan's reintroduction of the countertransference into the
analytic situation, Felman speculates that the reader is always already entangled in the snares worked out in the text. Reading is not

6. See especially Julia Kristeva, "The Bounded Text" (1966–67) and "Word, Dialogue,
and Novel" (1966), in *Desire in Language*, trans. Thomas Gora, Alice Jardine, and Leon S.
Roudiez (New York: Columbia University Press, 1980), 36–91.
7. See Fredric Jameson, *The Political Unconscious: Narrative as a Socially Symbolic
Act* (Ithaca: Cornell University Press, 1981).
8. McGee, *Paperspace*, 141.
9. Hayden White, "The Burden of History," in *Tropics of Discourse: Essays in Cultural
Criticism* (Baltimore: Johns Hopkins University Press, 1978), 27–50.

so much an enlightened decoding, however indeterminate, of the text's disguises as it is a repetition of the dynamics that fueled the text in the first place. Within this view, the corpus of criticism itself constitutes a "case study" subject to analysis, a point Felman makes with an interpretation of critical debates about Poe's work and James's *Turn of the Screw*.[10] The sheer mass of Joyce criticism, as well as its diversities and differences, suggests a ripe field for the analysis of the textual unconscious in Joyce as Felman defines it. No doubt such a textual unconscious exists implicitly in this volume, but it is not interrogated directly. We must leave it as a challenge to our readers to decode or "repeat" the repressed in our own readings—and those of Joyce studies in general—as a case in point of modernity and its discontents.

Joyce: The Return of the Repressed originated in a cluster of panels which I organized for the 1988 International Joyce Symposium in Venice. Joseph A. Boone, Marilyn L. Brownstein, Jay Clayton, Christine Froula, and I presented papers at the conference and have thoroughly revised and extended the arguments made in those initial papers. Ours have been joined with original essays, taking related approaches, by Laura Doyle, Ellen Carol Jones, Alberto Moreiras, Richard Pearce, and Robert Spoo. Our readings of the textual and political unconscious of Joyce's modernity fall into four sections: "Making the Artist of Modernity: *Stephen Hero, Portrait, Ulysses*"; "Repression and the Return of Cultural History: *Dubliners* and *Portrait*"; "Narratives of Gender, Race, and Sex: *Ulysses*"; and "Incest, Narcissism, and the Scene of Writing: *Ulysses* and *Finnegans Wake*."

Part I opens the collection with two essays that explore the psychodynamics of repression and return in Joyce's early narratives about the formation of the artist. My own essay, "(Self)Censorship and the Making of Joyce's Modernism," proposes a psychopolitical hermeneutic—based on Freud's grammar for the dream-work and his concept of dream series—for interpreting the production of Joyce's modernity as reflected in the changing representations of Stephen D(a)edalus. It treats *Stephen Hero, Portrait*, and, more

---

10. See Shoshana Felman, "Turning the Screw of Interpretation," in *Literature and Psychoanalysis*, ed. Felman, 94–207, and "The Case of Poe: Applications/Implications of Psychoanalysis," in *Lacan and the Adventure of Insight* (Cambridge: Harvard University Press, 1987), 27–51.

briefly, *Ulysses* as a textual series in which the revisions that made Joyce's texts "modernist" led to the increasing repression of the female subject and her insistent return, especially in the figure of Stephen's mother. In the essay I adapt poststructuralist methodologies for reading the textual unconscious but resist the teleological tendency in some poststructuralist readings of Joyce to view his transition from realism/naturalism to modernism/postmodernism as an unqualified "advance."

Alberto Moreiras, in "Pharmaconomy: Stephen and the Daedalids," investigates the repressed resonances of Stephen's formation as a writer in relation to Derrida's discussion of writing as *pharmakon* in "La pharmacie de Platon." Moreiras interprets the allusions to the Daedalus myth (Daedalus, Icarus, and the unnamed Talos) and the bird motifs (lapwing, partridge, *perdix*) in *Portrait* and *Ulysses* as trace representations of the *pharmakos*, the scapegoat figure who heals, kills, is killed, and returns in a cyclic process. The recurring flights of birds, he shows, inscribe the displacement and return of both mother and father within the son. These associations lead Moreiras to read against the grain of criticism that situates Stephen within the oedipal narrative of the displacement of the mother and the parricide of the father. Instead, Moreiras suggests that Stephen's entrance into writing involves suspended—ever repressed, ever returning—identifications with both maternal and paternal figures.

Part II contains three essays that examine social, political, and literary history as repressed discourses that erupt into the naturalist and modernist surfaces of Joyce's early work. In "Uncanny Returns in 'The Dead': Ibsenian Intertexts and the Estranged Infant," Robert Spoo argues that repetition of the once-familiar that has become strange accounts for the uncanny effects of the "incurable and incorrigible" final story of *Dubliners*. Adapting Freud's concept of the uncanny as a site of repression, Spoo reads "The Dead" as an uncanny repetition of Ibsen's *When We Dead Awaken*. He further argues that Gretta's recovery of her repressed rural past, represented by her dead lover, represents an uncanny birth of the lover as son, a birth in which Gabriel does not participate and which ultimately eludes his and the reader's gaze.

In "A Portrait of the Romantic Poet as a Young Modernist: Literary History as Textual Unconscious," Jay Clayton examines the debate about romanticism in Joyce by using two approaches to the interpretation of the textual unconscious: the first, represented by

Jonathan Culler, locates the textual unconscious in the reader's transferential repetition of the text; the second, represented by Peter Brooks, locates the textual unconscious in the text's structural interplay between the life and death instincts. With the first approach Clayton examines the text as discourse; with the second, as story. Romanticism (especially in the form of Wordsworth's "spots of time") as both discourse and story, Clayton argues, returns as a repetition of the repressed in Joyce's modernist narrative, *A Portrait of the Artist as a Young Man*.

Richard Pearce, in "Simon's Irish Rose: Famine Songs, Blackfaced Minstrels, and Woman's Repression in *A Portrait*," takes the song "Lilly Dale," which baby Stephen learned from his father, as its entry point for reading the social realities of gender, race, and class repressed in the stories of Simon and Stephen Dedalus. "Lilly Dale," Pearce notes, was a widely popular American song written in 1852 and often sung in Ireland in blackface after the U.S. minstrel tradition was imported into England and Ireland. Its lyric idealization of a woman's death represses the social realities of famine, pregnancy and motherhood, class, and race, a repression repeated in Joyce's characterizations in *Portrait* of Simon, Stephen, Stephen's mother, and Dante.

Part III focuses on the questions of desire, female subjectivity, the figure of the mother, and the interlocking psychodynamics of gender and race as they are inscribed in *Ulysses*. Paralleling Pearce's reading of the repressed cultural history of *Portrait*, Laura Doyle's "Races and Chains: The Sexuo-Racial Matrix in *Ulysses*," interprets the sexual and racial matrix in *Ulysses* as a modernist inheritance of a nineteenth-century preoccupation with pure and originary races and, in turn, with the purity of the women who mother those races. She argues that Joyce sought to complicate or cross boundaries of race and gender with Irish/English, Stephen as "jewgreek," and Bloom as "womanly man." But *Ulysses* also betrays mixed allegiances and an anxiety about cultural inheritances (for example, miscegenation and promiscuous women) which is projected onto mother figures. The narrative dislocations in *Ulysses* follow the path of the main characters' attempts to evade or contain the influence of racialized mother figures. At the text's closure, Doyle concludes, Joyce invokes an idealized rhetoric of mothers that leaves the reader, in deus ex machina fashion, with a sense of transcendence of conflicts—conflicts about racial and sexual inheritance that the text has been unable to resolve or repress.

Joseph A. Boone, in "Staging Sexuality: Repression, Representation, and 'Interior States' in *Ulysses*," interprets the "Circe" and "Penelope" episodes of *Ulysses* as instances of the return of the repressed in a double sense: first, they demonstrate Joyce's effort to represent what he called the "subconscious"; second, they inscribe eruptions of the textual unconscious of *Ulysses* itself. Boone examines Joyce's narrative strategies in the context of feminism and deconstruction to explore how the text is subverted by what it has repressed. The psychodramatic presentation of the unconscious in "Circe", he argues, celebrates a kind of polymorphously perverse sexuality, but its pyrotechnic display is a displacement of sexuality into the linguistic realm which continues to valorize masculine mastery. The interior monologue in "Penelope," he concludes, is the highly contested site of female subjectivity in which Molly eludes and subverts Joyce's attempt to appropriate female and feminine speech.

Part IV concludes the collection with three essays that probe the inscriptions of incest and narcissism in the paternal, filial, and artist figures in Joyce's later work. Marilyn L. Brownstein, in "The Preservation of Tenderness: A Confusion of Tongues in *Ulysses* and *Finnegans Wake*," uses Sandor Ferenczi's 1933 essay "Confusion of Tongues between Adults and the Child" (which calls for psychoanalysis to return to the repressed reality of father-daughter incest) to read the repressed narratives and discourses of incest in *Ulysses* and *Finnegans Wake*. It adapts Ferenczi's argument that incest involves a "confusion of tongues" between the child's language of tenderness and the parent's language of passion to a reading of father-daughter relations in Joyce's texts. It also uses Ferenczi's notion of healing based on a reconstruction of maternal language. The father's detachment and refusal to acknowledge incest mirrors the suppression of Bloom's incestuous desire for Milly. The incest desired in *Ulysses*, Brownstein argues, is acted out in *Finnegans Wake*, where the maternal language of loss in the final sections of the text reflects the attempt to heal the confusion of tongues in the act of writing.

Ellen Carol Jones, in "Textual Mater: Writing the Mother in Joyce," reads portions of *Ulysses*, especially the "Oxen of the Sun" episode, and selected passages from *Finnegans Wake* in conjunction with Kristeva and Derrida to argue that, in the economy and ideology of (re)production, writing is the space of repression, particularly of the mother. This erasure of the mother as speaking subject represents, according to the essay, a masculine appropriation of the maternal necessary for the creation of the word. Jones further argues that this appropriation institutes a poetics of incest in which the son penetrates the mother's flesh to (re)produce the word.

Christine Froula, in "Mothers of Invention/Doaters of Inversion: Narcissan Scenes in *Finnegans Wake*," rounds out the collection by returning to the issues about the artist raised in Part I, with reference to *Stephen Hero*, "The Dead," and *Portrait*, and in extended discussion of *Finnegans Wake*. Froula reads *Finnegans Wake* as the final text in a series of autobiographical "self-vivisections" that cross self-portraiture with cultural history. She explores the dynamics of desire visible in Joyce's Narcissan scenes and uses his self-reflexive depictions of his own art of self-portraiture to account both for the fluid dream-selves of *Finnegans Wake* and for the dreamer's pervasive crossings between "The form masculine. The gender feminine." Joyce's final volume, she concludes, represents a narcissistic return in which the book-as-self is indistinguishable from the book-as-world, in which Joyce inflates narcissistic self-portraiture to epic dimensions by re-creating the world in his own image.

No thematic organization for the collection does justice to the way the essays in this volume weave together, in their diverse ways, a number of common patterns with a variety of methodologies loosely connected by psychoanalysis and cultural studies. Nor can the essays be added one to another to come up with a single vision of Joyce. Rather, taken together, the essays contribute to ongoing debates in Joyce criticism around such issues as Joyce's representations of the artist, the feminine, the maternal, female subjectivity, and desire—debates evident in the recent work of critics including Derek Attridge, Shari Benstock, Sheldon Brivic, Kimberly J. Devlin, Daniel Ferrer, Suzette Henke, Karen Lawrence, Colin MacCabe, Patrick McGee, Vicki Mahaffey, Margot Norris, Jean-Michel Rabaté, Frances L. Restuccia, and Bonnie Kime Scott.

But if no single voice on Joyce emerges in this volume, an insistent return of issues contested in Joyce studies and contemporary literary studies in general is nonetheless evident. Common to the

disparate voices of the collection is the integration of psychoanalytic and historical methods. For the authors, the psychodynamics
of repression and return are represented textually in Joyce's oeuvre,
but they inscribe processes and positionalities that return us to
pressing questions of literary, cultural, and political history. In this
volume psychoanalysis is emphatically not a framework that allows
for an escape from history, as it has been for some poststructuralist/
psychoanalytic critics; rather, it becomes the occasion for a return
to the site of history making. Spoo and Clayton explore in particular
the traces of a repressed literary history—the romanticism of
Wordsworth, the realism/naturalism of Ibsen—that erupts into the
modern surface of Joyce's texts. Pearce and Doyle adapt psychoanalytic concepts of repression to a cultural studies project that interro-
gates the intersections of racial and gender discourses traversing
Joyce's texts. All the remaining essays locate an implicit or explicit
sexual politics in the markings of the textual unconscious in Joyce's
oeuvre.

The Joycean artist figure, and the poetics he promotes or embodies, is the focus of the first two and last two essays in the volume,
all of which develop in some form a version of the psychoanalytic
family romance as central to Joyce's artist narratives. My essay
reads Joyce's artist figures in relation to an oedipal narrative, in
which Joyce's transition to modernity is marked by the artist's increasing figuration of the maternal as an object of desire whose
silence makes possible the poet's speech. Instead of an oedipal narrative, Moreiras uncovers a hidden identificatory process whereby the
artist-son holds in suspension a contradictory identification with
both the maternal and paternal figures. Jones returns to the question
of the mother in Joyce's poetics, finding both the son's desire to *be*
the mother (that is, to appropriate her speech) and to penetrate the
maternal body in a signifying practice that is fundamentally incestuous. Froula argues that underneath the oedipal narrative of Joyce's
autobiographical artist figures lies a deeper narcissistic substrate
that not only reflects a solipsistic identification of self and other
but also represents the son's desire to return to a state of oneness
with the mother. Rather than see these excursions into Joycean
poetics as contradictory, I suggest we should understand their differences palimpsestically—as psychodynamic layers that coexist and
overdetermine the oedipal and pre-oedipal configurations of desire
in Joyce's representations of the artist.

Identity politics and the question of the subject—key issues in much contemporary criticism—stand behind another major cluster of essays. Does Joyce assert a phallogocentric subjectivity that suppresses female subjectivity, or subvert the masculine by speaking the feminine, or ventriloquize the feminine as a sign of masculine lack? These possibilities are much debated in Joyce criticism, especially as they are manifested in the figure of Molly Bloom, the readings of whom stand metonymically for various views of Joyce on the issue of subjectivity. In my essay I argue that Joyce's early realist/naturalist texts imagined (if not represented) a female subjectivity that is increasingly absent from Stephen's modernist poetics (though not necessarily from Joyce's own later work, in which forms of a repressed female subjectivity haunt the texts). Spoo argues that "The Dead" narrates (and thus exposes) the suppression of female subjectivity and its uncanny return through the story of Gabriel's fantasies of his wife and his failure to understand her past self, the Galway girl from the west of Ireland. For Pearce, *Portrait* participates in the repression of the cultural history of women's oppression during the Irish potato famine and its aftermath in its evocation of the idealized dead girl in the popular song "Lilly Dale," a song that itself covers over the realities of many Irish women's lives. Boone negotiates between these views by arguing that Joyce's linguistic displays in the "Circe" episode of *Ulysses* are displaced versions of masculine desire, but that in "Penelope" Joyce at least partially constructs a feminine speech that escapes masculine containment. Jones, in looking at *Ulysses* and *Finnegans Wake*, concludes that Joyce's deconstruction of the masculine subject represents an attempt to appropriate (and thus in some form erase) female subjectivity. Froula, with a retrospective look at Joyce's artist figures, finds in his pre-oedipal longings a narcissistic attempt to place himself in the mother's position, an attempt that results in an equation of the (masculine) self with the world and thus implicitly suppresses female difference.

If Joyce oscillates between critiquing and reifying his identification with masculine subjectivity, of what significance in this process is his status as (post)colonial Other in relation to the English? Pearce and Doyle both examine Joyce's Irishness as it relates to discourses of race and racialism in the nineteenth century. Pearce finds repressed in Stephen's opening song in *Portrait* the history of the ideological association of the Irish with Africans and African

Americans, as well as the Irish resistance to that identification. Doyle argues that *Portrait* and *Ulysses* invoke the racialist discourses of the nineteenth century which idealized racial purity in the form of the mother. But while *Portrait* reproduces these discourses, she suggests, *Ulysses* exposes and critiques them, to promote in their place a miscegenous and cross-gender mixing of races and sexes.

Overdetermining the question of subjectivity in Joyce's texts is the issue of desire, a focus of many of the essays in this volume. For all of them inscriptions of desire are inseparable from the subject's cultural positioning in the social order. Psychoanalytic theories of desire are adapted to explore the politics of desire motivating or inscribed in Joyce's texts. In my essay I suggest that oedipal narrative, a defining structure in Joyce's modernism, focuses his Stephen texts around the articulation of a male desire that precludes the possibility of a different, female desire. Spoo argues that "The Dead" exposes the way in which female desire, represented in the form of Gretta's love for Michael Furey, remains invisible to a man like Gabriel, caught in his own romantic fantasies of woman. Pearce shows how male desire for the idealized woman represented in "Lilly Dale" erases the existence of real women who suffered from poverty and patriarchal authority. Doyle examines the fear of and desire for the racialized maternal body in its pure and impure forms as both reified and critiqued in *Portrait* and *Ulysses*. Boone shows how male desire displaced into linguistic display in "Circe" reconstitutes a patriarchal authority seemingly deconstructed in the episode, while in "Penelope" Joyce represents not only a male fantasy of female desire but also a female desire that in some sense escapes his own attempt to appropriate it. Brownstein and Jones both raise the issue of incestuous desire. Brownstein suggests that the incestuous father-daughter desires that exist only as trace fantasies in *Ulysses* are acted out in *Finnegans Wake*, in which the final section represents the father's attempt to heal through identification with the maternal language of tenderness and with the daughter he desires and abuses. Examining incest within the oedipal/pre-oedipal framework, Jones examines the son's incestuous desire for the mother as essential to Joyce's poetics. Finally, Froula examines the manifestations of the artist's desire in Joyce's oeuvre, especially *Finnegans Wake*, as Narcissan scenes in which the boundaries between (masculine) self and (m)other, self and world, dissolve.

The figure of the mother, whether as historical subject or as image of the desired maternal body, forms a matrix in the volume that draws like a magnet all the other issues examined in the volume. If Joyce criticism initially focused on the father—the Dedalean paternal—as a central force behind and as a central subject of Joyce's work, in recent years critics have gone beyond the paternal configurations to the maternal constellations inscribed in his texts. This volume foregrounds the maternal as, in Freud's words, the "navel, the spot where it reaches down into the unknown."[11] For most of the essays, the maternal constellates the psychodynamics of repression and return. The figure of the mother and the desire for the maternal both function in Joyce's texts as knots whose (partial) unraveling leads us into the textual and political unconscious of modernity.

It remains a debate within this volume, as it is in Joyce criticism in general, just how fully Joyce was aware of or intentionally explored the processes of repression and return. Was Joyce, as the great Arranger, in full control of the psychodynamics his texts expose? Or are his texts the "symptoms" of his own and modernity's discontents? Do his representations of male desire and the erasure of female subjectivity, for example, represent a reification or a critique of the social order? Does he participate in the phallogocentrism that his texts deconstruct? Or does he perform the deconstruction of culture himself, brilliantly and subversively? As icon of modernity, did Joyce spearhead the dismantling of the Cartesian subject, as well as its related ontologies, epistemologies, and systems of gender, race, class, and sexuality? Or was he, as embodiment of modernity, a supreme example of modern man forever split and not fully known to himself?

Joyce: The Return of the Repressed does not present a single voice on these pressing questions. Rather, taken separately and as a whole, the essays in this volume implicitly suggest that it is the contestation between these two views that is itself inscribed in Joyce's work. If the challenge of the 1960s and 1970s for Joyce criticism was to recognize the ways Joyce's texts held the heroic and the ironic in perpetual oscillation and balance, then perhaps a project of the 1990s and beyond is for critics to learn to read the dialogue

---

11. Sigmund Freud, *The Interpretation of Dreams*, trans. James Strachey (New York: Avon, 1965), 564; see also 143.

(indeed polylogue) of cultural voices in Joyce's texts: both revolutionary and reactionary, both critiquing and subject to critique, both oppositional and ideological, both marginal and central.

PART I

Making the Artist of Modernity: *Stephen Hero, Portrait, Ulysses*

I

(Self)Censorship
and the Making of
Joyce's Modernism

Susan Stanford Friedman

> There is at least one spot in every dream at which
> it is unplumbable—a navel, as it were, that is its
> point of contact with the unknown.
>
> SIGMUND FREUD, *The Interpretation of Dreams*

> —Do you mean to say, said Stephen scornfully, that
> the President must approve of my paper
> before I can read it to your society!
> —Yes. He's the Censor.
> —What a valuable society!
>
> JAMES JOYCE, *Stephen Hero*

One of the "unplumbable" spots in the transforma-
tion of *Stephen Hero* into *A Portrait of the Artist as a Young Man*
is the disappearance of the Jesuit "Censor." In some three hundred
manuscript pages of *Stephen Hero* that survived Joyce's probable
destruction of his unfinished self-portrait, Stephen's two confrontations with the Censor represent key moments in the production of

A short version of this essay was presented at the 1988 International Symposium on
Joyce in Venice and published in the conference volume, *The Languages of Joyce*, ed.
Rosa Maria Bollettieri, Carla Marengo, and Christine van Boheemen (Amsterdam and
Philadelphia: John Benjamins, 1992). For their suggestions I am grateful to my co-panelists
in Venice, Jane Marcus and Daniel Ferrer, to Marilyn L. Brownstein, Robert Spoo, and my
colleagues in the Draft Group at the University of Wisconsin-Madison, especially Phillip
Herring, Cyrena Pondrom, Eric Rothstein, and Larry Scanlon.

his alienation as an artist in the making.[1] In the first instance McCann warns Stephen that his paper on Ibsen must have the permission of Father Dillon, the president of the college, before it can be read before the Debating Society. Whelan, the secretary of the Society, tells Stephen that his paper is "tabu" (*SH*, 89). Then Stephen defends himself before Father Dillon, who initially denies Stephen permission to read his paper but finally relents (*SH*, 90–98). In the second instance Stephen realizes that the monthly review that McCann edits is silently controlled by Father Cummins, the benign originator whose "discretionary powers" amount to censorship in spite of his relative open-mindedness (*SH*, 181–82).

But in *Portrait* the Censor has vanished, excised in the revision. Is the Censor's absence as character a symptom of his presence within the artistic process that governs the transformation of *Stephen Hero* into *Portrait* or the continuation of Stephen's story into *Ulysses*? The role of the state censor in the suppression of Joyce's writings for obscenity has been outlined at length by others. But have we satisfactorily identified the operation of the censor within Joyce himself as he came back again and again to the story of Stephen D(a)edalus? Have we found the traces of repression—(self)censorship—inscribed in his texts? Do we know what role this repression may have played in the production of Joyce's modernism? Can we chart the connection between repression and oppression, between individiual psychic processes and the ideological and material structures of the social order, in the making of a modernist artist? Finally, how might such a connection be marked by gender?

I pursue these inquiries by proposing a psycho-political hermeneutic for reading the texts in which Stephen appears. Some of these texts are commonly regarded as "drafts" leading up to the "final" text, *A Portrait of the Artist as a Young Man*—such as the 1904 narrative/essay titled "A Portrait of the Artist," and the "Epiphanies," many of which were adapted for *Stephen Hero* and *Portrait*.[2] *Portrait* and *Ulysses* are conventionally read as related but autonomous texts. I suggest that we read these texts as distinct parts of a larger composite "text" whose parts are like the imperfectly erased layers of a palimpsest, one whose textual and political unconscious

---

1. See James Joyce, *Stephen Hero*, ed. John J. Slocum and Herbert Cahoon (New York: New Directions, 1963), 89–98, 181–82; hereafter cited in the text as *SH*.
2. James Joyce, *A Portrait of the Artist as a Young Man: Text, Criticism, and Notes*, ed. Chester G. Anderson (New York: Viking Press, 1968); hereafter cited in the text as *P*.

can be read with a psychoanalytic, intertextual approach. This approach to interpreting Joyce's Dedalus texts adapts Freud's concept of the dream-work, his analysis of serial dreams, and his identification of "the return of the repressed" in the drama of transference.[3]

Freud's Hermeneutic and the Textual Unconscious

In his narrative of the psychodynamics of repression and desire in *The Interpretations of Dreams*, Freud personifies the psychic agency that forbids the drive to pleasure in the form of the "censor" or more generally "censorship."[4] As internalized agent of the cultural ethos in the realm of necessity, the censor attempts, with only partial success, to silence the forbidden desires of the unconscious. The linguistic processes that Freud calls the dream-work accomplish a compromise between the desire to express and the need to repress what is forbidden. Latent desire, buried deep within the unconscious, is transformed into the manifest content of dream or symptom by the grammar of the dream-work: the mechanisms of condensation, displacement, nonrational modes of representability (such as pictographics, symbolism, narrative juxtapositions, superimpositions, and transpositions), and secondary revision (the interpolation of connectors or structuring principles that arrange and order the dream content). These mechanisms distort the latent wish just enough to evade the censor. Freud himself likens the dream-work's negotiation between revealing and concealing to the delicate encoding of the political writer who must disguise dangerous con-

3. I first developed this approach in *Penelope's Web: Gender, Modernity, H.D.'s Fiction* (Cambridge: Cambridge University Press, 1990); "The Return of the Repressed in Women's Narrative," *Journal of Narrative Technique* 19 (Winter 1989): 141–56; and "Hysteria, Dreams, and Modernity: A Reading of the Origins of Psychoanalysis in Freud's Early Corpus," in *Reading the New*, ed. Kevin Dettmar (Ann Arbor: University of Michigan Press, 1992). After drafting this essay, I saw Margot Norris's "Portraits of the Artist as a Young Lover," in *New Alliances in Joyce Criticism: "When It's Aped to Foul a Delivery,"* ed. Bonnie Kime Scott (Newark: University of Delaware Press, 1988), 144–52. Norris also reads Joyce's Stephen texts as a palimpsestic, composite text; she includes *Finnegans Wake* in the series and sees the portrait of the artist in Joyce's final text as an exposé of *Portrait's* "dead subject" (144).

4. Sigmund Freud, *The Interpretation of Dreams* (1900), trans. James Strachey (New York: Avon, 1965), 175–78, 543–44; hereafter cited in the text as *ID*. The censor in this early text is a precursor of the superego introduced in 1923 in *The Ego and the Id*, trans. James Strachey (New York: Norton, 1961).

tent so as to fool the censor, who works on behalf of the oppressive state. He writes:

> A similar difficulty confronts the political writer who has disagreeable truths to tell to those in authority. If he presents them undisguised, the authorities will suppress his words. . . . A writer must beware of the censorship, and on its account he must soften and distort the expression of his opinion. According to the strength and sensitiveness of the censorship he finds himself compelled either merely to refrain from certain forms of attack, or to speak in allusions in place of direct references, or he must conceal his objectionable pronouncement beneath some apparently innocent disguise. . . . The stricter the censorship, the more far-reaching will be the disguise and the more ingenious too may be the means employed for putting the reader on the scent of the true meaning. (*ID*, 175–76)[5]

Freud's hermeneutic in turn fools the censor—undoes the repression of the psyche, the suppression of the social order—by a process that he names "decoding" and variously images as an archaeological dig, a journey into the labyrinth, an unraveling of woven threads, a translation of pictographic runes, a detective analysis of mystery and disguise, a removal of the layers in a palimpsest. Beginning in determinacy, his method ends in indeterminacy. Dreams *have* "authors," "intentions," and "meanings" to be decoded, he affirms. But their "overdetermination" necessitates an "overinterpretation" which never ends. The multiple layers of manifest form and latent content require an infinite regress of interpretation which ultimately leads to the "unplumbable" spot, what Freud names the "navel" of the dream, its contact point with the unknown (*ID*, 143). His metaphor for the gap or knot in the dream-text and in the text of dream interpretation suggests that the threshold of mystery is a point of contact with the maternal body, the irretrievable site of origins, as well as the origin of what is censored, what is disguised in the grammar of the dream-work. Ultimately, his figurative formulation suggests, the return of the repressed is the return of

---

5. For Freud's description of the dream-work, see *Interpretation of Dreams*, 311–546. Only in his so-called speculative writing, in which he theorized about the connection between the psyche and society—about, in other words, the psychological dimensions of social contract—did Freud seriously consider the significance of his comparison between state censorship and the internal censor. See especially *Totem and Taboo* (1913), trans. James Strachey (New York: Norton, 1950), and *Civilization and Its Discontents* (1930), trans. James Strachey (New York: Norton, 1961).

woman, of that mother/Other, to him forever unknown, untranscribable, untranslatable.

Freud's method for overinterpretation is fundamentally intertextual. In *The Interpretation of Dreams* Freud rejects what he calls the "symbolic" method of dream interpretation, which analyzes the dream as an autonomous unit with interrelating parts—a method that is strikingly consonant, by the way, with the theory of art Stephen expounds in *Stephen Hero* and *Portrait*. Freud proposes instead his psychoanalytic method, in which fragments of the dream become departure points into a labyrinth of associations that radiate without end into the dreamer's recent and distant past, the linguistic and visual artifacts of culture, and the events of history. The dream's meaning, however indeterminate, emerges in the dialogic exchange of analysis through a retelling—the creation of a new narrative whose constitutive parts are the intertexts of the individual and cultural past.[6]

Freud also breaks down the autonomy of the dream-text by reading dreams in relation to other dreams, decoding a series of dreams as a composite text. "A whole series of dreams," he writes, "continuing over a period of weeks or months, is often based upon common ground and must accordingly be interpreted in connecton with one another" (*ID*, 563). In "consecutive dreams," one dream often "takes as its central point something that is only on the periphery of the other and *vice versa*" (*ID*, 563). Reading serial dreams requires an analysis of the gaps in each that can be filled in by the others—the traces of displacement, condensation, and secondary revision that can be deciphered by juxtaposing and superimposing the texts in the whole series. The resonances among the dreams, the consonances and dissonances, can themselves be read for clues to unravel the disguise, undo the work of the censor. As he writes about dreams occurring in a single night:

> The content of all dreams that occur during the same night forms part of the same whole; the fact of their being divided into several sections, as well as the grouping and number of those sections—all of this has a meaning and may be regarded as a piece of information arising from the latent dream-thoughts. . . . [T]he possibility should not be overlooked that separate and successive dreams of this kind

6. For a discussion of narrative in the analytic situation, see Roy Shafer, "Narration in the Psychoanalytic Dialogue," in *On Narrative*, ed. W. J. T. Mitchell (Chicago: University of Chicago Press, 1981), 25–50.

> ... may be giving expression to the same impulses in different mate-
> rial. If so, the first of these homologous dreams to occur is often the
> more distorted and timid, while the succeeding one will be more
> confident and distinct. (*ID*, 369)

This formulation of repetitive dreams anticipates Freud's concept of the repetition compulsion and transference. Repressed desires, Freud later argues in his papers on technique, lead a person to "repeat" patterns of behavior as the person "transfers" the feelings from early childhood onto the contempotary adult scene. The analytic situation triggers the "transference": the analysand acts out with the analyst the patterns he or she once enacted with others, particularly parents, a repetition that is both a resistance to analysis and the clue that allows the analysis to proceed. The goal of analysis, Freud believes, is to move the analysand from repetition to remembering by "working through" the transference. Once an adult can remember the past, he or she is no longer doomed to repeat it.[7]

Freud's intertextual hermeneutic is richly suggestive for literary analysis because writing, like dreams, can enact a negotiation between desire and repression in which linguistic disguise accomplishes a compromise between expression and suppression. When the novel is autobiographical—like *Stephen Hero*, *Portrait*, or *Ulysses*—this negotiation is further heightened. Autobiographical self-creation recapitulates the developmental processes of the psyche, especially, as Colin MacCabe writes in *James Joyce and the Revolution of the Word*, "the construction of the subject in language."[8]

Like a palimpsest, both psyche and literary text are layered, with repressed elements erupting in disguised forms onto the manifest surface of consciousness. Building on the work of Julia Kristeva, critics such as Jonathan Culler, Shoshana Felman, Fredric Jameson, and Michael Riffaterre further suggest that a text has an unconscious accessible to interpretation through a decoding of its linguistic traces and effects. For Culler in "Textual Self-Consciousness and the Textual Unconscious" and Felman in "Turning the Screw of Interpretation," this textual unconscious is located in the interac-

---

7. See especially Freud, "The Dynamics of the Transference" (1912) and "Further Recommendations in the Technique of Psychoanalysis: Recollection, Repetition, and Working Through" (1914), both in his *Therapy and Technique*, ed. Philip Rieff (New York: Collier Books, 1963), 105–16, 157–66.

8. Colin MacCabe, *James Joyce and the Revolution of the Word* (London: Macmillan, 1978), 11.

tion between reader and text, which they see as a scene of transference in which the reader "repeats" the complexes of the text.[9] For Jameson in *The Political Unconscious* and Riffaterre in "The Intertextual Unconscious," the textual unconscious resides in the text, subject to the decoding of the reader, who occupies the authoritative position of the analyst. According to Riffaterre, the surface of a novel is narrative, but it has a lyric "subtext," a "verbal unconscious" buried etymologically and sylleptically inside the manifest words of the text.[10] For Jameson texts have a "political unconscious," which he defines as the repressed narrative of class struggle which a Marxist hermeneutic can interpret: "It is in detecting the traces of that interrupted narrative [of class struggle], in restoring to the surface of the text the repressed and buried reality of this fundamental history, that the doctrine of a political unconscious finds its function and its necessity."[11] From another perspective, Culler suggests, "the literary unconscious is an authorial unconscious, an unconscious involved in the production of literature; and the notion is thus useful for raising questions about the relation between what gets into the work and what gets left out, and about the sorts of repression that may operate in the production of literature."[12]

Combined with Freud's intertextual hermeneutic, all these approaches to the textual unconscious are useful for reading chains of related texts such as Joyce's works featuring Stephen D(a)edalus. "Drafts," such as *Stephen Hero*, can be read as the textual and political unconscious of the "final" text, *Portrait of the Artist*. The draft may contain elements that are repressed and transformed by the linguistic mechanisms analogous to the dream-work as the author revises the text. In becoming more "artful," the final version may indeed subject the draft to the process of linguistic encoding analogous to the production of a dream out of the forbidden desires restricted to the unconscious. In political terms, the repression of what is forbidden in the change from draft to final text may reflect the role of ideology as an internalized censor that allows the revela-

9. Jonathan Culler, "Textual Self-Consciousness and the Textual Unconscious," *Style* 18 (Summer 1984): 369–76; Shoshana Felman, "Turning the Screw of Interpretation," *Yale French Studies* 55/56 (1977): 94–207.

10. Michael Riffaterre, "The Intertextual Unconscious," *Critical Inquiry* 13 (Winter 1987): 385.

11. Fredric Jameson, *The Political Unconscious: Narrative as a Socially Symbolic Act* (Ithaca: Cornell University Press, 1981), 20.

12. Culler, "Textual Self-Consciousness," 369.

tion of a given story only if it is concealed through the mechanisms of the dream-work. Existence of the draft potentially aids the interpretation of what is hidden in the final text. The earlier text may erupt into the gaps of the later text just as cultural and political rebellion disrupts the social order. Textual repression can reflect cultural and political oppression. Representing "the return of the repressed," the draft version may contain a powerful and forbidden critique of the social order reflected in the final text.

And yet, a chain of drafts and texts with the same characters invokes Freud's theory of serial dreams and repetition. Stephen's reappearance in text after text suggests another form of the return of the repressed. Especially in autobiographical texts, *writing*, as well as reading, can be regarded as a scene of transference where the drama of repetition, resistance, and working through is enacted. Different drafts of a final text or texts in a series can be interpreted as repetitions in which the author is working through conflicts in an effort (conscious or unconscious) to move from repetition to remembering. Within this context the earlier drafts may well be the most repressed, most subject to resistance and transference, while the final text may represent in certain respects the author's capacity, achieved through language, to bring to conscious memory the issues repressed in the prior drafts. Similarly, in a series of texts with the same character, the early text may be the most distorted or timid, while the last text may represent the author's success in working through repetition to remembering.[13]

I am suggesting, in other words, the necessity of reading a chain of related texts "both ways"—on the one hand by refusing to regard the final text simply as aesthetically superior, the teleological endpoint of all the others, and on the other hand, by recognizing that repression can be present at the beginning as well as the end the process.[14] Rather than searching for the "authentic" version, I want to regard all versions as part of a larger composite text whose parts remain distinct yet interact according to a psycho-political dynamic to which we have some access with the help of Freud's grammar for the dream-work. This fluid method for reading a palimpsestic text further suggests that neither the beginning nor the endpoint in

13. See my *Penelope's Web*, 136–214, for an analysis of how this process works in H.D.'s *Paint It To-Day, Asphodel,* and *Bid Me to Live (A Madrigal).* For an analysis of writing as transference, see *Penelope's Web*, 281–354.

14. For a critique of the teleological attempt to find the "true" text in much textual criticism, see Jerome McGann, *A Critique of Modern Textual Criticism* (Chicago: University of Chicago Press, 1983).

a textual series should be privileged as the most or least repressed. Rather, all texts in the series can be read as sites of repression and disguised expression. In addition to reading both ways, we need to read the texts in a series relationally, recognizing that what may be condensed or distorted in one text may appear in less disguised forms in another. The object of this psycho-political hermeneutic is not a single, fixed reading of repression and expression, but rather perpetually shifting and relational readings that can give us some sort of access to the textual and political unconscious of a writer's oeuvre.

Stephen Hero and Portrait

If we superimpose *Portrait* on top of *Stephen Hero*, *Portrait* reads like a dreamscape and primer of the modernist break with the conventions of nineteenth-century realism, as many critics have argued. Reading Joyce's early development through the lens of *Finnegans Wake*, John Paul Riquelme finds the realist "muddles" of *Stephen Hero* a stage Joyce had to grow beyond to achieve the masterful sharpness of *Portrait*'s modernist style.[15] Riquelme's evident distaste for *Stephen Hero* is more overt than most critics', but his assertion that *Portrait* represents Joyce's emergence out of a realist/naturalist discourse into a recognizably modernist one is common.[16] Joyce's letters and conversations with friends, as well as the vast archive of manuscript material, suggest that he regularly engaged in an extraordinarily self-conscious process of layered writing and rewriting and thus foster the view that the difference between *Stephen Hero* and *Portrait* resulted from conscious aesthetic choice. Moreover, the contemporary privileging of modernism over realism (and postmodernism over modernism) has led to teleological readings of his revisions and developing oeuvre as necessarily progres-

15. John Paul Riquelme, *Teller and Tale in Joyce's Fiction: Oscillating Perspectives* (Baltimore: Johns Hopkins Press, 1983), 94.
16. For discussions of the differences between *Stephen Hero* and *Portrait*, see, for example, Riquelme, *Teller and Tale*, 48–55, 86–97; Richard Ellmann, *James Joyce*, rev. ed. (New York: Oxford University Press, 1982), 296–99; Bonnie Kime Scott, *Joyce and Feminism* (Bloomington: Indiana University Press, 1984), 15–17, 29–33, 48–53, 133–55; MacCabe, *James Joyce*, 39–68; Norris, "Portraits"; William York Tindall, *A Reader's Guide to James Joyce* (New York: Noonday Press, 1959), 101–3; James R. Sosnowski, "Reading Acts and Reading Warrants: Some Implication for Readers Responding to Joyce's Portrait of Stephen," *James Joyce Quarterly* 16 (1979): 43–63.

sive, with each text an "advance" over the one before.[17] I do not question the force of Joyce's conscious intention or the significance for literary history of his emergent modernism, but I want to suggest that revision, like composition, is an overdetermined process that incorporates unconscious motivations as well as conscious ones and cannot be fully understood solely in terms of poetics and literary history.

Traces of the unconscious processes of Joyce's revisions reside in the usefulness of Freud's grammar of the dream-work for reading the transition from realism to modernism marked by *Stephen Hero* and *Portrait*. The condensation of Stephen's family name from Daedalus in *Stephen Hero* to Dedalus in *Portrait* is symptomatic of the operation of the dream-work in the revision process. The absence of the *a* provides *Portrait*'s Dedalus with what Riffaterre calls a "verbal unconscious": the Greek name Daedalus is both there and not there in Stephen's name. This condensation disrupts an allegorical equation of Stephen with the brilliant Greek artificer Daedalus and introduces irony into Joyce's mythic analogue. The letter change questions, for example, whether Stephen's kinship is with the father or the foolhardy son Icarus; the sound change (from Daedalus to Dedalus) also puns on the word *dead*, which suggests Stephen's paralysis to come and his obsession with death in *Ulysses*.[18] "Names! What's in a name?" someone, echoing Shakespeare, asks Stephen in the ninth episode ("Scylla and Charybdis") of *Ulysses*.[19] The deletion of the *a* establishes an ironic indeterminacy, an open-

17. For examples of critics who read Joyce's development from *Stephen Hero* to *Portrait*, from *Portrait* to *Ulysses*, from the first (stylistic) part to the second part of *Ulysses*, or from *Ulysses* to *Finnegans Wake* in terms of a progressive metanarrative (from realism/ naturalism to modernism or from modernism to postmodernism), see, for example, Riquelme, *Teller and Tale*; MacCabe, *James Joyce*; Frances Restuccia, *Joyce and the Law of the Father* (New Haven: Yale University Press, 1988); Patrick McGee, *Paperspace: Style as Ideology in Joyce's Ulysses* (Lincoln: University of Nebraska Press, 1988); Sheldon Brivic, *Joyce between Freud and Jung* (Port Washington, N.Y.: Kinnikat Press, 1980); Karen Lawrence, *The Odyssey of Style in Ulysses* (Princeton: Princeton University Press, 1981); Brook Thomas, *Ulysses: The Book of Many Happy Returns* (Baton Rouge: Louisiana State University Press, 1982).

18. Joyce's pronunciation of both Daedalus and Dedalus was "Deedalus," according to Phillip Herring, a fact that might argue against a pun with "dead" in Dedalus. Herring suggests that the change might reflect Stephen's insistence that his name is Irish, not Greek (conversation with author). However Joyce pronounced the names, the fluidity and multilayered play with words that characterize his work suggest the possibility of a pun in Dedalus. The missing *a* in *Portrait* may have migrated to the name of Stephen's feminist friend, named McCann in *Stephen Hero* and MacCann in *Portrait*.

19. James Joyce, *Ulysses*, ed. Hans Walter Gabler et al. (New York: Random House, 1986), 9.901; hereafter cited in the text as *U* with episode and line numbers.

endedness that invites the reader to complete its interpretation—all qualities we have come to associate with modernism.

Condensation is clearly a major principle of revision in the transformation of *Stephen Hero* into *Portrait*.[20] Before Joyce abandoned the unfinished *Stephen Hero* in 1906, the manuscript was already about a thousand pages. Moreover, the 253 extant pages of *Stephen Hero* focus on a time period covered in 93 pages of *Portrait*.[21] More important, *Portrait* is stripped of what critics have called its naturalist setting and panoply of characters to focus entirely on Stephen. As Stephen himself prophetically states in *Stephen Hero*, "Isolation is the first principle of artistic economy" (*SH*, 33). Maurice and Isabel, Stephen's siblings in *Stephen Hero*, vanish, highlighting Stephen's alienation within the family. As Bonnie Kime Scott has pointed out in *Joyce and Feminism*, Emma Clery, a fully drawn character, a fellow student and feminist in *Stephen Hero*, is reduced to the initials E.C. in *Portrait*, a wraithlike fantasy of Stephen's desire instead of a woman who speaks her own mind.[22] Many episodes have been dropped from the later text. Stephen's delivery of his paper on Ibsen at the Debating Society and the traumatic death of his sister Isabel are two of the more important incidents to be erased.[23] Even the narrator in *Stephen Hero*, whose commentary is at times essayistic, disappears into a Jamesian center of consciousness which unrelievedly follows Stephen in *Portrait*. Accomplished in part by condensation, this focus on Stephen's subjectivity parallels what Freud calls the overwhelming egotism of the dream-world and embodies the foregrounding of consciousness that we associate with modernism.[24]

20. Although without reference to *Stephen Hero*, Maud Ellmann argues for *Portrait*'s modernity by demonstrating its synedochal economy and its radical transformation of "the tradition of the human subject" in "Disremembering Dedalus: 'A Portrait of the Artist as a Young Man,'" in *Untying the Text: A Poststructuralist Reader*, ed. Robert Young (London: Routledge and Kegan Paul, 1981), 197.

21. For the history of *Stephen Hero*'s composition and the fate of the manuscript, see Theodore Spencer's introduction to *Stephen Hero*, 7–17.

22. See Scott, *Joyce and Feminism*, 133–55.

23. Dropped from *Portrait*, Isabel may well have returned as Isabel in *Finnegans Wake*; but as Norris demonstrates, the *Wake*'s Isabel can also be read as a return of *Stephen Hero*'s Emma Clery ("Portraits," 149).

24. The discursive narrator in *Stephen Hero*, rooted in the ethical and aesthetic commentaries of narrators in the works of giants such as William Makepeace Thackaray, Charles Dickens, and George Eliot, is also a carryover from *Stephen Hero*'s 1904 precursor, "A Portrait of the Artist" (*P*, 257–60), the text that Richard Ellmann calls a "narrative/essay" (*James Joyce*, 147). For Freud's discussion of egotism in dreams, see *Interpretation of Dreams*, 301ff., 407. In *Stephen Hero*, Stephen is frequently the center of consciousness, but the narrator often adopts a discursive role, and Cranly at one point is the center of

Displacement also contributes to the transformation of *Stephen Hero* into *Portrait* in ways that highlight the later text's modernism. In *Stephen Hero*, for example, Stephen's aesthetic theory appears near the middle of the extant manuscript, at the beginning and end of Chapter 19, first in the narrator's discursive summary of his ideas and then in a dramatic episode in which Stephen expounds his Aquinian theory of the beautiful to the president of his college in defense of what the president calls his heretical paper representing "the sum-total of modern unrest and modern freethinking" (*SH*, 91). But in *Portrait*, Stephen's theorizing on *integritas*, *consonantia*, and *claritas* appears in direct dialogue with Lynch in the penultimate chapter, immediately preceding his decision to leave Ireland. His audience is not the Censor, who is won over by the brilliance of his defense in *Stephen Hero*, but rather the scatological and materialist collegemate, who is preoccupied with scratching his groin, swearing, thinking about his "yellow drunk" the night before, remembering how he ate cow dung as a boy, and connecting desire to writing his name on the backside of the Venus of Praxiteles (*P*, 204–10). Joyce's displacement of Stephen's aesthetic theory from the president's chambers to the walk with Lynch undermines Stephen's stance as romantic artist-hero in *Stephen Hero* and contributes to the modernist irony of Joyce's self-portrait in *Portrait*.

Stephen's composition of the villanelle in *Portrait* is both a displacement and a condensation of related events in *Stephen Hero*. In the earlier text Stephen hesitantly shows a poem of desire to his brother Maurice, who immediately asks "who she was" (*SH*, 36). Stephen does not name or even know his muse, but desire fuels his verbal longing: "The dawn awakes with tremulous alarms / . . . O, hold me still white arms, encircling arms!" (*SH*, 37). Emma Clery, with her "warm" body and inviting eyes, increasingly fleshes out his disembodied muse. Catching sight of Emma one day through the college window, Stephen madly rushes after her to say: "I felt that I longed to hold you in my arms—your body. I longed for you to take me in your arms. . . . Just to live one night together, Emma, and then to say goodbye in the morning and never to see each other again!" (*SH*, 198). Emma is hurt, angry, and confused. "You are mad,

consciousness for a sustained episode (*SH*, 123–25). For John Riquelme, the invisibility of the narrator in *Portrait* represents a merger of narrator and Stephen that is a mark of the text's modernist narrative point of view (*Teller and Tale*, 54). Sheldon Brivic writes: "Joyce, rewriting *Portrait* to see his mental struggle as central to his age, was first to build an understanding of neurosis as the force of culture (*Joyce between Freud to Jung*, 52).

Stephen," she says twice as she breaks away from him (*SH*, 198–99). Thereafter she refuses to acknowledge Stephen, including the moment when she pointedly ignores him and bows slightly to his friend Cranly (*SH*, 215). Stephen in turn is angry with what he sees as her conventionality, coupled with the inviting warmth of her body. Thinking of her as "the most deceptive and cowardly of marsupials," Stephen composes "some ardent verses which he entitled a 'Vilanelle of the Temptress'" (*SH*, 210–11).

In *Portrait* this matrix of Emma's anger and Stephen's desire, his frustration, and the villanelle is collapsed into a single episode in the final chapter, which reweaves words and images from the earlier text to suggest the origins of poetry in unfulfilled and displaced desire. In *Portrait* there is no discussion with Maurice, no early verses about "encircling arms," no mad proposition for a one-night tryst, no angry woman who is hurt and insulted. Instead, everything takes place within Stephen's mind. His distant and bitter observation from afar of E.C. with her companions leads him to lie half awake the next morning in the dawn of desire to compose lines about a woman he does not name. "It was that windless hour of dawn when madness wakes"; Stephen feels encircled in the "pale cool waves of light," and the opening line comes to him: "*Are you not weary of ardent ways?*" (*P*, 217). Four times this refrain punctuates Stephen's villanelle in *Portrait* (223–24), with "ardent" echoing its first appearance in the scene from *Stephen Hero* where Stephen composes "some ardent verses" called "Vilanelle of the Temptress" (*SH*, 211). The desire that led Stephen to his mad act of a proposition in *Stephen Hero* is sublimated in *Portrait* into the creation of a poem. The poem itself embeds the narrative that was acted out in *Stephen Hero*. The poet's question, "Are you not weary of ardent ways?" expresses Stephen's anger at a woman whose body invites but denies: "*And still you hold our longing gaze / With languorous look and lavish limb*" (*P*, 223). She is a "temptress," and Stephen's villanelle in *Portrait* is the poet's revenge for unrequited love. The transposition accomplished by this sublimating condensation of Stephen's desire suggests that the move to (male) modernism coincides with the production of woman as representation—as, that is, a signifier originating in and functioning for the subject who is male.

The condensation of Emma Clery into E.C. in *Portrait* is accompanied by a dramatic intensification of nonrational modes of representation. In contrast to *Stephen Hero*, *Portrait* is a lyric novel whose narrative is continually forwarded by the complex web of figurative language which encodes the kinetic movement of the plot. Bird motifs, color clusters, alternating binaries (for example, light/dark, warm/cool, fire/water, virgin/whore, holy/polluted, word/flesh, body/soul, and so on), linguistic and structural repetitions, rhythmic patterns, and sound play weave the text into a whole and disrupt the linear direction of the surface narrative. Such stylistic patterns in *Portrait* are well known and need no review. But their absence from *Stephen Hero* and presence in *Portrait* suggest a heightening of linguistic processes that Freud associates with the dream-work and that later analysts such as Lacan and Kristeva identify with the discourse of the unconscious. Kristeva in particular theorizes that all texts constitute the subject through a dialectical interplay of what she calls the semiotic and symbolic modes of discourse.[25] In modernist (and postmodernist writing), she suggests, the semiotic register, based in the pre-oedipal stage of psychosexual development, erupts more insistently into the symbolic register of the text than it did in premodernist writing. Nondiscursive and lyric, the semiotic mode is more evident in *Portrait* than it is in *Stephen Hero*.[26]

For Colin MacCabe, this lyric or semiotic dimension of *Portrait* signifies the later text's resistance to narrative and renunciation of "classic realism," the "meta-language" of the fathers. *Portrait*, he argues in *James Joyce and the Revolution of the Word*, "attempts to evade paternal identification and, in that evasion, to let the desire of the mother speak."[27] His view is consistent with those, such as Sheldon Brivic, who suggest that the modernist and especially postmodernist writing of Joyce represents a man "writing as a woman," forging *l'écriture féminine*, or speaking the discourse of the Other in a subversion of the phallogocentric discourse of the father.[28] I want to suggest in contrast that *Portrait*'s modernist revi-

25. Julia Kristeva, *Revolution in Poetic Language*, trans. Margaret Waller (New York: Columbia University Press, 1984), 23–24.
26. While Joyce was writing *Stephen Hero*, he was also seriously engaged in writing lyrics, ultimately published as *Chamber Music*. By the time he wrote *Portrait*, he had largely abandoned poetry in verse, but instead introduced the lyric mode into his fiction. The semiotic continues to intensify in Joyce's writing after *Portrait*. *Portrait* has a greater degree of the symbolic mode than *Ulysses*; the same is true of *Ulysses* in relation to *Finnegans Wake*.
27. MacCabe, *James Joyce*, 64.
28. See, for example, Sheldon Brivic, *The Veil of Signs: Joyce, Lacan, and Perception* (Urbana: University of Illinois Press, 1991), 23–29; Vicki Mahaffey, *Reauthorizing Joyce* (Cambridge: Cambridge University Press, 1988), 1–19; Suzette A. Henke, *James Joyce and*

sion of *Stephen Hero* represents the silencing of the mother, the erasure of her subjectivity, and the creation of the m/other who exists for and in the discourse of the son who thereby takes his place in the symbolic order of the father. This production of the mother as signifier of the son's desire is symptomatic of the repression of female subjectivity in general: the agency of women as mothers, lovers, and actors on the literary and political stage of modern life.

I arrive at this reading by focusing on what MacCabe ignores: the role of the dream-work in compromising with the strictures of the censor, that agency which represents the internalization of cultural ideology. What, in other words, is repressed or censored out of *Stephen Hero*? What in the earlier text is so forbidden that it must be disguised in the revision? The answer centers, I believe, on the issue of the mother and what she represents to Stephen. Freud's metaphor for the dream's knot as a navel is prophetic for the transformation of the maternal in the movement from *Stephen Hero* to *Portrait*.[29] In *Stephen Hero* the mother is a figure who is both inside and outside a patriarchal church and state from which Stephen must ultimately flee to become an artist. In *Portrait* Stephen's projected exile represents a repudiation of the maternal, which incarnates the suffocating forces of the Irish church and state.

Censored out of *Portrait* is Stephen's first confrontation with the censor, the president who represents the paternal authority of the church which stifles the modern, the freethinking, and the creative. Significantly, Stephen's debate with the Censor in *Stephen Hero* follows a lengthy discussion of Henrik Ibsen with his mother. Stephen reads the paper he has written celebrating Ibsen as the spirit of the modern to his mother as she stands ironing. To his surprise

---

the *Politics of Desire* (New York: Routledge, 1990), 1–11, 126–63, 205–12. McGee in *Paperspace* and Restuccia in *Joyce and the Law of the Fathers* also see the transition from Joyce's early realism to (post) modernism as a resistance to patriarchal authority and an attempt to put himself in the place of a woman. But Restuccia warns that not all antipatriarchalism is feminist and argues that Joyce does not speak as the feminine Other but rather "ventriloquizes" it as a symptom of his compensatory masochism (156–58). McGee sees Joyce's resistance to the symbolic as symptomatic of the "repressed desire animating patriarchal ideology: man's desire to be other, to be what he imagines a woman to be" (187); but he cautions: "Certainly, after feminism it is not in any simple sense woman's desire" that Joyce speaks (187).

29. See Maud Ellmann's discussion of Freud's metaphor in relation to *Portrait* in "Disremembering Dedalus," in which she reads the text as "omphalocentric," emphasizing the dissolution of identity (203–4). See also MacCabe, *James Joyce* (39–68), for a Lacanian reading of the move from the father to the mother in the two texts.

she likes the paper and asks to read Ibsen. At first he imagines that
all she wants is "to see whether I am reading dangerous authors or
not" (SH, 85). But to his shock she reveals that "before I married
your father I used to read a great deal. I used to take an interest in
all kinds of new plays" (SH, 85). His father's distaste for such things
led her to stop. "Well, you see, Stephen," she explains, "your father
is not like you: he takes no interest in that sort of thing" (SH, 85).
He is startled when she actually reads a group of plays "with great
interest" and is amazed to watch her try to persuade his baffled and
bored father to read the plays too. Stephen suspiciously asks
whether she thinks Ibsen is "immoral," writing about "subjects
which, you think, should never be talked about." Stephen tries, in
other words, to put his mother in the position of the censor, a role
she pointedly refuses. "Do you think these plays are unfit for people
to read?" he asks. "No, I think they're magnificent plays," she answers. "And not immoral?" he repeats. "I think that Ibsen ... has
an extraordinary knowledge of human nature," she says (SH, 87).

In liking Ibsen, Stephen is his mother's child, not his father's.
The role of moral censor that Stephen anticipated his uneducated
mother would play is actually acted out by her intellectual "supe-
riors"—first, among Stephen's classmates, the "young feminist"
McCann, who says the paper is a "bit strong," and the Irish nationalist Madden, who predicts that no one will understand it (SH, 105);
then the president of the college, the Jesuit authority Father Dillon;
and finally the audience, who react with general hostility. While
Stephen's father attends the Debating Society at which Stephen
speaks, Stephen's mother, the only one to appreciate his ideas, stays
home. Outside the college that does not admit women, outside the
Jesuit educational system, Stephen's mother has a certain freedom
the others do not possess to respond to Ibsen. The "modern" toward
which Stephen aspires is presented as a legacy from his mother, not
his father, a "freethinking" that can be nurtured only beyond the
reach of the Jesuit Censor.[30]

That Ibsen should be the playwright to introduce Stephen to the
mother who knows, the mother who speaks, the mother who thinks
outside the Jesuit hegemony is no arbitrary choice. Ibsen's women

---

30. The point Joyce makes here is similar to the one Virginia Woolf makes in A Room
of One's Own (New York: Harcourt Brace Jovanovich, 1957) after she was locked out of
the library at Oxbridge: "And I thought how unpleasant it is perhaps to be locked out;
and I thought how it is worse perhaps to be locked in" (24).

are powerful figures who insist on their status as human beings, as subjects in a patriarchal world that would confine them to what men desire them to be. Joyce's first formal publication was "Ibsen's New Drama," a lengthy review essay focused on Ibsen's *When We Dead Awaken*, which was published in the *Fortnightly Review* (1900). In it Joyce praised Ibsen's psychological realism, especially the "marvelous accuracy" of "his portrayal of women," whom "he seems to know . . . better than they know themselves."[31] Joyce wrote his brother in 1907 that Ibsen "was the only writer that ever persuaded me that women had a soul."[32] Much later still, Joyce defended Ibsen to Arthur Power by saying that "the purpose of *The Doll's House*, for instance, was the emancipation of women, which has caused the greatest revolution in our time in the most important revolution there is—that between men and women; the revolt of women against the idea that they are the mere instruments of men."[33] As with some of Ibsen's women, the potential for freedom that Stephen's mother represents is ultimately destroyed by the power of the church and the authority she is willing to give it. Her defense of Ibsen is ironically followed in Chapter 21 by her

31. James Joyce, *The Critical Writings of James Joyce*, ed. Ellsworth Mason and Richard Ellmann (New York: Viking Press, 1959), 64. Vicki Mahaffey also stresses the importance of this essay, but in contrast to my emphasis on Ibsen as a writer whose use of realist conventions fostered his representations of female subjectivity, she argues that "Ibsen's last play is a relentless inquest into the implications of realist representation" and became the starting point of Joyce's "lifelong search for alternative means of producing and reproducing human experience" (*Reauthorizing Joyce*, 196); this reading of the significance of Ibsen for Joyce ignores Joyce's praise for Ibsen's realism in his essay.

32. Ellmann, *James Joyce*, 287.

33. Arthur Power, *Conversations with James Joyce*, ed. Clive Hart (New York: Barnes-Harper, 1974), 35. In "Stifled Back Answers: The Gender Politics of Art in Joyce's 'The Dead,'" *Modern Fiction Studies* 35 (Autumn 1989): 479–506, Margot Norris argues that the political, socialist, and feminist Ibsen deeply influenced Joyce and contributed to Joyce's later ironic exposure of aestheticism as antifeminist in such texts as "The Dead" and *Portrait*. Although she offers a powerful reading of "The Dead" in conjunction with *When We Dead Awaken* and *The Doll's House*, I am not convinced that Joyce made the feminist critique she finds in the text and attributes to his conscious intention. The praise the eighteen-year-old Joyce heaped on Ibsen in "Ibsen's New Drama" mentions nothing political and centers on the extraordinary "genius" Joyce saw in him and his powerful representations of bourgeois life rendered with such "accuracy." Joyce's admiration for Ibsen's feminism expressed to Power does support Norris's reading. But I would suggest that Joyce's stance toward feminism was far more ambivalent than this statement allows. Norris's belief that Joyce retained an unchanging admiration for a feminist and political Ibsen throughout his life does not take into account how Ibsen drops out of *Stephen Hero* in the construction of *Portrait*. Similarly, Norris uses her reading of Joyce's feminist critique in "The Dead" as evidence that this critique is continuously present in *Portrait* and *Ulysses*, an assumption that ignores the development of Joyce's oeuvre from the social and psychological realism of *Dubliners* and *Stephen Hero* to the modernism of *Portrait* and *Ulysses*.

request for Stephen to perform his "Easter duty," which he refuses to do (*SH*, 131). In the context of her superiority to Father Dillon about Ibsen, her naive faith in the church represents a betrayal of the freethinking to which her position as a woman privileges her. In refusing her request, Stephen remains true to the legacy she has betrayed for herself but passed on to him.

In *Portrait* the paper on Ibsen has vanished, along with the mother who knows and the father who censors. What remains is his mother's request that Stephen perform his Easter duty and his ringing *non serviam*, displaced into the final chapter of *Portrait* and embedded in his last conversation with Cranly as the climactic preparation for his flight. As Hélène Cixous points out, *Portrait* portrays words as Stephen's legacy from his father, while the body that he both desires and hates is his inheritance from his mother. As a secondary revision of *Stephen Hero*, *Portrait* reorders the *Bildung* narrative of development along classically oedipal lines. The mother is the figure from whom Stephen must separate, for whom he must repress and ultimately sublimate his desire.[34]

As *Portrait*'s famous opening paragraph establishes, the father is the storyteller, the impresario of words, while the maternal is associated with the "moocow," taste, smells, blossoms, music, nonsense syllables, and warm urine—a sort of Kristevan semiotic (*P*, 7). Initiation at school involves learning that a boy shouldn't "kiss his mother before he goes to bed" (*P*, 14). Initiation as a youth, as Suzette Henke argues, means oscillating between desire for and loathing of the maternal body—in its pure form, the madonna; in its polluted form, the whore. Youth also means identification with the awesome power of the priest, whose word can bring the spirit of Christ into the flesh and blood of the Eucharist.[35] Even when Stephen rejects the power with which the Jesuit tempts him in Chapter 4, he takes on the priest's authority in the secular domain of art.

34. Hélène Cixous, "Reaching the Point of Wheat, or A Portrait of the Artist as a Maturing Woman," *New Literary History* 19 (Autumn 1987): 1–23. See also MacCabe, *James Joyce*, 56; and Christine Froula, "Gender and the Law of Genre: Joyce, Woolf, and the Autobiographical Artist-Novel," in Scott, *New Alliances*, 155–64. Froula argues that as an autobiographical artist novel *Portrait* "represents its own origins not as a birth from a mother but as a triumphant self-fathering. . . . [I]n *Portrait* Stephen/Joyce's actual maternal origin is strenuously overwritten by a symbolic paternal origin" (157).

35. Suzette A. Henke, "Stephen Dedalus and Women: A Portrait of the Artist as Young Misogynist," in *Women in Joyce*, ed. Suzette A. Henke and Elaine Unkeless (Urbana: University of Illinois Press, 1982), 87–88, 101–2. See also Restuccia's discussion of the Eucharist in *Ulysses* as a parody of the religious Law of the Father that Joyce invokes and then subverts through exaggeration (*Joyce*, 20–72).

Stephen's birth as an artist in Chapter 5, however qualified through irony, nonetheless represents his identification with the legacy of the fathers' exercising the authority of Logos. Within a Lacanian framework Stephen's *Bildung* follows the expected pattern of the son who has come to take up his position within the Symbolic Order according to the Law of the Father. The endless deferral of his desire—first for his mother, then for E.C.—is what allows him to occupy the position of the subject, the master of the signifier.[36]

The identification of Stephen's mother with the body instead of the word in *Portrait* is evident in the transposition of kitchen scenes between mother and son from *Stephen Hero* to *Portrait*. In the earlier text Stephen reads his paper while his mother irons, her thoughts moving back and forth with her arm (*SH*, 83–87). But in *Portrait* this scene is moved to the opening of the final chapter and represents the *only* substantial scene in the novel in which she appears directly, unmediated by Stephen's representation of her (*P*, 175–76).[37] Instead of discussing Ibsen, Stephen's mother agrees to bathe him, complains that "a university student is so dirty that his mother has to wash him," but does not contradict him when he "calmly" counters, "But it gives you pleasure" (*P*, 175). The mother who knows is replaced by the mother whose pleasure is to care for her son's body. As for his soul, she is convinced in *Portrait* that he has been corrupted by his reading: "Ah, it's a scandalous shame for you, Stephen, . . . and you'll live to rue the day you set your foot in that place. I know how it has changed you" (*P*, 175). In *Portrait* Stephen's mother occupies the position of censor she had repeatedly refused in *Stephen Hero*.

36. See, for example, Jacques Lacan, "Seminar on 'The Purloined Letter,'" in *The Purloined Poe: Lacan, Derrida, and Psychoanalytic Reading*, ed. John P. Muller and William J. Richardson (Baltimore: Johns Hopkins Press, 1988), 55–76; "The Signification of the Phallus," in *Ecrits: A Selection*, trans. Alan Sheridan (New York: Norton, 1977), 281–90. Mahaffey also associates the Stephen of *Portrait* and *Ulysses* with a "monological" and "transcendent" authority that originates in the Law of the Father (*Reauthorizing Joyce*, 1–63); Restuccia, however, believes, along with Margot Norris ("Portraits"), that Joyce intentionally subverts Stephen's association with the Law of the Father through parody and irony (*Joyce*, esp. 16, 137). I agree that in *Portrait* Stephen is already subject to irony, but in reading *Portrait* in relation to *Stephen Hero*, I am not convinced that Joyce's oedipal patterning of Stephen's *Bildung* in his revision represents a critique of that pattern. For a discussion of how Freud's *Interpretation of Dreams* represents a related oedipalization of desire and suppression of female subjectivity, see my "Hysteria, Dreams, and Modernity."

37. Stephen's mother speaks one brief sentence at four other points in the novel: three times during the fight at the Christmas dinner, when she asks for peace (*P*, 31, 32) and when she tells Simon not to speak coarsely before Stephen (*P*, 33); and once to Simon, when she says about Stephen's schooling, "I never liked the idea of sending him to the christian brothers myself" (*P*, 71).

With the removal of the Jesuit censors from *Stephen Hero*, the mother in *Portrait* remains the central force opposed to Stephen's flight into the modern. In this role she represents the suffocations of both church and state in Ireland. Ireland is the "fatherland" in *Stephen Hero*, a nomenclature reinforced by the power of the male priesthood, from whom Stephen must escape (*SH*, 53, 77).[38] In refusing the appeal to Irish nationalism made by Madden and other classmates, Stephen is denying his patrimony. In *Portrait* Stephen tells Cranly that he will not serve his "fatherland" (*P*, 247), but in the lyric web of the text Ireland has become feminized, frighteningly maternal. Stephen bitterly calls his country "the old sow that eats her farrow" (*P*, 203), a line that recurs in *Ulysses* and anticipates Stephen's association of Ireland with Old Gummy Granny in Nighttown (*U*, 15.4578–88). "When the soul of man is born in this country," Stephen tells the Irish peasant-student Davin, "there are nets flung at it to hold it back from flight. You talk to me of nationality, language, religion. I shall try to fly by those nets" (*P*, 203). The peasant woman who called Davin to her bed one dark night epitomizes that Irish net to Stephen. Absorbing Davin's story in horrified fascination, Stephen remembers

> [the] figure of the woman in the story [who] stood forth, reflected in other figures of the peasant women whom he had seen standing in the doorways at Clane . . . as a type of her race and his own, a batlike soul waking to the consciousnes of itself in darkness and secrecy and loneliness and, through the eyes and voice and gesture of a woman without guile, calling the stranger to her bed. (*P*, 183)

In the wake of this story, the request of Stephen's mother that he remember his religion is tantamount to the peasant woman's "calling the stranger to her bed." Cranly reminds Stephen of the constancy of a mother's love and concludes his appeal by softly singing an Irish tune: "*For I love sweet Rosie O'Grady / And Rosie O'Grady loves me*" (*P*, 244). But Stephen counters this conflation of mother love and Ireland by announcing his commitment to "unfettered freedom" (*P*, 246). In psychodynamic terms Stephen's exile is matri-

---

38. One reference to Ireland as "mother-country" does appear in *Stephen Hero*, when the nationalist in Mullingar, Mr. Heffenan, asks Stephen if he doesn't feel any "duty to your mother-country, [any] love for her" (*SH*, 247). But unlike *Portrait* and *Ulysses*, *Stephen Hero* does not regularly make use of the conventional association of Ireland with a poor old woman.

cidal. The final diary entry in *Portrait* represents the son's erasure of the maternal and identification and embrace of the Father: "21 *April*: Old father, old artificer, stand me now and ever in good stead" (*P*, 253).

What happens to Stephen's mother in *Portrait* is symptomatic of what happens to Emma Clery in the secondary revision of *Stephen Hero*. No doubt caught in the conventions of the patriarchal church and state, Emma nonetheles advocates an end to the exclusion of women from the university, refuses to be expended in the economy of Stephen's desire, and chooses to whom she will direct her attention in *Stephen Hero*. While none of these acts poses a radical challenge to Irish patriarchy, each demonstrates a degree of female agency that Stephen himself would deny her. His anger at her independence—akin perhaps to W. B. Yeats's frustration with Maud Gonne—anticipates Joyce's censorship of that agency in *Portrait*. As E.C. she is the temptress who flirts with the priest, the tease who leads Stephen on, lyrically linked to both virgin and whore. Scarcely ever a character who speaks and acts in *Portrait*, E.C. has become a representation of woman primarily existing in and for Stephen's subjectivity.[39]

The narrative of the mother who knows and the lover who speaks in *Stephen Hero* is the political unconscious of *Portrait*, censored out of the later text as Joyce forges the language of modernity. These transformations of the mother and lover suggest that the development of Joyce's modernism—and perhaps the phenomenon of male modernism in general—involves the repression of the mother, of woman, as subject. In Lacanian terms, woman in *Portrait* exists as the position of castration—as the Other (m/other) who cannot speak, but whose function as signifier within the chain of signification in the Symbolic Order is essential. To put it simply, a Lacanian theory of the subject, which is dependent on the presumption that the phallus is the transcendental signifier, suggests that the subject—a position implicitly reserved for men—cannot speak without the silence of the Other, a place occupied by women. While Lacan's concept of the subject in language is presented in universalistic terms, I am suggesting that it is itself an extension of the modern-

---

39. For further discussion, see Henke, "Stephen Dedalus and Women," on E.C. and Scott in *Joyce and Feminism* on Emma (133–55). Henke's article is reprinted in her *James Joyce and the Politics of Desire*, which also includes additional analysis of Joyce's maternal longings and loathings.

ism represented in Joyce's *Portrait*—the male modernism premised on the erasure of women's agency in language and women's reduction from subject to object in a male economy of desire.[40]

This censorship of women's speech in *Portrait* parallels the erasure of feminism itself as a discourse from *Stephen Hero*, prefigures the marginalization of women writers within the literary histories of modernism, and points to another dimension of the political unconscious of the later text. In *Stephen Hero* feminism, nationalism, and pacifism are the three political movements debated among the students. Stephen denies the relevance of all three to his development as an artist. But what is relevant here is the *presence* of feminism as an issue that Stephen must work through. One of the early extant chapters of *Stephen Hero* presents a sharp debate between Stephen and McCann about feminism. Formulaically identified at several points as "the young feminist," McCann argues forcefully for the rights of women to have access to all spheres of life. "Stephen delighted to riddle these theories with agile bullets," the narrator tells us, not only by bringing the authority of the church to bear, but also by linking feminism with McCann's prudish chastity and advocacy of abstinence from alcohol (*SH*, 49).[41]

In *Portrait* this debate has vanished; McCann is a greatly reduced character, and his feminism is condensed into one pejorative comment made about him by a mocker: "No stimulants and votes for the bitches" (*P*, 195). As in *Stephen Hero*, McCann in *Portrait* asks Stephen, without success, to sign the petition for the tsar on peace. But his role as serious advocate for feminism is repressed in the process of revision. The disappearance of Stephen's paper on Ibsen in *Portrait* can also be read as part of this general suppression of feminism in the discourse of (male) modernism. Ibsen's trapped but powerful heroines were frequently associated with "the woman question" at the turn of the century—most especially Nora in *The*

40. In various ways other critics have discussed the importance of woman-as-signifier in the development of (male) modernism and postmodernism. See, for example, Alice Jardine, *Gynesis: Configurations of Woman and Modernity* (New York: Columbia University Press, 1985); Sandra M. Gilbert and Susan Gubar, *No Man's Land: The War of the Words* (New Haven: Yale University Press, 1987); Teresa de Lauretis, *Alice Doesn't: Feminism, Semiotics, Cinema* (Bloomington: Indiana University Press, 1984); and Christine van Boheemen, *The Novel as Family Romance: Language, Gender, and Authority from Fielding to Joyce* (Ithaca: Cornell University Press, 1987).

41. See Scott, *Joyce and Feminism* (30–44), for a discussion of the model for McCann—Francis J. C. Skeffington, Joyce's close friend, a feminist who married another feminist friend of Joyce's, Hanna Sheehy. The Sheehy family served as the model for the Danielses in *Stephen Hero*.

Doll's House, a connection alluded to in Stephen's discussions with McCann and his mother (*SH,* 52, 86). Stephen's interpretation of Ibsen in *Stephen Hero* anticipates the erasure of Ibsen from *Portrait.* In touting Ibsen as the avant-garde of the modern, Stephen sees him "as free from any missionary attempt," free from the shackles of using "art to instruct, to elevate, and to amuse" (*SH,* 92, 79). Ibsen perfectly embodies for Stephen the aesthetic of Aquinas—"*Pulcra sunt quae visa placent.* . . . the beautiful as that which satisfies the esthetic appetite"—an advocacy of art based on "*integritas, consonantia, claritas*" (*SH,* 95–96). Unnamed in *Portrait,* Stephen's Ibsen in *Stephen Hero* is the textual unconscious buried within his description of the ideal dramatist in *Portrait:* "The artist, like the God of the creation, remains within or behind or beyond or above his handiwork, invisible, refined out of existence, indifferent, paring his fingernails" (*P,* 215).[42]

The censorship of debate about feminism evident in the revision of *Stephen Hero* in turn replicates the gradual erasure of feminism as part of the agenda of the modern in the heady days of prewar modernism. As Rachel Blau DuPlessis has argued, the name change of *The New Freewoman* to *The Egoist* in December 1913 is symptomatic of a shift in modernism.[43] Founded in 1911 by the militant feminist Dora Marsden, *The Freewoman* and its 1912 successor, *The New Freewoman,* advocated a broad-ranging cultural revolution that would affect not only the arts but also the institutions of sexuality, the family, work, and the state. What Marsden called "egoism" was central to her feminism, which promoted for both women and men a radical severing of the self from the confinements

42. In "Stifled Back Answers," Norris presents a different reading of Joyce's censorship of female subjectivity and feminism. She sees this erasure as itself the *subject* of Joyce's conscious critique. In her recuperation of Joyce for feminism, Norris reads *Portrait* and Stephen's aestheticism as "systematically ironized" (482). In "The Dead," she argues, Joyce's point is "that when a woman is transformed into a symbol by man, woman becomes a symbol of her social decontextualization, her silencing, the occlusion of her suffering, the suppression of her feeling" (483). Through Stephen's aestheticism in *Portrait* and *Ulysses,* "Joyce is able to critique art's own oppressive practices. . . . Joyce stages art's censorship of its own oppressiveness" by disrupting the text's "faith in an essentialist aesthetics" with incidents that reveal art as a "product of social forces" (502). I would counter that irony is often in the eye of the beholder and is notoriously difficult to locate in a text. I agree with the readings of *Portrait* (and *Ulysses*) that see the heroic and ironic in a perpetual state of contradiction; Norris too easily sees Joyce *staging* a deconstruction which her own deconstructive strategies have accomplished in unraveling the cultural and literary scripts of patriarchy to which Joyce himself powerfully, if ambivalently, contributes.

43. Rachel Blau DuPlessis, "Modernism: Agendas and Genders," paper delivered at the Modern Language Association Convention, December 1984.

of social obligation and convention. After *The New Freewoman* changed its name to *The Egoist* to reflect Marsden's philosophy, however, the feminist agenda of the journal was gradually marginalized as Ezra Pound, Richard Aldington, and T. S. Eliot increasingly used the journal to promote modernism.[44] Significantly, *Portrait*, which itself had censored feminism out of *Stephen Hero*, began its serialization in the newly named *Egoist* in February 1914.The textual and political unconscious of *Portrait* represented in *Stephen Hero* replicates the way feminism became the political unconscious of male modernism, the way women's writing became what was censored out of the literary histories of modernism itself.

Repetition and Remembering

Reading *Stephen Hero* as the textual and political unconscious of *Portrait* demonstrates how the psychodynamics of revision are based in the repression of woman as subject, an act of the internalized censor that replicates the oppression of women in history. But what about what I have called reading both ways? Freud's concept of serial dreams, whereby the earliest ones are the most repressed, suggests that *Stephen Hero* may itself represent the operation of the censor, while Joyce's later texts about Stephen may reflect his efforts to work through repetition to remembering. To chart this process through the succession of texts about Stephen, we must examine the origins of these autobiographical self-creations—textualizations of the self—in Joyce's own life. Central to these (re)productions of Stephen is the early death of Joyce's mother on August 13, 1903. The birth of Stephen D(a)edalus and the death of May Joyce are forever linked by the publication of Joyce's story "The Sisters" under the nom de plume "Stephen Daedalus" on the first anniversary of his mother's death.[45] I suggest that Joyce repeated this connection in every text featuring Stephen, and that what governs these transferential repetitions can be called an Orestes com-

44. For discussions of Marsden, see Scott, *Joyce and Feminism*, 85–88, 90–93; Gillian Hanscombe and Virginia Smyers, *Writing for Their Lives: The Modernist Women, 1910–1940* (Boston: Northeastern University Press, 1987), 129–77; Jane Lidderdale and Mary Nicholson, *Dear Miss Weaver: Harriet Shaw Weaver, 1876–1961* (New York: Viking, 1970). Harriet Shaw Weaver believed in and supported two people whom she regarded as geniuses: James Joyce and Dora Marsden.
45. Ellmann, *James Joyce*, 164.

plex: a repressed fear that his break from his mother was indeed matricidal, that his glorious flight into the modern required killing his mother, an act that, however necessary to his art, paralyzes him with guilt. Writing over and over again the story of Stephen represents for Joyce the exorcism of his mother's ghost and the search for expiation—a repetition, in other words, of the movement of Aeschylus's *Oresteia*.[46]

The key to this reading of Stephen's Orestes complex is a major displacement that both *Stephen Hero* and *Portrait* make in relation to the sequence of events in Joyce's life—namely, placing Stephen's refusal of his mother's request that he perform his Easter duty *before* his flight to Paris, instead of after his return. The telegram calling Joyce home from Paris with the words "MOTHER DYING COME HOME FATHER" arrived in April 1903. In a panic, Joyce scraped together the money to get home and found his mother not on her deathbed but quite ill and suffering from what her doctor diagnosed as cirrhosis of the liver. Fear of her impending death, according to Richard Ellmann, led May Joyce at this point to ask her son just after Easter to make his confession and take communion. Joyce absolutely refused, in spite of tears which led to her vomiting green bile into a basin. Joyce was disconsolate in the long months waiting for his mother to die from what was finally recognized as cancer. Her vomiting grew much worse over the summer. John Francis Byrne, Joyce's closest friend and the model for Cranly, chastised Joyce for not alleviating her suffering by going through the motions of confession and communion. "Whatever else is unsure in this stinking dunghill of a world a mother's love is not," Byrne recalls telling Joyce in his memoir *Silent Years*.[47] But Joyce still refused. While his mother lay in her final coma, Joyce's uncle ordered Joyce and his brother Stanislaus to kneel. Both refused. Later that night, after her death, Joyce and his sister Margaret got up at midnight to see her ghost. Margaret reported seeing her in the "brown habit in which she was buried." In spite of his refusals, Joyce later comforted his youngest sister, Mabel, by telling her: "Mother is in heaven. She

46. I posit the notion of an Orestes complex somewhat facetiously to counter the totalizing impact of the Oedipus complex as *the* explanatory myth of the human psyche in both psychoanalytic and literary discourse, as well as in much Joyce criticism. The Orestes narrative doubly complements the Oedipus story because (especially in the form Aeschylus gives it) it records the displacement of matricide as a punishable crime and the institution of the Law of the Father.

47. Byrne's statement is quoted in Ellmann, *James Joyce*, 130–31; for an account of May Joyce's death and its impact on Joyce, see ibid., 129–30, 134–37, 143–44.

is far happier now than she has ever been on earth. . . . You can pray for her if you wish, Mother would like that. But don't cry any more."[48]

In his tell-all letter to Nora Barnacle a year after his mother's death (August 29, 1904), Joyce took some responsibility for her death and justified his unwillingness to marry Nora as a refusal to participate in the institution of the middle-class Irish family which had victimized May Joyce: "My mother was slowly killed, I think, by my father's ill-treatment, by years of trouble, and by my cynical frankness of conduct. When I looked on her face as she lay in her coffin—a face grey and wasted with cancer—I understood that I was looking on the face of a victim and I cursed the system which had made her a victim."[49]

Not until *Ulysses*, however, was Joyce able to write overtly about his mother's death. But he did repeatedly write covertly about aspects of her dying. Elements of the biographical sequence appear in variously distorted forms in a chain of texts. These can be read according to Freud's notion of the dream series in which the first are the most "timid" while the last are the least censored. The series begins with a highly coded poem about grief; titled "Tilly," it was written shortly after May's death but not published until 1927. Starting out in the third person, the poem focuses on a cow-herd who drives the cows home with "a flowering branch before him." The cows listen to his voice that "tells them home is warm. / They moo and make brute noise with their hoofs." The final stanza switches into the first person to record surrealist images of inarticulate grief:

> Boor, bond of the herd,
> Tonight stretch full by the fire!
> I bleed by the black stream
> For my torn bough![50]

This poem suggests in condensed and nonreferential form some of the images that become associated with Stephen in later texts. For example, the cows longing for the warmth of home prefigure the maternal "moocow" that comes down the road in the opening sec-

48. Ibid., 136.
49. Ibid., 169.
50. For the text of the poem and discussion of its history, see ibid., 136–37.

tion of *Portrait*, as well as the multiple cows of *Ulysses*. The movement from "flowering branch" to bleeding "torn bough" suggests Stephen's "ashplant," which makes an occasional appearance in *Portrait* and serves as a major attribute of Stephen's weary sterility—the phallus that does not flower—in *Ulysses*. The alliteration of b's in "boor," "bond," "bleed," "black," and "bough" links the words together in a web of vile liquid that may displace his mother's vomit into an image of his grief and prefigure the snotgreen sea and bile of *Ulysses*.

As a lyric poem in which the personal has been made "invisible, refined out of existence," "Tilly" does not gesture at its autobiographical origins in the death of May Joyce.[51] Nor does "A Portrait of the Artist," the narrative-essay written in January 1904 about an unnamed adolescent forging the principles of his aesthetic. But the first paragraph focuses on the issue of memory and proposes that the past is not an "iron, memorial aspect" but is fluidly present as a successions of pasts in the consciousness of the moment (*P*, 257). A "portrait," Joyce states, follows "the curve of an emotion" (*P*, 258). The emotion in "A Portrait of the Artist" centers mainly on aesthetics, but a hint of the essay's textual unconscious resides in the distanced abstraction of an interchange between the youth and his friend: "Moreover, it was impossible that a temperament ever trembling towards its ecstacy should submit to acquiesce, that a soul should decree servitude for its portion over which the image of beauty had fallen as a mantle. One night in the early spring, standing at the foot of the staircase in the library, he said to his friend 'I have left the Church'" (*P*, 260). The narrator cryptically alludes in autobiographical terms to May Joyce's request that Joyce take communion and his refusal to do so for the sake of his art. But significantly, the essay contains not a single reference to the youth's mother, let alone her request about communion or her death.

Stephen Hero and *Portrait* come closer to reproducing this scene of the mother's dying request and the son's refusal. The youth's dramatic announcement to his friend about leaving the church is repeated in a more direct and expanded form in both *Stephen Hero*

51. In quoting Stephen's aesthetic for drama in *Portrait* in reference to the impersonalism of "Tilly" as a lyric poem, I realize that I am conflating two genres here; but I do so because Joyce's poem and Stephen's description of the personal made invisible in drama anticipate T. S. Eliot's 1919 formulation of impersonalism in lyric poetry in "Tradition and the Individual Talent," in *Selected Prose*, ed. Frank Kermode (New York: Harcourt Brace Jovanovich, 1975), 37–44.

(*SH*, 138) and *Portrait* (*P*, 238–39). But the mother's illness is still repressed, and the chronological sequence is still altered. Both *Stephen Hero* and *Portrait* place Stephen's refusal of his mother's request in a period *before* his flight to Paris, indeed as a metonymic representation of why he *must* go to Paris. In censoring May Joyce's illness and in displacing the chronology of her dying request, both texts avoid "remembering" the guilt and longing that impel the texts in the first place.

Joyce began writing *Stephen Hero* shortly after the magazine *Dana* rejected "A Portrait of the Artist" as incomprehensible. The discursive abstractions of the essay gave way to the direct narrative and dramatic dialogue of *Stephen Hero*. As we have seen, Stephen's mother appears regularly and centrally in the extant manuscript as a woman with whom he partially identifies and sympathizes. In addition to his mother's pleasure in Ibsen, Stephen is bonded to his mother in a moment of mutual horror just before his sister Isabel dies, a scene censored out of *Portrait*. The setting is deathlike: "He breathed an air of tombs" one evening as he "sat (silent) at his piano while the dusk enfolded him. . . . Above him and about him hung the shadow of decay, the decay of leaves and flowers, the decay of hope" (*SH*, 162). Suddenly, Stephen's "dismal" scene is interrupted by his mother's terrified voice calling out to him:

—What ought I to do? There's some matter coming away from the hole in Isabel's ... stomach ... Did you ever hear of that happening?
—I don't know, he answered trying to make sense of her words, trying to say them again to himself.
—Ought I send for the doctor ... Did you ever hear of that? ... What ought I do?
—I don't know ... What hole?
—The hole ... the hole we all have ... here. (*SH*, 163)

Vile liquid oozes out of the navel. The chapter ends abruptly in this hole of death—the navel, the point of contact with mystery, the maternal body, the knot of the dream-text according to Freud. Could this be a condensed and displaced dream-text for May Joyce's death as it remained in the textual unconscious of Joyce's autobiographical writing? Certainly Joyce's substitution of a sister for the brother, George, who died in 1902 of peritonitis is curious.[52] Joyce

52. See Ellmann, *James Joyce*, 93–94, in which he notes the displacement of George's death onto the death of Isabel in *Stephen Hero*. Joyce's feelings about his brother surfaced, according to Ellmann, in his decision in 1905 to name his son after his brother (94). Two

was, it is true, very disturbed by his brother's death. But why did he change a brother into a sister? We can read Isabel additionally as a screen for his mother. Stephen himself in *Stephen Hero* links mother and daughter as religious. Stephen "felt very acutely the futility of his sister's life," wasted not only by death but also by her devotion to the church (*SH*, 165). A "stranger to him," she "had acquiesced in the religion of her mother; she had accepted everything that had been proposed to her. If she lived she had exactly the temper for a Catholic wife of limited intelligence and of pious docility" (*SH*, 126). From Stephen's perspective, the church had stolen her freedom, just as it had his mother's.

In metonymic terms, the connection between Stephen's mother and Isabel lies even deeper. The odd emphasis on Isabel's "hole" in the exchange between Stephen and his mother—heightened further by the repetition of ellipses in the text—suggests the vaginal "hole" of the female body as well, a "hole" or "lack" that mother and daughter share. This links up with an equally odd passage describing Lynch, who prides himself on calling "the hymeneal tract" by the term "oracle" (*SH*, 136).[53] Stephen later uses "oracle" to mean a woman's invitation to sex by which she tantalizes men (*SH*, 191). In Lacanian terms, woman's "hole" or "lack" (state of castration) is an "oracle" that speaks in the cryptic, disguised grammar of the unconscious. Isabel's "hole," out of which the mark of her death oozes, signifies the constellation of death, birth, and sexuality that Stephen associates with the maternal body. In *Stephen Hero*, these associations exist only in a highly disguised form, but in Joyce's later texts these links are explored with increasing directness.

Portrait is no more direct than *Stephen Hero* in presenting the mother's dying or the son's denying. But while this memory remains in the textual unconscious of *Portrait*, the later text does come closer than *Stephen Hero* to characterizing the "curve" of Joyce's emotion in the months before his mother's death. The final chapter of *Portrait* contains puzzling contradictions in tone. On the

---

of the "epiphanies" about his brother's death that Joyce recorded in his notebooks were later incorporated into *Stephen Hero* in relation to Isabel. See ibid., 94; Robert Scholes and Richard M. Kain, *The Workshop of Daedalus: James Joyce and the Raw Materials for "A Portrait of the Artist as a Young Man"* (Evanston: Northwestern University Press, 1965), 29.

53. Robert Spoo has pointed out to me that Ian MacArthur, in "Stephen's Sexual Aesthetics," *James Joyce Quarterly* 25 (Winter 1988): 268–69, discusses Lynch's play on *vagina* when he responds to Stephen's aesthetic exposition with the expletive "Bullseye," slang for *vagina* (*P*, 212).

one hand, it includes Stephen's expositions of his aesthetic theory, the production of his villanelle, and the ringing *non serviam* announced to Cranly. In terms of structure, these actions lead in a linear direction toward the climactic escape from the labyrinth of Dublin for artistic freedom in Paris. But Stephen's affect is increasingly at odds with the narrative. Instead of tasting his coming freedom and power, Stephen wanders in weariness. Listening one night to the whirring flight and sharp cry of the swallows, Stephen is "jaded," "leaning wearily on his ashplant" (*P*, 226, 224): "A sense of fear of the unknown moved in the heart of his weariness, a fear of symbols and portents, of the hawklike man whose name he bore soaring out of his captivity on osierwoven wings" (*P*, 225). The final diary section shows him all the more trapped in Emma's net, as he records each glimpse he has of her. The truncated, near-inarticulate prose suggests more the discourse of illness than the prose of a poet-to-be. The final three diary entries reveal Stephen ready for flight, but the weary tone of the last chapter gives Stephen's "Welcome, O life!" a hollow sound. Freud's analysis of contradictory affect and story in a dream-text is perhaps relevant here (*ID*, 497–525). He argues that the affect of the dreamer's persona is the key to the latent content, which is distorted in the dream's narrative line. The Stephen who wanders Dublin wearily before his flight to Paris in *Portrait* parallels the Joyce who wandered those same streets as he waited for his mother to die.

The Stephen of Chapter 5 in *Portrait* is also akin in spirit to the Stephen of *Ulysses*. What separates them is the open discussion of the mother's death in the later text. In *Ulysses'* repetition of Stephen's story, the dying and reproachful mother who has been repressed in prior texts returns in a rectified sequence. Gone is the pretense that the request to perform his Easter duties came before he went to Paris. *Ulysses* is instead quite direct in its portrait of Stephen's obsession with his mother's death and the suffering his refusal caused her. The story of the son in *Ulysses* is the narrative of the son's guilt—"Agenbite of inwit. Conscience" (*U*, 1.481–82). Underlying that is the story of the son's ambivalent longing for and repulsion from the maternal body he has renounced and lost.[54] The

---

54. For other discussions of the repression and return of the mother and Stephen's guilty longing for her in *Ulysses*, see especially Daniel Ferrer, "Circe, Regret and Regression," in *Post-Structuralist Joyce: Essays from the French*, ed. Derek Attridge and Daniel Ferrer (Cambridge: Cambridge University Press, 1984), 127–44; van Boheemen, *The Novel as Family Romance*; McGee, *Paperspace*, 37–68, 115–49; Restuccia, *Joyce*, 92. For related

ooze of death from Isabel's hole in *Stephen Hero* reappears in *Ulysses* as the bile vomited by Stephen's mother.

In the first episode of *Ulysses* the irreverent and heretical Buck Mulligan initiates the chain of accusations that centrally occupy Stephen's thoughts throughout the day and night. As if he were the impresario of Stephen's unconscious, Mulligan points to the nickname he has given Stephen ("O, my name for you is the best: Kinch, the knifeblade"), invites Stephen to look at the sea ("A great sweet mother? The snotgreen sea. The scrotumtightening sea. . . . She is our great sweet mother. Come and look"), identifies their tower as the "omphalos" (the navel), and accuses Stephen directly of responsibility for his mother's death: "—The aunt thinks you killed your mother, he said. That's why she won't let me have anything to do with you. . . . You wouldn't kneel down to pray for your mother on her deathbed when she asked you. . . . You crossed her last wish in death" (*U*, 1.78–80, 88–89, 207–9, 212). The image of his dying mother wells up in Stephen's mind like the ghost that Hamlet sees and recapitulates the themes Mulligan introduced:

> Silently, in a dream she had come to him after her death, her wasted body within its loose brown graveclothes giving off an odour of wax and rosewood, her breath, that had bent upon him, mute, reproachful, a faint odour of wetted ashes. Across the threadbare cuffedge he saw the sea hailed as a great sweet mother by the wellfed voice beside him. The ring of bay and skyline held a dull green mass of liquid. A bowl of white china had stood beside her deathbed holding the green sluggish bile which she had torn up from her rotting liver by fits of loud groaning vomiting. (*U*, 1, 102–10)

For Stephen, the sea images the dual aspect of his mother as "a great sweet mother" and the green bile she vomits. Her arms enfold and suffocate. She is the place of life and death, the site of origin and end, the *omphalos* of his existence. She is the body that is both pure and polluted, a matrix of what is taboo—both desired and feared by the son. During the "history" lesson in the second episode ("Nestor"), *amor matris* is bedrock, the real (*U*, 2.165–66). But the "history" which constitutes "the nightmare from which I am trying to awake" is personal—the "history" of his mother's request, his refusal, her dying (*U* 2.371). As Stephen wanders on Sandycove in

---

discussions of Stephen's ambivalent desire for the maternal body in *Portrait*, see especially Brivic, *Joyce*, 17–86; Henke, *James Joyce*, 5–84.

the third episode ("Proteus"), he borders the sea, the maternal body. The sight of a drowned dog reminds him of a drowned man who is like a projection of himself, a man drowned in the snotgreen sea of a great sweet mother. In Stephen's Protean thoughts, the womb/ tomb of the "unspeeched" maternal body calls him to kiss—forever fusing love and death, desire and loathing, in a mother-son knot that bonds and binds:

> Bridebed, childbed, bed of death, ghostcandled. *Omnis caro ad te ven-iet.* He comes, pale vampire, through storm his eyes, his bat sails bloodying the sea, mouth to her mouth's kiss. . . . Mouth to her kiss. . . . Mouth to her mouth's kiss.
> His lips lipped and mouthed fleshless lips of air: mouth to her moomb. Oomb, allwombing tomb. His mouth moulded issuing breath, unspeeched: ooeeehah: roar of cataractic planets, globed, blazing, roaring wayawayawayawayaway. (*U*, 3.396–404)

Stephen's theory about Hamlet is often read in relation to the theme of paternity, but this emphasis on the father-son relationship can also be interpreted as a screen for an underlying incestuous mother-son matrix. "A side eye at my Hamlet hat," Stephen thinks in the passage that ends with his "mouth to her mouth's kiss" (*U*, 3.390, 399). Like Jesus to the rabbis in the temple, Stephen in the library expounds to Dublin's learned about how Shakespeare really identified with the cuckolded king in *Hamlet,* not with the son. This theory, based on a biographical reading, throws up an elaborate smokescreen, obscuring what Stephen shares with Hamlet: both are haunted by ghosts, both (according to a psychoanalytic reading which Joyce must have known) loved the forbidden flesh of their mothers.[55] Stephen concludes his intellectual tour de force by stating that he does not believe a word of it, but this denial is in turn a clever deflection of a biographical reading of his own dream-texts. Like Shakespeare, he has displaced and distorted what bothers him, what he wants to repress.[56]

55. For a related reading, see McGee, *Paperspace,* in which he argues that Stephen's mourning for his mother leads him to read Shakespeare's identification of Ann Hathaway with the maternal, with "the woman [as adulteress] who refuses to be the patriarch's other, who refuses to obey the law of the the father and support the symbolic rule of his name. Hers is the original sin against patriarchy and the original sin structuring Shakespeare's (and Stephen's) desire" (50–51).

56. For the connection between Hamlet and Stephen's thoughts about his mother, see also *U,* 9.800–57. In "Flesh and Blood and Love of Words: Lily Briscoe, Stephen Dedalus, and the Aesthetics of Emotional Quest," Jane Lilienfeld argues that "incest in *A Portrait*

In the Nighttown episode ("Circe"), the nightmare of Stephen's history returns yet again, this time without protective screens. Curiously, the dream sequence in which Stephen's mother appears to him shows the least evidence of dream-work distortions. Once more his mother makes her request, once more he refuses, and once more he "kills" her by declaring *"Non serviam!"* and swinging in a blind drunk with his ashplant at the chandelier (*U*, 15.4172–4245). Stephen declares his independence from the church—"The intellectual imagination! With me all or not at all. . . . No! No! No! Break my spirit, all of you, if you can! I'll bring you all to heel!" (*U*, 15.4227–36). But the dramatic confrontation between mother and son suggests that it is at base his mother, not religion, that he must deny. Stephen's refusal of the Irish church and state in *Portrait* and *Ulysses* is unveiled in "Circe" as a flight from the maternal. To be an artist, Stephen must repress the mother. This he cannot do. Caught in the cycle of repetition, Stephen can only play out in symbolic terms the game Freud used to describe the repetition compulsion, the child's endless enactment in "fort/da" of the separation from and return to the maternal body.

In relation to all the prior Stephen texts, *Ulysses* appears to accomplish for Joyce what Stephen within the narrative of the novel could not. It "remembers" what *Stephen Hero* and *Portrait* disguised and "forgot." It names the pattern of repetition and confronts head-on the medusa of longing, loathing, and guilt. In the transferential scene of writing, Joyce works through his repetitions to remember what Stephen can only repeat. At the close of the novel, Stephen remains caught in his paralysis, with only the faintest suggestion that his welcome in the home of Bloom and Molly as surrogate parents might foreshadow a fertile reconciliation with his own family ghosts. But as Stephen's creator, Joyce is not trapped in the same position as his character. Stephen in "Circe" tells his mother, "*(choking with fright, remorse and horror)* They say I killed you, mother. . . . Cancer did it, not I" (*U*, 15.4185–86). But in his self-confession letter to Nora of August 29, 1904, Joyce accepted what Stephen denies—his own complicity in his mother's death: "My

---

appears as a gap, an absence, an unmentionable arena of longing" which takes the form of Stephen's desire for "pure" women and revulsion from "impure" women (in Scott, *New Alliances*, 170–72). This gap in *Portrait*, I would argue, becomes the central narrative of Stephen's story in *Ulysses*.

mother was slowly killed, I think, by my father's ill-treatment, by years of trouble, and by my cynical frankness of conduct."[57]

The irony so characteristic of modernist texts distances Joyce from his portrait of his younger self and suggests that he sees himself as having moved beyond the psychic knot which tightens around Stephen. Bloom prophetically points to what might loosen the knot: "A girl. Some girl. Best thing could happen to him" (U, 15.4951). The way Joyce frames the autobiographical Stephen sequences is significant. Joyce cuts off his life story just at the point when he was about to meet Nora Barnacle on June 16, 1904. The day Ulysses takes place is the day Joyce's life changed dramatically, but the event that was to have such consequences is suppressed in the novel. Ulysses bears witness to the influence Nora had on Joyce, but the meeting itself and the courtship that ensued exist only in the textual unconscious of the date, although it may also be present in displaced form in the memories of Bloom and Molly about their epiphanic moment in Gibraltar.[58]

It is curious that Joyce chose not to portray directly the love that helped him untie the knot of his own paralysis. We can only speculate why. But one reason might well be the unconscious incestuous nature of that relationship for Joyce. Joyce sometimes called Nora "Ireland," and his letters to her in 1909 project onto her the same conflation of purity and pollution evident in Stephen's images of the maternal body as both virgin and whore in Portrait and Ulysses. On September 2, 1909, for example, Joyce wrote Nora: "I wonder is there some madness in me. Or is love madness? One moment I see you like a virgin or madonna the next moment I see you shameless, insolent, half naked and obscene!"[59] As a relatively uneducated woman of a class different from the middle-class circles in which the student Joyce traveled, Nora was markedly different from the educated, often self-identified feminist avatars of the "new woman" whom Joyce knew. Did Joyce project onto Nora the fantasies that he could not connect with women educated like himself? With Nora, did Joyce consciously or unconsciously hope to possess the

---

57. Quoted in Ellmann, James Joyce, 169.
58. Further evidence for the suppression of his courtship lies in the date of Joyce's brief residence in the Martello tower. Ulysses shows Stephen living in the tower when he had no attachment to any woman. But Joyce actually lived in the tower in September 1904, three months after he had met Nora and at a time when he was already deeply involved with her (Ellmann, James Joyce, 171–72).
59. Ibid., 287.

maternal body of his fantasy, the womanly woman, the m/other without agency? Perhaps some of his anguish in his marriage related to his discovery that Nora, like his mother, like Emma Clery, could at times have a mind of her own. The story of Bloom is the serial to the story of Stephen. Like the ultimate indeterminacy of the dream-text, like the interminability of analysis in Freud's schema, *Ulysses* only appears to "cure" the symptomatic complexes of its precursors. *Ulysses* and, after it, *Finnegans Wake* displace the problematics of male desire into new scenes of writing and reading.

"Reading both ways" with Joyce's various presentations of Stephen D(a)edalus appears to suggest two opposing views. From one perspective, *Portrait* and *Ulysses* are more repressed texts than *Stephen Hero* because in the later texts, woman-as-subject has been erased and replaced by the woman who exists for the male subject as a crucial signifier in the chain of signification. In *Portrait* the mother and E.C. are projections of Stephen's longing and loathing in a narrative of male individuation. In *Ulysses* Molly is not just Bloom's fantasy, but she speaks only in the discourse of the Other, a pole within the binary that still privileges male subjectivity.[60] And Stephen's mother in *Ulysses* is no longer the mother who reads Ibsen but only the mother who embodies the net of Irish church and state. From this perspective *Stephen Hero* is the textual and political unconscious of *Portrait* and *Ulysses*. But from the perspective of writing as a scene of transference and potential "cure," *Stephen Hero* (and the other early Stephen texts) is more repressed than the later versions, especially *Ulysses*. As early attempts to deal with Joyce's feelings about his mother's death, *Stephen Hero* and *Portrait* are more "timid" and distorted than *Ulysses*. Only after a series of textual repetitions can Joyce create a self-portrait that confronts the remorse, desire, and fear he repressed after his mother's dying.

60. Whether or not Molly's monologue represents female subjectivity, *l'écriture féminine*, woman-as-Other, ventriloquized femininity, stereotypical femininity, and/or a male fantasy of femininity has of course been hotly contested in Joyce studies for decades. For some recent views, see for example the essays in this volume by Joseph Boone and Ellen Carol Jones; Restuccia, *Joyce*, 158; McGee, *Paperspace*, 187; Brivic, *Veil of Signs*, 23, 27–29; MacCabe, *James Joyce*; Henke, *James Joyce*, 126–63; Derek Attridge, "Molly's Flow: The Writing of 'Penelope' and the Question of Women's Language," *Modern Fiction Studies* 35 (Autumn 1989): 543–68; Annette Shandler Levitt, "The Pattern Out of the Wallpaper: Luce Irigaray and Molly Bloom," *Modern Fiction Studies* 35 (Autumn 1989): 507–16; Diana E. Henderson, "Joyce's Modernist Woman: Whose Last Word?" *Modern Fiction Studies* 35 (Autumn 1989): 517–28.

What remains constant, however, in reading the process of censorship both ways is the centrality of the mother. In both cases the
creation of Joyce's modernist masterpieces depends on the censorship of the mother who speaks and acts, the mother who negotiates
some sort of agency in spite of and within the confinements of
patriarchy. What MacCabe calls Joyce's increasing renunciation of
"classic realism" carries with it a disturbing suppression of the
mother's speech. For MacCabe, we recall, Joyce's modernity "attempts to evade paternal identification and, in that evasion, to let
the desire of the mother speak." But for me, Joyce's modernity has
put into play the son's oedipal longing and Oresteian loathing for
the mother. The price of the son's speech is the mother's silence.

MacCabe's formulation of Joyce's move from a regressive realism
to a revolutionary modernism anticipates Alice Jardine's latter concept of gynesis. She defines *gynesis* as "the putting into discourse
of 'woman' as that *process* diagnosed in France as intrinsic to the
condition of modernity; indeed, the valorization of the feminine,
woman, and her obligatory, that is, historical connotations, as somehow intrinsic to new and necesssary modes of thinking, writing,
speaking."[61] The epistemological crisis of modernity, Jardine argues,
involves the dissolution of the unitary Cartesian subject fully
known to itself. The subject of modernity, in contrast, pushes at
the boundaries of the Other, the feminine, the unconscious, as
Joyce's texts increasingly do. This process, Jardine implicitly suggests, is largely found in male writing and has little to do with
"real" women. Although Jardine's *Gynesis* is in fundamental sympathy with MacCabe's view of the revolutionary potential of modernity, she wonders momentarily what "the putting into discourse of
woman" means for women:

> It is always a bit of a shock to the feminist theorist when she recog-
> nizes that the repeated and infinitely expanded "feminine" in these
> theoretical systems often has very little, if anything to do with
> women. If everyone and everything becomes Woman—as a culture
> obsessively turns itself inside out—where does that leave women,
> especially if, in the same atmosphere, feminism is dismissed as
> anachronistic along with Man and History? . . . The problem is that
> within this ever-increasing inflation of quotation marks around the
> word "woman," women as thinking, writing subjects are placed in the

61. Jardine, *Gynesis*, 27.

position of constantly wondering whether it is a question of women or woman, their written *bodies* or their *written* bodies.[62]

Within Jardine's framework, Joyce's texts about Stephen and his oeuvre in general increasingly perform "gynesis." But as these texts progressively appropriate or, in Frances Restuccia's terms, "ventriloquize" the feminine as a necessary enactment of his modernism (and postmodernism), they show an increasing inability to imagine "women as thinking, writing subjects." This economy raises the questions with which I conclude. Is the making of Joyce's modernism paradigmatic of male modernism in general? Is the silencing of women as subjects the linchpin to the production of the ever more artful voices of the men? Is the dominant literary history of modernism a "case history" of (male) readers who have been transferentially captured by the complexes of texts such as Joyce's *Portrait* and *Ulysses* in which women as subjects have been swallowed up into the productions and representations of male modernists?[63] Does male modernism, like Joyce's Stephen texts, have a textual and political unconscious censored by the censor that Joyce himself censored out of his premodernist work in the making of modernism?

62. Ibid., 35–37.
63. In reading literary history as "case history" in a scene of transference, I am borrowing from Shoshana Felman's "Turning the Screw of Interpretation" and "The Case of Poe," in *Lacan and the Adventure of Insight: Psychoanalysis in Contemporary Culture* (Cambridge: Harvard University Press, 1987), 27–51.

2

Pharmaconomy:
Stephen and the Daedalids

Alberto Moreiras

When the moon of mourning is set and gone.

JAMES JOYCE, *Finnegans Wake*

In a 1984 paper on Joyce, Julia Kristeva considers the return of the repressed in a literary text to be the "unveiling of intrapsychic identifications."[1] Freud's Imaginary Father of Individual Prehistory, "a primitive form that possesses the sexual attributes of both parents,"[2] is the site of a primary identification that would rule, from a distance, the development of a style of writing. The very decision to become a writer involves not only identificatory processes but, in particular, what Kristeva calls "the identificatory symptom,"[3] perhaps playing with the etymological meaning of *symptom* as "event." But a symptom can also mean in English a trace or vestige and in that sense it would be the sign of a disappearance.

For Kristeva, Joyce's insistence on father-son transubstantiation in *Ulysses* signals what she rather surprisingly calls "the real presence of a complex masculine sexuality. Without any repressions

This essay is dedicated to Laurence MacSheain.
1. Julia Kristeva, "Joyce 'the Gracehoper' or the Return of Orpheus," in *James Joyce: The Augmented Ninth: Proceedings of the Ninth International James Joyce Symposium, Frankfurt 1984*, ed. Bernard Benstock (Syracuse: Syracuse University Press, 1988), 169.
2. Ibid., 172.
3. Ibid., 172.

whatsoever."[4] Repression would be completely breached in the Joycean text through a clear welcoming of paternal identification. I do not think that Kristeva is suggesting that any writing can be reduced to the function of expressing or imitating the writer's unconscious. She seems in fact to be claiming the opposite: the unveiling of the identificatory symptom through the return of the repressed in writing releases writing into its own. Writing guards the trace of the writer's unconscious, but, as Jacques Lacan put it, a work "insofar as it is written, does not imitate the effects of the Unconscious. . . . It is real, and, in this sense, the work imitates nothing. It is, as fiction, a truthful structure."[5]

Jean Kimball, in her article on Joyce's use of Freud's essay on Leonardo da Vinci, quotes Freud's statement, in the context of his investigations of parental influence on the artist's development, that "the nature of the artistic function is . . . inaccessible along psycho-analytic lines."[6] Kimball's article shows how Joyce incorporated Freudian insights in order "to affirm the freedom and the power of the artist as self-created creator."[7] Such an affirmation, according to Kimball, necessarily passes through a release from the power of the phallic mother, which involves not so much an identification with the father as an identification with the mother's Other: "This release of the son from the power of the mother is . . . signaled by the replacement of Mut, the vulture-headed mother goddess of Freud's analysis of Leonardo, by the bird-headed Egyptian god Thoth," who was "self-begotten and self-produced."[8]

This essay questions the idea of artistic self-production as a struggle against the mother. Kimball's arguments, as well as the arguments of other scholars who have maintained that such a notion is dominant in Joyce's text, are certainly compelling. One of the most obvious reasons for the critical consensus is succinctly explained by Bernard Benstock:

Joyce's mother, May Murray Joyce, suffered the decline of the family

4. Ibid., 171.
5. Quoted by Jean-Michel Rabaté, "A Clown's Inquest into Paternity: Fathers, Dead or Alive, in *Ulysses*," in *James Joyce's Ulysses*, ed. Harold Bloom (New York: Chelsea House, 1987), 81.
6. Jean Kimball, "Freud, Leonardo, and Joyce: The Dimensions of a Childhood Memory," in *The Seventh of Joyce*, ed. Bernard Benstock (Bloomington: Indiana University Press, 1982), 70.
7. Ibid., 69.
8. Ibid.

into poverty and her husband's drunkenness shored by her Catholic
faith and her expectations that her eldest son James would find his
vocation in the priesthood. Her counterpart in *A Portrait* expresses
her disappointment and resentment as she watches her son go off to
his lectures at the National University. . . . The May Goulding Dedalus of *Ulysses* is even more memorable as the ghost haunting her
profligate son whom he attempts to exorcise from his guilt-ridden
consciousness. . . . It was May Joyce's terminal cancer that brought
her son back from his first attempt at self-exile in Paris when he was
twenty-one.[9]

Although there is ample textual evidence to support the notion
that the struggle against the mother is crucial for Stephen's constitution as a writer, such an interpretation tells only half the story.
There is another possibility for interpretation, which is not as
clearly suggested in the text because it remains largely encrypted,
buried in the textual unconscious. It is this: artistic creation in

9. Bernard Benstock, *James Joyce* (New York: Frederick Ungar, 1985), 9. Frances Restuccia, in *Joyce and the Law of the Father* (New Haven: Yale University Press, 1989), has
studied Joyce in the light of Gilles Deleuze's notion of masochism and has proposed a very
productive version of the Joycean game of parental identification. According to Restuccia,
Joyce's becoming-a-woman is a function of his attempt at subverting what she calls "the
law of the fathers/Father." Restuccia claims that "what is effected under the aegis of
Father/Son consubstantiality seems finally to be claimed or taken over by femininity"
(123) and then concludes that Joyce's turn to woman is the ploy of a Deleuzian masochist
to exclude and completely nullify the father (140). Inevitably, then, woman returns in
Joyce as a fetishized phallic Mother/Virgin. I have no quarrel—except perhaps at the level
of unstated if implied conclusions—with Restuccia's fascinating argument, which my
summary radically simplifies. This article in a sense supplements her book by locating an
alternative, but not necessarily contrary, possibility of interpretation. Patrick McGee's
Paperspace: Style as Ideology in Joyce's Ulysses (Lincoln: University of Nebraska Press,
1988) also disagrees with the largely consensual position that Stephen's self-constitution
occurs primarily in opposition to his mother. In Chapter 2 ("Between: A Name of the
Mother"), on "Scylla and Charybdis," McGee concludes: "Stephen writes his abjection;
he subverts the law of the father not by standing in the place of its imaginary opposition
but by standing on the edge of the symbolic, by pushing the law to its limit, where it
displays the folds in which we glimpse not the void but the infinite series of other possibilities" (68). For McGee these other possibilities are given by the name of the mother: "As
a unitary signifier, a unitary law of value or a feminine logos waging eternal war against
a male logos, there is no symbolic Name-of-the-Mother beyond Mother . . . ; there are
only the names of the mothers—proper names that, in a sense, lack the proper, that is, a
relation to property and legal constraint. . . . A name of the mother that has no place is
dissemination itself, not the negation of the father's name but its situation, its circum-
scription, its circumcision" (61). McGee's argument is forceful and seductive, but I would
hesitate to subscribe totally to his implied conclusions in this chapter, as they seem, like
Restuccia's, not to advance beyond the symbolic coordinates of the identificatory symptom even when questioning them (see also the "Epilogue," esp. 187–89, 195–97). Many
things in McGee's book, however, are of great value to me, for instance: "Stephen's discourse is perhaps the discourse of a lack, but a lack that from the beginning has been a
temporal fiction of the subject-in-process which effaces the boundary between subject and
object, self and other, father and mother. The subject-in-process is *between*" (61).

the Joycean text depends on a recognition of the undecidability of parental identification. Textual constitution goes through a radical negation of the mother as well as a no less radical assumption of the maternal name. Conversely, the paternal name, even if mediated and sustained by the idea of self-begetting, must also be negated, not just in parricide but also in what I call the suspension of maternal displacement. A strange logic obtains here: the logic of the identificatory symptom, as both event and vestige, unveiled.

In this essay I examine a particular identificatory phenomenon within the Joycean text in order to clarify the way "primary identification" is mediated in artistic expression. In part I am following Kristeva's suggestion: "The father dies in order that the son live; the son dies in order that the father be incarnated in his *oeuvre* and become his own son. In this labyrinth, indeed Daedalean, *chercher la femme.*"[10] I do not attempt to prove anything concerning Joyce's sexuality. As a matter of fact, my main point of emphasis involves the instituting function of the return of the repressed within Stephen Dedalus's theory of writing, over and beyond this same function within Joyce's writing practice. By looking at some conditions of textual constitution as they are offered in Stephen's conception of what it means to become a writer, I open a way to understanding the Joycean text's "truthful structure," that is, its presence as an art work. If the text's truthful structure, in the Lacanian phrase, is dependent on the text's being "real," it should be noted that the Lacanian notion of the real involves that which relates to the symptom in a certain way. If the symptom is "a principle of repetition that constitutes identity," it also undoes identity through repetition. Sheldon Brivic, in a remarkable book that intersects at many points with my arguments in this article, quotes Jacqueline Rose's definition of the Lacanian real: "Lacan termed the order of language the symbolic, that of the ego and its identifications the imaginary. . . . The real was then his term for the moment of impossibility onto which both are grafted, the point of that moment's endless return."[11] The real is that which returns and, returning, shakes imaginary identities and symbolic events. The real is that which, within the symptom, shows itself as the vestige of a disappearance.

I proceed in three steps. First, I give a preliminary definition of

10. Kristeva, "Joyce," 176.
11. Sheldon Brivic, *The Veil of Signs: Joyce, Lacan, and Perception* (Urbana: University of Illinois Press, 1991), 18.

what I call, using a Derridean notion, the pharmacological status of writing in *A Portrait of the Artist as a Young Man* and *Ulysses.* Second, I study the function of the *pharmakos* within Stephen's writing anxiety—and in the process I present my reasons for thinking that Stephen undergoes a fleeting semiconscious identification with Talos, Icarus's brother. The third part of my argument concerns Stephen's relation to writing itself, that is, not to the *pharmakos* but to the *pharmakon,* in the light of the Talos myth. This third part suggests that the text's truthful structure is marked by the undecidability of its own identifications; in that sense, textual structure is done as well as undone by the deployment, or the unveiling, of the paradoxes of the text's identificatory symptom.[12]

The Pharmacological Status of Writing

By pharmacological writing I mean first the associations evoked by Plato's description of writing as *pharmakon,* that is, at the same time "remedy" and "poison." In "Plato's Pharmacy" Jacques Derrida links *pharmakon* to *pharmakos,* the latter being the Greek term to designate a particular kind of threat to the community as well as the sacrificial victim who embodies it and conjures away the danger: the scapegoat.[13] I indicate some of the close connections between Stephen's conception of writing as expressed in certain passages of *Portrait* and *Ulysses,* and some Greek myths about the Daedalids. The Daedalids were, as we shall see, scapegoats, *pharmakoi.* I show those connections through an analysis of Stephen's fear of the unknown as expressed in the fear of the symbol, the fear of Daedalus, and the fear of Thoth. My hypothesis is rather modest at the level of analysis: I contend that a singular identification of Stephen with an almost forgotten pharmakic hero, Talos, is a part of the textual unconscious in both *Portrait* and *Ulysses.* As an unconscious presence, Talos is understood as plausibly in the text but never explicitly there: the identification remains a possibility, an it-just-might-have-happened, and this is all I need to

---

12. See Jacques Aubert, ed., *Joyce avec Lacan* (Paris: Navarin, 1987), for a selection of Lacan's writings on the Joycean "symptom." I have preferred not to include in this essay either a sufficient discussion or a presentation of Lacan's notion, in particular as it relates to the order of the real and to the task of writing. It remains to be done.

13. Jacques Derrida, "Plato's Pharmacy," in *Dissemination,* trans. Barbara Johnson (Chicago: University of Chicago Press, 1981), 63–171.

argue. This plausible identification as such would go a certain way toward illuminating Stephen's understanding of writing in relation to parentage and filiation. More specifically, this identification clarifies Stephen's understanding of writing as a passage of parentage, a taking "of" in the subjective and objective senses, in which what is decided goes beyond self-begetting toward an infinite return of parental identifications as well as their mutual cancellation.

In this infinite return an unveiling takes place in which the text shows itself at the same time bound by the identificatory symptom and radically resistant to it. The text shows itself marked by an originary constitution which is at the same time the site of its author's primary identification and of its abandonment and consequent entrance into the real. To prove this is the goal of this essay. I limit myself to some key passages for reasons of space.

In a 1964 article on Daedalean imagery in the first of Joyce's novels, David Hayman refers to Stephen's ambivalent feelings toward his father. "The Divine Father and his surrogates have been replaced by the inspiring image of the 'hawklike man' Daedalus, symbolizing for Stephen a yet undefined type of artistic creator."[14] For Hayman, Daedalus represents "the *ideals* of a creative youth," while Icarus symbolizes youth's "*achievements.*"[15] Stephen's misgivings about his self-conception and where it may lead him are given, according to Hayman, in the image of the "lapwing Icarus,"[16] which I hope to show is not Icarus but Icarus's brother, or stepbrother, Talos. Hayman does not explicitly refer to the *pharmakos*. His article, however, thematizes Stephen's obsession with wings and bird symbols, which we shall see as radical pharmacological motifs, to be related to Stephen's ashplant, the augural stick, through the curious mediation of an umbrella.

Hayman shows how Stephen's fear of birds carries him to a wary acceptance of destiny. He concludes:

> Stephen, who throughout his life has searched for the stability embodied in the person of a father, who has implicitly recognized that need in his Icarian cry, "Old father, old artificer, stand me now and ever in good stead," can solve his dilemma only by achieving the father

14. David Hayman, "Daedalian Imagery in *A Portrait of the Artist as a Young Man,*" in *Hereditas: Seven Essays on the Modern Experience of the Classical,* ed. Frederic Will (Austin: University of Texas Press, 1964), 51.

15. Ibid., 36.

16. Ibid., 36 and passim.

which is within him, by reconciling himself with his past, accepting his present, and thus freeing himself for the future.[17]

In my opinion that conclusion must be modified to suggest that, for Stephen, reaching the father within himself can be accomplished only through a particular form of parricide, which one might call suspended parricide. For Stephen the genealogical bonding is a poisoned gift mandating the obligation both to constitute and to dissolve identity. This is for me the double meaning of *Portrait*'s final words about "forging" conscience, an ending of the book which I would call not ironic but nostalgic, drawing upon the meaning of *nostos* as "return home." Penelope waits there.

The double inheritance, mother/father, which we shall see registered by Stephen has been studied by Derrida in his essay on Friedrich Nietzsche's *Ecce Homo*.[18] According to Derrida, Nietzsche's signature is his attempt to recover this double inheritance even at the moment when he is establishing his own legacy, the autobiographical moment. John Llewelyn puts it succinctly:

> *Entre*, between, in the way that the writer Friedrich Nietzsche and the writings to which he appended his name are between the father who died before him and the mother who died after him. Not only is the person who signs himself F. N. their heir, the heir of two sexes, their two laws (the civil law that Creon obeys and the law of the family followed by Antigone), but the heir of life and death.[19]

Inheritance and legacy: for Derrida all writing has a testamentary structure. Thus, we could raise the question of up to what point the intrapsychic identifications are also phenomena of mourning: of introjection and incorporation. Derrida writes: "Introjection/incorporation: everything is played out on the borderline which divides and opposes the two terms."[20] If *introjection* characterizes "normal" mourning as the process whereby we rearrange our libidinal investments after the death of a loved one, *incorporation* is the

---

17. Ibid., 54.

18. Jacques Derrida, *The Ear of the Other: Otobiography, Transference, Translation*, ed. Christie McDonald, trans. Peggy Kamuf and Avital Ronell (New York: Schocken Books, 1985), 15 and passim.

19. John Llewelyn, "Derrida, Mallarmé, and Anatole," in *Philosophers, Poets*, ed. David Wood (London: Routledge, 1990), 97.

20. Jacques Derrida, "Fors: The Anglish Words of Nicolas Abraham and Maria Torok," in Nicolas Abraham and Maria Torok, *The Wolfman's Magic Word*, trans. Nicholas Rand (Minneapolis: University of Minnesota Press, 1986), xvi.

"aberrant" phenomenon by means of which we manage to keep the dead alive inside, encrypted. In other words, incorporation implies the rejection of the loss: we have not lost anything. Writing, once accomplished, cannot claim one or the other without claiming both: like memory, writing resists loss; like memory, it can function only in loss. Between Scylla and Charybdis: there we have the passage into writing. It cannot be a cure without being at the same time a poison: it happens in life/death, and it happens as a curious form of survival, of resurrection. It is an impersonal resurrection which the suffering subject has given out while simultaneously giving up: the task of the writer.[21] For Llewelyn again:

> Not that the text speaks with the "voiceless voice" of what Levinas calls the *il y a* or of what Blanchot calls "nothingness as being, the idling *(désoeuvrement)* of being." The voice is a middle voice, neither simply active nor simply passive, that is incomprehensible within the categories of nothingness and being. It does not even *belong* to a person, and the personage through which the voice speaks has no selfconsciousness.[22]

This passage into writing is what is at stake in Stephen's pharmakic, borderline position. The "truthful" structure of the artistic text is here represented. Parental identification gives way to double inheritance. Writing enacts the task of mourning in that in it the mother-father identification must be radically introjected in a process of unveiling. But in a sense, writing will remain haunted: an always failed, disastrous introjection will become aberrant and will constitute the body of writing as an incorporated, alien body where the symptom reigns. From another perspective, however, the reign of the symptom in writing means that incorporation has abandoned the unconscious and is now a part of the real: for all to see, no longer a secret. By constituting itself as a passage between, writing gives itself over to primary identification at the very same moment that it withdraws itself from it. This is the signature effect, if you

21. Julia Kristeva writes in *The Black Sun: Depression and Melancholia*, trans. Leon Roudiez (New York: Columbia University Press, 1989): "The work of art that insures the rebirth of its author and its reader or viewer is one that succeeds in integrating the artificial language it puts forward . . . and the unnamed agitations of an omnipotent self that ordinary social and linguistic usage always leave somewhat orphaned or plunged into mourning. Hence such a fiction, if it isn't an antidepressant, is at least a survival, a resurrection" (51).
22. Llewelyn, "Derrida," 103.

will, and we shall see that Stephen calls it so. It is also the effect through which the structural truthfulness of the work of art announces itself. *Finnegans Wake* partially names it: "So why, pray, sign anything as long as every word, letter, penstroke, paperspace is a perfect signature of its own?"[23] In other words, why sign anything if everything is already incorporated, if nothing has ever been given up?

Pharmakic Anxiety

In this section I address the function of the *pharmakos* within Stephen's writing anxiety. It leads us into an exploration of the pharmakic characteristics of the Daedalean family, in the process unveiling the plausible presence in the textual unconscious of a rarely noted but important member of the family, Talos, also called Perdix.

Near the end of *Portrait* Stephen thinks of becoming a writer. The narrative includes these words:

> And for ages men had gazed upward as he was gazing at birds in flight. The colonnade above him made him think vaguely of an ancient temple and the ashplant on which he leaned wearily of the curved stick of an augur. A sense of fear of the unknown moved in the heart of his weariness, a fear of symbols and portents, of the hawklike man whose name he bore soaring out of his captivity on osierwoven wings, of Thoth, the god of writers, writing with a reed upon a tablet and bearing on his narrow ibis head the cusped moon.[24]

Placed at the temple, at the threshold of his inauguration into the theoretical or contemplative life of the writer, Stephen experiences three fears: of symbols and portents, of Daedalus, and of Thoth as the god of writing. This does not seem a transitional or progressive series, leading from one thing to the next.[25] There is a certain simul-

23. James Joyce, *Finnegans Wake* (Harmondsworth: Penguin, 1980), 115, 6–8; hereafter cited in the text as *FW* with page and line numbers.

24. James Joyce, *A Portrait of the Artist as a Young Man* (Harmondsworth: Penguin, 1982), 225; hereafter cited in the text as *P*.

25. In my opinion Roberto González Echevarría insufficiently interprets this series in a transitional sense, "desde los símbolos al dios de la escritura" (from symbols to the god of writing) in "BdeORridaGes (Borges y Derrida,)," in *Isla a su vuelo fugitiva* (Madrid: José Porrúa Turanzas, 1983), 209. About the function of the temple in Stephen's theory of writing, there is a splendid paper by Murray McArthur focusing on the "Library" chapter in *Portrait* and studying the temple as a *parergon* or frame in the Derridean sense: "The

taneity, a stasis, between the three fears or the three terms of the fear. These three fears are three versions of the same anxiety: the inaugural anxiety of writing. It comes to Stephen from the future: the future is anticipated as danger. Danger is at the heart of the portent, the portent of writing—of the inscription which the "Scylla and Charybdis" chapter in *Ulysses* calls "the intense instant of imagination, when the mind, Shelley says, is a fading coal, [and when] that which I was is that which I am and that which in possibility I may come to be."[26]

This ecstatic union of temporality in the supreme moment of creative vision is dangerous because it has to do, as production, with reproduction, with self-production, and therefore with parentage, with parental ghosts, and with mourning: "Through the ghost of the unquiet father the image of the unliving son looks forth" (*U*, 9.380–81). Freud remarks in his *Introductory Lectures on Psychoanalysis* that the act of birth is the prototype of all effects of anxiety. He then points out that it is "highly relevant that this first state of anxiety arose out of separation from the mother."[27] Stephen's association of anxiety with the decision to become a writer indicates not only the recognition of this separation but also the fact that in the new becoming, in the new birth, anxiety returns as a symptom of the essentially repressed, the primal separation. Writing, as a defense against anxiety, as an "anticathexis," will involve the transformation of the affect accompanying the separation into its opposite: it will seek the canceling out of the primal separation. Stephen's inaugural decision, as an act of birth, is also an antibirth, a defense against separation which takes place not only in the symbolic order but also in the order of the real. We can begin to see how and why the primary identification radically involves the negation of the mother. Freud's bisexed "Imaginary Father of Individual Prehistory," with whom intrapsychic identification takes place, is a function of this negation, an originary repression that makes of writing a task of essential mourning. In Stephen's anxiety we glimpse the *femme* that the father-son transubstantiation hides in the apparent liquidation of secondary, or "normal," repression.

Origin of the Work of Art in *Portrait* V," read at the Twelfth International James Joyce Symposium, Monte Carlo, June 1990.

26. James Joyce, *Ulysses*, ed. Hans Walter Gabler et al. (New York: Random House, 1986), 9.381–83; hereafter cited in the text as *U* with episode and line numbers.

27. Sigmund Freud, *Introductory Lectures on Psychoanalysis*, ed. and trans. James Strachey (New York: Norton, 1966), 397.

Thus, in the mother's negation, not dialectically but disastrously, a fundamental affirmation holds sway.

Let us examine carefully the paragraph just quoted. Stephen's association of symbols and portents needs to be noted. A portent is not only something prodigious but also whatever foreshadows a coming event. Hans-Georg Gadamer gives a good explanation of what is to be understood by *symbol* (even within its psychoanalytical definition):

> Originally [*symbol*] was a technical term in Greek for a token of remembrance. The host presented his guest with the so-called *tessera hospitalis* by breaking some object in two. He kept one half for himself and gave the other half to his guest. If in thirty or fifty years' time, a descendant of the guest should ever enter his house, the two pieces could be fitted together again to form a whole in an act of recognition.[28]

Stephen's fear of the coming event is a fear of the symbolic: a paranoid fear of encounter and recognition. He fears the return, in writing, of an identification with the (masculine) father, now projected as "the hawklike man whose name he bore." Kristeva points out that "whatever the variants of identification as a generic term, it presupposes the tendency inherent in the speaking being to assimilate itself *symbolically and in reality* to another entity separate from itself."[29] Stephen's reluctance to accept the paternal symbol in writing, although it proves nothing in itself, should be interpreted as an indication that for him, the paternal symbolic identification must be consummated; but this also means assumed and, therefore, transgressed. This double, self-contradictory mandate is not the origin of Stephen's anxiety; rather, it constitutes itself as

---

28. Hans-Georg Gadamer, "The Relevance of the Beautiful: Art as Play, Symbol, and Festival," in *The Relevance of the Beautiful and Other Essays*, ed. Robert Bernasconi (Cambridge: Cambridge University Press, 1986), 31. About "host" and "guest," two notions of essential importance in Joyce up to *Finnegans Wake*, see their ultimate symbolic identification, similar to the play of "heimlich" and "unheimlich," in Emile Benveniste's comments on *hospes* and *hostes* in *Indo-European Language and Society*, trans. Elizabeth Palmer (Coral Gables, Fla.: University of Miami Press, 1973). Stephen's preoccupation with "home" in the last section of *Portrait* is obviously rooted in that sort of experience. See also Jules David Law, "Joyce's 'Delicate Siamese' Equation: The Dialectic of Home in *Ulysses*," *PMLA* 102 (March 1987): 197–205, for connections with interiority and exteriority, patriotism and exile.

29. Kristeva, "Joyce," 171.

an (anxious) resistance to anxiety in the form of a symptom. Primal anxiety doubles itself in the inaugural passage of writing.[30]

Stephen calls Daedalus "hawklike." The association is at first sight enigmatic. Daedalus is of course a solar hero, and the osierwoven wings he used would seem to simulate those of an eagle, Zeus's emblematic bird, which as solar double of the king assumed the function of guarantor of the royal power for the Greeks. In Egypt, however, the hawk, or falcon, was the solar animal, the animal of Amen-Ra. It is said that at the moment of the Pharaoh's coronation a hawk descended upon him as a symbol of his investiture with divine power. Finding authority in J. H. Breasted, Freud mentions in *Moses and Monotheism* that the sun god Ra used to be represented as a hawk and a small pyramid.[31] From later representations in the shape of a beam-emitting sun, it would be possible to understand the pyramid as precisely the emanation of the hawk's surrogate power. Joyce is clearly associating Daedalus with Egyptian solar divinities, and the same association will be repeated in *Ulysses*. In my opinion it has the paramount purpose of connecting Daedalus with writing, through Thoth, while at the same time subverting that association, as we shall see.

Robert Graves explains that within Greek mythology the Daedalid myths seem "to combine the ritual of burning the solar king's surrogate, who had put on eagle's wings . . . with the rituals of flinging the partridge-winged *pharmakos*, a similar surrogate, over the cliff into the sea."[32] *Pharmakos* means "wizard," "magician," "poisoner." The *pharmakos* is someone whose function is ambiguous, double, because he can both heal and kill, a function then either benevolent or malignant, like that of the king with his paternal authority. The decision to get rid of him is cyclical and expiatory. It is a social decision through which the community, in the expulsion of what is threatening toward an abysmal outside, recreates its identity by reconstituting an inside. Derrida has this to say about the border-instituting function of the *pharmakos*:

30. Within anxiety, Stephen's fear of Daedalus is not only a fear of his father. It is ultimately a fear of his name, which links father, son, and brother and makes them doubles of one another: "Daedalus . . . Talos . . . and Hephaestus are shown by the similarity of their attributes to be merely different titles of the same mythical character; Icarus . . . may yet be another of his titles" (Robert Graves, *The Greek Myths*, vol. 1 [Harmondsworth: Penguin, 1984], 92.1).

31. Sigmund Freud, *Moses and Monotheism*, trans. Katherine Jones (London: Hogarth, 1951), 40.

32. Graves, *Myths*, 1:92.3.

> *Intra muros/extra muros.* The origin of the difference and division, the *pharmakos* represents evil both introjected and projected. Beneficial insofar as he cures—and for that, venerated, and cared for— harmful insofar as he incarnates the powers of evil—and for that, feared and treated with caution. . . . Sacred and accursed. The conjunction, the *coincidentia oppositorium,* ceaselessly undoes itself in the passage to decision or crisis.[33]

Through his paternal name Stephen has been given the name of a *pharmakos,* and he fears such an inscription when his inaugural decision to become a writer radically brings into question the opposition between inside and outside, home and the uncanny. Stephen reflects that he must leave forever "the house of prayer and prudence into which he had been born and the order of life out of which he had come" (*P,* 225) but that he must not do so at the price or in the manner of a mere abandonment; rather, he must leave as birds do, whose flight eternally recurs. Stephen's reading of his destiny, the augury from the temple, says precisely that: "What birds were they: He thought that they must be swallows who had come back from the south. Then he was to go away for they were birds ever going and coming, building ever an unlasting home under the eaves of men's houses and ever leaving the homes they had built to wander" (*P,* 225).

Stephen understands that his disruptive mission as a writer, like that of the *pharmakos,* will be the displacement of the dwelling place. As *pharmakoi* do, he will threaten the economy of inside and outside, and might therefore have to be sacrificed. Stephen is a Daedalid. Daedalus, Icarus, and Talos, artificers, are surrogates of the sun king, aquiline beings whose solar symbol will cost them their lives. All three are members of the Athenian royal family of Erechtheus, whose totemic emblem is the snake. Taking his cue from an old tradition, Nietzsche symbolized recurrence in the eagle and the snake. The realization of the recurrence of displacement in the home, and of home in the displacement, is one of Stephen's fears, a heavy burden indeed, "das grösste Schwergewicht," as Nietzsche calls it in *The Gay Science.* Stephen's version of the Eternal Return of the Same will be the price, as in Nietzsche, of the "intense instant of imagination," *Augenblick,* the blink of an eye

33. Derrida, "Pharmacy," 133.

(*Augenblick* is Luther's translation of the "twinkling of an eye," or ecstatic moment of salvation).[34]

Talos is Daedalus's surrogate son and therefore Icarus's brother. In Ovid's version of the myth, which Joyce certainly knew, we find that Daedalus had killed Talos because he was jealous of his reputation as an artificer. Graves adds that Daedalus also suspected Talos of an incestuous relation with his mother, Perdix.[35] Daedalus made Talos accompany him to the roof of the Parthenon and there invited him to contemplate the view. He then pushed Talos off the temple, into the abyss. Ovid says that at that point Pallas, "who looks favourably upon clever men, caught the lad as he fell and changed him into a bird, clothing him with feathers in mid-air."[36]

Another passage in *Metamorphoses* tells us that this bird was a partridge *(perdix)*. As Daedalus was burying Icarus on the beach at Samos, "a garrulous partridge came out of a muddy ditch [garrula limoso prospexit ab elice perdix], flapped its wings and crowed with joy."[37] But Perdix is Talos's mother's name. Talos is metamorphosed by Pallas into a bird in the form of his mother's name. Because of Daedaus's radical act of disinheritance, Talos retrieves his maternal name. This must be the meaning of Ovid's otherwise obscure verse: "Nomen, quod et ante, remansit" (his name remained the same as before; that is, as it was before he was given over to Daedalus as a surrogate son).[38] The nineteenth-century illustration accompanying this essay calls Talos by the name Perdix. The popular etymology that associates in Latin and the Romance languages the name of the bird with the word for "losing" *(perdere)* is important here. It is also important to note that *perdere* comes from *per* and *dare*, so that we lose something when we give it up completely. Talos is the disinherited one, the one without a father's name. And yet it was Pallas Athena, the goddess of truth, who saved him in the name of another inheritance, this time maternal, and by so doing made possible his pharmakic return, even in loss.

In "Scylla and Charybdis" Stephen will ask himself, "What's in a name?" (*U*, 9.927). He is thinking about Shakespeare and artistic

---

34. "Das grösste Schwergewicht" is the realization and acceptance of the idea of the Eternal Return of the Same. See Friedrich Nietzsche, *Die fröhliche Wissenschaft*, in *Werke*, ed. Karl Schlechta (Frankfurt: Ullstein Materialien, 1984), 2:436, aphorism 341. About the eagle and the snake, see Nietzsche, *Also sprach Zarathustra*, in *Werke*, 2:736–41, 3.13.2.
35. Graves, *Myths*, 1:92.1.
36. Ovid, *Metamorphoses*, ed. W. S. Anderson (Leipzig: Teubner, 1977), 8.251–53.
37. Ibid., 8.236–37.
38. Ibid., 8.255.

Perdix, the Nephew of Daedalus, transformed into a Partridge. A nineteenth-century print. Gift of John Miley to the author.

creation, parentage, but he is also living through the frustration of his return from Paris. The cause of Stephen's return, as we know, is a telegram from his father with an ominous misprint: "NOTHER DYING COME HOME FATHER" (U, 3.199). All editions prior to Gabler's say "MOTHER DYING COME HOME FATHER." "Nother" is not only "mother," for any reader must consider the possibility of a misprint, but also, uncannily, "not her" and "no other." Patrick McGee suggests that the scribal lapsus "expresses Stephen's secret refusal to let his mother die."[39] It would then be a symptom of incorporation. But if misprint there is, then it merely announces the need for normal mourning: the return home is the beginning of introjection. The telegram, written by Stephen's father, is a poignant text in which the radical ambiguity between introjection and incorporation announces itself. Is it a paternal ruse? Is his father killing him even when requesting his last return to mother?

The possibility of a paternal ruse, over and above his mother's agony, is what is worrying Stephen, who thinks about his return in terms of a meditation on his name: "Fabulous artificer. The hawk-like man. You flew. Whereto? Newhaven-Dieppe, steerage passenger. Paris and back. Lapwing. Icarus. *Pater, ait.* Seabedabbled, fallen, weltering. Lapwing you are. Lapwing be" (U, 9.952–54). The connection between the lapwing and Stephen's relationship with his mother has not, to my knowledge, been remarked upon. In my opinion it is significant, and it helps us understand the nature of Stephen's maternal phantasm. At the time of the narration Stephen's mother is, of course, already dead. Stephen failed to reconcile with her, and the fact haunts him.

As we saw, Hayman takes the lapwing to be Icarus. I would suggest the possibility that "lapwing" refers not to Icarus but to Icarus's brother, Talos, the partridge. At first glance there is of course no reason why "lapwing" should be made to refer to a partridge, but I will shortly give some reasons for my view. Should it prove plausible, we might conclude that in this passage Stephen, frustrated, thinks of Talos, a Daedalid who is Icarus's defeated brother, his double. We know from Ovid that Talos crowed with joy when Daedalus buried Icarus after his fall. Stephen, having returned from Paris, feels defeated, a fallen Icarus, "seabedabbled, fallen, weltering." And he feels a degree of hostility toward his father.

39. McGee, *Paperspace*, 58–59.

Let me make two preliminary points: the first is that when Stephen thinks of the lapwing, he has just been thinking of himself as a *pharmakos: "Autontimorumenos. Bous Stephanoumenos"* (*U*, 9.939). And: *"Stephanos*, my crown" (*U*, 9.47). The sacrificial crowned ox, *bous stephanoumenos*, is a substitute for the human *pharmakos* in some rituals. The one who destroys himself, *autontimorumenos*, is the pharmakic king, since he is the depository of the social power that will eventually decide on the sacrifice. These connections constitute clear textual evidence of the fact that Stephen associates himself with pharmakic figures. We find these mentions only in *Ulysses*, to be sure, but in a passage that has powerful internal links with the "Library" scene in *Portrait* on which I have been commenting. The borderline position of the *pharmakos* vis-à-vis society is one of the strongest motifs underlying Stephen's commitment to art: his self-definition from the quoted passage in *Portrait* has him forever leaving the house of prayer and prudence but also always building an unlasting home. This critical positioning of the decisive event of writing implies an impossibility of settling the question about displacement and parental murder. It is never for him only a question of taking over an inside, whatever the means and the reasons. It is never just an ethical question, precisely because the ethical—in its radical sense of *ethos*, the dwelling place, the familiar—is what the *pharmakos* first questions.

The second, minor, point is that in editions prior to Hans Gabler's the lapwing pasage reads "lapwing he" instead of "lapwing be." "Lapwing he" certainly makes it clearer that Stephen is thinking about a third person, perhaps a brother, with whom he momentarily identifies. Robert Scholes and Richard M. Kain, however, do not find this identification so momentary: "In *Ulysses* Stephen's main resemblance is clearly to this third lapwinged member of the Daedalian trinity [Talos]."[40] George L. Geckle calls Scholes and Kain's explication "implausible," although his reasons for denying the Talos-lapwing connection in the quoted passage seem arbitrary.[41] (Geckle's article goes on to examine the literary motif of the lapwing; he points out the etymological connection between *lap* and *hléapan*, and *wing* and *winchan*, which makes of the rather filthy

40. Robert Scholes and Richard M. Kain, eds., *The Workshop of Daedalus: James Joyce and the Raw Materials for "A Portrait of the Artist as a Young Man"* (Evanston: Northwestern University Press, 1965), 264.
41. George L. Geckle, "Stephen Dedalus as Lapwing: A Symbolic Center of *Ulysses*," *James Joyce Quarterly* 6 (Winter 1968): 104.

bird a bird capable of "leaping," shall we say, "in the wink of an eye." Faculties such as these open up the possibility of "intense instants of imagination"—*Augenblicken* in the Nietzschean sense.) I agree with Scholes and Kain.

But why the lapwing? What does it have to do with Talos? Mary M. Innes's popular English translation of *Metamorphoses* does translate *perdix* as "lapwing," even if in the index of contents she lists the bird as "partridge."[42] Innes obviously gave some thought to the issue. There is an interesting set of problems here, which I will mention briefly. Apparently Ovid's manuscript of *Metamorphoses* 8.237 reads, "Garrula ramosa prospexit ab ilice perdix." In his commentary on Book 8, A. S. Hollis calls this line "a famous crux,"[43] given that "ab ilice ramosa" implies that the *perdix* would be perching on a branching holm oak. But partridges do not perch in trees. The reading also conflicts with the whole point of the story, which Ovid tells in verses 255–59, namely, that *perdices* have developed a fear of heights since what happened to Talos.

A third problem concerning the *perdix* is that, in the words of Wilmon Brewer: "Ovid described [the partridge] as jubilantly beating his wings and immediately afterwards as crowing. For a partridge, this would not be in character. Ovid may have been thinking of a pheasant."[44] For my purposes it is enough to indicate that clear textual problems, of which Joyce may well have been aware, have traditionally problematized the immediate translation of *perdix* as "partridge." Innes renders "lapwing," not pheasant, for reasons of consistency. Verse 237 is nowadays generally taken to read: "Garrula limosa prospexit ab elice perdix." "Ab elice limosa" is translated as "from a muddy ditch." Lapwings do dwell in muddy ditches by the sea. The next verse, "et plausit pennis testataque gaudia cantu est," would also be consistent with a lapwing's rather rowdy general behavior, but not with a partridge's. My contention, in line with Scholes and Kain's, is that Joyce also chose to translate *perdix* as "lapwing." It would not in any case be out of character for him to hide the obvious and put Talos, the Perdix, under the wings of the lapwing. But, once we accept that there is some confusion between "lapwing" and "partridge" as translations of the Ovidian *perdix*,

42. Ovid, *The Metamorphoses*, trans. and ed. Mary N. Innes (Harmondsworth: Penguin, 1955).
43. A. S. Hollis, *Ovid: Metamorphoses Book VIII* (Oxford: Clarendon Press, 1970), 64.
44. Wilmon Brewer, *Ovid's Metamorphoses in European Culture*, vol. 2 (Boston: Cornhill, 1933), 182.

there is an even stronger reason, in my opinion, to suggest that Stephen is thinking about Talos in the passage in question.[45]

Stephen does not directly name Talos in his thought. Barely twenty lines after his first mention of the lapwing, however, the lapwing returns, this time explicitly juxtaposed to a Daedalean, pharmakic brother: "A brother is as easily forgotten as an umbrella. Lapwing. Where is your brother? Apothecaries' hall" (U, 9.974–77). In my interpretation Stephen is already abandoning his fleeting identification with Talos. Back in the persona of Icarus, Stephen now regards Talos as the easily forgotten brother, a distanced figure, left behind like an umbrella, or perhaps a caduceus, at the pharmacy among *pharmaka*. The presence in this segment of two references to a brother, coupled with two references to this pharmakic identity, point, I think, to the clear and distinct possibility that Talos is here that almost-already-forgotten presence, a withdrawing presence in the vanishing threshold of consciousness, a presence undergoing repression. The possibility that Talos is here the withdrawing presence, and that it is named as such, in withdrawal, seems to me to account better than any other for the text itself: "lapwing . . . a brother." But we still have to see why the umbrella should indeed be a reference to the Daedalean *pharmakoi*.[46]

Daedalus threw not only his son Talos off the cliff but also, according to the Second Vatican Mythographer (a compilation of myths), another man named Sciron. As in the Talos episode, Daedalus, himself a *pharmakos*, takes the position of the sacrificer and not of the sacrificed. The inversion is not surprising. Given the paradoxical condition of the royal figure, the *pharmakos* is always, in a certain sense, his own killer. His symbolic inscription is cer-

45. See also Franz Bömer, ed., *Metamorphoses: Buch VIII–IX* (Heidelberg: Carl Winer, 1977), 82–85. Incidentally, the partridge is not precisely an innocent bird itself. Bestiaries speak of it as a symbol of deceit. See T. H. White, ed., *The Bestiary: A Book of Beasts* (New York: Putnam, 1960), s.v. "partridge."

46. About Joyce and brother relationships in his writing, see Mary T. Reynolds, "Joyce and His Brothers: The Process of Fictional Transformation," *James Joyce Quarterly* 25 (Winter 1988): 217–25, and Jean Kimball, "'Lui, c'est moi': The Brother Relationship in *Ulysses*," *James Joyce Quarterly* 25 (Winter 1988): 227–35. Umbrellas are especially important in *Finnegans Wake*. See, for instance, John Bishop's comments in *Joyce's Book of the Dark: Finnegans Wake* (Madison: University of Wisconsin Press, 1987), 220, 232, 256, 275. See also Jacques Derrida, "I Have Forgotten My Umbrella," in *Spurs: Nietzsche's Styles/Eperons: Les styles de Nietzsche*, trans. Barbara Harlow (Chicago: University of Chicago Press, 1978), 123–43. The whole of Derrida's book suggests some unexpected connections between sailboats and umbrellas (unexpected, that is, if one forgets about the *pharmakos*). Umbrellas also turn up in Derrida, *Glas*, 2 vols. (Paris: Denöel/Gauthier, 1981), 1.35 and passim.

tainly burdensome. But Sciron means *umbrella* in Greek. Graves mentions a terra-cotta in which Sciron is represented falling through the air, toward the sea, grabbing an umbrella. The umbrella represents a bird's wings, but it is also a symbol of the house of Erechtheus, of which the Daedalids are of course members. The priest of this house, who is also chief of the Athenian cult of the snake, must carry an umbrella in the yearly procession of the Scirophoria festivals. Scirophorion was the last month of the Greek year, the month of return. Return is the goal of the *pharmakos*'s journey, after his cyclic sacrifice. It is symbolized by the ship that, in some representations, awaits the fall of the *pharmakos* to rescue him. The "Proteus" episode in *Ulysses*, in which Stephen muses over the possibility of falling "over a cliff" (*U*, 3.14), concludes: "Moving through the air high spars of a threemaster, her sails brailed up on the crosstrees, homing, upstream, silently moving, a silent ship" (*U*, 3.503–5).[47] We shall see reasons for hearing in this passage resonances of the "Library" scene in *Portrait*. The ship that picks up the fallen *pharmakos* is a representation of woman, according to old iconologies. It is associated with Pallas in the Talos myth. Without mentioning either Pallas or Talos, Derrida has also associated it with woman and the Nietzschean umbrella, following hints first developed by Luce Irigaray and Sarah Kofman.[48]

Fear and Truth

Now I am ready to comment on Stephen's third fear, the fear of Thoth, and thus to go from *pharmakos* to *pharmakon*, from the writer to writing itself. An examination of Stephen's third fear opens the way to understanding in what sense it is possible to claim that the text's identificatory symptom is undecidable and that it is this very undecidability that constitutes the experience of truth in which the text gives itself as writing.

The fear of Thoth is again confirmed in "Scylla and Charybdis": "Coffined thoughts around me, in mummycases, embalmed in spice

---

47. For the mythological references, see Graves, *Myths*, 1:96.
48. See the entire first part of Sarah Kofman, *The Enigma of Woman: Woman in Freud's Writings*, trans. Catherine Porter (Ithaca: Cornell University Press, 1985); also Luce Irigaray, *Amante marine de Friedrich Nietzsche* (Paris: Minuit, 1980). As for Derrida, see *Spurs*, 35–71 passim.

of words. Thoth, god of libraries, a bird, moonycrowned. And I heard the voice of that Egyptian highpriest. *In painted chambers loaded with tilebooks.* They are still. Once quick in the brains of men. Still: but an itch of death is in them" (*U*, 9.352–57). Writing and death: Thoth, god of writing, is also the god of death. And as a giver of death, he can also stop it, displace its power. He is the god of medicine, in charge of pharmacopoeia. *Pharmakon* is "drug," beneficent or malignant, medicament or poison. In the well-known myth of Thoth and Thamus, narrated in the *Phaedrus*, Thoth presents Thamus with writing as the *pharmakon* of knowledge. Thamus, who is a surrogate of the sun god Amen-Ra, if not the god himself, rejects the gift on the basis of its duplicity. Far from helping knowledge, writing supplants it, favoring only rememoration.[49]

Supposing that authentic memory is memory of truth, the rememoration that writing holds cannot but simulate that truth. Derrida writes:

> The subtle difference between knowledge as memory and nonknowledge as rememoration, between two forms and two moments of repetition: a repetition of truth *(aletheia)* which presents and exposes the *eodos;* and a repetition of death and oblivion *(lethe)* which veils and skews it because it does not present the *eidos* but re-presents a presentation, repeats a repetition.[50]

Writing is a repetition stopping death and another repetition reproducing and extending it, a medicament and a poison. Still, in "Scylla and Charybdis" Stephen meditates about poison, this time with an overt reference to writing and parricide: "They list, and in the porches of their ears I pour," Stephen thinks. "The soul has been before stricken mortally, a poison poured in the porch of a sleeping ear" (*U*, 9.465–67). Thus dies King Hamlet, opening the way for the portent.

If the *pharmakos* finds himself at the border between the inside and the outside, displacing it, mediating between home and the uncanny and thus threatening the very economy of their relationship, the *pharmakon* links, and thus subverts, *both* presence *and* forgetfulness. It is a violent operation. Writing is apparently committed to a necessary parricide, for it kills its origin as soon as it

49. Plato, *Phaedrus*, vol. 2 of *Platonis Opera*, ed. John Burnet (Oxford: Clarendon Press, 1901), 274c ff.
50. Derrida, "Pharmacy," 135.

shows up, negating its original dependence on the inscriber, the father of writing, or rather claiming to have supplanted the origin, to have suppressed in itself the need for an origin. Writing supplants the spoken word, but not merely by opposing it; on the contrary, making itself pass as its perfect mimesis, it is no longer an imitation of the model but a supplanted model. Derrida summarizes Thoth's attributes: "As a substitute capable of doubling for the king, the father, the sun, and the word, distinguished from these only by dint of representing, repeating, and masquerading, Thoth was naturally also capable of totally supplanting them and appropriating all their attributes."[51] Thus Thoth, parricide god and supplanter of the sun, is also a god of resurrection who "is less interested in life or death than in death as a repetition of life and life as a rehearsal of death, in the awakening of life and in the recommencement of death."[52] By absolutely impersonating his model, Thoth does not kill his model. It occupies its absence and thus suspends his parricide. Thoth, god of the passage between speech and writing, between life and death, god of the return of life in death and of death in life, is an uncanny god, worthy of fear.

Stephen fears his passage into writing because he fears the death operation in it. He thinks: "Through the ghost of the unquiet father the image of the unliving son looks forth" (U, 9.380–81). The moment of the passage into writing is the moment in which the father—and Derrida reminds us that *pater* is in Greek also "founder," "capital," and "good"[53]—must be displaced by the new action of founding, the new investment of capital, the new concealing of the good which all guests presuppose. But in this displacement there is no murder, only the confirmation of a previous absence that is now filled. The father must be reaffirmed, is indeed reaffirmed at the very moment of his supplantation, of his substitution. Stephen's fear of death is the fear of this portent, the symbolic alliance of death and life, recurrent. But his answer to such fears, like Nietzsche's, is acceptance and affirmation. In it something else is also given: the passage into writing, the move toward the constitution of artistic expression as nonsecondary truth. I will attempt to show this more clearly.

If Amen is pure self-presence, light and truth for himself, to sup-

51. Ibid., 90; the key word is "totally."
52. Ibid., 93.
53. Ibid., 81.

plant Amen—to be moon, son, scribe in the solar ship—is not to gamble for absence, shadow, and lies. This would be not a supplantation but a mere inversion. We could gamble for shadow, but only insofar as shadow guards us from the very alternative presence/absence. To supplant Amen is to think the simulacrum, not as an insufficiency representing the model but as a device that ultimately lets us think the model as a ghost of itself, if the unliving son is to become a life image.

Stephen turns toward the shadow because he needs it in order to write, as the "Proteus" episode makes clear. Returned from Paris, Stephen must follow a mythic itinerary that will lead him, as it leads the gypsy, toward the land of the dead: "Across the sands of all the world, followed by the sun's flaming sword, to the west, trekking to evening lands" (*U*, 3.391–92). "Turning his back to the sun he bent over far to a table of rock and scribbled words. . . . His shadow lay over the rocks as he bent, ending. Why not endless till the farthest star? Darkly they are there behind this light, darkness shining in the brightness, delta of Cassiopeia, worlds" (*U*, 3.406–10). The worlds in the delta: darkness shines. Toward them Stephen will trek in the garb of a *pharmakos* "with his augur's rod of ash," that is, his pharmakic token, the ashplant stick (*U*, 3.411).[54]

Before being the name for the alluvial deposit at the mouth of a river, and therefore before ever becoming a metaphor for female genitals, *delta* was the fourth letter of the Greek alphabet, the letter that initiates Stephen's paternal name. This is of course referred to in the already mentioned passage in "Scylla and Charybdis" about the name:

> What's in a name? That's what we ask ourselves in childhood when we write the name that we are told is ours. A star, a daystar, a firedrake, rose at his birth. It shone by day in the heavens alone, brighter than Venus in the light, and by night it shone over delta in Cassiopeia, the recumbent constellation which is the signature of his initial among the stars. (U, 9.927–31)

---

54. "Shadow" is *umbra* in Latin; hence "umbrella" as parasol. We can associate this trip with the trip between Scylla and Charybdis. Stuart Gilbert, in *James Joyce's Ulysses* (New York: Vintage, 1955), says, insufficiently, of Chapter 9: "The *motifs* of the sheer, steadfast rock of Scylla and the restless whirlpool of Charybdis, a sea of troubles, are utilized in a symbolic sense in this episode. The stability of Dogma, of Aristotle and of Shakespeare's Stratford is contrasted with the whirlpool of Mysticism, Platonism, the London of Elizabethan times" (224). But Gilbert also talks about "paired perils . . . the constraints of a dilemma" (225).

Whether Stephen's trekking to evening lands is an attempt to deal with his mother's death, for which he feels guilty, is open to question. It has been pointed out repeatedly that in *Ulysses* Stephen, in Jean-Michel Rabaté's words, "feels locked in a postmortem embrace with a mother who haunts him."[55] In this passage we see that Stephen does seek his paternal name, Dedalus. But how does the delta relate to his mother?

In his 1772 *Conjectural Observations on the Origin and Progress of Alphabetic Writing*, Charles Davy noted that "writing, in the earliest ages of the world, was a delineation of the outlines of those things men wanted to remember, rudely graven either upon shells or stones, or marked upon the leaves or bark of trees."[56] *Delta* is an old letter, supposedly borrowed from Cadmus from the original Hebrew or Samaritan alphabet, and thus identical to the Hebrew *daleth*, or *deleth*, meaning "door." In a curious work, *Sign and Design: The Psychogenetic Source of the Alphabet*, Alfred Kallir studies the letter *D* and its shape in many graphic systems to conclude its association with habitation, woman, vulva, moon, offspring. According to Kallir, for instance, Saint Ambrose gives "nativitas" for the meaning of the Hebrew letter *daleth*. But more important are the triangular outlines that define abode and femininity in many different traditions.[57] Closer to home, a delta is the siglum Joyce employed for Anna Livia Plurabelle in the *Finnegans Wake* notebooks and in *Finnegans Wake* itself (*FW*, 119.19–22). (Hayman notes the use of delta to refer to Nora Joyce in Notebook VI.B.5.)[58]

Both searches, for a paternal name initialed with the delta of Dedalus and for a maternal reconciliation in the trip to the evening lands, following the example of Odysseus, become one and the same, and therefore neither. One is the *pharmakon* of its other. Stephen, even in his fear of mourning, in his persistent attempt at encryption of his mother in the search for artistic self-production, is forced to recognize the mutual interdependence of parental identifications. What we have here is a rejection of the image of the artist as an accomplished Oedipus. The impossibility of deciphering

55. Rabaté, "A Clown's Inquest," 85.

56. Charles Davy, *Conjectural Observations on the Origin and Progress of Alphabetic Writing* (London: T. Wright, 1772), 1.

57. Alfred Kallir, *Sign and Design: The Psychogenetic Source of the Alphabet* (London: James Clarke and Co., 1961), 201–10. I wish to thank Juan Carlos Temprano for having brought these alphabetical matters to my attention.

58. David Hayman, "'I Think Her Pretty': Reflections of the Familiar in Joyce's Notebook VI.B.5," *Joyce Studies Annual* 1 (1990): 42.

the delta away from Dedalus is only the counterpart to the impossibility of erasing the loss in Perdix's name. Following Stephen's primary identifications, we will not have a consummated introjection of father and an aberrant incorporation of mother. Conversely, the introjection of the mother in the work of mourning cannot function without an equally explicit dislodging of the father. The passage into writing negotiates this difficult economy of parental mourning not by consummating mourning but by transferring it away from the unconscious into the real of expression. Joyce does not solve his problems, but Stephen does.

Stephen says: "As we, or mother Dana, weave and unweave our bodies . . . from day to day, their molecules shuttled to and fro, so does the artist weave and unweave his image" (U, 9.376–78). There is a hesitation in the sentence which makes it almost unintelligible: Is it we, or mother Dana? Who is the artist? Where does he get his strength? Who might mother Dana be? She is a maternal divinity. It would be comforting to decide that mother Dana is the region for the parricidal battle, the site upon which all filial displacements as well as all births take place—a place, a ground at least. Talos would be happily redeemed by a maternal act of salvation. Daedalus would not have to be feared—or not much. The symbolic would be the entrance into the maternal name. Stephen's three fears would be radically appeased once the passage into writing was consummated. Can that be Stephen's theory, his inaugural view from the temple? It is particularly important in this context to note that Stephen's mention of the "intense instant of imagination" in which the writer becomes one with himself, in the ecstatic moment in which past, present, and future come together, a moment of ultimate self-conception, self-parentality, comes right after this mention of mother Dana, the female divinity which is an obvious counterpart to Freud's "Imaginary Father of Individual Prehistory":

> So does the artist weave and unweave his image. And as the mole on my right breast is where it was when I was born, though all my body has been woven of new stuff time after time, so through the ghost of the unquiet father the image of the unliving son looks forth. In the intense instant of imagination, when the mind, Shelley says, is a fading coal, that which I was is that which I am and that which in possibility I may come to be. (U, 9.377–84)

Going back to *Portrait*, Stephen's temple vision is a contemplation. It gives him fear. Martin Heidegger explains how *contemplari* is the vision from the *templum*, and how the *templum* is precisely the place that is visible from all points, and thus also the place from which everything is visible: a site, then, of encounter between seeing and being seen, and therefore a place of passage, of crisis between both perspectives. This privilege makes of the temple the region for all inauguration and all auguries: "The Latin *templum* means originally a sector carved out in the heavens and on the earth, the cardinal point, the region of the heavens marked out by the path of the sun. It is within this region that diviners make their observations in order to determine the future from the flight, cries, and eating habits of birds."[59] *Contemplatio* is the Latin translation of *theoria*. *Contemplatio* is, of course, the fearful vision that Daedalus forced on his son before killing him. Talos's vision before his fall is a theoretical vision, at the edge of the abyss. *Theorein*, Heidegger explains, is *thean horan*, that is, "to look attentively on the outward appearance wherein what presences becomes visible and, through such sight—seeing—, to linger with it."[60] *Thea* means "aspect," and it is related to *theater*. It is not just anecdotal that the Athenian theater of Dionysos, where tragedy cyclically represented the theory of the world, lies directly beneath the Parthenon in the Acropolis. But Heidegger has called attention to the fact that in *theoria* there is also *theá*, the goddess, and "it is as a goddess that *Aletheia*, the unconcealment from out of which and in which that which presences, presences, appears to the early thinker Parmenides."[61]

Daedalus, father and teacher, throws his son from the temple after he has his theoretical vision. Pallas is the goddess of the theoretical vision. As we know from Ovid, Pallas, "who looks favourably upon clever men, caught the lad as he fell and changed him into a bird." The "Library" scene in *Portrait* reflects Talos's fearful contemplation. The passages there that express Stephen's inaugural decision, once made, read:

> A soft liquid joy like the noise of many waters flowed over his memory and he felt in his heart the soft peace of silent spaces of

59. Martin Heidegger, "Science and Reflection," in *The Question concerning Technology and Other Essays*, ed. and trans. William Lovitt (New York: Harper Torchbooks, 1977), 165–66.
60. Ibid., 163.
61. Ibid., 164.

fading tenuous sky above the waters, of oceanic silence, of swallows flying through the seadusk over the flowing water.

A soft liquid joy flowed through the words where the soft long vowels hurtled noiselessly and fell away, lapping and flowing back and ever shaking the white bells of their waves in mute chime and mute peal and soft low swooning cry; and he felt that the augury he had sought in the wheeling darting birds and in the pale space of sky above him had come forth from his heart like a bird from a turret quietly and swiftly. (P, 225–26)

I would suggest that these passages be interpreted in the light of the Talos-Daedalus myth. Stephen is falling into the sea, repeating the fall of the Erechtheionid *pharmakos*. Stephen has become a bird; he is flying in a trance; the augury is manifested to him. Should we not associate that "lapping and flowing" with the lapwing? Of course, this passage was written years before "Scylla and Charybis" was even conceived. And yet, that Book 8 of *Metamorphoses*, where the story of Talos is narrated, was clearly important for Joyce when he was composing *Portrait* is clearly established by the fact that the epigraph of the book ("et ignotat animum dimittit in artes") comes from it. The source of the illustration accompanying this essay is undoubtedly a Renaissance representation, in which the background to the metamorphosis of Talos into a partridge is not the Parthenon but, precisely, a turret. The importance of the sea, and of images of liquidity and softness which hint at the maternal bosom, is also obvious in a different connection.

Jean Kimball thinks that "when Stephen . . . watches the birds outside the library, it is to escape the raw emotion of his struggle with his mother, her 'sobs and reproaches,' in the cool contemplation of the flight of birds, which, he reminds himself, Swedenborg links to 'things of the intellect.'"[62] I differ: in his contemplation, in his passage into the abyss, Stephen is, like Talos the artificer, phantasmatically recovering a maternal name. His identificatory symptom concerning the feminine goes well beyond what will later be implied in *Ulysses:* guilt before his mother's death.

In Stephen's pharmakic projection into the flight of birds "ever coming and going" a return begins, patterned in the flight of the swallows. The inside/outside, the remedy/poison, the paternal/maternal, the imitation/truth, the symbolic/imaginary are all sus-

---

62. Kimball, "Freud," 68.

pended precisely through the intrapsychic identifications that constitute Stephen in his inaugural moment as a writer. Stephen's signature is not only given in his negation of paternity, not only given in his displacement from his mother. Rather, as we have seen, both paternity and maternity return, as inheritance to be sure, but also as legacy for the reader. In this return there is nothing cyclical. It means, it figures, the textual projection of itself as a truth that has nothing to do with secondariness, with representation. The text thus announces its abandonment of the symbolic and its entrance into the real. "*Wo ich war . . .*"

Rabaté has developed the Lacanian theme of the Name-of-the-Father in connection with *Ulysses*. He explains very concisely what is at stake:

> For Lacan, the acquisition of language is contemporary with the Oedipal stages. When first I speak, I accept a symbolic castration in that I have to renounce my intense desire for fusion with the mother: as I learn the rules of language, I accept the externality of a symbolic code which existed prior to my unique connection with the other and even predetermined it. . . . This paternal complicity explains the guilt lying within language's very foundation, the guilt of having to displace the mother and to kill the father as presence.[63]

It has been a habit of Joycean criticism to interpret Stephen's passage into writing in the light of this oedipal ideology, even when Lacan was not invoked. I hope to have shown, through the pharma-conomical connections, that Stephen's passage into writing, and therefore the textual conception of itself as an artistic object, is a mode of resistance to the situation explained in Rabaté's summary: a working-through, or even a reaction against, such paternal complicity whose effect is, precisely, the suspension of maternal displacement and of paternal murder. But if the symbolic is first made possible by both events, then the work of art consummates the symbolic. The logic of the symbol is broken precisely because the broken parts of the symbol no longer fit. In the impossibility of deciding the sign of primary identification, in the impossibility of understanding the relative hierarchy of the mother-father inheritance, the symbol shatters, and a particular kind of opacity shines forth. The text offers itself no longer as an effect of meaning but as

63. Rabaté, "A Clown's Inquest," 90.

the site where meaning regresses; abandoning the symbolic, the text reverts into the real. To that extent, the work does not imitate the unconscious. To that extent, the return of the repressed, within the work of art, is not a symptom but a catharsis; and all cathartic drugs are, inevitably, poisonous remedies.

I began by quoting Kristeva's definition of the return of the repressed within the literary text as "the unveiling of intrapsychic identifications." We can subscribe to such a definition if we understand "unveiling" in the sense in which Heidegger interprets Greek truth, *aletheia*, to be an "unveiling." The literary text unveils an intrapsychic primordial phenomenon only to show its own truth not as the bringing-into-light of a series of previously repressed identifications but as the unveiling itself. In other words, its radical importance is on the side of expression, not of manifestation. Because it expresses, and not because it manifests, the literary text is the site where the identificatory symptom meets its undoing: in the very materiality of its presence, which outlasts manifestation and has therefore the quality of survival. Stephen's double inheritance becomes a legacy, which is (to be) read.

To give up what in art is manifestation of intrapsychic content in favor of art's "truthful structure," to use the Lacanian phrase, is to place art on the side of whatever in ethics is fundamentally beyond ethics: not a remedy, not a poison, not familiar, not uncanny, not maternal, not paternal, and so on, but the very possibility of their ruinous coincidence. This is ultimately what Stephen's theory of writing has to offer. If Stephen writes *between*, the radicality of his position as a writer depends on the impossibility of holding fast to subject positions created at the imaginary or the symbolic level. Which is to say that writing, as an experience of the real, offers no ethical or political comfort except to those who come to writing hoping to be comforted, and who thereby negate the experience of writing.

PART II

Repression and the Return of Cultural History: *Dubliners* and *Portrait*

3

Uncanny Returns in "The Dead": Ibsenian Intertexts and the Estranged Infant

Robert Spoo

"The Dead" might be described as Joyce's first sustained fictional enigma. The other fourteen *Dubliners* stories, all composed earlier, contain local puzzles and opacities, but these seem integrated and explicable when compared to the persistent unassimilated strangeness of the final story. This element of the "strange" (a word that echoes throughout "The Dead") exists on all levels of the text—plot, character, language, imagery, the very act of narrating—and is particularly arresting in that it emerges within the homely context of the Misses Morkan's annual Christmas dance. In this story the uncanny (*das Unheimliche*, or the "unhomely") makes its home precisely in *das Heimliche*, in that which is familiar and familial, so that the ambivalent etymological journey that Sigmund Freud in his essay "The 'Uncanny'" (1919) traces for the word *heimlich*—from "comfortable" and "homelike" to "hidden," "secret," and "dangerous"[1]—is played out in Gabriel Conroy's relationships with members of his family, in particular with his wife, Gretta.

We are assured in the opening pages of "The Dead" that the party "was always a great affair. . . . For years and years it had gone off in splendid style as long as anyone could remember."[2] This investment

---

1. Sigmund Freud, "The 'Uncanny,'" in *The Standard Edition of the Complete Psychological Works*, ed. and trans. James Strachey et al. (London: Hogarth Press, 1955), 17:222–26; hereafter cited in the text as Freud.

2. James Joyce, *Dubliners*, ed. Robert Scholes, in consultation with Richard Ellmann (New York: Viking Press, 1967), 175–76; hereafter cited in the text as *D*.

in a carefully controlled repetition of success sets the stage for ironic appearances of the uncanny and the emergence of unanticipated, ghostly "wit" at the expense of hyperconscious sociality. This process is repeated at the level of individual psyches, notably in the gradual dismantling of Gabriel's vigilant, self-absorbed aplomb. Joyce's text generates an uncanniness in which the frightening is not always distinguishable from the comic (as it occasionally is not in E. T. A. Hoffmann's tale "The Sand-Man," which Freud analyzes in "The 'Uncanny'").[3] This range or instability of affect, representing one of the chief obstacles to determining meaning, gives "The Dead" dim affinities, haunting in their elusive precocity, with *Finnegans Wake*.

Freud begins "The 'Uncanny'" with the complaint that neither aesthetic theory nor medico-psychological literature has adequately accounted for the experience of uncanniness. He notes that in 1906 Ernst Jentsch defined the uncanny as a feeling of "intellectual uncertainty" in the face of the novel and unfamiliar—uncertainty, for example, about whether an animate being is really alive, or, conversely, whether a lifeless object such as a doll or automaton might not be animate (Freud, 226–27). While crediting Jentsch with important insights, Freud contends that uncanny feelings arise primarily from something other than intellectual uncertainty, something less uncertain and far more disturbing. Taking "The Sand-Man" as a notable instance of the uncanny in literature, Freud asserts that the source of uncanniness in this tale is not the living female doll, Olympia (as Jentsch would have it), but rather the student Nathaniel's castration complex and his struggle with the father imago, a condition represented in the text by "the theme of the 'Sand-Man' who tears out children's eyes" (Freud, 227). Freud thus posits repressed infantile complexes, the once-familiar returning in terrifying forms, as the chief source of Nathaniel's uncanny experiences, an interpretive move that reinforces Freud's lengthy lexicographical demonstration that the meaning of the word *heimlich* "develops in the direction of ambivalence, until it finally coincides with its opposite, *unheimlich*" (Freud, 226).

Thus, according to Freud, the uncanny is "something which is familiar and old-established in the mind and which has become alienated from it only through the process of repression" (Freud,

---

3. For a discussion of the relationship between the uncanny and the joke, see Elizabeth Wright, *Psychoanalytic Criticism: Theory in Practice* (London: Methuen, 1984), 137–50.

241). He distinguishes between two classes of uncanniness: the re-surfacing of primitive religious beliefs that have been "sur-mounted" by modern civilization (such as the belief in the omnipotence of thoughts, secret injurious powers, the return of the dead); and an analogous revival of infantile complexes that have been "repressed" in the adult (castration complex, womb fantasies, and so forth). Two forms of the uncanny hold a special fascination for Freud: the encounter with a double, which results from a "divid-ing and interchanging of the self," a splitting of the ego into observer and observed (Freud, 234); and involuntary repetition, "a 'compul-sion to repeat' proceeding from the instinctual impulses and prob-ably inherent in the very nature of the instincts—a compulsion powerful enough to overrule the pleasure principle, lending to cer-tain aspects of the mind their daemonic character" (Freud, 238).[4]

This brief, necessarily selective summary of "The 'Uncanny'" provides a starting point for a discussion of "The Dead" as well as a basis for rethinking aspects of Freud's essay and extending its implicit but largely undeveloped ideas about literary representation. With minimal extrapolation the uncanny might be defined as a mode of psychic and/or textual representation that disguises re-pressed affects by means of what Freud calls "estrangement." The alienated luster that estrangement lends to these affects appears at the intersection of the familiar and the unfamiliar, the homely and the hidden, giving uncanny events their special quality, at once harrowing and perversely seductive.[5]

"The Dead" is an uncanny narrative the strangeness of which derives in part from a number of such "estrangements"—seemingly marginal moments in the text where the once-familiar can be fleet-ingly glimpsed under its incognito. By adopting a flexible psycho-analytic approach and not restricting it to individual characters' psyches or insisting that all estrangements can be traced to the conscious or unconscious mind of the author, I hope to shed light on a variety of textual "impediments," to use Jacques Lacan's term: discontinuities, bizarre figurations, and flashes of wit that signal

4. Freud alludes here to his theory of the repetition compulsion in *Beyond the Pleasure Principle* (1920), a work he drafted in the same year that he completed "The 'Uncanny.'"
5. I have intentionally blurred the distinction between the uncanny in life and the uncanny in fiction on the grounds that much of psychic life is inaccessible to us except in represented forms (such as accounts of dreams). Wright, in *Psychoanalytic Criticism*, 143–50, argues that Freud makes a positivistic effort to keep this distinction intact in "The 'Uncanny'" but that the effort fails in a number of "uncanny" ways.

the operation of the unconscious.[6] By the "unconscious" I do not mean some absolute event or psyche immanent in the text but rather a dynamic, problematic convergence of uncanny *experiences* elicited by the act of reading: the experiences of characters in the story, for example, when they encounter such things as doubling and involuntary repetition, as well as the reader's response to analogous phenomena on the level of textual and intertextual play. In the case of intertextual uncanniness, the once-familiar of a prior text is felt to haunt the present text in estranged yet recognizable forms.

It is important to stress that this convergence of experiences is so overdetermined in Joyce's text that the "sources" of the uncanny cannot easily be traced at any point. Moreover, as Freud himself noted, the uncanny in literature differs from the uncanny in life inasmuch as literature "contains the whole of the latter and something more besides, something that cannot be found in real life" (Freud, 249). This "something more," this representational excess, points to the unauthored, autogenetic quality of the uncanny as it operates within the peculiar language of literature.[7] The uncanny is itself uncanny when it makes its home in aesthetic discourse.

This broadly textual adaptation of the uncanny seems warranted by Freud himself, who proposes the concept initially as a way of accounting for aesthetic phenomena not amenable to such traditional categories as the sublime and the beautiful (Freud, 219–20). Unfortunately, Freud's scientific and clinical interests lead him to focus almost exclusively on the *content* (what he calls the "events" or "particulars") of Hoffmann's tale, reducing its complex texture to a quarry for corroborative instances. As a result, Freud's attention to the formal, aesthetic dimension of the uncanny, and to the rich grammar of representation implied in his own theory of repression and alienated return, gives way to a bustling positivism and an efficient etiology; *Wahrheit* easily displaces *Dichtung*, authoritatively converting writing into exemplarity, the signifier into the signified.

Even so, Freud offers some promising directions for exploring the relation between the uncanny and textuality. He notes, for example, that fairy tales, while they often contain uncanny elements, pro-

6. Jacques Lacan, *The Four Fundamental Concepts of Psycho-Analysis*, trans. Alan Sheridan (New York: Norton, 1981), 25.
7. For a parallel use of the term "autogenesis" to point to the ambiguity of a text's representation of individual minds, see Elizabeth Brunazzi, "La Narration de l'autogenèse dans *La Tentation de saint Antoine* et dans *Ulysses*," in *"Scribble" 2: Joyce et Flaubert*, ed. Claude Jacquet and André Topia (Paris: Minard, 1990), 123–24.

duce no feeling of uncanniness because they postulate a world of unreality from the start, whereas writers who set their tales "in the world of common reality" readily achieve uncanny effects (Freud, 250). Although Freud does not develop the point, it might be argued that realism and naturalism represent a "secularization" of literature—a sacrifice, in the interests of verifiability and clear-eyed mimesis, of the poetic and the figurative—analogous to the surmounting of primitive beliefs which Freud says paves the way for the return of those beliefs in estranged forms. Thus, the realistic or naturalistic mode—Joyce's fictional mode in *Dubliners*—would seem to be an especially fertile ground for uncanny visitations by virtue of the resolute rationality of its discourse, a discourse in which surmounted or repressed literariness, the excess of the signifier, returns to haunt the reader.

I largely avoid what in many ways continues to be, despite recent revisionary assaults, the standard approach to "The Dead," which traces Gabriel's progress toward a final epiphany of enlightenment, whether liberating or paralyzing.[8] Instead I will focus on marginal elements that have resisted incorporation into this master narrative and as a result have undergone a sort of critical repression, or at least have remained, for the most part, below the threshold of critical articulation. Various uncanny elements will be considered, but the chief enigma involves the figuring of Michael Furey—the boy who died of love for Gretta Conroy when she was a girl—as Gretta's *child*, a mystery the text hints at in various ways but never directly confronts. As a consequence, Gretta's own passion play of repression and return will emerge as one of the deep, driving forces in the

---

8. Interpretations that resist the standard reading of "The Dead" in one way or another include Ruth Bauerle, "Date Rape, Mate Rape: A Liturgical Interpretation of 'The Dead,'" in *New Alliances in Joyce Studies*, ed. Bonnie Kime Scott (Newark: University of Delaware Press, 1988), 113–25; Ross Chambers, "Gabriel Conroy Sings for His Supper, or Love Refused," in *Modern Critical Interpretations: James Joyce's "Dubliners,"* ed. Harold Bloom (New York: Chelsea House, 1988), 97–119; Tilly Eggers, "What Is a Woman . . . a Symbol Of?" *James Joyce Quarterly* 18 (1981): 379–95; R. B. Kershner, "'The Dead': Women's Speech and Tableau," in *Joyce, Bakhtin, and Popular Literature: Chronicles of Disorder* (Chapel Hill: University of North Carolina Press, 1989), 138–50; Garry Leonard, "Joyce and Lacan: 'The Woman' as a Symptom of 'Masculinity' in 'The Dead,'" *James Joyce Quarterly* 28 (1991): 451–72; Margot Norris, "Stifled Back Answers: The Gender Politics of Art in Joyce's 'The Dead,'" *Modern Fiction Studies* 35 (1989): 479–503; and Vincent P. Pecora, "Social Paralysis and the Generosity of the Word: Joyce's 'The Dead,'" chap. 6 of *Self and Form in Modern Narrative* (Baltimore: Johns Hopkins University Press, 1989), 214–59. None of these critics ignores, or fully succeeds in escaping, the traditional focus on Gabriel, and my reading is no exception in this respect. Chambers and Kershner in particular note "uncanny" elements in "The Dead."

text; her experience will be recognized as a problematic "double" of Gabriel's more conspicuous psychodrama. In addition, I consider a number of uncanny textual and intertextual returns, including Ibsen's *When We Dead Awaken* and some of the earlier *Dubliners* stories. The discussion of intertexts within *Dubliners* is preliminary to, and paradigmatic for, the discussion of Ibsen and "The Dead."

Resonant Intertexts

Whether the uncanny takes the form of the once-familiar returning in masquerade, or of doubling, or of involuntary patterns and coincidences, the common factor in all cases is the element of repetition. Yet, clearly, repetition alone does not explain the feeling of uncanniness, for even after the repressed element has been extricated from its estranged husk and revealed as the common denominator of a series of psychic and/or textual enigmas (as in Freud's oedipal decoding of "The Sand-Man"), a residue of the unexplained remains, and this residue continues to haunt. That the aura of the uncanny cannot be wholly exorcised by rational processes points to the abiding mystery surrounding the source or cause of uncanny events, and to the fact that estrangement, as a mode of representation, does not function merely as a mask that can be peeled away and discarded but actually plays a *constitutive* role in the psyche or text.

These two aspects—the sense of a secret or untraceable "author" of uncanniness and the realization that the transformations worked by estrangement are ineradicably part of the psyche's development—contribute to the feeling of helplessness that Freud notes in the experience of uncanny repetition (Freud, 237). Stephen Dedalus's definition of Aristotelian terror as "the feeling which arrests the mind in the presence of whatsoever is grave and constant in human sufferings and unites it with the secret cause" is as much about the inscrutability and durability of the uncanny as it is about the tragic emotion.[9]

The foregoing distinctions between kinds of repetition should

9. James Joyce, *A Portrait of the Artist as a Young Man,* ed. Chester G. Anderson and Richard Ellmann (New York: Viking, 1964), 204.

help us explore the quality of strangeness in "The Dead." Not all instances of repetition, even when they contribute to the register of the "terrifying," qualify as uncanny. For example, certain phrases in the text seem calculated to reinforce the pervasive sense of death: "My wife here takes three mortal hours to dress herself" (*D*, 177); "Both of them kissed Gabriel's wife, said she must be perished alive" (*D*, 177); "As the subject had grown lugubrious it was buried in a silence of the table" (*D*, 201). These thematic promptings are not in themselves uncanny, largely because we can see Joyce building up his effect by specific, programmatic repetitions, not unlike his unabashed deployment of rhetorical figures in the "Aeolus" episode of *Ulysses* to underscore that episode's theme of rhetoric. This kind of repetition is intentionally strained and verges on the compulsive clowning of Joyce's later writings. In "The Dead" it produces a droll effect of simulated gothic terror. An analogous case might be that of the uncanny in fairy tales, which, as we have seen, Freud regards as devoid of uncanny effect.

Other forms of repetition in "The Dead" are more haunting and haunted, however. For example, the phrase "the snow falling faintly through the universe and faintly falling, like the descent of their last end, upon all the living and the dead" (*D*, 224) grows out of at least two earlier moments in the text: at dinner Mary Jane said that the monks have coffins "to remind them of their last end" (*D*, 201); and later, as the guests are leaving, we learn that "the sky seemed to be descending" (*D*, 212). The return of these phrases in Gabriel's final meditation produces an effect of uncanniness, in this particular case because he could have heard only one of the phrases (Mary Jane's), but more generally because the swelling rhythmic sonority and expanding perspective render all attempts to assign the final paragraphs to a single consciousness, to find a psychic home for them, as futile as Gabriel's efforts to hold on to his old, stable ego. Here, the uncanny emerges in the space between psyches, in the breakdown of the text's ostensible commitment to a relatively stable psychogenesis and a naturalistic basis for narrative voice, together with the corresponding ideology of the sovereign subject. The "fading out" of Gabriel's identity both results from and is a precondition for the strange authority of the final paragraphs, an authority that is paradoxically and disconcertingly "authorless."[10]

10. The last scene of John Huston's generally successful film adaptation of "The Dead" (Vestron Pictures, 1987) fails in attempting to convert what I call this strange authority

Certain intertextual returns from earlier *Dubliners* stories add to the uncanny quality of "The Dead" and further erase the boundaries of identity and narrative voice. In the opening story, "The Sisters," the young boy imagines a terrifying visitation from his recently deceased friend, the old priest (of whom one of the characters remarks that "there was something uncanny about him" [*D*, 10]): "I drew the blankets over my head and tried to think of Christmas. But the grey face still followed me. . . . I felt my soul receding into some pleasant and vicious region" (*D*, 11). The similarities between this passage and the final scene of "The Dead" are striking: stretching himself "cautiously along under the sheets," Gabriel begins to be aware of ghostly "forms." "His soul," we are told in a distinct echo of the earlier story, "had approached that region where dwell the vast hosts of the dead" (*D*, 223). Authority for this resonant repetition is impossible to determine, and the problematic nature of narrative voice in "The Dead" is ironically underscored by the irruption of language from a most definitely "authored" first-person narrative into this "authorless" final section. This erasure of the boundary separating the realistic from the fantastic—the rational and narratable from the haunted and unspeakable—produces an uncanny effect of the type noted by Freud in his discussion of realistic fiction in "The 'Uncanny.'" The intertextual "haunting" in the final paragraphs of "The Dead" hints at the presence of a dialogism—to be fully realized in *Ulysses* and *Finnegans Wake*—in which the vast hosts of discourses that make up the "realistic" mode are permitted to have their ghostly say.

Similarly, a passage from "A Little Cloud" anticipates Gabriel's vision of universal snow:

> He turned often from his tiresome writing to gaze out of the office window. The glow of a late autumn sunset covered the grass plots and walks. It cast a shower of kindly golden dust on the untidy nurses and decrepit old men who drowsed on the benches; it flickered upon all the moving figures—on the children who ran screaming along the gravel paths and on everyone who passed through the gardens. He watched the scene and thought of life; and (as always happened when he thought of life) he became sad. (*D*, 71)

---

into Gabriel's own first-person voice. The naturalistic premise is simply no longer viable at this point. For different approaches to the question of voice and narrative authority in "The Dead," see Hugh Kenner, "The Uncle Charles Principle," chap. 2 of *Joyce's Voices* (Berkeley: University of California Press, 1978); and Janet Egleson Dunleavy, "The Ectoplasmic Truthtellers of 'The Dead,'" *James Joyce Quarterly* 21 (1984): 307–19.

The human panorama, the comprehensive sympathy, the sweeping cadences intimating a soul on the verge of swooning suggest that this scene is an attenuated "double" of the final passage of "The Dead," especially if we allow for the substitution of the sunset's "golden dust" for snow and of Little Chandler's feeble (and pointedly ironized) meditation on life for Gabriel's night thoughts on death. It is important, however, to avoid ascribing these instances of repetition to intentionalistic practices such as Joycean self-parody, pastiche, allusion, prolepsis, cross-reference, or other features of a text conceived of as consciously predetermined and teleological. One reason why the spontaneous, autogenetic quality of such inter-textual returns may seem disorienting, especially to readers whose response has been conditioned by the criticism, is that Joyce critics have consistently argued for a text that is infallibly self-conscious, the product of an almost superhuman authorial intention. The concept of an invisible but ubiquitous "Arranger," which in one form or another has been invoked for most of Joyce's fiction, is limited precisely insofar as it cannot adequately account for a text such as *Finnegans Wake* or for the pervasive strange or "estranged" quality of "The Dead."[11] The doctrine of the Arranger has the further drawback of eliding or masking the role of interpretation in constituting the ingenuity of Joyce's texts, providing a blanket rationale for narcissistic projections of the reading process onto this convenient authorial demiurge. The Arranger is the "blank check" in the economy of the Joyce industry.

Another range of textual "impediments" (to recur to Lacan's term) concerns the pervasive military imagery in "The Dead." We encounter such phrases as "an irregular musketry of applause" (*D*, 192); "Freddy Malins acting as officer with his fork on high" (*D*, 206); "Mary Jane led her recruits" (*D*, 184); "Between these rival ends ran parallel lines of side-dishes" (*D*, 196); "three squads of bottles . . . drawn up according to the colours of their uniforms" (*D*, 197). Although these metaphors can be rationalized as objective correlatives for the putative battle between Gabriel Conroy and his rival Michael Furey, or as symbolic outcroppings of Gabriel's conflict with himself, such readings seem too monotonal and tenden-

---

11. The "Arranger," a sort of emanation of Joyce himself deduced from the elaborate interconnections in *Ulysses*, was first proposed by David Hayman in *"Ulysses": The Mechanics of Meaning* (Englewood Cliffs, N.J.: Prentice-Hall, 1970), and developed ingeniously thereafter by Hugh Kenner in his writings on Joyce.

tiously thematic to be fully persuasive. I suggest that this imagery represents a resurfacing, with an estranged difference, of the military and quasi-military metaphors of "Two Gallants," where the cynical insensitivity with which Corley conducts his love affair is linked to what Joyce called "the moral code of the soldier and (incidentally) of the gallant."[12] Joyce adopted this equation from his recent reading of the Italian historian and sociologist Guglielmo Ferrero, whose *L'Europa giovane* (1897) and *Il Militarismo* (1898) attacked the militaristic mentality and the related concept of *galanteria*, with its barely submerged agenda of domination and misogyny.[13]

The possibility that Ferrero's writings and "Two Gallants" are intertexts is further suggested by such phrases as "Mr Browne . . . gallantly escort[ed] Aunt Julia" (D, 192) and "[Gabriel] raised his glass of port gallantly" (D, 205). Gabriel's attitude toward Gretta becomes increasingly "gallant" as the evening progresses; at the end of the party he is feeling "proud, joyful, tender, valorous" and longs to "defend her against something and then to be alone with her" (D, 213). When his aroused chivalry is later checked by her unresponsiveness, he restrains himself from "brutal language" and desires "to be master of her strange mood" (D, 217). In part, no doubt, Gabriel is reincarnating the attitudes Joyce satirized in Corley and Lenehan, but the broad, unstable deployment of military imagery in "The Dead" (most of it concentrated in the early part, long before Gabriel becomes gallant) cannot be accounted for solely in terms of Gabriel's psyche or Joyce's satirical intent. Military figures occur so randomly and exhibit such a wide range of tone— including the ghostly "wit" I mentioned earlier—that they overwhelm all attempts to ground them in some specific psychogenesis or intentionality. In this respect the text as a whole mirrors Gretta's homely yet quite *unheimlich* and disconcerting inscrutability;

---

12. Joyce's letter of May 5, 1906, to Grant Richards, in *Letters of James Joyce*, vol. 2, ed. Richard Ellmann (New York: Viking Press, 1966), 133; hereafter cited in the text as *Letters*.

13. For analyses of Ferrero's influence on Joyce, see Edward Brandabur, *A Scrupulous Meanness: A Study of Joyce's Early Work* (Urbana: University of Illinois Press, 1971), 95– 98; Dominic Manganiello, *Joyce's Politics* (London: Routledge and Kegan Paul, 1980), 46– 57; Susan L. Humphreys, "Ferrero Etc: James Joyce's Debt to Guglielmo Ferrero," *James Joyce Quarterly* 16 (1979): 239–51; and Robert Spoo, "'Una Piccola Nuvoletta': Ferrero's *Young Europe* and Joyce's Mature *Dubliners* Stories," *James Joyce Quarterly* 24 (1987): 401–10.

"The Dead" simply refuses to allow the reader to be master of its strange mood.

The centrality that "The Dead" gives to the female as impediment to interpretive mastery is focused in a series of social and personal failures that Gabriel experiences in the course of the evening. His suavity and control are baffled in turn by Lily the caretaker's daughter, Molly Ivors (his professional and intellectual equal), and Gretta in a pattern so marked as to raise the possibility that he is in the grip of a repetition compulsion. Gabriel's repetition of error, yet another sign of uncanniness in the story, hints at a "death drive" on his part that may connect with his later experience of self-dissolution and communion with the dead. It might also be argued that these repetitions, along with the recurrent image of snow in the story, contribute to a structure of delay, and that, as Elizabeth Wright observes of "The Sand-Man," "what is delayed is death."[14]

Gabriel's need for reiterated proofs of control and his aunts' desire for the annual success of their party reflect in different ways an obsession with keeping the unfamiliar from entering the circle of the "home," be it psychic or social. This industrious staging of homely experience prepares the way for *das Unheimliche*, which in turn will reintroduce *das Heimliche*, the once-familiar, in estranged and threatening guises. Late in the story, when Gabriel is coming to see the futility of his desire for a night of honeymoon passion with Gretta, he passes in front of the cheval glass and sees "the face whose expression always puzzled him when he saw it in a mirror" (*D*, 218). The feeling of uneasiness at encountering one's reflected image—what Freud called the uncanny effect of the "double" (Freud, 248n)—results from an unconscious defamiliarizing of the familiar, which in Gabriel's case is related to his intense conscious willing of the familiar, his need for experience that is predictable and controllable.

The bibulous Freddy Malins, in almost every way the antithesis of the responsible Gabriel, is nevertheless Gabriel's "bad" double, mirroring him in his intense though conflicted relationship to a dominating mother and even in certain personal habits, such as "the mechanical readjustment of his dress" (*D*, 185). (Gabriel fusses with his clothes and pats his tie nervously throughout the evening.)

14. Wright, *Psychoanalytic Criticism*, 147.

As Gabriel's double, the docile, unmarried Freddy uncannily embodies Gabriel's buried self (passivity, oedipal dependence, potential for infantile regression), a self that keeps him perpetually staging or "scripting" his own experience, as if, for Gabriel, Eros needed vigilant coaching lest Thanatos supervene in the form of entropic repetitions of error, as in any case it seems to do. The attempt to predetermine Gretta's erotic response and the ironic, leading questions he puts to her about Michael Furey are crucial examples of his scripting of experience, and they open the way for the full emergence of the uncanny late in the story.

The exasperating unreadability of women in "The Dead" suggests that there may be an intertextual relationship with the plays of Henrik Ibsen, in particular with *When We Dead Awaken*, which Joyce read with admiration and discussed in an article in the *Fortnightly Review* for April 1, 1900.[15] *When We Dead Awaken*, Ibsen's last play, is an uncanny work in its own right, mixing symbolic and naturalistic elements with such daring that Ibsen's great English exponent, the translator William Archer, decided that the play was "purely pathological," a piece of "self-caricature, a series of echoes from all the earlier plays, an exaggeration of manner to the pitch of mannerism."[16] Archer's annoyance has to do with what he deems uncharacteristic and unworthy elements of *repetition* (self-caricature, echoes, mannerism), and he comes close to accusing the senescent Ibsen of a repetition compulsion. Archer's strategy is to rationalize uncanny elements in terms of Ibsen's alleged irrationality and aesthetic irresponsibility. The unreliable Arranger that he posits in this psychogenetic move would seem to be the antithesis of the infallible Joycean Arranger, yet in principle the two figures are similar.

The action of *When We Dead Awaken* revolves around the chance meeting of the sculptor Arnold Rubek and his model Irene, who

---

15. Although critics have noticed connections between *When We Dead Awaken* and Joyce's *Exiles*, surprisingly little attention has been paid to the relevance of the play to "The Dead." Richard Ellmann does not include it among the sources he adduces in "The Backgrounds of 'The Dead,'" chap. 15 of *James Joyce*, rev. ed. (New York: Oxford University Press, 1982). For general treatments of Joyce and Ibsen, see also James R. Baker, "Ibsen, Joyce, and the Living-Dead: A Study of *Dubliners*," in *A James Joyce Miscellany*, 3d ser., ed. Marvin Magalaner (Carbondale: Southern Illinois University Press, 1962); and B. J. Tysdahl, *Joyce and Ibsen: A Study in Literary Influence* (New York: Humanities Press, 1968).

16. *Collected Works of Henrik Ibsen*, ed. and trans. William Archer, vol. 11 (*Little Eyolf, John Gabriel Borkman, When We Dead Awaken*) (London: William Heinemann, 1910), xxvii; hereafter cited in the text as *Ibsen*.

years before had sat for his most famous work, *The Resurrection Day*, an image of a young woman "awakening from the sleep of death" (*Ibsen*, 371). The theme of the living dead runs throughout *When We Dead Awaken*, and Rubek's meeting with Irene, herself recently awakened from a mental collapse which she prefers to call her "death," stirs him to realize that his marriage of several years to Maia has been a conventional death-in-life. "It is simply and solely I myself," he tells Maia, "who have once more undergone a revolution . . . an awakening to my real life" (*Ibsen*, 399). Irene states the case more bleakly: "We see the irretrievable only when . . . we dead awaken" (*Ibsen*, 431). All these elements—a marriage dulled by routine, a peripeteia brought about by a figure returning from the past, the half-conscious sufferings of the living dead, awakenings that only confirm a sense of loss and emotional aridity—return to haunt Joyce's story intertextually. Moreover, *When We Dead Awaken* resembles "The Dead" in its general movement from scenes of social interaction (at a bathing establishment on the coast) to the final act with its intense focus on Rubek and Irene as they ascend a mountainside and are engulfed by a snowstorm. Rubek likens the menacing blasts of wind to "the prelude to the Resurrection Day" and exhorts Irene to "let two of the dead—us two—for once live life to its uttermost—before we go down to our graves again!" (*Ibsen*, 454).

Determined on a death pact that will paradoxically restore to them "the beautiful, miraculous earth-life," the two figures climb toward the Peak of Promise, where, Rubek tells Irene, "we will hold our marriage-feast" (*Ibsen*, 455). As Gabriel follows Gretta up the stairs to their room in the Gresham Hotel, he too believes that they are about to experience a renewal of passion and, like Rubek, feels a violent impulse to seize his wife even before they reach their destination. Later, joining her under sheets which are also shrouds for the newly awakened dead, Gabriel has his vision of snow "general all over Ireland" (*D*, 223), and the couple's white-sheeted forms extend the quiescent snowscape into the hotel room. Similarly, at the end of *When We Dead Awaken*, Irene and Rubek can be dimly discerned "as they are whirled along with the masses of snow and buried in them" (*Ibsen*, 456); one of the characters even remarks of the approaching storm clouds that "soon they'll be all round us like a winding-sheet" (*Ibsen*, 448).

In his *Fortnightly Review* article, "Ibsen's New Drama," Joyce lingers over that final image of Rubek and Irene, claiming that they "hold our gaze, as they stand up silently on the fjaell, engrossing central figures of boundless, human interest."[17] In Joyce's reading, Rubek and Irene become mythic figures as their identities, like Gabriel's and Gretta's, are extinguished in the immense avalanche of newly discovered life. Joyce's portrait of the awakening Rubek anticipates what critics have described as Gabriel's change of mind and heart: "There may be lying dormant in him a capacity for greater life, which may be exercised when he, a dead man, shall have risen from among the dead" (CW, 66). In Rubek's "conversion," writes Joyce, "there is involved an all-embracing philosophy, a deep sympathy with the cross-purposes and contradictions of life, as they may be reconcilable with a hopeful awakening—when the manifold travail of our poor humanity may have a glorious issue" (CW, 66).

But it is the uncanny figure of Irene that fascinates Joyce most. Pale and slender, dressed in a white gown and a large white shawl, Irene moves about the stage with erect carriage and phantomlike demeanor. She is the picture of a beautiful, shrouded corpse, and throughout the play she tells Rubek that she has returned from the dead and that it is he who killed her. In "Ibsen's New Drama" Joyce devotes a long passage to Irene in which he first asserts that Ibsen's treatment of her shows how thoroughly he "knows" women. "He appears," Joyce says, "to have sounded them to almost unfathomable depths" (CW, 64). But after naming several Ibsen heroines and assigning them to literary genres (tragic, comic), he admits that Irene "cannot be so readily classified; the very aloofness from passion ... forbids classification" (CW, 64). Irene's ghostly impassiveness eludes aesthetic categories in the same way that the uncanny, according to Freud, resists being classed under the sublime or the beautiful. Following Ibsen, who describes Irene in the stage directions as "the strange lady" (Ibsen, 359), Joyce acknowledges her uncanniness by also characterizing her as "strange." He refers at one point to the meaning hidden beneath her "strange words" (CW, 53) and their transformative effect on Rubek, and later says that "she interests us strangely—magnetically, because of her inner power of character. . . . She holds our gaze for the sheer force of her intellectual capacity" (CW, 64).

17. James Joyce, The Critical Writings of James Joyce, ed. Ellsworth Mason and Richard Ellmann (New York: Viking Press, 1959), 61; hereafter cited in the text as CW.

"Strange" is a word consistently associated with Gretta Conroy also, especially in the latter part of the story, and with Gabriel's reaction to her revelations about Michael Furey ("a strange friendly pity for her entered his soul" [D, 222]). Just as, according to Joyce, Irene's strange magnetism "holds our gaze," so Gabriel, at the conclusion of the party, is hypnotized by Gretta as she stands on the stairs in the shadow, listening to an old ballad being sung in an upstairs room. As he remains below, straining to hear the air and "gazing up at his wife," he notices that there is "grace and mystery in her attitude as if she were a symbol of something," and tries to master the strangeness of this spectacle by mentally turning it into a conventional piece of art, by assigning Gretta to the popular aesthetic category of the tableau: "*Distant Music* he would call the picture if he were a painter" (D, 210).[18]

This painting of the uncanny female is also a sign of repression of the maternal body. According to Freud the latter is both strange and familiar, at once a magical cave and a long-lost home: "This *unheimlich* place [the female genitals] . . . is the entrance to the former *Heim* [home] of all human beings, to the place where each one of us lived once upon a time and in the beginning" (Freud, 245). Gabriel's own struggle with his mother and with the maternal imago—a struggle he consciously casts as resentment of her disapproval of his "country cute" wife (D, 187)—is projected upon Gretta and her body, which he characterizes here in terms of "grace and mystery." Gabriel's reduction of Gretta's uncanny power proves only temporary, however; her strangeness will reassert itself, and in a new register, once they reach the hotel room.

Gabriel's aestheticizing of Gretta has its intertextual double in Rubek's sculpture, *The Resurrection Day*, for which Irene modeled. Irene informs Rubek, to his horror, that the sacrifice she made for his art brought about her death, that she remained dead for years and gradually came to hate Rubek, "who had so lightly and carelessly taken a warm-blooded body, a young human life, and worn the soul out of it—because you needed it for a work of art" (*Ibsen*, 410).[19] Instead of giving her love, Rubek conferred on her an artistic immortality which spelled the death of her soul. The aesthetic act

18. On the tableau and its centrality to Gabriel's erotic imagination, see Kershner, *Joyce, Bakhtin, and Popular Literature*, 144–45.

19. Margot Norris notes the theme of symbolic murder through aestheticization in *When We Dead Awaken* and "The Dead" in "Stifled Back Answers," 483–84.

becomes an act of murder inasmuch as it must raze human individuality before it can rear in its place a universalized art form. Art
murders to create. Irene resists all of Rubek's assertions about the
greater glory of art and reminds him that the artist-model relationship is a strongly gendered one. When he says exultantly, "You gave
me all your naked loveliness," she bitterly adds, "To gaze upon"
(*Ibsen*, 378). The role played by the male gaze in the aesthetic act is
another important intertext here, linking with images of fascinated
males and female cynosures in both "The Dead" and "Ibsen's New
Drama."

Although Irene regrets giving up her youthful soul and body for
Rubek's art, she consoles herself with the knowledge that *The Resurrection Day* is famous, and insists on referring to it as "our child."
She tells Rubek that, although she secretly hated him while she
was exposing herself to his gaze, "that statue in the wet, living clay,
that I loved—as it rose up, a vital human creature, out of those raw,
shapeless masses—for that was our creation, our child. Mine and
yours" (*Ibsen*, 411–12). Her discourse seems calculated to produce
an effect of estrangement as it merges maternal and biological images with the more traditional aesthetic rhetoric of transcendence
and immortality, hinting at the link between male fascination with
the aestheticized female form and the fear and loathing inspired by
the *unheimlich* maternal body. By persistently figuring the statue
of herself as her own child, by conjoining the animate and the inanimate (as in the doll Olympia in "The Sand-Man"), Irene introduces into an otherwise relatively realistic plot a perverse element
of the uncanny. This paradoxical offspring, a love child born of hatred, a statue that, according to Irene, is both living and dead, provides what may be the deepest, most enigmatic intertextual link
with "The Dead."[20]

The Uncanny Babe

Joyce devotes a paragraph of "Ibsen's New Drama" to Irene's
bizarre motherhood and "the child of her soul," as he calls it: "By

20. Margot Norris reminded me that in *Hedda Gabler*, Thea Elvsted refers to Løvborg's
manuscript as her child and feels that in destroying it, as he claims he has done, he has
killed the child. It is interesting to compare a letter Joyce wrote Nora in 1912 during his
abortive effort to get *Dubliners* published in Dublin. He referred to the book as "the child
which I have carried for years and years in the womb of the imagination as you carried in
your womb the children you love" (*Letters*, 308).

her child Irene means the statue. To her it seems that this statue is, in a very true and very real sense, born of her. Each day as she saw it grow to its full growth under the hand of the skilful moulder, her inner sense of motherhood for it, of right over it, of love towards it, had become stronger and more confirmed" (CW, 57). Joyce emphasizes Irene's maternal sense and, if anything, exaggerates her claims over the child. Whereas Ibsen's Irene usually refers to the statue as *"our* child," Joyce gives the impression that Irene is the sole parent, thereby reinforcing the deconstruction of male creativity that the play itself effects and underscoring the turbulent drama taking place in Irene's mind.

Gretta Conroy undergoes a trauma very similar to Irene's. She, too, is haunted by the past and by a sense of regret for things done and opportunities missed. At the end of the party, as Gabriel stands gazing up at her and transforming her into a tableau, she is listening to the distantly intoned words of a song, "The Lass of Aughrim," which a boy named Michael Furey used to sing when she was living in Galway. The song's strange, elusive lyrics tell of a love affair between Lord Gregory and a peasant girl, her abandonment by him, and her return one night in the rain with her child to seek admission at his door. Only a snatch of the song appears in the text:

> O, the rain falls on my heavy locks
> And the dew wets my skin,
> My babe lies cold . . .
>
> (D, 210)

Gretta tells Gabriel that when Michael learned that she was leaving Galway, he left a sickbed and stood below her window in the rain, and a short while later died. "I think he died for me," Gretta says (D, 220). Her descriptions of this frail boy—"a young boy . . . very delicate" (D, 219), "such a gentle boy" (D, 221)—are maternal in their tenderness, and the image of Michael shivering beneath her window suggests a connection with the cold babe lying in the arms of the peasant mother in the song.[21]

This mother-child relationship is hinted at in other ways, but so unobtrusively that the surface of the narrative is barely broken by

---

21. Richard Ellmann observes that Gretta is "a woman with genuine maternal sympathy, which she extends both to the dead boy who loved her and to her inadequate husband," in *James Joyce*, 295.

the emergent figurations. When Gabriel wonders if she had been in love with Michael, Gretta answers, "I was great with him at that time" (D, 220). Her West Country dialect is as strange and multivalent as the language of "The Lass of Aughrim," and the faint merging here, beneath the literal sense of her words, of the roles of lover, mother, and unborn infant generates an uncanny music of otherness that calmly subverts Gabriel's jealous cross-examining.[22] His questioning of Gretta—a reversal of the catechism he himself underwent earlier at the hands of Miss Ivors—has the unintended effect of assisting at the birth of Gretta's long-gestating memory of Michael and her girlhood. Earlier, as they climb the stairs to their hotel room, Gretta is described as being "bowed in the ascent, her frail shoulders curved as with a burden, her skirt girt tightly about her" (D, 215). She is delivered of this burden of the past with the help of Gabriel's unwitting midwifery. (The maieutic method of Socratic dialectic may be a remote analogue here.) After she has fallen asleep, her labor over, Gabriel muses on "how she who lay beside him had locked in her heart for so many years that image of her lover's eyes when he had told her that he did not wish to live" (D, 223).

This image of the past locked away in the womb/heart—a metaphor that recurs throughout *When We Dead Awaken*—reappears in *Ulysses* when Stephen is helping his student Sargent, another delicate boy, with his algebra. Stephen finds him "ugly and futile," but decides that "someone had loved him, borne him in her arms and in her heart."[23] Sensing a similarity between Sargent and himself at that age, he thinks of their pasts in terms of repression and return: "Secrets, silent, stony sit in the dark palaces of both our hearts: secrets weary of their tyranny: tyrants, willing to be dethroned" (U, 2.170–72). Much later, at the end of "Circe," Bloom's long-dead infant son, Rudy, magically appears to him with "a delicate mauve face" (U, 15.4965). In this theatrically uncanny finale to an episode in which Bloom gives birth to a brood of dream children, the return of his painful past is figured as a delicate boy, dead for years but

22. Kershner, *Joyce, Bakhtin, and Popular Literature,* 150, notes in passing that the "ambiguities surrounding fathers, mothers, and lovers are echoed faintly in Joyce's story by the suggestions that Michael is a sort of son to Gretta, just as Gabriel is a sort of father."

23. James Joyce, *Ulysses,* ed. Hans Walter Gabler et al. (New York: Random House, 1986), 2.140; hereafter cited in the text as U, with episode and line numbers.

reanimated, like Michael Furey, by a series of psychological shocks administered to the parent.[24]

Freud suggests that the uncanny feeling produced by dolls and automata may originate in the childhood belief that dolls are alive or can be brought to life (Freud, 233). Marginal, easily ignored images of dolls, infants, and children appear in "The Dead" long before the hotel room scene. During Mary Jane's piano piece, Gabriel's wandering attention lights on embroidered pictures of "the balcony scene in *Romeo and Juliet* . . . [and] of the two murdered princes in the Tower" (*D*, 186), pictures which combine themes of *Liebestod* and *Kindermord* to the point of overdetermination (suggesting also Gretta's sense of responsibility for Michael Furey's death). Earlier, noticing that Lily has grown into a young woman, Gabriel realizes that he "had known her when she was a child and used to sit on the lowest step nursing a rag doll" (*D*, 177). A few minutes later, stung by Gretta's flippancy about his insistence that she wear "goloshes," Gabriel retorts, "It's nothing very wonderful but Gretta thinks it very funny because she says the word reminds her of Christy Minstrels" (*D*, 181). By "Christy Minstrels" Gabriel probably means blackface minstrels in a general sense (for by this period the term no longer referred exclusively to the American troupe of that name), or the phrase may even be a polite circumlocution for "negro" or "black." (Later in the story Freddy Malins praises the singing of the "negro chieftain" in the pantomime, to the embarrassment of the other dinner guests [*D*, 198].) In any case, it is the *word* "goloshes" that reminds Gretta of black or blackface figures, and the missing verbal link is evidently "golliwog," the popular term for a grotesque black doll inspired by a series of children's books featuring an animated doll named Golliwogg.[25]

24. Images of pregnancy and babies in "The Dead" may have been influenced by the circumstances of the story's composition. Joyce conceived the idea for the story, or at least its title, in Rome in 1906, but was too overworked and unhappy to begin it. When he did come to write it almost a year later, he was recovering from rheumatic fever and had to dictate the ending to his brother Stanislaus. The story was finished in September 1907 (see Ellmann, *James Joyce,* 263–64). This long gestation combined with Joyce's illness may have rendered the process of composition itself somewhat uncanny, as it was for T. S. Eliot when he drafted parts of *The Waste Land* almost without conscious thought (or, as he put it, "in a trance") while recovering from a nervous breakdown. It may also be relevant that Joyce's companion, Nora, was pregnant during this period; their daughter Lucia was born on July 26, 1907.

25. The American-born British illustrator Florence Upton (d. 1922) was the originator of the *Golliwogg* series, picture books with simple rhymes written by her mother, Bertha; the first Golliwogg story was published in London in 1895, and a dozen more titles ap-

It is interesting that "golliwog," the vaguely homophonic link with "goloshes," does not actually emerge into the text but remains beneath the surface, hinted at but never directly indicated. This black doll or dark infant is submerged in the same way that Gretta's relationship with Michael Furey has remained buried for so many years. (Joyce later referred in a poem to the Michael Furey figure as a "dark lover.")[26] Critics have suggested that the galoshes are a symbol of sterility and prophylaxis; it might be added that what Gabriel is preventing conception *of* is Gretta's relationship to her past. Only fleetingly glimpsed at this point in terms of dolls, her girlhood will come to full term later in the evening in the form of the babe/lover Michael Furey.

The "impossible" imaging of Michael as Gretta's infant never reaches full articulation in the text, but remains below the threshold of textual consciousness and acquires a good deal of its uncanny power from precisely this occultation. Like other enigmas in "The Dead," the uncanny babe might be said to be an "encysted" element, a pocket of repressed material (in this case, Gretta's) resisting assimilation into the text and receiving its particular form through the work of estrangement.

Joyce's notes for *Exiles* shed some light on this repressed material. Written in 1913, seven years after he completed "The Dead," these notes allowed Joyce to set down memories (chiefly those of his companion, Nora) that might help him with the writing of his semi-autobiographical play. In order to give depth to the character Bertha (the figure based on Nora), Joyce recorded snippets of Nora's early life in Galway, including images of her young admirer, Sonny Bodkin, the original of Michael Furey: "Graveyard at Rahoon by moonlight where Bodkin's grave is. He lies in the grave. She sees his tomb (family vault) and weeps. The name is homely. . . . He is dark, unrisen, killed by love and life, young. The earth holds him" (*E*, 152). By "the earth" Joyce partly means Bertha/Nora herself (associ-

---

peared between that time and 1908. The term "golliwog" was in general use at the turn of the century, most often in reference to the golliwog doll. Debussy composed a piece for piano titled "Golliwogg's Cake Walk" (probably based on a doll his daughter owned), which he included in his suite *Children's Corner* (1908). In the "Nausicaa" episode of *Ulysses*, Cissy Caffrey is described as having "golliwog curls" (*U*, 13.270). Golliwog dolls, still given to children in Britain and Ireland, are topped with fuzzy shocks of hair.

26. In "She Weeps over Rahoon," a poem revisiting the Michael Furey theme which Joyce composed in 1912, a female figure mourns her dead "dark lover"; *Collected Poems* (New York: Viking Press, 1957), 50. The phrase also appears in Joyce's notes for *Exiles* (New York: Viking Press, 1951), 152; hereafter cited in the text as *E*.

ated, like Molly Bloom, with that element) or, more specifically, her *womb*. A few lines later, relating Bodkin's grave to the poet Shelley's in Rome, Joyce writes, "Shelley whom she has held in her *womb or grave* rises" (emphasis added). When Ibsen's Irene learns from Rubek that the statue has been placed in a museum, she feels that their child has been locked away in a "grave-vault" (*Ibsen*, 412–13).

As intertexts and interconnections multiply, the submerged figure of the uncanny babe in "The Dead" begins to take on a more definite form. The womb/tomb of Bertha/Nora is a later secondary revision of what Joyce had first figured as Gretta's "heart," in which she had "locked . . . for so many years that image of her lover's eyes" (*D*, 223). In the notes for *Exiles* Joyce writes further of Sonny Bodkin that he is "her buried life, her past," and adds: "His attendant images are the trinkets and toys of girlhood (bracelet, cream sweets, palegreen lily of the valley, the convent garden)" (*E*, 152). Just as Bodkin represents Bertha/Nora's past, so Michael Furey is an estranged figure for Gretta's girlhood, her "buried life." Burial was one of Freud's favorite metaphors for repression, the process "by which something in the mind is at once made inaccessible and preserved, [a] burial of the sort to which Pompeii fell a victim." [27] Gretta has had to bury her past in order to become the wife of Gabriel Conroy, a man who feels ashamed of his wife's simple, rural origins and unconsciously agrees with his mother's class-based assessment of her as "country cute" (*D*, 187). Gretta has had to put away her childhood, to repress it for the sake of her marriage, but it returns on the evening of the Misses Morkan's party in the form of the babe/lover Michael Furey. The alienated, intensely charged form in which this past returns is some measure of how violently Gretta has had to deny it.

Here, too, *When We Dead Awaken* proves a resonant intertext. Reminding Irene of her sacrifice for his art, Rubek says, "You renounced home and kindred—and went with me" (*Ibsen*, 372). Rubek's wife, Maia, has experienced a similar uprooting, which she recounts in the form of a parable to her new companion, Ulfheim: "There once was a stupid girl, who had both a father and a mother—but a rather poverty-stricken home. Then there came a high and mighty seigneur into the midst of all this poverty. And he took the

27. Sigmund Freud, *Delusions and Dreams in Jensen's "Gradiva,"* in *The Standard Edition*, 9:40.

girl in his arms—as you did—and travelled far, far away with her"
(*Ibsen*, 440–41). Like Gretta Conroy, these women have been taken
away from home and family at a young age, and, although the elope-
ment may have brought them advantages, it also meant renunciation and irreparable loss. It is worth noting that Maia's bitter parable
about a poor girl rescued by a "high and mighty seigneur" bears
a distinct resemblance to the dramatic situation of "The Lass of
Aughrim," in which Lord Gregory seduces and impregnates a peasant girl. In a poignant moment in *Ulysses*, Stephen Dedalus thinks
of his deceased mother's girlhood in terms of random souvenirs she
kept: "Her secrets: old featherfans, tasselled dancecards, powdered
with musk, a gaud of amber beads in her locked drawer" (*U*, 1.255–
56). This inventory is not unlike the list of items Joyce assigned to
Bertha/Nora's girlhood in the notes for *Exiles*. Mrs. Dedalus's past,
like Gretta's and Bertha's, was scrupulously "locked" away, buried
by her in an effort to accommodate a socially superior husband.[28]

Discussing Freud's analysis of "The Sand-Man" and his emphasis
on oedipal themes, Hélène Cixous notes that his "minimizing of
[the female doll] Olympia leads to the focus on Nathaniel."[29] Similarly, critics have made much of Gabriel Conroy's "journey westward" (*D*, 223), but less attention has been paid to the fact that it
is Gretta who travels *back* to her origins in the West, that "The
Dead" is as much about her journey of reunion as about her husband's discovery of new psychic terrain. Whatever Gabriel's final
swoon into self-dissolution may mean, whether it is spiritual death
that beckons to him or some other undiscovered country, his wife
has already reached the bourne of the once-familiar, a very specific
locale long known to her but in recent years under ban. Gretta's
deracination has so thoroughly alienated her from her life in Galway, from family and friends, that it has taken years for this "buried
life" to resurface, and when it does, it returns in the weird, estranged form of a boy lover who doubles as her own infant. She was

28. Discussing Torvald in *A Doll's House* and Gabriel Conroy, Norris ("Stifled Back
Answers," 487) points out that these husbands, "ashamed for different reasons of their
provincial wives, go to enormous lengths to alienate them from their origins, isolate
them from families and friends, and silence their memories and feelings. Through this
suppression, they make their wives strangers to their husbands and estrange the women
from themselves."

29. Hélène Cixous, "Fiction and Its Phantoms: A Reading of Freud's *Das Unheimliche*
(The 'Uncanny')," *New Literary History* 7 (1976): 535.

"great with him at that time," even before she met Gabriel, and the slow, dark birth has taken half a lifetime to reach full term.

It is interesting to compare this uncanny babe/lover with a similar fantasia in H. D.'s *Helen in Egypt*. H. D.'s revisionary epic begins with the countermyth that Helen spent the Trojan War safely hidden away in Egypt while a phantom Helen paced the ramparts of Troy. In this new telling, Helen and Achilles become lovers after the war, and, at one point in her life, Helen concludes that Paris is the child of this union:

> he of the House of the Enemy,
> Troy's last king (this is no easy thing
> to explain, this subtle genealogy)
>
> is Achilles' son, he is incarnate
> Helen-Achilles; he, my first lover,
> was created by my last.[30]

Paris, Helen's "first lover," becomes her child, and her last lover, Achilles, the child's father. Helen's relationship to her past, like Gretta Conroy's, is troubled and censored, and this blockage gives rise, in the course of Helen's intense broodings, to uncanny figurations, as in Joyce's text. Just as Achilles has sired his enemy and eventual slayer, so Gabriel is the "father" of Michael Furey, the "impalpable and vindictive being" he senses "coming against him" as Gretta unfolds her past in the hotel room (D, 220). Gabriel has created Michael in the sense that he is largely responsible for Gretta's renunciation of her origins. But the "subtle genealogy" that makes Gretta the mother of her own first lover also strangely empowers her in relation to her last one, and by the end of the story it is Gabriel who considers his past futile and negated. The uncanny proliferation of female roles is a sign of Gretta's new-found power and self-knowledge.

Gretta's psychodrama is the dark "double" of Gabriel's more conspicuous sufferings, partly because hers is the narrative that is most frequently and conveniently ignored by critics, and because the true source of Gabriel's sufferings—his wife's occluded past—lies hidden from him even as it functions deep within his psyche, playing a large part in his self-definition as an Irishman and in his relationship

---

30. H. D. [Hilda Doolittle], *Helen in Egypt* (New York: New Directions, 1961), 184–85.

with her. Gretta has already set out for Galway by the time Gabriel reaches his decision to journey westward. Her return to the womb/tomb of her past is like Irene's determination to seek out the museum that contains *The Resurrection Day*, that image of and monument to her youthful passion. "I will make a pilgrimage," Irene declares, "to the place where my soul and my child's soul lie buried" (*Ibsen*, 413). Gretta's journey is already fully under way in the strange replies Gabriel elicits from her in the hotel room; his pilgrimage, by comparison, is imitative and of a lesser intensity. Where Gretta already is, Gabriel can only hope to be.

But speculation about the characters' afterlife (in both senses of the word)—and such speculation is common in criticism of "The Dead"— is always a covert attempt to contain the problematic nature of the text. The "textual energetics" of the story (to use Peter Brooks's phrase),[31] which I have argued arise from the pervasive, multivalent operation of the uncanny, refuse containment and closure, just as they cannot be traced to a single source or set of sources, however construed. I have largely resisted, for example, the text's invitation to an oedipal reading, though Gabriel's mother conflict and the virtual absence of his father in his conscious thoughts might be read as a "source" of the uncanny babe figuration, making the latter a sort of magic-lantern projection of Gabriel's unmastered infantile scenario. The oedipal clue might equally be traced to Joyce himself, whose relationship to Nora quickly became infantile and filial in times of stress, as when he wrote her from Dublin in 1909 just after being informed (falsely) of her infidelity: "O that I could nestle in your womb like a child born of your flesh and blood, be fed by your blood, sleep in the warm secret gloom of your body!" (*Letters*, 2:248). (Curiously, Joyce mentions in the same letter that he has just been to the Gresham Hotel, the setting for Gretta's revelations about Michael Furey.) But the oedipal scenario as such, with its male agenda and its limited exegetical power outside Gabriel's (or Joyce's) personal narrative, is unlikely to elicit and at the same time respect the multiform strangeness of this text, which seems in any case to be generated by female scenarios and occlusions of female experience. [32]

31. Peter Brooks, *Reading for the Plot: Design and Intention in Narrative* (New York: Vintage, 1985), 123.
32. Though beyond the scope of this essay, Freud's reading of the female Oedipus complex and its "resolution" in the birth of a child which symbolically compensates for the absent penis could be related to Gretta and the uncanny babe figuration. See especially

Although I have linked the uncanny power of Michael Furey to Gretta's repression of her past, I have not intended this as an exhaustive psychogenetic explanation of the uncanny in the story. The babe/lover figure—only one "symptom" of the uncanny among many here—is overdetermined, just as the multiple intertexts I have discussed (and there are numerous others) represent a surplus of "backgrounds" for "The Dead." That the uncanny cannot be "cured" by critical exegesis points also to what I have called the constitutive role of estrangement. As a mode of representation, estrangement is not merely a mask covering the pain of the once-familiar but is actually fused to the textual-psychic face beneath. In this respect, as in others, "The Dead" may have more in common with *Finnegans Wake* than with any other work by Joyce.[33] As critics have noted, the bizarre verbal density of *Finnegans Wake* is generated by a kind of dream-work, a process that renders manifest and latent contents inseparable from each other in the same way that estrangement constitutes signification in "The Dead." Moreover, both texts are autogenetic and authorless, and refuse, or perpetually absorb, efforts to account for them in terms of sources, authors, Arrangers, or other finite causes of textual effects. Like *Finnegans Wake*, "The Dead" is incurable and incorrigible.

Lacan's analysis of this female oedipal scenario, in *Feminine Sexuality*, ed. Juliet Mitchell and Jacqueline Rose; trans. Jacqueline Rose (New York: Norton, 1985), 101ff. I am grateful to Joseph A. Kestner for reminding me of this possibility.

33. In *Wandering and Return in "Finnegans Wake": An Integrative Approach to Joyce's Fictions* (Princeton: Princeton University Press, 1991), Kimberly J. Devlin uses Freud's conception of the uncanny to characterize the experience of reading the *Wake*, arguing that Joyce's previous writings return in distorted yet ultimately recognizable forms in his final work.

4

A Portrait of the Romantic Poet as a Young Modernist: Literary History as Textual Unconscious

Jay Clayton

The question of the unconscious in Joyce could be taken as an inquiry into unconscious processes in the author, in the characters, or in the text. The first, a tried-and-true procedure of older Freudian criticism, has become discredited in many circles over the course of the last thirty years: too many reductive critical works have treated books as little more than the symptoms of their authors' personal neuroses. The second has often been applied to the characters in Joyce, leading to attempts to illuminate the phantasmagoria of the "Circe" chapter, say, by psychoanalyzing Bloom. Only in recent years, principally in the work of Shoshana Felman, Jonathan Culler, Peter Brooks, and Fredric Jameson, has the third procedure been explored. This approach depends on an analogy between the text as a dynamic system, complete with manifest and latent contents, and the psyche—an analogy authorized by and indebted to Jacques Lacan's interpretation of the Freudian unconscious as structured like a language.

If one takes such an analogy seriously, one needs to clarify what it means to say that a text rather than an author possesses an unconscious. Two basic models of this position have some currency. The first, represented in the work of Felman and Culler, locates the textual unconscious in a relation of transference between reader and text. The second, found in the work of Brooks and Jameson (despite their many differences on other points), locates the unconscious entirely within the text, as a distortion in the story produced by something that has been repressed. Most of the critics who use this term do not comment on the ways in which their usage differs from that of others, but significant consequences follow from the differences between these two models.[1] I end this essay by playing off one version against the other in order to arrive at a more adequate account of how this concept can help us think about Joyce. Here, however, I want to comment on the special role of narrative in these theorists' discussions.

All four theorists elaborate their models in the course of developing accounts of narrative. What is the connection between the two topics? Is the association fortuitous, or is there a reason why a model of the textual unconscious should be produced as part of a theory of narrative? At first glance the topics seem far apart. Narrative is deeply related to temporality,[2] whereas the unconscious is the one psychic state in which time has no meaning. As Freud put it, "Unconscious mental processes are in themselves 'timeless.'"[3] Equally, the linearity of narrative seems far removed from mental processes that follow no sequential pattern, that are fluid, mobile, and reversible, that scorn the law of noncontradiction. But we soon discover that this incompatibility is essential to the critics' efforts to think about the textual unconscious. For Brooks, narrative proves necessary precisely because of its intractable qualities; its stubborn linearity provides a textual equivalent of the pleasure principle and satisfies our desire for coherence, causality, and teleological order. For Felman, narrative becomes the vehicle of transference and fulfills the same need for intelligibility: "We are here prompted to raise the question whether the acting-out of the unconscious is always in effect the acting-out of a *story*, of a narrative."[4] In return for doing such unglamorous work, narrative receives compensation from the critics in the only coin they have to offer: a more sophisticated theory. They hope to replace the static models prevalent in narratology by proposing dynamic models of narrative, models that account

---

1. Culler does set his definition in relation to Felman's and in contradistinction to Jameson's. His distinctions, however, are based on different coordinates from the ones I employ here.

2. See Paul Ricoeur, *Time and Narrative*, trans. Kathleen McLaughlin and David Pellauer, 3 vols. (Chicago: University of Chicago Press, 1984–88).

3. Sigmund Freud, *Beyond the Pleasure Principle*, trans. James Strachey (New York: Liveright, 1961), 22.

4. Shoshana Felman, "Turning the Screw of Interpretation," in *Literature and Psychoanalysis: The Question of Reading: Otherwise*, ed. Shoshana Felman (Baltimore: Johns Hopkins University Press, 1982), 133; hereafter cited in the text as Felman.

not only for the linear dimension of texts but also for the effects of reading and repetition.

Although Felman, Culler, Brooks, and Jameson all connect the textual unconscious with narrative, they do not focus on the same level of narrative, nor do they invoke the same concepts from psychoanalysis. Felman and Culler concentrate on what narratologists call "discourse" and on the psychoanalytic notion of transference; Brooks and Jameson focus on "story" and on the instincts, repression, and mechanisms of displacement.[5] The differences between these two models stem from their alternative objects of attention. In narratology, the distinction between story and discourse has an almost foundational status. Seymour Chatman's influential synthesis of narrative theories takes its title from this distinction, which he traces from the Russian formalists, through the structuralists, to current poststructuralist accounts of narrative. According to Chatman, "narrative has two parts: a story, the content or chain of events . . . , and a discourse, that is, the expression, the means by which the content is communicated. In simple terms, the story is the *what* in a narrative that is depicted, discourse the *how*."[6] Under various names, and despite occasional challenges to the validity of the distinction, the division of narrative into these two levels remains central to most narrative theory today.[7] More important, the division plays a crucial although unacknowledged role in both of the models of the textual unconscious I have outlined.

In her influential essay on psychoanalysis and literature, "Turning the Screw of Interpretation," Shoshana Felman argues that we should look for the unconscious not in the author of a text nor in its characters but in the transaction between the reader and the text. The unconscious becomes visible at those moments when the reader gets caught up in the text and assumes a role in the drama that the text has already marked out. When we think that we are

5. Brooks also discusses transference, but his treatment of this concept comes in the second half of *Reading for the Plot*, which is not concerned with working out a theory of the textual unconscious.

6. Seymour Chatman, *Story and Discourse: Narrative Structure in Fiction and Film* (Ithaca: Cornell University Press, 1978), 19.

7. For challenges to the concept, see Barbara Herrnstein Smith, "Narrative Versions, Narrative Theories," *Critical Inquiry* (Autumn 1980): 213–36, and Jonathan Culler, "Story and Discourse in the Analysis of Narrative," in *The Pursuit of Signs: Semiotics, Literature, Deconstruction* (Ithaca: Cornell University Press, 1981), 169–87. For a response to Culler's argument, see Seymour Chatman, "On Deconstructing Narratology," *Style* 22 (Spring 1988): 9–17. Whether or not this distinction is ultimately valid makes little difference in the current context because all four critics I consider implicitly rely on it.

merely interpreting a narrative, we are actually implicated in its conflicts. "The critical interpretation, in other words, not only elucidates the text but also reproduces it dramatically, unwittingly *participates* in it" (Felman, 101). When critics argue with one another about the meaning of a text, they "act out" or perform that meaning in the course of their debate rather than reveal it through their finished interpretations. This process, according to Felman, is analogous to the situation of transference in psychoanalysis, where the analyst plays a role in the analysand's drama.

The question of Joyce's romanticism provides a striking example of this phenomenon. This controversial issue has frequently tempted critics to assume transferential roles, and for good reason. How one assesses Joyce's relation to romanticism is important since it influences one's stance toward the Joycean epiphany, and in particular toward those scenes in Chapters 4 and 5 of *A Portrait of the Artist as a Young Man* in which Stephen turns away from his church, family, and nation and decides to dedicate himself to art. These are self-reflexive moments. They force one to reflect on the discourse one is reading as well as on the events of the character's life. Any passage that draws attention to the work's immediate precursors and to its place in literary history will have a self-reflexive dimension, but those concerning Stephen's decision to become an artist are among the most self-conscious in the novel.[8] Jonathan Culler argues that such episodes, more than any others, seem to engage readers in transference. This point, in fact, represents his chief addition to Felman's theory of the textual unconscious. After accepting her account of transference, he proposes that the "literary unconscious at work in this transference makes itself felt in the text at what we call moments of self-consciousness."[9] If Culler is right, then these passages are promising places to begin a search for the textual unconscious in Joyce.

Joyceans are divided about whether or not the epiphany is a romantic visionary moment, and their debate bears all the marks of transference. The opinions of Morris Beja and Hugh Kenner can be

8. Joyceans have not neglected to connect such passages to the level of discourse. Colin MacCabe points to them as evidence for his argument that the level of discourse in *Portrait* characteristically dominates that of story; see his *James Joyce and the Revolution of the Word* (New York: Barnes and Noble, 1979), 62, 64. John Paul Riquelme also employs the story-discourse distinction suggestively in *Teller and Tale in Joyce's Fiction: Oscillating Perspectives* (Baltimore: Johns Hopkins University Press, 1983).

9. Jonathan Culler, "Textual Self-Consciousness and the Textual Unconscious," *Style* 18 (1984): 373; hereafter cited in the text as Culler.

taken as representative of the opposing camps. Beja says unequivocally that "the concept of the epiphany itself is of course extremely Romantic, as is Joyce's presentation of it."[10] Scholars of romanticism have been quick to agree. As part of a general reassessment of the continuity between romanticism and modernism, Robert Langbaum and M. H. Abrams have identified the Joycean epiphany as the modern culmination of the romantic "moment of vision"— what Wordsworth called "spots of time."[11] These critics can point to the evidence of Joyce's letters, where he wrote in 1905: "In my history of literature I have given the highest palms to Shakespeare, Wordsworth and Shelley," and "I think Wordsworth of all English men of letters best deserves your word 'genius.'"[12] Joyce gave a lecture on Blake in 1912,[13] and his allusions to that poet in *Ulysses* and *Finnegans Wake* have been documented by a roll call of distinguished Blakeans, including Northrop Frye, Morton Paley, S. Foster Damon, Robert Gleckner, and others.[14] Joyce's references to Shelley are nearly as extensive, if not so thoroughly documented.[15] There has also been significant work on Byron and Joyce, as well as several articles on Joyce's relation to Keats.[16] There is, however, a strange

10. Morris Beja, *Epiphany in the Modern Novel* (London: Peter Owen, 1971), 79.
11. See Robert Langbaum, "The Epiphanic Mode in Wordsworth and Modern Literature," *New Literary History* 14 (1983): 335–58, and M. H. Abrams, *Natural Supernaturalism: Tradition and Revolution in Romantic Literature* (New York: Norton, 1971), 421–22.
12. *Letters of James Joyce*, ed. Richard Ellmann (New York: Viking, 1966), 2:90, 91.
13. See James Joyce, *The Critical Writings of James Joyce*, ed. Ellsworth Mason and Richard Ellmann (New York: Viking, 1959), 214–22.
14. See Northrop Frye, "Blake and Joyce," *James Joyce Review* 1 (1957): 39–47; Morton D. Paley, "Blake in Nighttown," in *A James Joyce Miscellany*, 3d ser., ed. Marvin Magalaner (Carbondale: Southern Illinois University Press, 1962), 175–87; Robert F. Gleckner, "Joyce and Blake: Notes toward Defining a Relationship," in *A James Joyce Miscellany*, 3d ser., 188–225, and "Joyce's Blake: Paths of Influence," in *William Blake and the Moderns*, ed. Robert J. Bertholf and Annette S. Levitt (Albany: State University of New York Press, 1982), 135–63; S. Foster Damon, "The Odyssey in Dublin," in *James Joyce: Two Decades of Criticism*, ed. Seon Givens (New York: Vanguard Press, 1963), 203–45; L. A. G. Strong, *The Sacred River* (New York: Pellegrini and Cudahy, 1951); John Clarke, "Joyce and Blakean Vision," *Criticism* 5 (1963): 173–80; and Frances Motz Boldereff, *A Blakean Translation of Joyce's Circe* (Woodward, Pa.: Classic Non-Fiction Library, 1965).
15. See Timothy Webb, "'Planetary Music': James Joyce and The Romantic Example," in *James Joyce and Modern Literature*, ed. W. J. McCormack and Alistair Stead (London: Routledge and Kegan Paul, 1982), 30–55.
16. See Hermione de Almeida, *Byron and Joyce through Homer: "Don Juan" and "Ulysses"* (New York: Columbia University Press, 1981); Hazard Adams, "Byron, Yeats, and Joyce: Heroism and Technic," *Studies in Romanticism* 24 (1985): 399–412; Wylie Sypher, "Portrait of the Artist as John Keats," *Virginia Quarterly Review* 25 (1949): 420–28; M. A. Goldberg, "Joyce, Freud, and the Internalization of Order," in *The Poetics of Romanticism: Toward a Reading of John Keats* (Yellow Springs, Ohio: Antioch Press, 1969), 151–60; and Michael Seidel, "Coronal Embarrassments: Joyce and Keats," *James Joyce Quarterly* 19 (1982): 186–89.

absence of research on Joyce's relation to Wordsworth, the romantic poet who most clearly anticipated the Joycean epiphany.[17]

Hugh Kenner, by contrast, thinks the epiphany is decidedly not romantic because it is objective rather than subjective. He sees an ironic dimension intervening between Stephen's views and Joyce's own.[18] It was Kenner, of course, who taught us to see the irony in Joyce's fiction. Kenner claims that Joyce is mocking the pomposity and sentimentality of Stephen in those ecstatic scenes that lead him to dedicate himself, in a highly romantic phrase, as "a priest of eternal imagination."[19] And one could point to the scene from the "Nausicaa" chapter in *Ulysses*, where Bloom gazes at a young woman on the beach, as a parody of Stephen's bird-girl vision in *Portrait*.

For convenience, we might identify these two positions with common critical stances, the first with that tendency of contemporary scholarship that Jerome McGann has called "romantic ideology," the habit of reading the texts of the past two hundred years through "romanticism's own self-representations."[20] The second position is characteristic of New Criticism; it looks for irony and ambiguity where the romanticist might find sincerity and authenticity, and it undercuts expressionist assumptions by focusing on point of view, authorial distance, and dramatic situation. But these stances find reflections not only in the critical scene at large but also within the texts of Joyce. The reductio ad absurdum of romantic ideology exists in one of Stephen's fellow students in the fifth chapter of *Portrait*, the pathetically sincere "emotionalist" Temple, who declares Stephen "the only man I see in this institution that has an individual mind" (*P*, 201). Temple takes Stephen's romantic

17. In an essay reviewing sixty years of research on *Portrait*, Thomas Staley comments that "far more scholarship has been devoted to the influence of *A Portrait* on later works than to the influence of other works on Joyce in the writing of the novel"; see Thomas F. Staley, "Strings in the Labyrinth: Sixty Years with Joyce's *Portrait*," in *Approaches to Joyce's "Portrait": Ten Essays*, ed. Thomas Staley and Bernard Benstock (Pittsburgh: University of Pittsburgh Press, 1976), 22. Although some progress has been made since Staley offered this comment, the situation is largely unchanged in respect to Wordsworth.

18. See Hugh Kenner, *Dublin's Joyce* (Boston: Beacon Press, 1956), 132–33.

19. James Joyce, *A Portrait of the Artist as a Young Man*, ed. Chester G. Anderson and Richard Ellmann (New York: Viking Press, 1964), 221; hereafter cited in the text as *P*. In an essay urging the importance of further study of Joyce's relation to romanticism, Hermione de Almeida comments: "The artist as priest is a notion of Wordsworth's"; see her "Joyce and the Romantics: Suggestions for Further Research," *James Joyce Quarterly* 20 (1983): 352.

20. Jerome J. McGann, *The Romantic Ideology: A Critical Investigation* (Chicago: University of Chicago Press, 1983), 1.

self-representations at face value, even when he must brave the jeers and blows of scoffers such as Cranly. Less reductively, the aspect of Stephen himself that pledges "to forge in the smithy of my soul the uncreated conscience of my race" (*P*, 253) is an example of romantic ideology for believing uncritically in his own self-representations. Another aspect of Stephen, however, gives us an excellent example of the New Critical stance toward literature, and this is the part of him that articulates an impersonal theory of art, just a few pages before he composes an embarrassingly personal villanelle.

Each of these critical postures plays a role within the drama of Joyce's novels, so that, in Culler's words, "when the critics claim to be interpreting the story, standing outside it and telling us its true meaning, they are in fact caught up in it, playing an interpretive role that is already dramatized in the story. The quarrels between critics *about* the story are in fact an uncanny repetition of the drama *of* the story" (Culler, 371). The critics' repetition of Joyce, then, becomes a kind of drama of transference, and it is this drama—the history of our unending engagements with the text, not a buried or repressed content within Joyce's novels—that corresponds to Felman and Culler's definition of the textual unconscious.

Felman and Culler do not seem to notice, however, that their theories concentrate on what narratologists call discourse and ignore the level of story. Culler reveals the level at which he is working when he comments that the textual unconscious is not a "hidden or repressed" dimension of the story; rather, it manifests itself at moments "when the text talks about itself," at moments, that is, which draw attention to the discourse (Culler, 370, 372). What happens if we look at the romantic elements not in the discourse but in the story? Can we uncover a textual unconscious on the level of story, or are Felman and Culler correct in locating it only in a particular kind of discursive situation—transference? This question asks us to supplement Freud's theory of the analytic encounter with his meditations on the instincts.

Peter Brooks does exactly that, looking at hidden or repressed features of the story and modeling his theory of narrative's unconscious processes on the opposition between what Freud calls the life and the death instincts. For Brooks, narrative with its linear movement toward an end is the "life" of a novel, but within narrative itself there exist repetitions, returns of the repressed, which cast the novel back on itself, and this repetition compulsion within narrative might be compared to the death instinct. The conflict between these two impulses, between the forward movement and the compulsion to repeat, is what Brooks identifies as the textual unconscious.[21] In contrast to Felman and Culler, for Brooks the textual unconscious exists on the level of story, not discourse.

The same can be said of Fredric Jameson's concept of the political unconscious. In seeking to recast many of the central problems of Marxist theory, Jameson unabashedly turns to contemporary narrative theory: he aims "to restructure the problematics of ideology, of the unconscious and of desire, of representation, of history, and of cultural production, around the all-informing process of *narrative*, which I take to be . . . the central function or *instance* of the human mind."[22] He develops a hermeneutic for uncovering in the story of a literary work a repressed political content, which is itself structured as narrative.[23] He writes: "It is in detecting the traces of that uninterrupted narrative, in restoring to the surface of the text the repressed and buried reality of this fundamental history, that the doctrine of a political unconscious finds its function and its necessity" (*PU*, 20). This hermeneutic is vastly more complicated than that of Brooks, but it shares with the latter the ambition of supplementing static narratological accounts of story with the "more active terms of production, projection, compensation, repression, displacement, and the like" derived from psychoanalysis (*PU*, 44). For both, the textual unconscious becomes visible on the level of the story as an irruption or return of a repressed content, a story beneath the story.

Let us look at how these two conceptions of the textual unconscious might help us understand the romantic moment in Joyce. The first thing to note is that on the level of story, a romantic visionary experience has a very disruptive effect. One can see this effect clearly in one of Wordsworth's most disturbing visionary epi-

21. See Peter Brooks, *Reading for the Plot: Design and Intention in Narrative* (New York: Knopf, 1984), 90–112. For a more extended account and critique of Brooks's theory, see Jay Clayton, "Narrative and Theories of Desire," *Critical Inquiry* 16 (Autumn 1989): 33–53.

22. Fredric Jameson, *The Political Unconscious: Narrative as a Socially Symbolic Act* (Ithaca: Cornell University Press, 1981), 13, italics in original; hereafter cited in the text as *PU*.

23. For an illuminating application of Jameson's method to *Ulysses*, see Patrick McGee, *Paperspace: Style as Ideology in Joyce's "Ulysses"* (Lincoln: University of Nebraska Press, 1988), 189–94.

sodes, the Penrith Beacon incident in the *Prelude*, which is where
he coins the phrase "spots of time." The poet, who is alone and
lost, stumbles upon the ruins of a gibbet where a murderer was once
executed. Wordsworth takes a single look at this spot and starts
running the other way. The act of turning away receives a curious
stress, as it does in several other spots of time: the Simplon Pass
episode and the encounter with the blind beggar in London. Reaching the bare common, the poet has one of his most famous visions,
famous even though it is composed, like Stephen's vision of the
bird-girl, of the humblest materials—a pool, a beacon, and a young
woman whose clothes are tossed by the wind:

> I fled,
> Faltering and faint, and ignorant of the road:
> Then, reascending the bare common, saw
> A naked pool that lay beneath the hills,
> The beacon on the summit, and, more near,
> A girl, who bore a pitcher on her head,
> And seemed with difficult steps to force her way
> Against the blowing wind. It was, in truth,
> An ordinary sight; but I should need
> Colours and words that are unknown to man,
> To paint the visionary dreariness
> Which, while I looked all round for my lost guide,
> Invested moorland waste, and naked pool,
> The beacon crowning the lone eminence,
> The female and her garments vexed and tossed
> By the strong wind.
>
> . . . .
>
> Oh! mystery of man, from what a depth
> Proceed thy honours. I am lost, but see
> In simple childhood something of the base
> On which thy greatness stands. . . .[24]

This vision, like Stephen's, ratifies for Wordsworth his calling as
a poet. The entire *Prelude*, in fact, is subtitled "The Growth of a
Poet's Mind," and shares with Joyce's later novel a structure elabo-
rated around a series of these crucial, epiphanic episodes. There are
several points I want to draw attention to in Wordsworth's experi-

---

24. William Wordsworth, *The Prelude*, in *Poetical Works*, ed. Thomas Hutchinson, rev.
Ernest de Selincourt (London: Oxford University Press, 1969), 12.246–75; hereafter cited
in the text as *Prelude*, followed by book and line numbers.

ence. To begin with, the vision has an economic structure: the epiphanic image comes as a defense against a prior fear. Throughout
Wordsworth's work—and in Joyce's as well—the sublime moment
comes in response to and as compensation for some traumatic experience. Romantic vision is not, as so many readers assume, a naive
affirmation of imaginative power, but rather a compensatory gesture that allows the writer to transform an upsetting experience into
a sign of poetic greatness. Second, the romantic vision interrupts the
progress of Wordsworth's narrative—as it does Joyce's—at the very
moment when the conflict between the life and death instincts
within the narrative becomes too overwhelming. Third, this defensive interruption of the narrative works by shifting our attention
away from the level of story and onto the level of discourse. The
story of Wordsworth's journey as a boy disappears, replaced by an
account of the kind of discursive situation that gave rise to the
poem we are reading. Again, this shift is characteristic of Joyce's
writing, too. The self-reflexive dimension of *Portrait*, which is most
unavoidable in scenes such as the bird-girl vision, gives us an account of how the artist who wrote the work we are reading had his
character formed.[25]

When Stephen turns seaward from the road at Dollymount in
Chapter 4 of *Portrait*, he too is fleeing from a scene of anxiety: his
father's conference with the tutor about Stephen's entrance into the
university. As in Wordsworth, the novel parallels the physical act
of turning seaward with Stephen's mental revolution: "When the
moment had come for him to obey the call he had turned aside,
obeying a wayward instinct" (*P*, 165). Stephen seems to hear "notes
of fitful music" (*P*, 165), which might remind us how often Wordsworth shuts out something troubling in the visible world and listens
to visionary strains, "to notes that are / The ghostly language of the
ancient earth, / Or make their dim abode in distant winds" (*Prelude*,
2.309–11). For Stephen, the music "was an elfin prelude, endless
and formless; and, as it grew wilder and faster, the flames leaping
out of time, he seemed to hear from under the boughs and grasses
wild creatures racing, their feet pattering like rain upon the leaves"
(*P*, 165).[26] This little vision soothes him, but his anxiety is renewed

25. For more on the structure of romantic visionary moments and their effect on narrative, see Jay Clayton, *Romantic Vision and the Novel* (Cambridge: Cambridge University
Press, 1987), 1–26.
26. Can one hear in Joyce's "elfin prelude" a distant echo of "elfin pinnace" from the
stolen-boat episode in the *Prelude* (1.373)?

when he passes a squad of Christian Brothers who are marching two-by-two across the bridge; they remind him that in renouncing the university, he has renounced the oils of ordination as well.

By the time he reaches the beach, Stephen feels the need for a compensatory gesture of some sort, and, characteristically, he turns to language, murmuring a "phrase from his treasure": "A day of dappled seaborne clouds" (P, 166). These words provoke in him a reverie, during which he drifts away from the world around him, until finally he seems to hear "a voice from beyond the world . . . calling" (P, 167). This fade-out is characteristic of romantic vision-ary experiences and appears in all of Wordsworth's spots of time, most famously in the Simplon Pass episode, "when the light of sense / Goes out" (Prelude, 6.600–601). Stephen's reflections on why he prefers the "rhythmic rise and fall of words" to the "reflec-tion of the glowing sensible world through the prism of a language manycoloured and richly storied" (P, 166–67) even resemble Words-worth's meditation on the "power in sound / To breathe an elevated mood, by form / Or image unprofaned" (Prelude, 2.304–6). In both cases the passages delicately shift our attention from the events of the story to the discourse in which it is written, thus constituting self-reflexive moments in the works.

Stephen's reverie is interrupted, however, by the cries of school friends. He has to shake himself out of his trance. As he returns to consciousness, he feels isolated from his acquaintances, and he makes unflattering observations on their "pitiable nakedness" as they swim (P, 168). He ends these unattractive comments with a sentence about himself: "But he, apart from them and in silence, remembered in what dread he stood of the mystery of his own body" (P, 168). The text moves from a guilt about his choice of life to a different source of anxiety: his feelings of physical inadequacy. In response to this anxiety a second, more intense vision appears, the well-known image of the "fabulous artificer" (P, 169), his namesake, flying above the waves. The defensive character of this vision is not hard to discern, and the self-reflexive element in the passage is equally clear. Stephen chooses to interpret this "winged form" as "a prophecy of the end he had been born to serve and had been following through the mists of childhood and boyhood, a symbol of the artist forging anew in his workshop out of the sluggish matter of the earth a new soaring impalpable imperishable being" (P, 169).

Voices again call Stephen back to earth, and he moves away, wan-

dering until he finds himself alone. Then he encounters his third
and final vision—the one which, like Wordsworth's vision at Penrith Beacon, confirms for him his vocation as a poet. Stephen sees
a girl who "seemed like one whom magic had changed into the
likeness of a strange and beautiful seabird" (P, 171). The romanticism of this bird-girl vision is of a distinctly Wordsworthian sort:
"It was, in truth, / An ordinary sight" (Prelude, 12.253–54), but one
that has taken on a visionary hue. Her stillness, her solitude, and
the quiet patience with which she suffers Stephen's gaze evoke
those solitary figures who populate Wordsworth's verse. The power
of these figures, for Stephen as for the poet, lies in the compensation
they provide for a deeply felt loss. Stephen has renounced church,
family, and country to become a poet, and poetic visions will have
to make up for all that he has abandoned.

I have gone over these familiar passages to emphasize that each
of Stephen's romantic moments comes as a defense against some
prior pain. Joyceans have sometimes held this fact against Stephen's
visions, saying that it proved their inauthentic character, but we
should not lose sight of the point that romantic visionary poetry
followed the same compensatory pattern. Many readers have found
the content of Stephen's visions silly. But their content is less important than their compensatory structure. If Stephen's experiences
are viewed structurally rather than thematically, they remain interesting as stages in the movement of the poetic mind away from
something painful in the story and toward something exalting on
the level of discourse.

Remaining on the level of story, where Brooks and Jameson locate
the textual unconscious, one observes that Stephen's visions inter-
rupt the narrative at the same point where Wordsworth's intervened: the moment of intensest conflict between the life and death
instincts within the narrative. In order for the story of Stephen as
an artist to live, to continue moving forward, it must turn away
from all that has made up his life in the past; and the return of this
repressed past, in his naked friends and in the line of Christian
Brothers, reminds him of the death instinct at work in the new turn
his story has taken.

We could define Stephen's visions, structurally, as defenses
against the textual unconscious of his story and, like all defense
mechanisms, as evidence of the existence of repression. Then

should one conclude that Brooks and Jameson are right, that the textual unconscious exists at the level of story, not discourse? Such a conclusion would be premature. The compensatory mechanism in both Stephen's and Wordsworth's visions operated, we remember, by shifting the reader's attention away from the story and onto the discursive level. And there, in the self-reflexive moment in the work, the reader is caught up in the relation of transference that Felman and Culler identified as the textual unconscious. So what we really have are two unconsciouses—the story's and the discourse's—each thoroughly textual. One, the story's, is logically prior to the other. But that does not make it more fundamental, for our only access to it is through the other, the discourse's. We encounter the textual unconscious of the discourse, and are situated by it, *before* we begin to (re)construct the textual unconscious of the story. Then should one conclude that Felman's and Culler's accounts of the textual unconscious identify the more fundamental principle? Again, I think not. I would suggest, instead, that neither the textual unconscious of the story nor that of the discourse is primary, and that neither can be considered in isolation from the other.

Let me conclude by indicating how playing off one concept against the other can aid us in reading Joyce. The problem with conceiving the textual unconscious entirely as a buried or repressed content within the story—whether that content is political (Jameson) or instinctual (Brooks)—is one of reduction. This is the danger that Susan Stanford Friedman acknowledges in her contribution to this volume when she reads the textual unconscious as more repressed in the finished work and less repressed in an early draft such as *Stephen Hero*. We end up with an authoritative master narrative—about the repression of the mother, say—which determines (by distortion) our reactions to all other versions.[27] And yet, the danger in conceiving the textual unconscious merely in terms of transference is not reduction to an authoritative master narrative but the erasure of the story altogether. The meaning of a work becomes ensnared in the mechanics of the interpreter's transference,

27. See Susan Stanford Friedman, "(Self)Censorship and the Making of Joyce's Modernism" Chapter 1 in this volume. Friedman's strategy for avoiding reduction involves reversing her procedure and also reading the textual unconscious as more repressed in the early drafts and less repressed in the finished work. This strategy of double reading avoids the pitfall of reduction, but by different means from the kind of double reading suggested here, for both of her readings concentrate on the level of story.

and we are left with the kind of empty mise-en-scène that climaxes so many unskillful deconstructions. We need some sense of the story and its repressions, even if that story is endlessly revised, repeated, and worked through in our interpretive transference. To lose sight of the story is to lose sight of a crucial historical and political dimension of literature. Felman and Culler substitute another history and another politics—that of the struggle among successive critical interpretations—and I would not want to lose sight of this dimension of the reading experience either. Both seem to me indispensible.

In many of the essays in this volume there is an emphasis on the need for reading in two directions, for recognizing the doubleness in Joyce, for consulting both the story and the discourse. Is the unconscious of *these* essays to be found in our transference with the Joycean texts we so love—and so love to quarrel with—or in our master narratives about politics, gender, the repression of the mother, and incestuous family relations? Perhaps the only answer is a double one.

5

Simon's Irish Rose: Famine Songs, Blackfaced Minstrels, and Woman's Repression in *A Portrait*

Richard Pearce

A Portrait of the Artist as a Young Man begins with Stephen's father telling him a story. Stephen's father has a hairy face, and is looking down through what looks like a glass. The father's story, like the story of the first father, begins at an ideal point in time, when a very good time it was—or, as Mikhail Bakhtin calls it, "the epic absolute past . . . the single source and beginning of everything good."[1] It is designed to follow the road, past where Betty Byrne sold lemon platt, to a logical conclusion. The logic of the story that Mr. Dedalus begins to tell, and that continues from Stephen's point of view, leads to the development of the artist, and points in the direction of separation, independence, success, and power. This is what Nancy Miller calls the "ambitious story."[2]

I thank the following people for leading me into new fields of scholarship: Mary Lowe-Evans, Ruth Bauerle (an authority on Joyce and music), Rosemary Cullen (curator of Brown University's John Hay Library), Sheila M. Hogg (Assistant Music Librarian at Brown University's Orwig Music Library), Cheryl Herr, Elsie Mitchie (who helped me with facts of Irish history and theories of colonialization), and Ulrich Schneider (an authority on popular culture in Ireland, who led me to understand the theoretical complexities of studying popular culture and the uses of Antonio Gramsci).

1. Mikhail M. Bakhtin, *The Dialogic Imagination: Four Essays by M. M. Bakhtin*, trans. Caryl Emerson and Michael Holquist, ed. Michael Holquist (Austin: University of Texas Press, 1981), 13–15.

2. Nancy K. Miller, "Emphasis Added: Plots and Plausibilities in Women's Fiction," *PMLA* 96 (1981): 36–48.

Seeking to achieve its goal, the authorial voice—which is identified with the voice of the father even though it focuses on Stephen's rebellious consciousness—represses stories that do not fit into or that threaten its plot line by overlooking, denying, displacing, reforming, or appropriating them.[3] The little boy in the father's story may require the services of Betty Byrne, or may need to overcome her temptations, but he requires no knowledge of her. Nor will we learn anything about Betty Byrne from *Portrait*. We know that Elizabeth Byrne was a real woman who appears in *Thom's Dublin Post Office Directory of 1886* as a grocer at 46 Main Street in Bray (where both Joyce and Stephen lived as children). But to develop her as a character in the novel would divert or threaten the (male) story line. It would raise questions such as: Was she a widow or a spinster? How old was she? Was she supporting a large family? Did she take over the business from her husband or her father? Did she build up the business herself? What did it mean for a single woman to be running a business of her own? What would she have said about the little boy from a well-to-do family who was brought in to buy lemon platt? While Stephen will rebel against traditional forms of authority and search for new kinds of stories, his father's kind of story prevails. Betty Byrne is never mentioned again, and the stories of the women who are central to his childhood are repressed, transformed, and appropriated.

I want to look at the stories told about and by women in the opening pages of *Portrait* which introduce and initiate young Stephen: the stories of Mrs. Dedalus and Dante, but first the story of Lilly Dale, the woman of baby Stephen's abbreviated song, whose very name is elided. And I want see how their stories, though central to Stephen's world, are repressed by the authorial voice that is identified with the father and that tells the story of the artist as a young man. I also want to show on the basis of historical evidence what is repressed into the novel's political unconscious and how it was repressed and managed by the popular discourses of the late nineteenth century.

After hearing the father's story, cast into the form of an Irish children's tale, baby Stephen tells a story in the form of a song,

---

3. In *The Politics of Narration: James Joyce, William Faulkner, and Virginia Woolf* (New Brunswick: Rutgers University Press, 1991), I argue that the authorial voice contends with a rebellious voice that disrupts and subverts the ambitious story in ways that Joyce would develop in *Ulysses*, but the authorial voice prevails.

transforming *"O, the wild rose blossoms / On the little green place,"* to *"O, the green wothe botheth."*[4] The song is called "Lilly Dale," and it begins:

> *Twas a calm, still night,*
> *And the moon's pale light,*
> *Shone soft o'er hill and vale.*
> *When friends mute with grief,*
> *Stood round the death bed,*
> *Of my poor lost Lilly Dale.*

> *Oh! Lilly, sweet Lilly, dear Lilly Dale,*
> *Now the wild rose blossoms o'er her little green grave,*
> *Neath the trees in the flow'ry vale.*[5]

But, although Stephen sings "Lilly Dale," it is nonetheless his father's song—obviously one he heard his father sing, and one that Simon Dedalus might have sung with his drinking companions before coming home to serenade his son. Even though Stephen changes the words, his song is not much different from his father's. Nor is it much different from his fantasy of the "unsubstantial" Mercedes, or his idealization of the girl on the beach, or the lyric he writes as an aspiring artist, or the "ambitious" bildungsroman form in which his story is set. For Stephen is caught in the nets of a discourse that was being woven in the stories and songs in the opening section of *Portrait*—and that Joyce was exposing in a way that would become much more explicit in *Ulysses*.

"Lilly Dale" is about the love of a sweet, dead woman; the "green place" is actually a "green grave." Singing about a sweet, dead woman, a very popular tradition, was a way of transforming her death into a beautiful, nostalgic song. Or, as Margot Norris points out in another context, it is a way of taking pleasure in her pain, and repressing her physical, social, and political reality.[6] Nothing in the song leads us to imagine, let alone know, what Lilly Dale looked like, how old she was, whether she was a young maid or a married woman, what kind of a home she came from, or what she

---

4. James Joyce, *A Portrait of the Artist as a Young Man: Text, Criticism, and Notes,* ed. Chester G. Anderson (New York: Viking Press, 1968), 7; hereafter cited in the text as *P*.

5. H. S. Thompson, *Lilly Dale* (Oliver Ditson: Boston, 1852).

6. Margot Norris, "Stifled Back Answers: The Gender Politics of Art in Joyce's 'The Dead,'" *Modern Fiction Studies* 35 (Autumn 1989): 479–503.

died of. Nonetheless, the range of possibilities is limited. "Lilly Dale" was written in 1852 and was very popular in the years after the Great Famine. So there is a fairly good chance that what Lilly died of—or the physical, social, and political reality well known by all who sang and heard her song but repressed by her lyric idealization—was starvation, some form of malnutrition, or one of the other very prevalent secondary effects of the potato famine: dysentery, scurvy, or cholera. As Mary Lowe-Evans convincingly argues, the Great Famine of 1845–51 established a discourse that deeply pervaded the Irish consciousness for two generations.[7] This discourse was a way of expressing but also managing the feelings, thoughts, and behavior of those being exploited by the forces of colonization. And one of the ways they managed those feelings was through the sentimental idealization of social reality and death in popular songs.

"Lilly Dale" came to Ireland from America. It was written by H. S. Thompson, about whom nothing is known except that he also wrote the music for what became the Cornell alma mater. Like many songwriters, he probably sold his songs for a few dollars, leaving the profits to the managers, performers, and sheet music companies. And, if we may judge by the sheet music that spun off from and helped commodify "Lilly Dale," it was enormously popular. It was published in 1852 and again in 1853, inspiring an illustrated *Lily Dale Songster*. It was transformed into "Lilly Dale arranged with Variations," the "Lilly Dale Schottish," the "Lilly Dale Quickstep," and then published in *Heart Songs* in 1909 as one of the four hundred most popular American songs as selected by twenty thousand respondents to a national ad. It traveled to Europe as Sigmund Thalberg's "Lilly Dale, Air Americain varié pour le Piano."[8] It was sung in London at Jullien's famous concerts by Madame Anna Thillon after their American tour of 1850–54 (the sheet music with Anna Thillon's picture on the cover also lists W. H. Currie's 1853 adaptation "The Grave of Lilly Dale"). And the song was popular in English and Irish concert halls, music halls, pubs, and parlors at

7. Mary Lowe-Evans, *Crimes against Fertility: Joyce and Population Control* (Syracuse: Syracuse University Press, 1989).

8. Annotation to H. S. Thompson, *Lilly Dale* (Boston: Oliver Ditson, 1852), by S. Foster Damon, in the Harris Collection of American Poetry and Plays, John Hay Library, Brown University. *Heart Songs Dear to the American People*, published by Joe Mitchell Chapple (Boston, 1909), reprinted with introduction by Charles Hamm (New York: Da Capo Press, 1983).

least until 1886, when Simon Dedalus would sing it to young Stephen.

The point of this brief history is not only that dead maidens made good songs. It is that they made especially good songs, lively dances, and music hall numbers when their gender, class, exploitation, and suffering were repressed, sentimentalized, idealized, or sublimated. And Simon Dedalus, like many Dublin men who spent their time (and their family's money) drinking and singing in the pubs, gave beautiful form to the stories of dead—safe—women, repressing and sublimating into art the reality of gender, poverty, deprivation, over-work, exploitation, and colonization.

But there is more to the social and political reality that Stephen's father may have been repressing. Simon Dedalus was shaped by social pressures: his class, his colonized status, the lack of opportu-nities, the need to prove his manhood, as well as the pressures to conform, to repress his sexual urges, to have a large family, and passively to accept his social status. The social picture I want to fill out begins with the fact that he was modeled on Joyce's father, who, typical of many men of his class, went from relative prosperity in 1880, when he married, to poverty by the time his wife died in 1903. During the twenty-three years of their marriage, May Joyce experienced seventeen pregnancies. Indeed, Ruth Bauerle points out that she was pregnant at least fourteen times during the first fifteen years, as they were forced to move from one house to another, and the houses became smaller, and the family became larger, and (I would add) her husband spent more of his money in the pubs singing songs such as "Lilly Dale." Bauerle also asks a series of illuminating questions: "Did John Stanislaus, returning home truculent and vengeful, forcibly demand conjugal rights of his overburdened wife? He could attempt to kill her. He could shout, as she lay dying, 'Die and be damned to you!' The children were witnesses to, even participants in these violent scenes. Can we doubt that he insisted on his sexual rights with verbal and possibly physical violence? Given the small, crowded homes, could the children—especially James, the sensitive eldest—escape hearing scenes of mate rape?"[9] And we might also ask whether Joyce could have separated this

9. Ruth Bauerle, "Date Rape, Mate Rape: A Liturgical Interpretation of 'The Dead,'" in *New Alliances in Joyce Studies: "When It's Aped to Foul a Delfian,"* ed. Bonnie Kime Scott (Newark: University of Delaware Press, 1988), 119–20. Bauerle's own citation in this passage is to Richard Ellmann, *James Joyce* (Oxford: Oxford University Press, 1982), 136.

image of his father from the image of the father who sang "Lilly Dale" to Stephen when he was an infant. Or whether "mate rape" wasn't a normal and accepted part of the treatment of Irish-Catholic wives and therefore inherent in Simon Dedalus's characterization. Women dying of starvation, women dying in childbirth, women dying from overwork, women being exploited and raped by lovers and husbands who sang songs of pure love and beautiful dead women: these are some of the social realities that Mr. Dedalus might well have been suppressing, and that contribute to the novel's political unconscious.

There is still another layer of social reality repressed in the song of Stephen's father. "Lilly Dale" was originally an American "plantation"—that is, minstrel—song. So what is also being repressed is race and the dark side of colonialism. According to Charles Hamm, the prototype of "Lilly Dale" was "Miss Lucy Neal," written in 1844 by the American James Sanford and popularized, though not for long, by the crusading Englishman Henry Russell. But unlike in the sentimental "Lilly Dale," the social and historical content is manifest. It begins:

> I was born in Alabama
> My master's name was Meal
> He used to own a yellow gal,
> Her name was Lucy Neale.

In the next nine stanzas the singer tells how he fell in love with Lucy, how they were separated when his master sold him, and how, unable to find his way back, he hears that:

> Miss Lucy she was taken sick,
> She eat too much corn meal.
> The Doctor he did gib her up.[10]

10. Charles Hamm, *Yesterdays: Popular Song in America* (New York: W. W. Norton, 1979), 137. According to Hamm "Mary Blane," sung by the Irishman J. W. Raynor, was an earlier example of the song in which the singer's lover did not die but was sold: "I often asked for Mary Blane, / My Massa he did scold, / And said you saucy nigger boy, / If you must know, she's sold." Both "Mary Blane" and "Miss Lucy Neal" were representative of a new group of songs in pseudo-black dialect emerging in the 1840s but tied to the sentimental ballad, which treated black characters sympathetically and portrayed a "whole gallery" of southern slave women. "Lilly Dale," Hamm contends, was an offshoot that had no connection with black minstrelsy, since there is no trace of dialect or reference to slaves or the South (136). Nonetheless, it is listed in *Minstrel Songs Old and New*, which was published in 1910 by Oliver Ditson of Boston, the original publisher of "Lilly Dale," and in other standard minstrel listings. And the *Lilly Dale Songster* is illustrated with pictures of blackface singers and dancers in courtly dress.

Nor would audiences, hearing the tragic announcement of her death in the final stanza, have judged this a case of overeating. Slaves were often underfed when rations were too closely calculated by an owner trying to maximize his profit, or when times were hard, or when extravagances came to more than was anticipated. John Blassingame quotes a "carefully reasoned economic treatise written in 1844," which says that, while free laborers required a hundred dollars a year for food and clothing, a slave could be and often was supported on twenty.[11] Moreover, most slave autobiographers report that they had at least one owner who did not give them enough food, and that with other owners provisions sometimes ran low.[12] The young slave woman, then, died of malnutrition—as did many young Irish women during the potato famine. So the migration of "Lilly Dale" from the world of American slavery to the world of the Irish famine has a historical logic. Indeed, as I will show, there is a deep relationship between enslaved Africans and colonized Irish, not only in their manner of exploitation but in the popular discourse of the colonizers.

The cover of the London song sheet, which pictured Anna Thillon singing at one of Jullien's concerts, also promoted "Lilly Dale" as one of the "Christy Minstrel New Songs."The Christy Minstrels were a popular group that spawned a large number of plagiarists and soon became the generic name for the "nigger" minstrelsy. Although they often played as part of a music hall program, they also developed their own independent minstrel shows which, in contrast to the music halls, were legitimate, and hence respectable, theater, and could appeal to a wider spectrum of society. Indeed, minstrel shows were so respectable that Gabriel Conroy would take his wife to see them—and she would tweak him about the "galoshes" he made her wear: "The word reminds her of Christy Minstrels."[13] The

11. John W. Blassingame, *The Slave Community: Plantation Life in the Antebellum South* (New York: Oxford University Press, 1979), 265.

12. Ibid., 254. There is an even more cynical explanation of Lucy Neal's death. Frederick Douglass describes how, when slaves ran through their food allowances and applied for more, the enraged master would often compel them to eat until they got sick (*Narrative of the Life of Frederick Douglass, an American Slave,* in *The Classic Slave Narratives,* ed. Henry Louis Gates, Jr. [New York: New American Library, 1987], 301).

13. James Joyce, *Dubliners: Text, Criticism, and Notes,* ed. Robert Scholes and A. Walton Litz (New York: Viking Press, 1969), 181. Music hall owners and managers tried to woo the middle class by breaking with the public house tradition, banning the sale of drinks from the auditorium, replacing tables with rows of seats, cleaning up the songs and skits, controlling the audience's behavior, inviting dignitaries, and opening the show with the national anthem. Yet, as Dagmar Höher argues, the middle class did not flock to the music halls in the 1890s, for there were a considerable number of anti–music hall cam-

Christy Minstrels probably brought "Lilly Dale" to Ireland in the 1850s, about the same time as Anna Thillon's London concert, where it remained popular in concert tours, music halls, and minstrel shows for at least thirty years. It is very likely, then, that Simon Dedalus would have heard and seen it during the 1850s performed not only by a concert artiste but also by a blackface minstrel playing the role of a slave. And the sheet music which he might have seen on the pianos of both parlors and pubs was associated with both kinds of performance.

What would Simon Dedalus have thought and felt about the representation of black slaves on the Irish minstrel stage? And how would he have reconciled the image of a blackface Lilly Dale with the pure white image that would have come to mind when he heard the song on the concert stage or when he imitated that formal style in a pub such as the Ormond? To answer these questions we must see what happened when the minstrels came from America to England and then to Ireland. And this rather long digression will lead us to understand much about some popular discourses that inform the novel and about their dynamics of repression.

In the United States minstrels were tied to the social reality of southern slavery. According to Charles Hamm, early minstrels represented the black slave as a "ridiculous, grotesque, marginally human creature," but this image was displaced, especially by singers who communicated their grief over the death of a beloved in the tradition of the sentimental ballad.[14] It seems, however, that the representations continually alternated and overlapped. Sometimes slaves were represented as people with human emotions suffering tragedies brought about by their inhumane treatment. But at other times they were animalistic caricatures, heightened by the incongruity of the black face and the cultured style, the lyric voice and stereotyped gestures. Moreover, the minstrel could satisfy the need

---

paigns ("The Composition of Music Hall Audiences, 1850–1900," in *Music Hall: The Business of Pleasure*, ed. Peter Bailey [Philadelphia: Taylor and Francis, 1986], 86). Höher is referring only to the English music halls, but in Ireland the middle class was at least as conservative. Eugene Watters and Matthew Murtagh describe Dan Lowrey's continual battle to gain legitimacy for his Star of Erin, especially since the legitimate theaters were rightly concerned about the competition of "people's fun" (*Infinite Variety: Dan Lowrey's Music Hall 1879–97* [Dublin: Gill and MacMillan, 1975], 38). More important, the church had a great deal of control. And, as Cheryl Herr points out, the music hall was considered antinationalistic, a way of importing English performers into Irish culture (*Joyce's Anatomy of Culture* [Chicago: University of Chicago Press, 1986]).

14. Hamm, *Yesterdays*, 136.

of free white Americans, no matter how they were exploited, to see slaves as radically Other, especially when free blacks threatened whites in the northern job market, and it is important to note that minstrels first became popular during the depression of 1842. When a man in blackface sang a sentimental ballad such as "Lilly Dale" without dialect or reference to the social reality of slaves, he could evoke sympathy for a fellow human being. But, incongruously dressed in formal attire and singing in the style of a concert performer, he would also evoke laughter at high culture, like that of Julien's "epic" concerts, where Madame Anna Thillon sang "Lilly Dale" on the American tour before taking it to England. And by exploiting the black stereotype to satirize high culture, he enabled whites of the working class to feel superior to their black counterparts, if not temporarily satisfied with the system that exploited them both.

According to Michael Pickering, in Britain, where there were few black people, the popularity of the minstrels was in large part due to a curiosity about the New World.[15] And at least in industrialized England—where comparisons between slave labor and wage slavery were common—"minstrelsy was as much about English social relations as it was about a scantily known Afro-American population. . . . Race relations abroad were perceived in the light of class relations at home. It is this which links, in official and popular discourses, the derogatory images of 'negroes,' Jews, Irish, hooligans, working-class 'roughs,' criminals and whores: essentially they all belonged to a perpetually lower order that was defined by its antithetical contrast with English gentility."[16] Moreover, the minstrel could offer the lower classes, the unemployed, and the disaffected an "inverted image of all that was held comely, respectable, and proper in a civilised society and all that meant success in a commercial world and an enterprise culture"[17]—that is, the work

15. Michael Pickering, "White Skin, Black Masks: 'Nigger' Minstrelsy," in *Music Hall: Performance and Style,* ed. J. S. Bratton (Philadelphia: Milton Keynes and Open University Press, 1986), 84. Hans Nathan traces the literary interest in black people back to Thomas Southerne's *Oroonoko* (1695); what he describes as a "humanitarian trend" in the eighteenth century "culminated in a vogue for the oppressed" (*Dan Emmett and the Rise of Early Negro Minstrelsy* [Norman: University of Oklahoma Press, 1962], 4). But Nathan's history lacks the social density of Pickering's. Also see J. S. Bratton, "English Ethiopians: British Audiences and Black-Face Acts, 1835–1865," in *The Yearbook of English Studies: Literature and Its Audience, II,* ed. G. K. Hunter and C. J. Rawson (London: Modern Humanities Research Association, 1981), 11:127–42.
16. Pickering, "White Skin, Black Masks," 84.
17. Ibid., 88.

ethic. Mark Osteen, focusing on the big spenders in the "Cyclops" chapter of *Ulysses* but also explaining the dissipation of Simon Dedalus, points out that in colonized Ireland, rejecting the work ethic was a way of rejecting British values. Drinking to excess was related to a "potlatch" competition in buying drinks; it was a "sacrificial politics," a self-defeating "impulse for independence."[18] And this helps us understand at least part of what Simon Dedalus felt while watching the comic excesses of the blackface minstrel with his gratuitously genteel love song to an idealized dead woman.

But the British minstrels had yet another dimension: blacking up in England was a form of masking assimilated into popular custom and vernacular drama. It was a form of license. The minstrel performance took place in "a cultural space bracketed off from the moral rules and regulated behavior of mundane reality, but it did this at once via an association with black people in a new dynamic theatrical format and within a developing professionalism and commercial provision of popular entertainment. It was the coalescence of all these factors which made the minstrel mask so volatile in its meanings."[19] And the meanings became even more volatile as a result of the creative disparities, the contradictions arising from the mixture of dress, song, and language. As Pickering writes: "The humor of minstrelsy . . . hinged crucially on the incongruity of blackface impersonations, as did the whole effect of 'coon' love songs, which in varying degrees comically subverted the tone and content of the Victorian parlour ballad, not only by treating the theme of romance with a flippant lightheartedness, but also by using the coon buffoon caricature to ironically send up a mawkish sentimentalism."[20]

The British masking tradition resulted in carnivalesque fusions that broke down traditional hierarchies—but at the same time reaffirmed them.[21] Music halls and minstrels were subversive, but they

18. Mark Osteen, "Narrative Gifts: 'Cyclops' and the Economy of Excess," in *Joyce Studies Annual*, 1990, ed. Thomas F. Staley (Austin: University of Texas Press, 1990), 162–96.

19. Pickering, "White Skin, Black Masks," 79.

20. Ibid., 79.

21. It is important to recognize the variety of forces at work in the music halls and minstrel shows and to understand the creative dynamic, the dissonant fusions of styles and messages that undermine traditional hierarchies. But the carnival tradition, from which the masking tradition derives, is at best ambiguous, for it was traditionally licensed by authority. The Roman Saturnalia, the Kalends of January, and the English Feast of Fools were legitimized ways to release pent-up energies. They were situated outside of normal time. But, at a predetermined moment in time, order would be restored. Also, see Peter

were capable of managing subversive feelings. They appealed to people of all classes, who enjoyed sitting together under the same roof, but the classes were segregated according to the price of their seats. The cross-class appeal was heightened by characters addressing each different part of the audience. But they held the spirit of democracy in check by pitting one class against the other in a spirit of sport.

Moreover, the spontaneity that drew audiences together could be exposed as manipulative and exploitive in the very act that engaged the audience as happy accomplices to the manipulation and exploitation. J. S. Bratton describes a music hall song that epitomizes one form of this contradiction.

> I've just been informed by the manager here
> That the reason I'm back at the Empire this year,
> Is because it states on my contract quite clear,
> I must sing a song with a chorus;
> I've found one at last—it's a terrible thing,
> But still it must go with a rush and a swing;
> So when I've sung it once, for goodness sakes sing,
> And bring down the roof that is o'er us.
> If the song doesn't go, well I do, that's all,
> So here and outside this chorus please bawl:
> O, O, Capital O, Why should it be so I really don't know,
> O, O; now let it go!
> If you don't know the chorus, sing O, O, O.[22]

As Bratton points out:

> The singer and the audience, the management and the song, are described as being locked into a network of relationships that is acknowledged as exploitive and phoney, even as the song is generated and enjoyed. The spontaneous audience participation supposedly at the heart of music hall's "popular" status . . . is exposed as a deliberate fabrication written into the contract by the management, which rewards the performer according to his ability to sell his manufactured bonhomie to the audience. But the song is not a bitter denunciation of the system; the response it invites is the same participation at which it scoffs, and the singer would have failed indeed if the audience were not singing heartily by the end.[23]

Stallybrass and Allon White's introduction to *The Politics and Poetics of Transgression* (Ithaca: Cornell University Press, 1986).

22. Words and music by J. W. Knowles, song by Wilkie Bard (1903); quoted in J. S. Bratton, Introduction to *Music Hall: Performance and Style*, ed. J. S. Bratton (Philadelphia: Taylor and Francis, 1986), vii.

23. Bratton, Introduction, vii.

Bratton illuminates what historians of popular culture, building on Antonio Gramsci, see as a site of exchange, negotiation, and continuing struggle for ideological hegemony.[24] In the Irish music halls this struggle takes another form as the English, who brought the shows from Liverpool to Dublin, became the butt of satiric laughter. For audiences would enjoy the satire of English ideology at the same time they were literally buying into it. Indeed, Cheryl Herr argues that the music hall ultimately "served . . . to *contain* lower-class frustration by making expression into a form of commodity to be purchased by the worker." While it consciously satirized the English upper classes, it "manipulated the Irish into enacting roles more beneficial to the ruler than the rule. . . . If laborers . . . could be made to accept, however ironically, the minimal utopia of an urban garden (as portrayed in the music hall song, 'That Little Back Garden of Mine') and a secure but colorless marriage (as in 'My Old Dutch') so much the better."[25]

Two of the figures Irish audiences most loved and bought into were the stage Irishman and the blackface minstrel. And these two figures are deeply related. As Perry Curtis shows, the Irish were considered "white Negroes" by the English. They were told that, according to a well-respected scientific formula, they had a high "index of Negrescence." And they saw themselves "simianized," depicted with apelike characteristics, in Victorian cartoons in magazines ranging from *Punch* to the penny weeklies.[26] Building on Curtis, Elsie Mitchie points out that the Irish were identified as blacks in the dominant English discourse that pervaded the novels of the Brontë sisters as well as the popular press. They were called "blacks" and "white monkeys," caricatured as apes, and identified with "primitive" Africans (as American slaves had been) as a way of justifying the masters' treatment—especially during the famine.[27] And Harriet Jacobs claimed, "I would ten thousand times

24. For an excellent survey of theoretical issues in the study of popular culture, see Peter Bailey, "Leisure, Culture, and the Historian: Reviewing the First Generation of Leisure Historiography in Britain," *Leisure Studies* 8 (1989): 107–25; his discussion of Gramsci is on 113.

25. Cheryl Herr, *Joyce's Anatomy of Culture* (Urbana: University of Illinois Press, 1986), 190.

26. Perry Curtis, *Apes and Angels: The Irishman in Victorian Caricature* (Washington, D.C.: Smithsonian Institution, 1971).

27. Elsie Mitchie, "Heathcliff, Rochester, and the Simianization of the Irish," *Novel* 25 (Winter 1992): 125–40.

rather that my children should be the half-starved paupers of Ireland than to be the most pampered of the slaves in America."[28]

Irish audiences, then, could sympathize with black American slaves as a result of being lower class and colonized. But their enjoyment (like that of the exploited American workers) may have come from the opportunity to distance themselves from the blacks being represented. If their enjoyment was based on distancing themselves from the scapegoat, the English were not only making money on the popularity of minstrels but also finding another way to contain the frustration of their colony. The blackface minstrel—who sang songs such as "Lilly Dale" in the attire, manners, and diction of a middle-class white gentleman—could generate both tears and laughter. He could effect identification but also a distancing that resulted in a repression of the social reality, or the relation between black slaves and white Irishmen. But the repression was more complex, for fantasizing the death of a young woman was a way of repressing the reality of her exploitation and the audience's complicity in it. Moreover, the linking of simianized slaves, colonized Irishmen, and exploited women establishes the mutuality of simianization and feminization. It suggests that forces of self-hatred, displacement, and projection are at work in the desire for a beautiful woman's death. The minstrel's obvious satirizing of the sentimental style of the concert stage (where Simon Dedalus might also have heard "Lilly Dale") competed with but did not undermine the powers of repression inherent in the colonialized discourse of the most popular forms of entertainment.

Cheryl Herr persuasively argues in *Joyce's Anatomy of Culture* that Joyce recognized the subversive potential of the music halls as well as of the minstrels. But Simon Dedalus did not. From all we know of him in *Portrait* and from hearing of the way he and his cohorts sang in the "Sirens" episode of *Ulysses*, he took his sentimentalism straight. He would have wrung every tear out of the song he sang to his young son, using the emotion as a way of displaying his voice. And the tears would have been some measure of the social reality he repressed.

28. Harriet Jacobs [Linda Brent], "Incidents in the Life of a Slave Girl," in *The Classic Slave Narratives*, ed. Henry Louis Gates, Jr. (New York: New American Library, 1987), 363. American slaves identified themselves with the Irish, or at least made use of the discourse regarding them. Recalling his departure from Colonel Lloyd's plantation for Baltimore at eight years of age, Frederick Douglass called up the proverb: "Being hanged in England is better than dying a natural death in Ireland" (*Narrative*, 272).

Stephen is introduced and initiated by a father's story that takes Baby Tuckoo past Betty Byrne and a father's song that entertains him as he sings it in his childish way. The story and song characterize the father as nurturing, protective, and benevolent. And this characterization is achieved at least in part by the repression of the women's stories and of the physical, social, and political reality in which they played an important part. But Stephen is also initiated by what one might call a mothers' story and a mothers' song, or chant. I am pluralizing *mother* to focus on the relationship between Stephen's mother and his nurturing Dante, who gave him cachous and fed his imagination by teaching him about far-off places. But I am also pluralizing *mother* to show how women are generalized as well as repressed and idealized in the opening pages, and how such generalization is a form of devaluation and marginalization, and leads to their characterization as agents of repression.

While the father's song and story reflect him as nurturing, protective, and benevolent, the mothers' story and song reflect them as repressive, threatening, and malevolent. When Stephen says that he is going to marry Eileen someday, his mother revises his story: "O, Stephen will apologise" (*P*, 8). Dante threatens with an alternative version: "O, if not the eagles will come and pull out his eyes" (*P*, 8). And their story is followed by a terrifying chant—"Pull out his eyes, / Apologise" (*P*, 8)—which is not attributed to any character and issues from some generalized author-ity.

The implications of the women's story and the song (which they do not sing but for which they are nonetheless held responsible) become clear when we see how Joyce revised his original epiphany. In the original, Mr. Vance is the active agent who revises Stephen's story and provides the threatening alternative: he comes in with a stick, saying "he'll have to apologise. . . . Or else . . . the eagles'l come and pull out his eyes." Then Mrs. Joyce assents: "O yes. . . . I'm sure he will apologise." And Joyce, hiding under the table, chants to himself: "Pull out his eyes, / Apologise."[29] By giving Mrs. Dedalus Mr. Vance's lines, Joyce turns her from an assenting subordinate into an active agent of repression. By giving Dante the young boy's lines, he shows how the women who nurture Stephen not only are implicated but actively contribute to the very power that

29. James Joyce, "Epiphanies," in *The Workshop of Daedalus: James Joyce and the Raw Materials for "A Portrait of the Artist as a Young Man,"* ed. Robert Scholes and Richard Kain (Evanston: Northwestern University Press, 1965), 11.

represses them—most specifically by becoming the locus of guilt for the next generation of repressed men. And by displacing the source of the terrifying chant, he shows the women to be agents of an unidentifiable, generalized, ubiquitous, terrifying force, which should be labeled totalitarian. He shows that they are repressing not only the particular desire to marry a Protestant but, as we see throughout Stephen's development, sexual desire in general. But he also shows how they are identified with the pervasive and incomprehensible forces that victimize them.

To understand more fully the totalitarian nature of this repression, its interrelated sources, and the way it was internalized by those whom it most repressed, we need to turn back to the time in which the mothers of Mrs. Dedalus and Dante were having children, and to the discourse of the Great Famine. In *Crimes against Fertility: Joyce and Population Control*, Mary Lowe-Evans shows how the English had accepted as part of their laissez-faire policy the Malthusian doctrine—that overpopulation would be controlled naturally as it outstripped the food supply—as a way of dealing with the growing population of Ireland. Laissez-faire was a form of repression that depended on the repression of social recognition and responsibility. It naturalized, generalized, and therefore suppressed the locus and agency of repression, which is how it achieved its totalitarian form.

From 1845 to 1851 the Irish population was diminished and physically as well as psychologically enervated as a result of starvation, malnutrition, epidemics of dysentery and scurvy and cholera, lack of fuel and bedding, ubiquitous corpses, enormous rats, a general feeling of despair, and—except for those who emigrated—a paralyzing passivity. Contributing to the despair and passivity was the impotence of the starving Irish as they daily faced the fact that there was plenty of food in Ireland. For it was only the potato—the most sustaining crop they could grow on the little land allotted them—that was blighted. The crops of the landlords flourished and brought prices in the English markets that the Irish could not afford.

What also contributed to the apathy and passivity, and hence the repression, was the Irish church. Cheryl Herr describes the range and pervasiveness of its repressive discourse. One of the ways it contributed to the passivity was through a form of idealization reflected in a letter written by the bishop of West Cork. In his history of Ireland (which Joyce owned), Michael Davitt tells of John O'Con-

nell, M. P. (eldest son of the Liberator), reading this letter in Conciliation Hall, Dublin: "'The famine is spreading with fearful rapidity,
and scores of persons are dying of starvation and fever, but the
tenants are bravely paying their rents.' Whereupon O'Connell exclaimed, in proud tones, 'I thank God I live among a people who
would rather die of hunger than defraud their landlords of their
rent!'"[30]

Idealization, sentimentalization, the repression of social reality,
and the repression of most active choices (including emigration) led
to the passivity and paralysis that Joyce illuminated in *Dubliners*
and *Portrait* and that he associated with the church. He also illuminated the church's most potent, pervasive, and successfully naturalized form of repression: the promotion of large families linked to
the repression of sexual desire. It is important to focus on the implications of this paradox, or apparent paradox. For, while to "increase
and multiply" (as Leopold Bloom would put it) seems at odds with
the English desire to decrease the Irish population, it was a way of
contributing to the Malthusian momentum. And of course it meant
contributing to the supply of cheap labor. Moreover, it also contributed to Irish passivity. The price of large families was largely paid
by women. And, while the price of sexual repression was paid by
both genders, the men, once married, achieved the most, and sometimes the only, gratification, for they could leave the family behind
all day and gain their conjugal rights when they returned at night.

Sexual repression—requiring celibacy until marriage, considering
masturbation a form of perversion and the body a source of sin—
was part of the church's discourse, from sermons to the confessional, that is, from the most public to the most private places of
association. And the contradictory message—be chaste and multiply—was a form of obfuscation which Joyce would expose in *Ulysses*. The church, then, added a psychological burden of confusion
and obfuscation to the physical and psychological burdens of the
large families that survived the Great Famine. When we consider
how the church enlisted mothers and nurturing women to become
its potent advocates, we can better understand the discourse of control, and what Joyce did first by picturing Stephen's mother and
Dante as agents of the repression, and then by displacing the dramatic source of the terrifying—indeed paralyzing—chant. He helps

30. Quoted in Lowe-Evans, *Crimes against Fertility*, 29.

us understand how the discourse of the church served the empire, and how the blame for its complicity and its victimization is projected onto the victims. If victimized lovers are idealized through beautiful songs of their death, victimized mothers are transformed into threatening agents of repression.

Dante requires special attention, for she is not a mother but a de facto spinster because of her power in the opening scene, and because of the role she plays in the climactic scene of little Stephen's life.[31] At the Christmas dinner the ineffectual men, Stephen's father and Mr. Casey, begin by talking of Christy, who manufactured "champagne for those fellows"—that is, bombs for the Fenians (*P*, 28). They go on to vituperate against the priests for betraying Parnell and rending him "like rats in the sewer" (*P*, 34). This leads into Mr. Casey's story, which concludes with his bending down to the "harridan" who was "bawling and screaming" about Kitty O'Shea and spitting a mouthful of tobacco juice, "*Phth . . . right into her eye*" (*P*, 37).

Dante opposes the men, but it is important to realize that she collaborates in telling their story by goading them on. One response actually incites Mr. Casey to tell the story of the famous spit. "I will defend my church and my religion," Dante tells Mrs. Dedalus, "when it is insulted and spit upon by renegade catholics" (*P*, 34). And her reactions are voiced in the violent language of the church against the Protestant Parnell: "*It would be better for him that a millstone were tied about his neck and that he were cast into the depths of the sea rather than he should scandalise one of these, my least little ones.* That is the language of the Holy Ghost" (*P*, 32). Indeed, she slams out of the room shouting, "Devil out of hell! We won! We crushed him to death!" bringing tears to the men's eyes (*P*, 39).

Mr. Casey and Dante become caricatures as they caricature the very language that builds on violence and denies them individual self-realization. But Mr. Casey's characterization is positive, indeed heroic, in contrast to Dante's. He may be a blowhard, but we empathize with his outrage, exult in his victory, and share in his laughter. Moreover, he gets the chance to tell his own story—and to picture himself as a kind of hero. Dante, by contrast, is identified with the harridan, the villain of Mr. Casey's story, and with the power of the church, even though she is victimized by its patriarchy and colonialist complicity. She is not allowed a story of her own. In fact, her story is

---

31. The discussion that follows has been adapted from my *Politics of Narration.*

shaped by Stephen's father, who was identified with the authorial voice in the opening of the novel. Mr. Dedalus had told Stephen that Dante "was a spoiled nun and that she had come out of the convent in the Alleghanies when her brother had got the money from the savages for the trinkets and the chainies" (P, 278). That is, he situated her in the unknown American frontier which excited the imagination of both the colonizers and the colonized. Ironically, he identified her not with the cowboys but, since she is rescued by her brother, with the Indians of the captivity stories. He also identified her by association with Africans and slavery. And, conversely and paradoxically, he identified her by implication with those who profited from slavery and colonialism, thereby identifying the victim with the forces of colonialism. But how did Dante get to America? Why did she enter the convent? Did she choose the convent as a positive alternative to the patriarchal family, as so many women did in the nineteenth century? What did she do in the convent? Did she come out of the convent willingly? What are we to make of her being rescued by a brother who exploited "savages"?

It helps to know that Dante was modeled on a woman "embittered by a disastrous marriage," who had been on the verge of becoming a nun in America when her brother, having made a fortune in Africa, died and left her £30,000.[32] But it helps more to know that the Allegheny convents were not what was pictured by the male imagination, that they were not houses of captivity or benighted retreats from the world but centers of care and learning, that they adapted to the customs and needs of the New World rather than perpetuate the traditions of the European closed convent, that they developed the first professionally trained nurses in the country, that they had the most advanced education for wealthy girls, that the tuition helped pay for educating the poor, that some sisters managed businesses to support their charitable work, that many orders had their own constitutions, which meant they were under the jurisdiction of neither a European motherhouse nor a bishop and were therefore freer than nuns, and perhaps all women, anywhere else in the world.[33]

Knowing all this might lead us to imagine a story for Mrs. Riordan that neither Stephen's father nor the novel's primary narrator could

32. Ellmann, *James Joyce*, 25.
33. See Mary Ewens, *The Role of the Nun in Nineteenth-Century America* (New York: Arno Press, 1978). I also learned about American nuns from conversations with James Kenneally, who has long been a historian of Catholic women.

tell. Dante would probably have been one of the poor girls, educated in sewing rather than Latin. But when she entered the order, her education would have changed. Indeed, we know she was exposed to books, had an appetite for knowledge and an attraction for what was beyond. After all, she taught Stephen "where the Mozambique Channel was and what was the longest river in America and what was the highest mountain on the moon (*P*, 10–11). Had she not been rescued by a brother who made a fortune exploiting "savages," she might well not have become the narrow-minded harridan pictured in *A Portrait of the Artist as a Young Man.*

I do not mean to rewrite Dante's story, only to show how it is shaped to identify her with the repressive power of the church and the forces of colonialism, how she becomes an instrument to perpetuate a power from which as an Irish-Catholic woman she is most excluded, how indeed she becomes its scapegoat in the novel's most dramatic scene. As with Betty Byrne, Lilly Dale, and Mrs. Dedalus, her story has been repressed, transformed, and appropriated to fit into the "ambitious" story of a young man seeking independence and power.

All four characters had stories that were central to the physical, social, and political reality of Stephen's world. But Betty Byrne is not recognized as a businesswoman. Lilly Dale's death is sentimentalized to repress its relation to the reality of women's overwork and sexual exploitation, of malnutrition and starvation, of colonization and slavery, of the discourses that feminized and simianized the colonized Irish. And the forces of repression are projected onto Stephen's mother and the nurturing Dante, who, while having internalized the ideology of the British colonizers and the Irish church, were among the most excluded and victimized by them. The women who participate in Stephen's introduction and initiation are appropriated by an authorial voice which positions them in Stephen's "ambitious" story, the bildungsroman, where a young man grows from innocence and marginality to experience and a position of social recognition and power. But the women are also repressed, transformed, and appropriated by equally powerful elements that enhance the authorial voice: the popular discourses of Ireland in the late nineteenth century, which would become more and more central to Joyce's interrogations in *Ulysses* and *Finnegans Wake.*

PART III

Narratives of Gender, Race, and Sex: *Ulysses*

6

Races and Chains:
The Sexuo-Racial
Matrix in *Ulysses*

Laura Doyle

In their encounter in Nighttown, Leopold Bloom urges Cissy Caffrey: "Speak, woman, sacred lifegiver!"[1] He wishes her to intervene in the scuffle between her companion, Private Carr, and Bloom's companion, Stephen Dedalus, who has insulted the king of England and now faces Carr's fist. Bloom calls upon Cissy, "the link between nations and generations" (*U*, 15.4648), the maternal paragon, to smooth over this blood feud as she smoothed over her younger brothers' sand castle fight on the beach. In this essay I show how *Ulysses*, as this scene hints, unearths a deeply embedded cultural matrix in which feuds over race or nationality and claims of "sacred" motherhood depend on each other. In this cultural matrix, racial and sexual myths cooriginate. In addition to exposing the fused roots of these myths in parodies such as the one just cited, the novel teases out the contradictory metaphysics of those myths and simultaneously pushes narrative toward a body logic—what could be called a somalogic—which challenges these myths' racialized and gendered metaphysics.

I begin by establishing the cultural construction, both ideological and historical, of the sexuo-racial mythologies parodied in *Ulysses*. I then go on to highlight *Ulysses*'s exposure of the dangerous, fool-producing power of Western sexuo-racial myths, especially in their hierarchical division of bodies by gender and race. Next, I argue that

---

1. James Joyce, *Ulysses*, ed. Hans Walter Gabler et al. (New York: Random House, 1986), 15.4648; hereafter cited in the text as *U*, with episode and line numbers.

structural features of the narrative challenge the hegemony of this mythology over the powers and intimacies of bodies, counterpointing that hegemony with what can be understood as an "intercorporeic" narrative structure. Finally, I propose that, despite its further unraveling of conservative bodily mythologies, the final "Penelope" section nonetheless remains attached by a single strong thread to the racialized mother figure of the older myths. In other words, Joyce leaves his book, with all of its parodic racial, sexual, and narrative shatterings, to be swept up and redeemed by the mother figure's overworked body. The very burdens of racial and sexual embodiment and disembodiment which the book shows to be too much hers—as in the parodic scene with Cissy—nonetheless remain hers at the end of *Ulysses*.

This reading is meant to indicate some of the ways in which modernism, or, more precisely, experimental modern fiction, allows the simultaneous return of racial and sexual repressions—revealing these repressions as inextricable from one another. If modernism develops in the context of a "war of the sexes," that war develops in the context of a "war of the races." Therefore, to the extent that sexual repressions return in modernist literature, the legacy of race surfaces with them. A few examples of the nineteenth- and early twentieth-century conception of a hierarchy, struggle, or war of the races must serve, for the purposes of this essay, to recreate the climate of racialism in which Joyce and modernism developed, especially in connection with the "battle of the sexes" which critics have of late considered formative to modernist experiments.[2]

The rise of new ideologies of womanhood in the eighteenth and nineteenth centuries has attracted the attention of feminist scholars, among them literary critics, for several decades. Scholars have shown that the separation of middle-class economic spheres into the private and the public derived authority in part from a new "science of woman," which pronounced women constitutionally

2. Sandra Gilbert and Susan Gubar document a "battle of the sexes" raging behind modernism in *No Man's Land: The Place of the Woman Writer in the Twentieth Century*, vol. 1 (New Haven: Yale University Press, 1988). Other works that frame modernism in terms of gender, of which there is an increasing number, include Bonnie Kime Scott, ed., *The Gender of Modernism* (Bloomington: Indiana University Press, 1990); Rachel Blau DuPlessis, *Writing beyond the Ending: Narrative Strategies of Twentieth-Century Women Writers* (Bloomington: Indiana University Press, 1985); and Shari Benstock, *Women of the Left Bank, Paris, 1900–1940* (Austin: University of Texas Press, 1986).

unsuited to intellectual and professional endeavors.[3] Brain measurements, nerve theories, skeletal drawings, and case studies furnished scientific support for this cultural and economic enclosure of middle-class women. Meanwhile, throughout the nineteenth and early twentieth centuries, similar kinds of data were gathered in support of what Nancy Stepan has called the "chain of races," fashioned after the Renaissance idea of a "chain of being," and arranging races in descending order from the lightest to the darkest.[4] These scientific theories of race and sex often became interlaced to a degree that deserves closer scrutiny from scholars of Western culture. At the least, given that these theories sometimes constructed explicit analogies between "higher" and "lower" races and sexes, one is justified in suspecting a deep structural interdependence between sexual and racial mythologies. I suggest that study of the shared matrix of these ideologies illuminates the stories and the narrative practices of modern novels, including *Ulysses*.

Many scientific theories claimed the existence of actual physical analogies between races and sexes, such as that "the female skull approached that of the infant, and in still further respects that of lower races, whereas the mature male of many lower races resembled in his pendulous belly a Caucasian woman who had had many children."[5] In such formulations races are gendered and sexes are racialized; the two systems of hierarchic value depend mutually on each other. The metaphor of "the couple" epitomizes this tautological circle of race-sex references. For instance, Gustave d'Eichthal suggested in 1839 that "the white race represented the male and the black race the female,"[6] and Gustave Klemm philosophized similarly that "humanity, in its entirety is, like man, one being which is divided into two parts, each necessary to the other, the

3. For evidence of the medical and scientific fortifications of the domestic enclosure of women, see, among others, Barbara Ehrenreich and Deirdre English, *For Her Own Good: 150 Years of the Experts' Advice to Women* (New York: Anchor Books, 1978); Londa Schiebinger, *The Mind Has No Sex? Women in the Origins of Modern Science* (Cambridge: Harvard University Press, 1989); Joan N. Burstyn, "Education and Sex: The Medical Case against Higher Education for Women in England, 1870–1900," *Proceedings of the American Philosophical Society* 117 (April 1973): 79–89.

4. Nancy Stepan, *The Idea of Race in Science: Great Britain, 1800–1960* (Hamden, Conn.: Archon Books, 1982); On scientific racial theories of the nineteenth and early twentieth centuries, see also Leon Poliakov, *The Aryan Myth: A History of Racist and Nationalist Ideas in Europe*, trans. Edmund Howard (London: Chatto Heinemann, 1974); George Stocking, *Race, Culture, and Evolution* (New York: Free Press, 1968).

5. Nancy Leys Stepan, "Race and Gender: The Role of Analogy in Science," *Isis* 77 (1986): 261–77.

6. Quoted in Poliakov, *Aryan Myth*, 221.

active and the passive part, the male and the female."[7] In these comparisons gendered polarities of passive and active provide metaphors for racial polarities, the neat fit of which in turn strengthens the effect of the gendered polarities. It is clear, at least on the level of metaphor, that racial and sexual mythologies grew and expanded together. Joyce parodies these intermingled mythologies, as we shall see.

Such gendered racialism has roots not only in the colonial European and American pasts but further back in the European history of conquering and conquered "races."[8] Thus, German nationalists of the sixteenth century belittled Europe's "Romano-Welsche" or southern peoples by characterizing them as a "woman-race, a crowd of weaklings."[9] With the rise of nineteenth-century colonialist racialism, and in the wake of class revolutions in Europe, which were very much perceived as race revolutions in which the native conquered finally took up arms against their foreign conquerors, such gendered racial theories again found wide expression. In the mid-nineteenth century Otto von Bismarck claimed that "the German, the teutonic race, may be regarded as embodying the virile, the fertilizing principle in Europe; but the Celtic and the Slav peoples are womanly races, passive, unproductive."[10] Likewise, Ludwig Feuerbach theorized that "the heart—the feminine principle, the sense of the finite, the seat of materialism—is French; the head—the masculine principle, the seat of idealism—is German."[11] Note here that nationalities become essentialized by being conflated with races, as they often were in sexuo-racial theories of a century ago. Joyce works within this contemporary conflation. He also particularly examines the metaphysics implicit in these racial and gender mythologies.

We do know that Joyce owned several books which "proved" the biological hierarchy of races and sexes. Marilyn Reizbaum has es-

---

7. Quoted ibid., 252.
8. For a thorough study of the importance of race in early European history, see Poliakov, *Aryan Myth*, and the older but classic work by Magnus Hirschfeld (produced in forced exile from Nazi Germany), *Racism*, trans. and ed. Cedar Paul and Eden Paul (New York: Kennikat Press, 1938). See also two early works by Jacques Barzun, *The French Race* (New York: Columbia University Press, 1932), and *Race: A Study in Modern Superstition* (London: Methuen, 1940). These works establish the European affiliation of nation and race which Joyce inherits.
9. Poliakov, *Aryan Myth*, 82.
10. Quoted in Hirschfeld, *Racism*, 169.
11. Quoted in Poliakov, *Aryan Myth*, 364.

tablished that Joyce had a sizable library of books on racial theory, especially books concerning the "Semitic race."[12] Among the sexuoracial theorists who seem to have made their way directly into *Ulysses* are Jules Michelet, mentioned explicitly (*U*, 3.167), and Otto Weininger, whose book *Sex and Character* (1903) Joyce owned.[13] In *Sex and Character*, Weininger argues that Jews are womanish and that all women are as deceitful as Jews. Some critics have suggested that Joyce used Weininger's work *uncritically* in creating his women and his Jews in *Ulysses*.[14] In contrast, I agree with Reizbaum that Joyce's creation of Leopold Bloom—the "new womanly man" who advocates intermarriage between races—*critically* parodies such gendered racialism (though sometimes with double-edged irony).

This interpretation of gendered racialism in *Ulysses* finds support in Joyce's nonfiction writings. In his lecture "Ireland, Isle of Saints and Sages," Joyce rejects racial categories and racial accounts of history, insisting instead on the fertility and inevitability of racial mixture. He points to Ireland's complicated history of invasions and migrations, holding up the country as a "vast fabric, in which the most diverse elements are mingled," and concluding that "in such a fabric it is useless to look for a thread that may have remained pure and virgin."[15] Joyce's choice of the phrase "pure and virgin" calls attention to the sexual mythology entwined with the racial mythologies he debunks here. In the conclusion of his lecture, Joyce's antiracialism leads him to question "the purpose of bitter invectives against the English despoiler" (*CW*, 173). In *Ulysses*, as we shall see, he implicitly questions invectives against both the English and the Jewish "invaders" and, in addition, exposes these invectives' masculinist interests.

As with most of his characters and materials, Joyce's parodic dis-

12. For documentation of Joyce's familiarity with racial theories, see Marilyn Reizbaum, "James Joyce's Judaic Other: Texts and Contexts" (Ph.D. diss., University of Wisconsin, 1985). Her appendix includes a list of books in Joyce's library related to racial theory. For Reizbaum's argument that in *Ulysses* Joyce critiqued Otto Weininger's book *Sex and Character* (cited in n. 13), see her essay "The Jewish Connection Cont'd," in *The Seventh of Joyce*, ed. Bernard Benstock (Bloomington: Indiana University Press, 1982).

13. Otto Weininger, *Sex and Character* (1906; rpt. New York: AMS Press, 1975). For a discussion of Michelet as a racial thinker, see Poliakov, *Aryan Myth*, 32–34.

14. Richard Ellmann, *James Joyce* (New York: Oxford University Press, 1972), 477. See also Reizbaum, "Jewish Connection," 229–30.

15. James Joyce, "Ireland, Isle of Saints and Sages," in *The Critical Writings of James Joyce*, ed. Ellsworth Mason and Richard Ellmann (New York: Viking Press, 1959), 165; hereafter cited in the text as *CW* with page reference.

tancing serves purposefully to separate him from those cultural inheritances which he once embraced but perhaps cannot be expected
to have let go altogether. For as a young man Joyce did, at least
briefly, embrace racialism. In an early college essay titled "Force,"
he defends the virtues of subjugation. He points to man's subjugation of the earth for farming, to his subjugation of the animals and
jungles to make way for civilization, and to the subjugation of the
"lower races of the world" by the higher, stating matter-of-factly
that "among the human families the white man is the predestined
conqueror."[16] All of these subjugations, the young Joyce ultimately
argues, demonstrate the necessity of man's "subjugation of his own
mental faculties" (CW, 22) for the development of high art and culture. As an adult Joyce had the originality to reject this kind of
masculinist racialism—most publicly by writing a novel that both
parodies that racialism and creates the very "chaotic mazes" and
"huge shapelessness" against which he warns "unsubdued" artists
in this essay (CW, 22). It nonetheless seems to me that the epic
scale of Joyce's parody in Ulysses reflects, among other things, both
the global scale of that racialism and the heroic effort required for
the purge, which inevitably leaves some trace of original attachment.

I mention Joyce's youthful absorption of racialism in large part
because it indicates, perhaps better than the books in his library,
the pervasiveness of gendered racialism at the turn of the century.
Joyce lived in an era of gendered racialism; it colored the world
narratives of philosophy, history, government, and science. He imbibed it as much as others did, and so he had his purging, parodic
work cut out for him. In fact, in the years of Joyce's coming of age
the rhetoric of gendered racialism became increasingly intense. At
the dawn of the twentieth century, in the decades before and during
the First and Second World Wars, thinker after thinker spoke of "the
vast rivalry" of world races, "the struggle of the Western races for
the inheritance of the future"[17] or the "ceaseless racial struggle for
dominance that no number of platitudes about brotherly love will
obviate."[18] An important element of this historical atmosphere is
the eugenics movement.

---

16. James Joyce, "Force," in Critical Writings, 22, 20.
17. Benjamin Kidd, The Control of the Tropics (New York: Macmillan, 1898), 1–2.
18. S. D. Porteus and Marjorie Babcock, Temperament and Race (Boston: Gorham Press, 1926), 327.

Eugenics epitomized the racialized, survival-of-the-fittest view of history that was dominant at the turn of the century, and it explicitly named that history's dependence on gender systems. Emerging near the end of the nineteenth century, eugenics was in a sense a science of how to win the race war. It promoted and received government funds for projects that aimed to institutionalize the feebleminded and the drunken, inhibit the procreative habits of the unfit and the colonized, and encourage early marriage and many children among the "best and the brightest."[19] It is the science of what the noted early twentieth-century eugenicist Caleb Saleeby, author of *Parenthood and Race Culture*, proudly called "race culture," an ideal of culture which assumes that each race has a form of culture (implicitly lower or higher) proper to it and that a racial culture propagates itself through proper intraracial marriages. Like others, most notably the Nazis, Saleeby believed that society's racial eugenics program should begin in grade school by teaching "the boy and the girl . . . that the racial instinct exists for the highest of ends. . . . To be manly is to be master of this instinct."[20] If to be competitively race conscious is to be manly, it should not surprise us to learn that "Woman is Nature's supreme instrument of the future" of race culture (*PRC*, xv). Man has the racial instinct; Woman serves as that instinct's instrument through procreation. In his 1911 book Saleeby advocates quite explicitly this interdependence between the dominant culture's racial and sexual programs when he proposes that "the modern physiology and psychology of sex must be harnessed to the service of Eugenics" (*PRC*, xv). In other words, the "science" of sexuality should be harnessed to the "science" of race.

And "harnessed" it was: prominent practitioners of the emergent science of "sexology," such as Havelock Ellis, considered racial improvement one of their more laudable potential contributions to society. While Ellis and others often favored the lifting of prohibitions on women's sexuality, for such thinkers that sexuality nonetheless reached its "highest" end in marriage, which served *its*

19. On the eugenics movement, see David Kevles, *In the Name of Eugenics* (New York: Alfred A. Knopf, 1985); Donald A. MacKenzie, *Statistics in Britain, 1865–1930* (Edinburgh: Edinburgh University Press, 1981); Mark H. Haller, *Eugenics: Hereditary Attitudes in American Thought* (New Brunswick, N.J.: Rutgers University Press, 1963, 1984); and G. R. Searle, *Eugenics and Politics in Britain, 1900–1914* (Leyden: Noordhoff International Publishing, 1976). On eugenics as rationalized and practiced in Nazi Germany, see Hirschfeld, *Racism*, esp. chap. 16.

20. Caleb Williams Saleeby, *Parenthood and Race Culture* (New York: Moffat, Yard and Company, 1911), xiv; hereafter cited in the text as *PRC*.

highest end in the reproduction of a race and, therein, a culture.[21] At the more repressive end of the spectrum, such harnessing of women's reproductive powers for racial ends found enforcement in the antimiscegenation laws in the United States and in Nazi Germany as well as in the anti–birth control pressures on racially "fit" mothers and the sterilization of the racially "unfit."[22]

Racial and sexual sciences, and the forms of dominance they underwrote, thus intersected and depended on each other. They intersected most crucially in what can be called racialized mother figures. Mothers took on a newly articulated importance not just as instruments and objects of men's power but also as pawns and vessels of white men's *racial* power. Saleeby's chapter on the "Supremacy of Motherhood" implicitly touts motherhood as the foundation for another kind of supremacy—a racial supremacy.[23]

In short, in the early twentieth century, cultural and material power had a perceived basis in (white) racial power, which in turn had its perceived basis in gender practices. Therefore, racialized mothers become focal points in early twentieth-century political and literary experiments. The concept of a sexuo-racial "matrix" points toward this mother-grounded center of sexual and racial mythologies. When we consider the charged appearance of nationalized or racialized mother figures in works by Thomas Hardy, Djuna Barnes, Jean Toomer, William Faulkner, Virginia Woolf, Jean Rhys, Zora Neale Hurston, Samuel Beckett, Ralph Ellison, and others, we may begin to see that experimental novelists—white and black, male and female, Jewish, Catholic, and Protestant—reshaped and

21. See, for example, Havelock Ellis, *Little Essays of Love and Virtue* (New York: George H. Doran, 1922), which includes chapters titled "The Objects of Marriage," "The Love-Rights of Women," and, at the end of the book, "The Individual and the Race." Whereas for the "lower races" what Ellis calls the "animal end of marriage" remains "the sole end of marriage" (64), among the "higher" races sex within marriage serves a spiritual end that may also be rationally directed toward securing the survival of the "fittest" races. If women experience a little sexual pleasure in this process, that is, Ellis assures us, a risk well worth the "future of the race."

22. For a discussion of miscegenation laws in the United States, see Haller, *Eugenics*, 158–59, and on such ideas and practices in Europe, see Hirschfeld, *Racism*, chap. 16 and Appendix C. On birth rates and sterilization practices, see Haller, *Eugenics*, 79–82, 130–41, 180; see also Hirschfeld, *Racism*, Appendix D.

23. Thought-provoking documentation of the nineteenth-century ideology of motherhood (although not in a racial context) appears in Mary Ryan, *The Empire of the Mother: American Writing about Domesticity, 1830–1860* (New York: Haworth Press, 1982). See also Barbara Welter, "The Cult of True Womanhood, 1820–1860," *American Quarterly* 18 (1966): 151–64.

rewrote the master narratives of racial and sexual lineage partly through these figures. Certainly Joyce did so.

For many such modern novelists, and quite consciously for Joyce, the assumption that most requires scrutiny in these mother-charged, sexuo-racial mythologies is that of metaphysics, particularly its subordination of materiality and the body. I suggest that modern authors witnessed the unraveling of metaphysical (or binary, mind-based) values insofar as these values were contradictorily woven into a racist and sexist but deeply materialist science.[24] On the level of historical event, we can observe that the flowering—or mushrooming—of racial and sexual biology in the form of Nazi Germany and Hiroshima finally withered that science, at least temporarily, with the spectacle of its millions of victims. Likewise, on the level of logic, racial and sexual science suffered from its own hubristic overreaching. That is, when racial and sexual science attempted to make biology the highest authority and the final cause of value while maintaining the body's status as the lowest, most debased value, attributing "bestiality" to women, blacks, Jews, and others, it mounted a contradiction. In practical terms, biology's study of the powers of the body handed collateral over to those who worked and produced and gave birth with their bodies, even as that science attempted to use a discourse of the body to sustain the oppression of those bodies. Science thus jeopordized the authority and logic of metaphysics when, in order to conserve sexuo-racial mythologies, it mingled metaphysics with its antimetaphysical materialism.

Experimental novelists such as Joyce fastened on this contradiction, with varying degrees of self-consciousness. They narrated,

---

24. The famous nineteenth-century racial theorist Robert Knox epitomizes this ambivalent attitude toward materiality in his book *The Races of Men* (Philadelphia: Lea and Blanchard, 1850), when he proudly claims that "the basis of the view I take of man is his Physical structure" (2), but then denigrates those he casts as *merely* physical, such as the Celts, who "never could be made to comprehend the meaning of the word liberty" (21), or the Bushmen, who are "content to live and perish like the beasts of the field" (158). Knox closes his book with this poignantly contradictory reverie: "For how many centuries yet to come, but for the interposition of the Saxon and the rifle, might not the stately giraffe with the gazelle eye, have adorned . . . the Calihari . . . ? Who shall say? The wild man was obviously unequal to their destruction" (309). What does it mean to be "unequal" to the destruction of stately beauty? The glories of the physical world are, for Knox, best met with a destructive subjugation that is nonetheless infused with nostalgia. The works of Charles Darwin exercise more propriety in tone but, on close reading, also may be seen simultaneously to celebrate and subjugate "physical structure."

whether intentionally or not, how that body logic worked and how it collapsed the mind-body binarism of metaphysics. Joyce pushed this collapse to the heart of a Western and Christian aesthetic committed to transcendence both of and through materiality. More generally, modern novelists including Joyce experimented with how the body moving through the world might be used to give the fictional world a new order: their narrators move down streets and into houses with the *bodies* of Joe Christmas, Leopold Bloom, Clarissa Dalloway, Sasha Jansen, and Janie Starks, recording a world absorbed through characters' flesh, creating a kind of narrative flesh perception. These bodies do indeed lean under the weight of sexual and racial codings, but they also move into interstices and gaps, into literal and metaphorical outbuildings, where such codes fail to enter. Ultimately, whether we see them as following or trumping the lead of science, experimental novelists put authority—authorship— in the hands of the body, letting materiality narrate identity, fragmentarily, exuberantly, painfully, conservatively, alternatively.

This narrative body logic, or somalogic, is also what led many authors to the mother figure: ideologically and historically, mother figures have been given responsibility for the reproduction of bodies, especially their racial and sexual status. As we shall see, narration through bodies that are in turn oriented toward embodying racialized mother figures is at least part of what Joyce attempts in *Ulysses*.

The Sexuo-Racial Matrix: A Day at the Races

Hence Cissy Caffrey. In her first appearance in the novel Cissy saunters along the contested borders of racial, sexual, and maternal identity. Watching her on the beach, Gerty MacDowell and Bloom, respectively, identify Cissy as a "tomboy" (*U*, 13.480) and as "the dark one with mop head and nigger mouth" (*U*, 13.898). Thus Cissy crosses to the other side of the norms of both girlishness and whiteness. The two violations seem to go hand in hand, set in comic contrast to the idealized qualities of the ever feminine and ever so white Gerty ("her face almost spiritual in its ivorylike purity" [*U*, 13.87]). Furthermore, Cissy openly, physically flouts proper sexual and racial boundaries. While Gerty flirts secretly with Bloom (the "dark-eyed" "foreigner" on the rocks [*U*, 13.416]), Cissy strides uninhibitedly over to him to ask the time. Similarly, Gerty feels repulsed by the noisy children and irritated by their interruptions of her blossoming sexual fantasies; Cissy easily mixes sexuality and maternalism, scolding and caressing and diapering her brothers seemingly all at once. Her language, which Gerty admires but rejects for herself, speaks crassly and boyishly of things bodily. Cissy's cluster of qualities places her in titillating opposition to the culture's idealized, purified sexuo-racial mythology. For Bloom, the "foreigner," her intermingling of sexual, maternal, and racial qualities makes her especially worthy of the role as a "link between nations and generations" (U, 15.4648).

Yet in Nighttown Cissy senses her own precariousness as she stands on the charged borderlines of sex and race. She responds to Bloom's appeal with "alarm." She "seizes" the British Private Carr's sleeve and insists: "Amn't I with you? Amn't I your girl? Cissy's your girl" (U, 15.4651). Cissy chooses in this scene not to get caught in the cross fire over men's blood feuds or arguments about the superiority of their respective races. She sides with the one in power, though she later attempts inconspicuously (and unsuccessfully) to deter him from smacking Stephen in the mouth. Cissy abdicates the racially and sexually mixed throne on which Bloom has placed her, evading the humiliations to which Bloom, in his Nighttown ascent (descent?) to that same throne, has just been subjected. Cissy knows that Bloom's ideals of open intercourse between nations and generations are eccentric and that Bloom himself is marginal: he has been labeled, as we shall see, "a bloody dark horse" (U, 12.1558) in the race among races.

Moreover, Cissy seems to know that a woman in her position has even more to fear than a man in Bloom's. For women who mix sexually with "other" races initiate, according to long-standing mythologies invoked repeatedly in Ulysses, that entrance of "strangers" into a nation that spells its destruction. Helen of Troy epitomizes the woman who betrays "her" nation to another; many a nation has succumbed to such betrayal, as several men in Ulysses emphasize. These characters, in explaining the downfall of their races and nations, ultimately always return to this model of history. Deasy bemoans that "england is in the hands of the jews. . . . Wherever they gather they eat up a nation's vital strength" (U, 2.346–50). He traces the presence of such strangers to the sins of woman, citing famous cases from history and the Bible: "A woman brought sin into the world. For a woman who was no better than she should be, Helen, the runaway wife of Menelaus, ten years the Greeks made war on Troy. A faithless wife first brought strangers to our shore here, MacMurrough's wife and her leman, O'Rourke, prince of Breffini. A woman brought Parnell low too" (*U*, 2.390–94). Thus, women bring whole nations "low" in allowing sexual infection by "strangers." Or, in the words of the song that shadows both Stephen's conversation with Deasy and the "Nighttown" scene, "The harlot's cry from street to street / Shall weave old England's windingsheet" (*U*, 2.356; 15.4641). Given that the "harlots" of Nighttown tend to be (or play-act being) of African descent (Zoe identifies herself as black [*U*, 15.1333] and "FlorryZoe" are called "jujuby women" [*U*, 15.4123]), such a lament implicitly places both sex *and* race at the heart of defensive definitions of nationhood.[25]

In the course of the novel, this sexuo-racial mythology about national destinies and downfalls weaves its own windingsheet, parodied from so many angles that finally the manifest destiny of the sexuo-racial argument itself meets its downfall. The notorious citizen mouths it in "Cyclops," the chapter of blindness and bad vision: "A dishonoured wife . . . that's what's the cause of all our misfortunes. . . . The adultress and her paramour brought the Saxon robbers here. . . . The strangers . . ." (*U*, 12.1156–58). In addition to Joyce's demystification of such accounts of Irish history in his lecture "Isle of Saints," here his epic-parodying narration makes laughable the transparent and defensive self-aggrandizement of such attitudes: "He said and then lifted he in his rude great brawny strengthy hands the medher of dark strong foamy ale, and uttering his tribal slogan, Lamb Dearg Abu, he drank to the undoing of his foes, a race of mighty valorous heroes . . ." (*U*, 12.1210–13). Joyce comically accumulates heroic adjectives and parodies what might be called the jargon of sexuo-racialist warrior legend—"tribal," "mighty race," "brawny strengthy," "heroes." The word "slogan" particularly hints at the critique implicit in the parody.

But even more telling is the narrational turn in the next paragraph to the Gold Cup, the horse race won by Throwaway, "a rank outsider" (*U*, 12.1219), says the older Lenehan, and lost by Sceptre, the unfortunate (phallic) betting choice of Lenehan and all his mates.

---

25. Zoe borrows from the Song of Solomon the line "I am black, but comely, O ye daughters of Jerusalem." See Don Gifford with Robert J. Seidman, *Ulysses Annotated*, 2d ed. (Berkeley: University of California Press, 1988), 470; hereafter cited in the text as *UA*.

Joyce's frequent and strategic interjection of the topic of horse races and in particular the winning of the Gold Cup by a "dark horse outsider" and the loss of it by Sceptre suggests its importance to the men's sexuo-racial posturing throughout June 16, 1904.[26] References to the horse races surface repeatedly in the men's conversation and serve to reveal an undercurrent of warriorism in their talk. In "Nestor" we learn that pictures of horses stand "in homage" on Deasy's walls; and Stephen, as he listens to Deasy's sexuo-racialist ranting, quoted earlier, imagines increasingly bloody and chaotic horse races, climaxing in an image of "jousts, slush and uproar of battle . . . a shout of spear spikes baited with men's bloodied guts" (U, 2.314–18). Stephen tries to imagine himself "among them" but is ridiculed by a voice that laughs, "You mean that knockkneed mother's darling who seems to be slightly crawsick?" Stephen thus falls short of the eugenic standards of a masculine warrior race, and therefore, as will become clear, he begins to deride the sexuo-racial matrix by which eugenic ideals are buttressed and protected.

In "Oxen of the Sun" the young men engage in pseudoscientific discussion of ideal child-bearing conditions in terms of "the future of a race" (U, 14.832) and of what is most "beneficial to the race . . . in securing the survival of the fittest" (U, 14.1284–85). This eugenic, Darwinian discussion echoes the pronouncements of early twentieth-century politicians and scientists which I alluded to earlier. Strengthening this connection, Joyce intermingles the boys' eugenic spoutings not only with an anti-Semitic diatribe against Bloom (who has chastised the young men for their "frigid genius") but also with an account of the Gold Cup horse race, on which both Madden and the younger Lenehan have lost owing to the "dark horse Throwaway" (U, 14.1132). Bloom, himself a member of an "other" race within Irish culture, is repeatedly associated in the text with this Gold Cup "dark horse"—this defeater of Sceptre (see note 26). In "Cyclops," for instance, the false rumor that Bloom won money on Throwaway yet still buys not a single round of drink ignites the race riot which so dramatically closes that section. The reader's knowledge of the falseness of the rumor exposes the scapegoating, self-defensive impulse of race races.

26. In addition to the references to horse races discussed in this essay, see also U, 5.526–48; 6.559; 7.385; 8.156; 8.813–45; 8.1008–19; 12.1550–65; 15.2140; 15.2936; 15.3965–90; 15.4862; 16.1242–80; 18.424–26. For an essay that pays similar attention to these horse race references, see Vincent Cheng, "White Horse, Dark Horse: Joyce's Allhorse of Another Color" in Joyce Studies Annual 2 (Summer 1991): 101–28.

The "Nighttown" scene with Private Carr also climaxes with a nationalistic race, and Joyce's sly use of the word "race" implies yet again how a racial paradigm underlies competitive nationalism. After the cry "Dublin's burning!" we learn in a long parenthetical description of brimstones and artillery and shrieks that "a chasm opens. . . . Tom Rochford, winner, . . . arrives at the head of the *national* hurdle handicap and leaps into the void. He is followed by a *race* of runners and leapers. In wild attitudes they spring from the brink. Their bodies plunge" (*U*, 15.4672–76, emphasis added). Especially since characters such as the "one-legged" sailor hold up the Irish as the "best jumpers and racers" (*U*, 16.1017), the word "race" in the Nighttown catastrophe clearly points in two directions—toward competitive running and toward a particular group of humanity—collapsing these two meanings into the implication that the human races race one another, a race of races ending in catastrophe.

That, in this scene, the "race of runners" is led by their hero and winner into "the void," and that the whole catastrophic moment is an imaginary inflation of a street scuffle, flaunts the idiocy of such racial mythology. But the insidious pervasiveness of this mythology—present not only among the younger and older men in *Ulysses* but also in, for example, the self-mythology of the white-skinned, blue-eyed Gerty as against the mop-headed Cissy—demonstrates that it is a force to be reckoned with on many levels and in many situations. In addition, that the race race climaxes when the runners' "bodies plunge" "in wild attitudes" into a void suggests that eugenic racing, despite its aim of physical racial improvement, actually distorts and sacrifices the bodies of its runners to an ideological void. An extended look at Stephen Dedalus's inner turmoil within this society illuminates more closely the "body" problems created by this ideological interdependence of race and gender.

The Sexuo-Racial Matrix: Stephen's Mother-Troubled Metaphysics

Stephen Dedalus is among the few in the book (Leopold and Molly being two others) who mock the idea that women's promiscuity invites strangers who bring on the downfall of the "original" race. Bawdily parodying the Bible, pagan myth, Shakespeare, scholarship, and himself all at once, he pronounces early in the "Oxen of the Sun" section:

> Bring a stranger within thy tower it will go hard but thou wilt have the secondbest bed. . . . Remember, Erin, thy generations and thy days of old, how thou settedst little by me and by my word and broughtedst in a stranger to my gates to commit fornication in my sight and to wax fat and kick like Jeshuram. Why hast thou done this abomination before me that thou didst spurn me for a merchant of jalaps and didst deny me to the Roman and the Indian of dark speech with whom thy daughters did lie luxuriously? Look forth, now, my people, upon the land of behest, even from Horeb and from Nebo and from Pisgah . . . .
> (U, 14.372–76)

Here Stephen parodies the biblical God himself as an adherent of the sexuo-racialist myth (as indeed he is) that identifies the promiscuous "miscegenation" of women ("thy daughters") as the curse of nations. Stephen's irreverent sexual puns, such as "it will go hard," and his loose intermingling (like Bloom's) of Erin and Palestine or Jews and Irish imitate this feminine promiscuity: his conflated references commit in language the "mixing" of values or referents that cross-national or cross-racial sexuality commits in blood. His inflated language also implicitly deflates that mythology which grandly equates the Hebrews and the Irish as chosen, wronged peoples. Stephen's parodic language hints that such epic racial equations perpetuate the very racialism by which their adherents are victimized.

Stephen feels and expresses these ironies as an emotional outsider who, according to race and gender, should be in the inner circle of Irish insiders. But for the same reason he also embodies most sharply the contradictions at the heart of what I call the sexuo-racial matrix. In many ways throughout *Ulysses*, Stephen identifies and is identified with "strangers" and with women, those welcomers of strangers. At the same time he moves among those who reject strangers and defame women; he himself sometimes openly defames or rejects women and Jews. At heart Stephen shares gendered racialism's contradictory attitude toward the world of the body; the contradiction afflicts his relationship to art, to religion, and to his mother.

In *A Portrait of the Artist as a Young Man*, we learn of Stephen's ambition to merge sensuality and ideality, or body and mind. As an aspiring artist he searches for the best means of folding the world of physical phenomena into what he conceives of as the spiritual energy of creation. He bucks the Irish Catholic suppression of sensuality, finally rejecting the Jesuit calling; but, in *Portrait*, his conception of spirit and matter conforms to the Western and Judeo-Christian tradition of feminizing matter and masculinizing the "immortal" shaping spirit of art. Feminist critics,[27] myself included, have noted the gender coding implicit in Stephen's desire, as expressed in *Portrait*, to transform the "sluggish matter of the earth [into] a new soaring imperishable being."[28] That women are merely a passive element, "sluggish matter," transformed by men into immortal art, is suggested by the text's juxtaposition of this fantasy against Stephen's sexually charged encounter with the girl on the beach, from whom he "turned away . . . suddenly" to thoughts of his art; her "image had passed into his soul forever," serving "the holy silence of his ecstasy" (*P*, 172).

Accordingly, in *Portrait* Stephen answers the question raised by Cranly as to whether a mother—as bodily origin—is "the only true thing in life" with a resounding no. His artistic ambitions are more "real." The question arises in his discussion with Cranly over Stephen's refusal to attend Easter Mass. Cranly insists that "whatever else is unsure in this stinking dunghill of a world a mother's love is not. Your mother brings you into the world, carries you first in her body. . . . Whatever she feels, it, at least, must be real. What are our ideas or ambitions? Play" (*P*, 242). Cranly chides Stephen specifically for denigrating the mothering body in relation to mind or "ideas." But Stephen silently objects; he cherishes a transcendent paternal autonomy realized by "mind." Cranly's comments move Stephen to his crucial decision about their friendship and about his vocation as a metaphysical artist: "Cranly had spoken of a mother's love. He felt then the sufferings of women, the weaknesses of their bodies and souls: and would shield them with a strong and resolute arm and bow his mind to them. Away then: it is time to go" (*P*,

27. I made this argument in a paper given at the "Ideologies of Modernism" Conference, West Chester University, West Chester, Pennsylvania, October 1986. For other related readings of Stephen, see the essays in Suzette Henke and Elaine Unkeless, eds., *Women in Joyce* (Urbana: University of Illinois Press, 1982), esp. Henke's "Stephen Dedalus and Women: A Portrait of the Artist as a Young Misogynist," 82–108.

28. James Joyce, *A Portrait of the Artist as a Young Man* (New York: Viking Press, 1982), 169; hereafter cited in the text as *P*.

245). As in the earlier scene on the beach, Stephen's response to the mortal reality of women is a turning away to "imperishable" art. He will not "bow" mind to body. Moreover, the secular aesthetic Stephen embraces at the end of *Portrait* is explicitly an aesthetic of the father and his race. He commits himself, in his closing journal entry, to pursuit of "old father, old artificer," and he expects, through that commitment, to "forge . . . the uncreated conscience of my race" (*P*, 253). As we have seen, in the early twentieth century, to follow the father's secular aesthetic is indeed to "forge" a culture mined from the resources of something called race. As with modern biological sexuo-racial ideologies, Stephen imagines that he will use the feminized body to found and substantiate a powerful racialized world of masculine spirit.

At the end of *Portrait*, then, although Stephen has rejected the priesthood, he has sustained a gendered and racialized metaphysics. At the same time, however, and without acknowleging it, he has inherited the metaphysical problematic epitomized in the Christian Easter event. Easter, of course, commemorates both the resurrection of Christ's body and its disappearance upward into the realm of divine spirit. Easter thus celebrates the merging of spirit and matter in the resurrected body of Christ at the same time that it rejoices in the dissolution of that merging as body gives way to the ascension to impalpable spirit. In comparison to the Old Testament, Christianity may move Western monotheism earthward, toward a fuller embrace of materiality in the person of Christ. But Christianity never approaches anything like a radical or eternal fusion of spirit and matter. Even in the literally phenomenal event of the Christian Easter, spirit in the end separates from matter and achieves its highest end in that separation. And yet that highest end could not have been reached without the body; in the story of Christ, spiritual transcendence needs, and values, the body as vehicle, as instrument. Christianity in short—in a way that prefigures the contradictory body logic of racial and sexual science—maintains a paradoxical relationship to materiality, both raising and denigrating it.

Hence, in choosing Easter Sunday to show his rejection of his mother's Catholicism, Stephen unconsciously signals his own ambivalent attitude toward the world of matter. His confusion remains unconscious all the way through *Portrait*. The high ambitions of his closing journal entries take flight not only toward a transcendent racial father but away from this ambivalent confusion. The height of Stephen's masculine, racial ambitions may in fact be in exact proportion with the depth of his maternal, alienated confusion.

I differ, however, with those who would consider this critique the last word on Stephen. I suggest that the sexual and racial metaphysical formula of transcendence (toward the racial father's masculine impalpable through the feminine palpable) is one that Stephen depends on at the end of *Portrait* but which in *Ulysses* he questions and parodies as well as sometimes reiterates. In *Ulysses*, that is, Stephen lets surface his conundrum; he allows the return of repressed contradictions and costs. He begins silently to acknowledge that his fearful sense of his own "feminine" characteristics (as a "knockkneed mother's darling") partly underlies his distaste for the idea of shielding women "with a strong and resolute arm"—for he may not have such an arm. More important, he keeps returning to—or allowing the return of—the image of his mother's body, a return that forces him to consider his attachment to and dependence on things feminine. The charge that he killed his mother's body for "ideas" haunts him partly because he has a deep, positive attachment to her body and partly because, if he *has* killed her body, or his connection to it, he has also killed his chances for folding the feminized body into a masculine, transcendent art.

In *Ulysses*, in short, Stephen realizes that to live in his body, to watch his "woman's hand" (*U*, 15.3678) hold a mirror for Buck Mulligan, to see the "white breast of the dim sea" (*U*, 1.244) and smell sea breath, to do these things is to recall his mother and her birthing of his body. Yet to recall his mother is also to be reminded of her decision to "bow" her mind *and* body to the church. She urges him, on her very deathbed, in the last gasps of bodily life, to accept the church. He refuses her plea and in so doing denies his own "blood." But to accede to her would also have been to conform to a church that denies his "blood"—not only in its sexual prohibitions but in its making a mere "servant," as we shall see, of the embodying mother. As long as his mother believes in the Easter version of the spirit-body relation—the body dies for the spirit—and as long as she urges that view on Stephen, he cannot wholly reconnect with his own body, which comes from her body. Stephen's body is on the rack, pulled in two directions.

Thus, although Stephen in *Ulysses* becomes more conscious of his dilemma, he cannot readily find a substitute for the transcendental formula he espouses at the end of *Portrait*. Publicly he parodies in *Ulysses* the old myth of racialized, masculine transcendence. Privately he suffers both longing for and bitterness toward the mother who holds his body captive. Repeatedly he sets up an antagonism between mother figures and children. At the beach he sees two midwives carrying their medical bags and suspects them of carrying an aborted or unwanted baby whom they will dispose of in the sea (*U*, 3.30–36). In the "Oxen of the Sun" chapter Stephen alone argues that in childbirth the infant's life should be saved before the mother's. His opinion would seem to have implications for his own situation, wherein he must sacrifice his subservient mother if he is to pursue his aesthetic desires—although, as we have seen, this solution cannot altogether succeed either. In his vision of his mother in Nighttown he at first gladly and without bitterness beseeches her, asking her to name that word that merges maternalism and sexuality, or transcendent and corporeal womanhood—love— but when she turns instead to prayer and damnation, his bitter alienation returns.

At the same time, among the newspapermen Stephen expresses contempt for asexual women in his tale of the two lifelong virgins who climb Nelson's column but are too frightened to take in the view it affords them. Not only is this story suggestively interspersed with a paperboy's cries offering a "racing special!" (*U*, 7.914), but also, when Stephen finishes his anecdote, the professor comments that Stephen reminds him of Antisthenes, who was the "son of a noble and a *bondwoman*," and about whom "none could tell if he were bitterer against others or himself" (*U*, 7.1035–37, emphasis added). As we shall see, Stephen sees his own mother as a bondwoman—her body in thrall to a paternalistic church—whose bondage he himself must serve. His position makes him bitter toward himself *and* others.

For Stephen does not blame his mother only. He sees beyond her supplication to the conditions of paternity and racial paternalism that make her, like Cissy Caffrey, "serve her conqueror," or that make her "pray," as Cissy does in effect to Private Carr, for favor with the conqueror. Early in the "Telemachus" chapter, through Stephen's memories, we learn of May Dedalus's "secrets: old featherfans, tasselled dance cards, powdered with musk, a gaud of amber beads in her locked drawer. . . . Phantasmal mirth, folded away: muskperfumed" (*U*, 1.255–63). That these baubles of Stephen's mother's adolescent sexuality are "folded away" or kept in "locked drawers," and that he dreams of them here, may well indicate an oedipal relation. But what is an oedipal relation other than the struggle with an artifical paternal law against sexuality in the mother, a law deeply baffling to children who have felt the mother's caresses and known her body as intimately as anyone? If fathers caressed and fed and cleaned as much as mothers, and the split between virgin motherly home and licentious fatherly polity were absent, children might not feel with such deep nostalgia that desire for the acknowledgment and continuation of the mother's desire. For it seems to me that the tone of Stephen's feeling when he thinks of "the white breast of the dim sea" together with tasseled dance cards and phantasmal mirth (folded away) is not sexual lust for the mother but nostalgic sadness for her lost sensual past—and sadness for her as much as for him. That Stephen returns to these images of his mother's past and recognizes how they are "folded away" suggests his sympathetic understanding of the limitations within which she lived her life.

The wider social conditions that set up these limits emerge more clearly in Stephen's thoughts about the milkwomen. Just as Mrs. Dedalus has her "secrets" and comes to Stephen decaying and "silent" in a dream, so the milkwoman enters the opening chapter "old and secret . . . maybe a messenger" (*U*, 1.399–400). Stephen imagines her as "the lowly form of an immortal serving her conqueror and her gay betrayer," (*U*, 1.405). After she demurs to the mocking Buck Mulligan and the condescending Haines, Stephen reflects that "she bows her old head to a voice that speaks to her loudly, her bonesetter, her medicineman: me she slights" (*U*, 1.418–19). He goes on, puzzled by but resigned to her deference "to the voice that will shrive and oil for the grave all there is of her but her woman's unclean loins, of man's flesh made not in God's likeness, the serpent's prey. And to the loud voice that bids her be silent" (*U*, 1.420–22). Stephen refers here to the Catholic practice of anointing a dying man's genitals but not a woman's, suggesting again that the milkwoman defers to a tradition that scorns her sexuality yet buys her milk.

Stephen's equation of the loud voices of Haines and Mulligan with those of the church fathers—though neither Haines nor Mulligan is particularly reverent—suggests that Stephen is thinking of his mother and *her* deference to "her conqueror and her gay betrayer" as

well as of the milkwoman's. This link implies that Stephen understands his mother as conquered by a tradition that says man's but
not woman's flesh is made in God's likeness; he recognizes that the
muteness of what he earlier called his mother's "mute secret
words" (U, 1.272) is enforced by the "loud voices" of the church
fathers that "bid her be silent."

If Stephen's mother is a servant, Stephen is, as he calls himself
just before this passage, "the server of a servant," for he is flesh of
her ungodly flesh (U, 10.312). Moreover, he too demurs repeatedly
to, or serves, the loud voices of Mulligan and Haines; if he could,
he would be "among them," as he says in the horse-racing fantasy
quoted earlier. Like the women, he serves in order to share the
society of his gay betrayers. Not surprisingly, then, he has his
mother's face and his sister's eyes (U, 10.865, 15.4949, 16.1804).
Likewise, his hands, which hold up the mirror by which the brash,
manly Mulligan shaves his coarse, thick beard, are a "woman's
hands" (U, 15.3678).

Most of all, as befits the sexuo-racialist order of his society, Stephen's phrase "server of a servant" associates him with an "other"
race as well as the other sex. This phrase places both his and the
women's servitude in the context of a long history of such service
codified along racial lines, for it alludes to the fate of Ham's son
Canaan. According to biblical lore and as emphasized by nineteenth-century racialists, Ham, the cursed son of Noah, is the ances-
tor of the African peoples. And why were Ham's descendants cursed
by Noah to be "servers of a servant"? Because Ham was the son
who saw Noah naked as he drunkenly slept. Ham knew the naked
body of his father, saw behind the clothes and the roles of Noah's
patriarchal stance to his bare and inebriated body. For this bodily
knowledge of the father's vulnerability, his descendants were condemned to serve Japheth, Shem, and their descendants. And likewise, as nineteenth-century racial theorists reasoned, because of
Africans' tendency to indulge their sensual curiosity, these descendants of Ham were fit only for bodily service to the chosen servants
of God: the whiter descendants of Japheth and Shem.[29]

29. Perhaps the most famous racial theorist to use these biblical brothers as the basis
for racial theories is the Frenchman Count Arthur de Gobineau in his influential book
The Inequality of the Races (1853–54). Gobineau is also one of those who aimed to discredit darker "races" by associating them with femininity and to discredit women by
association with darker "races." For accounts of the place of the curse of Ham and other
religious arguments in the rise of nineteenth-century racial theory, see Martin Bernal,

Even in the earliest pages of *Ulysses*, then, Joyce invokes the sexuo-racial matrix which fixes the oppressive center of Western—in this instance Anglo-Irish—culture. By reference to that culture's racial framework, the text associates Stephen, his mother, and the milkwoman with an other-racial sexuality, just as later, by reference to a gender framework, Stephen's jeering friend associates him with an other-gender racial mixing: Stephen, the "jewjesuit" (*U*, 9.1159), practices "woman's reason. Jewgreek is greekjew. Extremes meet" (*U*, 15.2096–97). In both cases Joyce hints at the interdependence of race and gender constructs. He makes clear how race lines serviceably mark an "other" side by which sexuality that does not serve the claims of paternal lineage can be cast as "dark" and "impure" and "slavish." And he suggests how femininity likewise provides an "other" category by which those who violate or subvert racial boundaries that uphold paternal lineage can be shamefully cast as "womanly," "feminine," or "knockkneed." The text of *Ulysses* positions Stephen and his mother within this sexuo-racial framework, and it develops that gendered and racialized relationship as constitutive of Stephen's aesthetic and sexual conflicts.

The Sexuo-Racial Matrix: Implicating Shakespeare

In espousing his critique of paternity through Shakespeare, Stephen ferrets out an even more precise interdependence between ideologies of race and sex. He suggests, using Shakespeare as an example, that the invisibility of men's paternity provokes anxiety—especially because property and power are at stake—which motivates a mythology of race. That is, as his theory suggests, traceable physical characteristics of race together with an *idea* of ethnic or racial purity can support the claims of an otherwise untraceable fatherhood. For any dominant group, identifying and celebrating group or racial characteristics may become an economically and politically driven obsession which, when generalized within a tribe, becomes a mythology of race. The "endogamous" or "exogamous" circulation of women in marriage has served to construct—to fortify

---

Black Athena, vol. 1 (New Brunswick: Rutgers University Press, 1987), and Poliakov, *Aryan Myth*, 7–8.

or extend—such ethnic or racial boundaries, and therein partly to define men's economic and political claims.[30] Within such race- or group-bounded marriage practices, mothering women serve at least two valuable political and economic functions: they "preserve" by their (enforced) fidelity the men's racial characteristics; and they channel within the group, according to proper racial or class or ethnic inheritance boundaries, men's political and material power. With an idea of race in place, in other words, men can sustain a racial paternity which takes the pressure off an otherwise ever challenged individual paternity and which legitimizes men's control of property or resources, both through and including women.

As Stephen sees it, renowned artists who become spiritual "fathers of a race" are in the most enviable position: they can, through their art, lay claim to the body of every woman of the race and therein play the part of every man of the race. But, as Stephen also shows, they thus come face to face with the contradictions of metaphysical aesthetics. In his theorizing about Shakespeare, Stephen again compares Western culture's contradictory aesthetic metaphysics with its paradoxical Christian metaphysics. He also borrows, as he did in his identity as the "server of a servant," from the point of view of a racial "other," calling upon the authority of "Sabellius, the African, subtlest heresiarch of all the beasts in the field" (U, 9.862). Sabellius claimed, in his own Christian complication of the spirit and matter relation, that "the Father was Himself His Own Son" (U, 9.863). Stephen takes a similarly heretical view of Shakespeare, identifying him not only with the put-upon hero Hamlet but with Hamlet's father, the vengeful ghost, as well. Stephen suggests that, as an artist, Shakespeare could be father, son, mother, and wife, which raises him above the role of "father of his own son merely" and allows him to make himself instead "the father of all his *race*" (U, 9.868, emphasis added). Thus, as artistic father of a *race* of men (or of a corpus of cultural self-definitions around which members of the white race have rallied), Shakespeare seemingly transcends the limits of being one man or another.

But Stephen goes on to expose Shakespeare as a man sunk in paternal blood jealousies, one who strives for transcendent racial

30. Suggestive evidence on the economic and structural function of the circulation of women in marriage can be found in Gayle Rubin, "The Traffic in Women: Notes toward a Political Economy of Sex," in *Toward an Anthropology of Women*, ed. Rayna Reiter (New York: Monthly Review Press, 1975), 157–210, as well as in the anthropological studies of Jack Goody and Claude Meissailloux.

paternity over and against those sexual and blood jealousies—as did Stephen at the end of *Portrait*. Shakespeare remains caught, Stephen argues, in the contradiction of having to borrow from that blood life to create his transcendent art. Stephen points out, first of all, that "all events brought grist to [Shakespeare's] mill" (including instances of "witchroasting" and "jewbaiting" [*U*, 9.748–54]); and then Stephen links Shakespeare's personal life to the familial drama of *Hamlet*. The character Hamlet is Shakespeare's son Hamnet, and the vengeful ghost is Shakespeare himself speaking to his real son about the possible relationship of his real wife, Ann Hathaway, with Shakespeare's real brother Richard.

Yet Stephen makes sure to deflate any sentimental sympathy for Shakespeare that this scenario might evoke when he establishes Shakespeare as a man of double standards who himself "dallied . . . between conjugal love . . . and scortatory love" during twenty years of marriage (*U*, 9.631–32). He paints him as a rich man and a lender who "drew Shylock out of his own long pocket" and furthermore as "a man who holds [as] tightly to what he calls his rights over what he calls his debts [as he does] to what he calls his rights over her whom he calls his wife" (*U*, 9.788–91). Furthermore, Stephen argues that, although Christians attribute avarice to Jews, Shakespeare was vulnerable to that "avarice of the emotions" in which "love given to one near in blood is covetously withheld from some stranger who, it may be, hungers for it" (*U*, 9.781–82). Shakespeare aimed to ensure that "no sir smile neighbour shall covet his ox or his wife" (*U*, 9.790). Stephen thereby points to the economic stakes in racial and sexual jealousies and boundaries; and he heretically argues that such an economy produces the complicated "mortal" underpinnings of Shakespeare's "immortal" art.

Thus Stephen challenges the view of Shakespeare as a universal "myriadminded" man and offers one exposing his petty entanglement in the blood jealousies endemic to the interdependent practices of racial division and patriarchal marriage. In this way Stephen involves Shakespeare and other canonized artists in the same metaphysical dilemma with which he himself struggles. Like him, such artists need the blood life to create their art, as he needs the feminine "sluggish matter"; but the point of their art, its advantage to them, is exactly to transcend that blood matter and transform it and themselves into masculine "impalpable, imperishable" beings, made immortal by association with a "race." In his most powerful moment among Irish insiders (the floor is his), then, Stephen ironically uncovers the control-seeking racialism and paternalism at the heart—and the height— of "universal" Western art.

Stephen's recognition of this central metaphysical contradiction indicates how he has shifted his attitude since the end of *Portrait*. Perhaps his most penetrating insight is that traditional aesthetics lead, after all, not to a triumphantly transcendent art but to a covertly "androgynous" art—which, in a racial-patriarchal context, is an assailable, vulnerable achievement. And yet Stephen ends by parodying the possibilities of a more overt androgyny in art, mocking aesthetic androgyny and therein encouraging it to remain covert. When Stephen concludes that *Hamlet* "foretold" an "economy of heaven" in which "there are no more marriages, glorified man, an androgynous angel, being a wife unto himself" (*U*, 9.1051–52), he not only parodies Hamlet and Saint Matthew (*UA*, 250) but also hints that Renaissance family dramas such as *Hamlet* point toward the (modernist) day when the sexuo-racial logic would stumble into its own metaphysical contradictions, perhaps giving way to an "economy" that no longer rests on group-bounded, patriarchal marriage. While this prophecy is provocative, its comic image of "glorified man, an androgynous angel, being a wife unto himself" stops short of imagining truly radical alternatives—alternatives in which the patriarchally charged word "wife," for instance, has no place.

Hence, although parody serves as Stephen's means of purging himself of sexuo-racial mythologies, the absence of any other kind of intersubjective performance by him suggests an inability to step outside the world of those mythologies. His parodic pose fixes him, in fact, within that world. We should remember that Stephen fabricates this entire deconstruction of Shakespeare, Christianity, and gendered racialism to win a hearing inside, not outside, his culture—among the intellectuals of Dublin. To *some* extent the same is true for Joyce, in a European context, as we shall see in my conclusion. First, however, I emphasize the opposite: Joyce's supplement to Stephen's strictly parodic pose, in which we find that Joyce authors a somalogical narrative order in *Ulysses* that surpasses parodic performance.

Narrative Embodiment: The Aesthetic of Intersection

With Stephen in *Ulysses*, Joyce moves at least to a position of parody of transcendent aesthetics and unfolds a psychological critique of the sexuo-racial matrix of patriarchal culture, especially as it debilitates the "insider" son's long-term relation to an "insider" mother such as Mrs. Dedalus. With the character of Leopold Bloom, by contrast, Joyce delves into the daily intersubjective dialectics of a racial "outsider," one who is at once excluded from, oriented toward, and essential to the dominant culture. In bringing together Stephen and Bloom, Joyce continues his revision of the sexuo-racial order. By temporarily placing the insider son in the mixed motherly-fatherly and Jewish-Irish hands of the outsider, Joyce suggests that fatherhood must give up both its gender and its racial loyalties if the Stephens of the world are to find what they need.

Moreover, Joyce challenges the metaphysics of the sexuo-racial order by focusing on the bodily sensibility of his cross-gendered and cross-racial character Bloom. In other words, through Bloom, Joyce himself looks at the racial and sexual specimen pinned under the microscope of contemporary science. He sheds science's contradictory attention to and abhorrence of humans' physical structure, instead tracing the body's activities and powers with unflagging fidelity and astonishing linguistic enthusiasm. In doing so with Bloom's character, Joyce moves toward an anatomy of what I call intercorporeity—or bodily situated intersubjectivity.

The term *intercorporeic*, which I use to characterize these textual practices, is borrowed from the French phenomenologist Maurice Merleau-Ponty.[31] Intercorporeity, whether inside or outside texts, may be most simply understood as the bodily corollary to intersubjectivity. That is, in part we orient ourselves toward one another, know one another, and know the world by way of our bodily presences, gestures, paces. Our bodies shape, gesture, stage, and display our orientations, even as they measure and move in concert or tension with the orientations of other bodies. Bodies continually pass and absorb hugely important messages, giving contour to an intentionality that is neither the body's alone nor the mind's. Furthermore, this interbody knowledge rests on a shared medium of materiality; or, in other words, human-to-human intercorporeity depends on human-to-phenomenal-world intercorporeity: the air allows or invites us to see one another, the ground allows our steps' movement toward or away from one another. Finally, most headily, it may be that the air and the ground live out an intercorporeity

31. See especially Maurice Merleau-Ponty, "The Intertwining—The Chiasm," in *The Visible and the Invisible* (Evanston: Northwestern University Press, 1968).

among themselves, among the nonhuman things of the phenomenal world. This is a layer of intercorporeity which Virginia Woolf in particular, more so than Joyce, aims to represent. Joyce is most preoccupied with human-to-human intercorporeity, such as with Bloom's quiet experience of the men's knees pressed together in the funeral carriage.

I should acknowledge that the word *body*, in this context, becomes as inaccurate as *mind*, implying a mind-body separateness counter to the essence of the idea of intercorporeity. Yet I often use the word *body* here, working as I do within a transitional state of our culture, as well as of my perception. The move toward a de-separated concept of mind and body must begin with a shift in emphasis, highlighting materiality as active, and interactive, rather than simply the "sluggish matter" catalyzed by mind. Thus, to use the word *body* is a compromise, but for now a necessary one.

Joyce's representation of intercorporeity has at least two dimensions. First, Joyce's Leopold Bloom lives out rather felicitously the crass bodiliness with which nineteenth- and early twentieth-century racial theories frequently associated Africans and Jews—a bodiliness the text reveals as more than merely crass, verging instead at times on the exquisite or the inspired. Joyce's narrator minutely records, even merges with, Bloom's bodily sensibility. Second, and more broadly, Joyce organizes his narrative around the intersections of bodies, an organization that imitates the preoccupations of his character Bloom. (In both of these narrative features *Ulysses* bears comparison to William Faulkner's *Light in August*.)[32] In organizing his narrative around the literal path crossings of differently embodied characters—of Bloom and Stephen, or Bloom and Boylan, or Cissy and Bloom and Gerty, or Stephen and Molly—Joyce finds structural representation for his challenge to the path-segregating narratives of dominant sexuo-racial mythologies.

Stephen Dedalus *strives*, as we have seen, for corporeal groundedness—"Hold to the now, the here, through which all future plunges to the past" (*U*, 9.89)—and he supplements Bloom's dramatization of intercorporeity with his theoretical meditations on dialectic and his dialogue with Bloom. But Stephen rarely relaxes

32. In Faulkner's novel, for instance, bodies in motion define intersecting narrational horizons, as with Lena Grove and Armstid in the novel's opening scene; likewise the novel uses spatial organization to represent a collapse of gender and racial boundaries when its racially and sexually ambiguous characters converge on the town of Jefferson.

into the world of sensation. He never seems to achieve that for which he strives, although in temporarily giving himself over to Bloom he follows a good instinct. In the end it is Bloom whom Joyce's text most pervasively—even if sometimes parodically—emulates, especially in its narrative structure of physical intersection. One could say the text projects its coveted values onto Bloom, a move by which it attempts to recover, or re-father *and* re-mother, Stephen. But I will return to these suggestions later, following their "return" in the latter part of the text.

To say that Bloom is a man particularly sensitive to sensation and to bodies is to state the obvious. His bodily sensitivities as rendered by Joyce, positively impinge on the reader. In its first sentence about him the text relishes Bloom's own "relish" of "inner organs" (*U*, 4.1), and Molly, at the other end of the book, admires him for knowing "a lot of mixedup things about the body and the inside" (*U*, 18.180). We might wish Bloom somewhat *more* indifferent to the comings and goings of Nosey Flynn's nose phlegm, in fact. But we accept these so as also to delight in his delicate attention to intercorporeic sensation in small, quiet moments, such as when he notes that the funeral carriage, which he shares with Dedalus, Cunningham, and Power, on one of its turns "united noiselessly their unresisting knees" (*U*, 6.228).

It might be argued that this perception belongs to the narrator rather than to Bloom. I agree that the narrator narrates this line. But part of my point here is that the narrator observes and structures the world of *Ulysses* through the bodies of characters. If this observation seems to belong to the narrator because it describes a sensation of several characters at once, I would point out that the narrator *can* speak at once of several characters because their bodies touch, or unite, at this moment. As in Woolf or Faulkner or Toni Morrison, the intercorporeic narrator in Joyce synchronizes character perceptions *through* the material world the characters inhabit in common. The "break in the hedge" in *To the Lighthouse*, for example, both *joins* the perceptions of Lily and Mr. Bankes and *pivots* the text's narration of Lily's and Mr. Bankes's perceptions. In varying degrees such authors' narrators may themselves be said to inhabit the material world, recording characters' lives as they impinge on that world (that is, constantly) or on one another through it.

In short, I would argue that the line belongs to Bloom as well as to the narrator: what Bloom and the narrator have in common is their bodily perceptiveness. Like the narrator, Bloom achieves intersubjectivity through bodily signals, such as with the blind man ("Knows I'm a man. Voice" [*U*, 8.1102]) or when he thinks in the pause that follows the lowering of Dignam's coffin, "If we were all suddenly somebody else" (*U*, 6.836). That is, Bloom (like the narrator) pursues a desire to place himself inside others' bodies and by this means know their point of view. Accordingly, Bloom (like the narrator) dwells on the "meetings" of eyes, or of gazes, as with Mrs. Breen ("Look straight into her eyes. I believe in you. Trust me" [*U*, 8.250]); and he appreciates the complex dynamics of watching oneself be watched or watching oneself watch, as Kimberly Devlin has detailed in her analysis of Bloom's visually enacted sex with Gerty MacDowell.[33] In general, Bloom repeatedly espouses the value of "see[ing] ourselves as others see us" in a way that merges subjective with physical "seeing" (*U*, 8.662; 13.1058).

For Bloom, then, a person so sensitive to intercorporeity, or the physical-subjective intersections of one body with another, his unintended yet seemingly fateful meetings with Blazes Boylan in the course of his day have a potent impact. Bloom marvels at his repeated near collisions with his rival, especially when "just that moment I was thinking [of him]" (*U*, 6.197). As this comment suggests, these meetings display for Bloom the affinity or equivalence between internal and external, mind and matter. On the same day that Boylan and Bloom's wife will consummate their affair, Bloom sees Boylan from the funeral carriage, avoids him at the barroom of Miss Douce and Miss Kennedy, swerves out of his sight into the museum. The intersecting orbits of these bodies with common interests seem to place motive and matter in a magnetic, interactive relation rather than an active-passive, mind-willing-matter, hierarchical one. For we can hardly say that Bloom wills these intersections, even unconsciously, when it is not at all clear that he desires them. In fact, we can read Bloom's response to his sightings of Boylan in two ways: one could argue either that, in sighting but avoiding Boylan, Bloom shrinks from a face-to-face encounter with his rival (as he does later with his sexual partners Gerty and Molly); or that, in sighting but avoiding Boylan, he takes wonder-struck note of unintended daily intersections of bodies and yet respectfully honors those bodies' separate trajectories, honoring those encounters and trajectories even when they conflict with his desires.

33. Kimberly Devlin, "The Female Eye: Joyce's Voyeuristic Narcissists," in *New Alliances in Joyce Studies*, ed. Bonnie Kime Scott (Newark: University of Delaware Press, 1988), 135–43.

In the treatment of Bloom in Nighttown the text seems to explore both readings of him—as cowardly cuckold/pervert who engages in sordid, unmanly encounters and as sensitive champion of unscripted meetings. He is scourged as a ridiculous man of "Mongolian extraction" (U, 15.954) who foolishly "so wants to be a mother" (U, 15.1817). He is sat upon and spat upon as a grotesque "example of the new womanly man" (U, 15.1798–99). But a dissenting faction also gains the floor and elects him the messianic mayor of Dublin, whose call for "mixed races and mixed marriage," "union of all jew, moslem, and gentile" (U, 15.1686) meets with cries of approval. His advocacy of "intersections" or overlappings of sexes and races wins him both admiration and condemnation. The envelope of parody encasing both of these views of Bloom and many others in the book has left readers with few clues as to Joyce's view, a state of things that probably best fulfills Joyce's intentions.

Joyce reveals his earnestness to some degree insofar as he privileges structures of intercorporeic encounter in the same way Bloom does. In tracing the paths of his different characters, his narrative extends or enacts the structure of intersection epitomized in the experiences of Bloom with Boylan. In the case of the criss-crossing paths of Boylan and Bloom, it is significant that at one point Bloom nearly intersects with Boylan unaware: Boylan flirts inside with a shopgirl while Bloom peruses the books outside at a nearby bookstall. Both men are choosing presents at this moment for Molly Bloom (U, 10.315). This coincidence appears as the text's special knowledge, revealed to the reader but unknown to the characters. In unveiling this near intersection the text may evoke in the reader Bloom's own experience of and conviction about the wonder of intercorporeic coincidence: the magnetic pull of two "opposite" bodies which have a shared ground or interest.

Or the text may be parodying Bloom's foolish attention to such chance intersections. To load coincidental meetings with meaning, as Bloom does, might be comically to overvalue the realm of physicality, which perhaps remains purely nonreferential and literal, unreadable. From this angle the text's stylized pattern of coincidental path crossings may be read as a comic or parodic treatment of intercorporeity. Certainly Joyce arranges comic collisions, such as when Father Conmee stumbles upon Vincent in the bushes with his girl. I maintain, however, that, even if parodic, Joyce's structure of physical intersection reflects his investment in the intercorporeic, especially when considered together with other features of the text such as his minute linguistic attention to sensuous phenomena. To a considerable degree the text depends on intercorporeic intersections for its narrative order, thus extending the perceptual practices of Bloom. In the end, Joyce's comical narrative stylization of intercorporeity, for which authors such as Faulkner or Woolf or Morrison may be said to have found a more nuanced, phenomenal form, may indicate the limits of Joyce's imagination of intercorporeity at least as much as it reveals a mocking intention. Despite the essentially comic, caricature-tending strain of his imagination, Joyce nonetheless takes seriously, as a philosophical or cosmic ground for human experience, the world-making phenomena of intercorporeity.

Consider as a further example of patterned narrative intersections the text's attention to the flyer handed to Bloom proclaiming "Elijah is coming." Bloom throws the flyer away, but he returns again and again to the possibility of Elijah's coming. Likewise, the novel is studded with references by Stephen and other characters to Elijah or a Messiah. More important, on the level of narrative structure the text reiterates Bloom's meandering yet pregnant pattern of intersections by following the course of the thrown-away flyer. Cast here and there by wind and water, the flyer appears and reappears in the paths of various characters throughout the text. The text weaves this flyer into its critique of the sexuo-racial mythology by repeatedly refering to it as a "crumpled throwaway" (U, 10.294; 10.1096), thus associating it with the "dark" horse Throwaway who wins the Gold Cup. In this way Joyce not only, by way of Bloom, invades the center of his text with cultural lore which many Irish citizens would consider foreign, but also keeps that lore beckoning from the interstices of his text by his own quite separate tracing of the path of the flyer. In doing so the text shares Bloom's fascination with chance yet signifying, intercorporeic intersection.

Narrative Embodiment: Intercorporeity and Dialectic

The final meeting of Stephen Dedalus and Leopold Bloom represents the climax of intercorporeic encounter, for both Bloom and the text. Their early chance encounter at the door of the library links, through Stephen, into a chain of associations that helps us interpret the value of all the novel's intercorporeic intersections. This chain of associations points toward a dialectical philosophy of physical encounter that further encourages us to read Joyce's stylized narrative structure of intersection as more than merely comic or parodic.

Foreshadowing their final prolonged interaction (ending at the doorway to Bloom's house), at the library door the paths of Stephen and Bloom so precisely intersect that Stephen must step aside to let Bloom pass. Stephen thinks of the word "portico" as Bloom passes (*U*, 9.1205), which, it turns out, evokes his prior analysis of the life of William Shakespeare and hints at those implications of intercorporeic intersection that most interest Joyce.

That is, in answer to the characterization of Shakespeare's marriage as a mere error, Stephen had countered with the claim that such "errors" are, rather, "portals of discovery." The mismatched joinings of Socrates and Xanthippe or Shakespeare and Ann Hathaway, he insisted, are in fact doorways into a dialectic not unlike that which finally develops between the older, Jewish Bloom and the younger, Irish Catholic Stephen. The meeting of differences, or even opposites, Stephen suggests, opens doors. The late-night dialogue between Bloom and Stephen bears out this suggestion.

In this dialogue the direct acknowledgment of differences between Stephen and Bloom continually opens into another question or comparison between them. When the text asks, "What two temperaments did they individually represent?" the answer implies just such a meeting of opposites: "The scientific. The artistic" (*U*, 17.560). And when the narrator asks, "Did he [Bloom] find four separating forces between his temporary guest and him?" the answer names the four socially "separating forces" or "name, age, race, and creed" (*U*, 17.402–3). As the dialogue proceeds, however, suppressed affinities surface and cut through these "separating forces"—such as Bloom's and Stephen's exploration of the similarities between the ancient Hebrew and Irish languages (*U*, 17.731 – 60). Meanwhile, the text's mock-learned account of their discussion luxuriates in the balancing and sometimes oxymoronic language of dialectic: their conversation reveals "similar differences," "counterproposals," "points of contact," "connecting link[s]" (*U*, 17.893, 960, 745, 478).

The phenomenology of such a dialectical meeting significantly finds its most dense expression at the point where Bloom meditates on their racial difference. We learn that "neither" of them "openly allude[s] to their racial difference" (*U*, 17.525) but that they interpret each other's thoughts about it: "He thought that he thought that he was a jew whereas he knew that he knew that he knew he was not" (U, 17.530). In both halves of the sentence we begin with Bloom's perspective. Bloom thinks that Stephen thinks that Bloom is a Jew, whereas Bloom knows that Stephen knows that Bloom knows that Stephen is not a Jew. The "whereas" between the "thought" and the "knew" clauses implicitly contrasts the hiddenness of Jewishness with the public normalness of Irishness and Catholicism. But the ambiguous use of "he" grammatically collapses the separation between the two men so that the reader must sort through the phrasing to separate them again. In the meantime, any such reader has considered at least one or two alternative ways of referencing the pronoun—alternatives which, even if ultimately rejected in favor of one that seems "right," subvert the strict separation of persons and types on which the sexuo-racial system depends.

Roy Gottfried has demonstrated how midsentence shifts in syntax characterize Joyce's prose in *Ulysses*.[34] I would suggest that these shifts in syntax particularly give rise to ambiguous pronoun references, to confusion about the "subject" of the sentence. Together with shifts in person (that is, mixing of first and third person) and "stacked" pronouns (as in the example just given), this syntactic shifting conspires to undercut a fixed stance in the reader. Readers must change positions as the prose slips from one pronoun to another, and our struggle for orientation reveals our dependence on categories and oppositions in determining the grammatical and the existential subject. In this way, Joyce's prose realizes the social and grammatical potential for confusion, convergence, collapse—recovering in the end, however, into a reorientation with difference enfolded. Thus again, the text contrives the linguistic as well as corporeal convergence of differences—*within* Cissy or Molly or Stephen, and *between* Bloom and Stephen or Molly—exactly to open "porticos" which allow egress from the purist, separatist mythology of the sexuo-racial matrix.

The Return Home to the Racial Mother

The final "portico" of *Ulysses* leads into Molly's bedroom and, from there, out of the text. In Molly's room, Bloom and Molly

34. Roy K. Gottfried, *The Art of Joyce's Syntax in Ulysses* (Athens: University of Georgia Press, 1980).

"unite noiselessly," but, even more, within herself Molly mingles sexual and racial differences. Molly is a mother, a married woman; she lives safely indoors; yet she is sexual, both with other men and, in fantasy, toward women. Molly is also polyracial—Irish, Jewish, and possibly Spanish. Molly is "impure," then, both sexually and racially. Yet Joyce gives this "other" woman a voice. In fact, he gives her the last word.

In this final word Molly explicitly continues the text's subversion of racial and especially sexual mythologies, even extending that subversion to the positions of Stephen and Bloom. Previously instruments of comic deflation, Bloom and Stephen themselves become *objects* of deflation in Molly's monologue. At the same time, Molly celebrates sensuality among and between women and men, delighting in its polymorphous flux. In sum, Molly's monologue involves both sexuo-racial critique and intercorporeic vision.

At the same time, Joyce achieves his final intercorporeic vision *through* this monologue, through Molly. In a sense Molly is for the text what Cissy Caffrey is for Bloom: an exciting embodiment of boundary-crossing identity. In closing his text with such a figure, Joyce underwrites Molly's transgressive, intercorporeic body; but he also rides upon it. The sudden separate singled-outness of Molly's compact closing monologue contains the energy of a reversal. That energy betrays, even as it struggles away from, an old attachment to the opposite viewpoint, to an ethic of sexuo-racial subjugation. Joyce's aim in *Ulysses* is radical: to collapse the body-subjugating binarism of metaphysics by riding into, rather than up and away from, the physical. But his vehicle, the racialized mother, remains familiar, a relic of the very metaphysical mythologies he critiques.

Because many readers, feminist and otherwise, have considered Molly a flat or stereotyped female character, I begin this last section by attending to the details of Molly's monologue that give her dimension, both sharp edges and curving depths. Only in recognizing these dimensions of Molly can we appreciate her simultaneously critical, visionary, and conservative roles in the text's closure, and at the same time avoid the errors of Bloom in his understanding of Molly.

Of primary importance to Molly's subversion of racial and sexual mythologies is simply the fact that in Molly's monologue we learn *her* perspective on the men who have commented on her and on the racial and sexual heterogeneity she embodies. Molly's comments recast even the sympathetic, sensual Bloom. Although we have by now gathered that Bloom fantasizes freely about all sorts of inventions and gathers schemes for money-making, for instance, we have not been aware of the degree to which he dissembles or even lies about his skills and plans. Molly recalls their near shipwreck at Bray, Bloom having told the boatman he knew how to row when it was barely true. She remembers his plan to start "a musical academy on their first floor drawingroom with a brassplate or Bloom's private hotel he suggested," neither of which ever materialized, "like all the things he told father he was going to do" (U, 18.980–83). At one point, when his latest scheme has failed and money is short, he suggests to Molly that she pose nude for a local painter (U, 18.560). Molly feels she was a "born fool to believe all his blather" (U, 18.1187), but she nonetheless admits that "he used to amuse me the things he said" (U, 18.1185). Even more, she acknowledges her attraction to his oddity: "I kiss the feet of you senorita theres some sense in that didnt he kiss our halldoor yes he did what a madman nobody understands his cracked ideas but me" (U, 18.1405). Bloom's kissing of Molly's "halldoor" hints that between them, too, intersecting differences open "portals of discovery."

In light of Molly's sympathetic yet frank account of Bloom's failings, Bloom's complaints about Molly's lack of "intelligence" (U, 17.674–702) carry less of a punch. Juxtaposing Molly's criticism of Bloom against Bloom's criticism of Molly sets up a comic mutuality between wife and husband. But, even beyond the countering of Bloom's criticisms, Molly's comments and background on herself significantly revise our understanding of her. Through the comments of Bloom and other men we have the impression of Molly mainly as a buxom, flirtatious, nonmonogamous woman with a singing voice but no brains. Molly offers us fragments of her personal history that both explain and recast this picture of her.

Molly depicts herself as a polycultural woman. She explains her "harumscarum" personality ("I know I am a bit") as the result of having spoken different languages and lived in many places and on many streets ("and all the bits of streets Paradise ramp and Bedlam ramp and Rodgers ramp and Crutchetts ramp and the devils gap steps well small blame to me if I am a harumscarum" (U, 18.1468–70]). In the course of her monologue Molly defensively speaks a little Spanish to show "I havent forgotten it all" (U, 18.1472), but her larger point is that she is the put-upon victim, not the proud master, of polylingualism. Molly sees herself as having been uprooted repeatedly by men—whether by her father, by her husband, or by the threat of war. The resulting exotic and mixed background that attracts Bloom to her also leaves her uncommitted to and unschooled in the codes of any one culture and positioned at one remove from the codes of all.

Molly points out specifically that her charged position within constructs of both motherhood and racialism at the time Bloom met her—as a young, sexual Jewess tending her dying mother—was partly what attracted him to her ("I suppose on account of my being a Jewess looking after my mother" [U, 18.1184]). Rather like Cissy Caffrey, Molly straddles borders of sexuality, maternalism, and race in a way that challenges dominant racial and sexual mythologies— and excites Bloom. Molly as sexually and racially "impure" daughter (and later mother) makes a titillating touchstone for Bloom's wandering desires. But, although Bloom finds excitement in Molly's sexual and racial multiplicity, he fails to see that this multiplicity underlies what he considers her "deficient mental development" (U, 17.674–702). His incomprehension of her personality in relation to her polyhistory reveals his contradictory attachment, like Stephen's, to a gendered metaphysics. That is, even Bloom, the "new womanly man," easily reduces Molly to a body without a brain, overlooking the complicated history which gives rise to her different sensibility.

The text, it is important to note, avoids this habitual error; in this closing section Molly does present her own history. Furthermore, within Molly's monologue the text establishes that what appears to Bloom as Molly's lack of intelligence turns out to be a consciously adopted anti-intellectual, antimetaphysical position on her part. She takes this position in resistance to the very misogyny and racialism inherent, as we saw and as she implicitly sees, in Western metaphysics.

Repeatedly Molly challenges traditional definitions of intelligence. For Molly, intelligence is the ability to read people, not books: "When I put my hat and gloves in the window to show I was going out not a notion what I meant arent they thick never understand what you say even youd want to print it up on a big poster for them . . . where does their great intelligence come in" (U, 18.704–9). She contrats her pleasure in "rivers and lakes and flowers and colours springing up even out of the ditches primroses and violets" to what men call knowledge, saying, "I wouldnt give a snap of my two fingers for all their learning" (U, 18.1561–63). As for intellectual atheists, she suggests, "Why dont they go and create something" (U, 18.1564). Molly pits the resources of bodily gesture and palpable nature against the uses of explanatory language and impalpable learning. Even though her oversimplified reversal of the metaphysical position may fail, finally, to subvert that metaphysics, one should remember to ask whether this simplistic reversal is only Molly's or also the text's. There is reason to consider Molly's simplifications the text's simplification of Molly.

Meanwhile, other of Molly's observations cut deeper into the heart of sexuo-racial metaphysics. In the spirit of Stephen, she attacks men's metaphysical pretensions as hypocritical. She points to the hidden sensual indulgence in priests' learned tracts, such as one about "a child born out of her ear because her bumgut fell out" (U, 18.489). And she considers the material ramifications, for women, of men's supposedly mind-inspired "inventions." Men's most clever invention, according to Molly, is simply "for him to get all the pleasure" (U, 18.158). Men, for instance, produce women's restrictive clothing: "these clothes we have to wear whoever invented them expecting you to walk up Killney hill then for example at that picnic all stayed up you cant do a blessed thing in them" (U, 18.627). Similarly, men have invented a sexual double standard: "they can pick and choose what they please a married woman or a fast widow or a girl . . . but were to be always chained up" (U, 18.1388). Finally, again buttressed by a myth of men's intelligence and invention, men leave women with the unacknowledged physical work of raising children: "if someone gave them a touch of it themselves theyd know what I went through with Milly nobody would believe cutting her teeth too" (U, 18.159); and later: "they wouldnt be in the world at all only for us they dont know what it is to be a woman and a mother" (U, 18.1440). With these comments Molly hints that, through the mythology of transcendent intelligence, men both pursue bodily desires and avoid bodily drudgery, meanwhile denying women's bodily desire and heaping them with bodily labors. Molly takes her stand clearly against such bondage, not least in laying her claim to the pleasures of sexuality. She insists: "theyre not going to be chaining me up" (U, 18.1391).

Yet, although Molly has successfully worked around the restrictions on her heterosexual liaisons, her less noted attachments to women have suffered repeated sunderings at the hands of men. Joyce critics have made much of Molly's recollections of her various male lovers; but Molly also describes her sensual memories of women— from whom she has been separated. These separations occur not just psychologically but physically as she or other women are moved from place to place by fathers or husbands or wars. She thinks of a former neighbor of hers and Bloom's who was "a lovely woman magnificent head of hair down to her waist . . . 1st thing I did every morning to look across see her combing it . . . *pity I only got to know her the day before we left*" (U, 18.477, emphasis added). Likewise, she thinks longingly, and with much sensual detail, of her old friend Mrs. Stanhope, who used to write calling her "dearest Doggerina" and telling her how she had "just had a jolly warm bath" or how she "will always think of the lovely teas we had together scrumptious currant scones and rasberry wafers I adore" (U, 18.612–21). Because of the war, it seems, Mrs. Stanhope left and "never came back" (U, 18.667). When she left, Molly remembers, "she kissed me six or seven times didnt I cry yes I did or near it my lips were taittering when I said goodbye she had a Gorgeous wrap of some special kind of blue colour" (U, 18.673).

This memory moves Molly to comment on her lonely and paternally determined state at that time, especially as a girl bereft of her own mother ("thats what I never had" [U, 18.1442]): "after they went I was almost planning to run away mad out of it somewhere" for she knows that as a woman she will not be allowed simply to travel or live single. Her complaint against marriage—"were never easy where we are father or aunt or marriage waiting always waiting to guiiide him toooo me waiting" (U, 18.676–78)—flows directly into a complaint against the war: "their damn guns bursting and booming all over the shop especially the Queens birthday and throwing everything down in all directions" (U, 18.679–80). That the bombing happens worst on the queen's birthday seems a particular insult to Molly, perhaps because of the way the war has separated her from her "queen," her surrogate mother Mrs. Stanhope. Thus, the text indicates that war (over race races) and marriage, two cornerstones of the patriarchal racialist order, intervene rudely between Molly and the women with whom she desires intimacy. That the text portrays Molly as desiring intimacy with women at all, rather than considering women simply as antagonists in a heterosexual contest, further testifies to its transgression of old sexuo-racial divisions.

Moreover, even as the text shows the destructive effects of men's dominance over women's intimacy, it manages also to suggest that the interplay of men's and women's "worlds" can potentially increase the pleasures in each, as in Molly's memory of her girlfriend Hester: "we used to compare our hair mine was thicker than hers she showed me how to settle it at the back . . . we were like cousins what age was I then the night of the storm I slept in her bed she had her arms around me then we were fighting in the morning with the pillow what fun he was watching me whenever he got an opportunity at the band . . ." (U, 18.638). This passage perfectly demonstrates how Molly's unpunctuated prose permits a bisexual slippage from homosocial to heterosocial pleasures, how Joyce's method carries us toward such a slippage, and how Molly's personality delights in this slippage. The text represents Molly's sexuality as capable of overriding conventional boundaries of sex and race.

We might even draw a parallel between Stephen's and Bloom's pleasure with each other over Molly in their parting scene, on the one hand, and Hester's and Molly's pleasure with each other in the context of a watching boy, on the other hand. In the "Ithaca" section, after a light in Molly's room "attract[s] Bloom's who attract[s] Stephen's gaze" and leads Bloom to describe his attraction to Molly, the men become "silent, each contemplating the other in both mirrors of the reciprocal flesh of their hisnothis fellow faces" (U, 17.1183). Similarly, the boy in Molly's memory of Hester adds an exciting self-consciousness to their intimacy. Of course, in both cases the men watch and the women are watched. Yet Joyce's arrangement does imply, again as Kimberly Devlin has shown in her reading of the Gerty scene, that the women are watching too: Hester and Molly "watch" the boy who watches, and Molly is aware of, if not watching, the men who stand below watching her. As in the sentence "he knew he knew he knew," Joyce uncovers layers of interrelated watching and reading of the other's readings. This intersubjective dynamic, embedded in intercorporeic concreteness, moves with an energy that overrides divisions of hetero- or homoerotic, pure or impure. Such an intercorporeic dynamic thrives on the mutual *differences* of self and other, men and women, dark-skinned and light. That all bodies are oriented toward all other bodies yet each remains separate and different exactly *in* body makes the body an exquisite merging of sameness and difference and makes the spaces *between* bodies "portals" seductively open to the intersections *of* bodies.

This joyous, high comic reading of *Ulysses* requires a final quali-fication, however. The fact remains that most of *Ulysses* lives in-side the lighter-skinned men. African men and women, after all, serve mainly as tropes in *Ulysses*, an outer ring of associations used to define certain lighter-skinned characters as outsiders to the dominant light-skinned patriarchal order. And even Molly, in the context of the many pages that precede her, appears most of all as a final lens through which to view Stephen and Bloom, as well as the final vehicle for our exit as readers from the parodic text.

In short, Joyce above all desires to know his men, especially his Irish Catholic men. As an inheritor of a moderately "other" racial tradition, for most of the text Bloom serves Joyce's desire: it is through immersion in Bloom as a sensual "other" man that Joyce can reconstruct his bond to himself—that is, to himself in the per-son of Stephen, the fallen-away Catholic sensualist. The perspective of Molly, the other sex and race combined, completes the attempt: Molly's view allows him to get the final angle on these men who lead him to the most multiple, most intercorporeic man in himself.

This transgressive self-embrace, instrumental as it is to the proj-ect of surpassing old racial and sexual mythologies, begs other texts to pick up where it leaves off—to risk a fuller face-to-face embrace with the transgressive mother figure. Molly's closing "Yesyesyes" nostalgically *recalls* a moment of face-to-face sexuality with Bloom; it does not surge *forward* within such a moment. Likewise, consider the "blocked" spatial rendering of Molly: she never leaves her house, not to mention her bed, for the text depends, multiply, on her fixed presence there.

Other modern novels repeat this limitation. Novels such as *Cane* and *Light in August* circle back to the mother, reenacting their protagonists' and the culture's dependence on her as touchstone of embodiment. Novels such as *To the Lighthouse* and *Beloved*, how-ever, heed the call implicitly issued by Molly's monologue. Woolf and Morrison often begin with the mother and reenact narratively an intercorporeic sensibility originating with her; but they ulti-mately find grounding beyond the mother in her culture-servant role—in Lily Briscoe or Denver or Paul D.

More important, however, than these distinctions between such

modern novelists is the project they undertake in common: to subvert and revise a racialized, gendered metaphysics, specifically by
converting a body-grounded silencing into a body-grounded speech
and vision. Together with Toomer, Woolf, Hurston, Faulkner, Morrison, and others, Joyce continues his culture's latest experiments
with the racial and sexual body, allowing the body's testimony to
unravel the culture's racial and sexual metaphysics from within.

7

Staging Sexuality: Repression, Representation, and "Interior" States in *Ulysses*

Joseph A. Boone

I would like to begin by confessing that the task I have set for myself is a nearly impossible one: to investigate what are perhaps the two most elusive chapers of *Ulysses*—"Circe" and "Penelope"—in order to evaluate how issues of sexuality and narrative inevitably impinge on each other in Joyce's attempt to represent states of consciousness. At stake in such an investigation is of course the relation between the representation of gendered subjectivity and the endeavors of many modernists to shift novelistic representations of "reality" from the vantage point of the seemingly objective or external to that of the individual's inner life. As Virginia Woolf put it in her epoch-defining essay "Modern Fiction" (1919), life is not a "series of gig lamps symmetrically arranged" but rather "a luminous halo, a semi-transparent envelope surrounding us from the beginning of consciousness to the end"; and she proceeds to suggest that one consequence of resituating the narrative eye within "an ordinary mind on an ordinary day" is that "the point of interest" for the "moderns" will "very likely [lie] in the dark places of psychology."[1] The way in which the act of exploring the

An earlier version of this essay was presented at the 1988 International Symposium on Joyce in Venice and published in the conference volume, *The Languages of Joyce*, ed. Rosa Maria Bollettieri Bosinelli, Carla Marengo, and Christine van Boheemen (Philadelphia: John Benjamins, 1992).

1. Virginia Woolf, "Modern Fiction" (April 1919), rpt. in *The Norton Anthology of English Literature*, 4th ed. (New York: Norton, 1979), 2: 23, 24.

flux of mental activity almost inevitably extends into this "darker" underside of "consciousness" is corroborated, albeit in more melodramatic language, by Joyce's comment to Arthur Power that the "modern theme" concerns "the subterranean forces, those hidden tides which govern everything and run humanity counter to the apparent flood: those poisonous subtleties which envelop the soul, the ascending fumes of sex."[2] Or, as Joyce explained his goals in writing *Ulysses* to Djuna Barnes in a 1992 *Vanity Fair* interview: "I have recorded, simultaneously, what a man says, sees, thinks, and what such seeing, thinking, saying does, to what you Freudians call the subconscious."[3]

The succinctness of Joyce's description belies the monumentality of the endeavor to represent, in Woolf's phrase, "an ordinary mind on an ordinary day," as the psychosexual complexity summoned forth by his formal innovations attests. Tellingly, having just identified "what you Freudians call the subconscious" as one of his representational aims, Joyce abruptly interrupts himself, Barnes reports, in order to dismiss psychoanalysis, in no uncertain terms, as "neither more nor less than blackmail"[4]—a statement we might do well to read in the light of Jacques Lacan's observation, paraphrased by Patrick McGee, that "Joyce the symptom illustrates the psychoanalysis that Joyce the subject refuses."[5] For, indeed, not only did the attempt to represent linguistically the "tides" of "consciousness," as well as the "subterranean" depths of what Joyce here calls the "subconscious," help revolutionize the twentieth-century novel; by creating a spatial dimension within narrative evocative of the atemporal, nonchronological, associative processes of mental and libidinal activity, Joyce created the fictive illusion of "interiority" precisely by articulating the fundamentally split nature of identity—"those hidden tides . . . run[ning] humanity counter to the apparent flood"—which has been the most radical contribution of

---

2. Arthur Power, *Conversations with James Joyce*, ed. Clive Hart (London: Millington, 1974), 54.

3. Djuna Barnes, "James Joyce," *Vanity Fair* 18 (1922): 65.

4. Ibid.

5. This is McGee's paraphrase of Lacan's wording in "Joyce le symptôme," in *Joyce in Paris, 1902.....1920—1940.....1975*, 2 vols., ed. J. Aubert and Maria Jolas (Paris: Editions du C.N.R.S., 1929), 1:13–17. See Patrick McGee, *Paperspace: Style as Ideology in Joyce's "Ulysses"* (Lincoln: University of Nebraska Press, 1988), 2. See also Lacan's comment that "I shall speak of Joyce, who has preoccupied me much this year, only to say that he is the simplest consequence of a refusal . . . of psycho-analysis, which, as a result, his work illustrates," in *The Four Fundamental Concepts of Psycho-Analysis*, ed. Jacques-Alain Miller, trans. Alan Sheridan (New York: Norton, 1978), ix.

psychoanalysis to modernity. And in harnessing both the power and slipperiness of language to express the dilemmas and impossible desires of the radically split self, Joyce's experiments in representing consciousness simultaneously call into question the very distinction between "interior" and "exterior" on which a classical metaphysics of coherent identity has depended.[6]

What particularly intrigues me is how this metaphoric opening up of narrative form made space for the representation of what Joyce called those "ascending fumes of sex"—that is, those incalculable psychosexual forces that shape as they subvert human subjectivity. Hence my focus on "Circe" and "Penelope," the two episodes in *Ulysses* that most thoroughly reject traditional methods of realistic narration, and particularly traditional techniques for representing states of inwardness, in order to simulate the erotics of mental activity. In the one case we see this effect accomplished through an *exteriorization* of what are largely Bloom's subconscious fantasies and unconscious desires, and in the other through an *interiorization* of Molly's stream-of-consciousness reveries in a self-contained monologue. I am arguing that in both these narrative instances Joyce self-consciously stages a return of his own "Freudian" version of the (sexually) repressed—"those hidden tides which govern

6. This problematic distinction between "interior" and "exterior" is related to the assumptions embedded in the often unquestioned use of metaphors of surface and depth to describe psychic activity. Such metaphors not only are implicit in modernist rhetoric (note Woolf's "dark places," Joyce's "subterranean forces") but also characterize both popular and psychoanalytic definitions (thus *consciousness* consists of "the *upper* level" of mental life, while the *subconscious* indicates those mental activities "just *below* the threshold of consciousness, as *Webster's* informs us). The demarcation of such boundaries *within* the self parallels the construction of the boundary between interior and exterior, self and other, that subtends a Western humanistic conception of coherent identity. Indeed, in a fascinating footnote to her essay "Word, Dialogue, and Novel," in *Desire in Language* (trans. Thomas Gora et al. [New York: Columbia University Press, 1980]), Julia Kristeva argues that "what is persistently being called 'interior monologue'" is modern Western civilization's last-gasp effort to preserve a traditional norm of identity as "organized chaos" and "transcendence." For Kristeva, this "limited literary effect," rather than being avantgarde, still operates within the realist premise that the "self" can somehow be captured in narrative, an illusion of "an internal voice" that Freud's "'Copernican' revolution (the discovery of the split within the subject) [has] put an end to" (90). While I would agree with Kristeva that Freud's theorization (continued by Lacan) of the split within subjectivity spells an end to the fiction of interiority insofar as it posits the subject's "radical exteriority in relation to, and within, language," I argue in an ongoing project of which this essay is a part (in a chapter titled "Modernism's Theaters of the Mind") that modernists such as Joyce, Woolf, and Barnes, in their novelistic attempts to represent the erotics of mental activity, also recognize "interiority" to be a linguistic aftereffect, the refraction of a series of external surfaces, masks, and roles that call into question the assumed distinction between interior and exterior, self and other, and hence are *using* what Kristeva dismisses as a "limited literary effect" to address the very division within subjectivity that Kristeva sees representations of mental activity as threatening to erase.

everything"—in order to celebrate the breakdown of unitary or normative conceptions of sexuality, identity, and narrative. At the same time, I want to account for the way in which what might be called *Ulysses*'s own "unconscious"—*Joyce's* repressed—complicates, indeed at times overwrites, the authorial effort to open up a textual space for an unrepressed sexuality, for polymorphous free play, within the text. "Circe," in this light, inadvertently reveals an investment in those mechanisms of narrative control that compromise the section's celebratory evocation of sexual and textual plurality, while "Penelope" paradoxically gives (and gives over) expression to a speaking subject in Molly, one whose discursive construction tantalizingly evades Joyce's authorial impositions even as her *enacted* subjectivity remains part of the masquerade of self and sexuality which "Penelope," no less than "Circe," seeks to expose.

"Circe's" Mental Theater

"Imagine the underside of a text," Hélène Cixous writes of "Circe," "where discourse becomes detached and fantasies imprint their anxiety." Indeed, to read the fifteenth segment of *Ulysses* for the first time is to find oneself in such a surreal, defamiliarizing realm, a realm of the "underside" in which repressed guilts and libidinous desires, subconscious fantasies and symbols of the unconscious mingle indiscriminately, jockeying for position and displacing one another in turn. All this occurs, moreover, on a textual plane composed of oddly familiar but estranging words, images, phrases—all of which we may vaguely recall having read before but, now pried loose from their meaning-bestowing contexts, seem to have become open-ended, floating signifiers. And if "fantasies imprint their anxiety" on this "underside of the text," it is at least in part because "Circe's" setting in Dublin's Nighttown or red-light district evokes, as Cixous also so aptly puts it, "a feast day of the repressed" in Bloom as well as in the text itself.[7]

Of course, Bloom's "repressed" has never been entirely absent from the narrative proper. The interior monologue technique that Joyce has intermittently used since "Calypso" to reveal the ongoing

7. Hélène Cixous, "At Circe's, or the Self-Opener," *boundary* 2 3 (Winter 1975): 390, 388–89.

stream of thoughts coursing through Bloom's mind has indirectly revealed—through its approximation of the verbal slippages, condensations of meaning, metaphoric substitutions, telltale gaps, ellipses, and associative leaps that characterize the thought process— a great deal about Bloom's subliminal fears, guilts, and desires; we are encouraged to read his "quoted" thoughts as an analyst would read a patient's chain of associations, as keys to what remains *unsaid* or suppressed. For, by definition, however much the unconscious may operate according to linguistic rules, its activities do not take verbal form. Accordingly, one task of "Circe" is precisely to delve into "the ellipses of the stream-of-consciousness passages of the early chapters," as Karen Lawrence notes.[8] To represent these unconscious and subconscious processes, however, Joyce must resort to a radically different narrative technique. Hence the shift, in "Circe," from third-person narration, with its intermittent internal monologues, to the genre of dramatic script. The reader's eye is immediately assaulted by stage directions, scripted dialogue, rapid scene shifts, changes of costume, and multiple levels of role playing—all signs that we have entered a realm of mental theater, one in which the repressed is rendered "visible" in the form of *enacted* fantasy. Joyce's method of rendering psychic processes in this episode, then, is expressionistic and psychodramatic, and thus the majority of the surreal "events" that subsequently unfold function as literalized metaphors, as externalized embodiments, of unexpressed, indeed often inexpressible, desires and fears. It is important to note, however, that the language in which these fantasies are expressed is not specific to any one character's verbal tics or thought patterns; rather, the words that compose "Circe" well up from the text's entire repertoire of figures and images—from, if you will, the dreaming unconscious of *Ulysses* itself.[9]

This expressionistic dissociation from any mimetic relation to

8. Karen Lawrence, *The Odyssey of Style in "Ulysses"* (Princeton: Princeton University Press, 1981), 153. See also Dorrit Cohn's observation concerning "Circe" that the Freudian unconscious "can never be quoted directly"; hence in this episode Joyce abandons "the realistic monologue technique in favor of a distinctly surrealistic dramatic phantasmagoria," in *Transparent Minds: Narrative Modes for Presenting Consciousness in Fiction* (Princeton: Princeton University Press, 1981), 88.

9. Explains Lawrence: "It is important to stress that the 'dream of the text' is not equivalent to the fantasies or dreams of the characters. . . . For the psychological boundaries of the characters' minds are wildly, extravagantly transgressed . . . ; that is, the narrative memory of the book provides the resources for this extraordinary drama, often in violation of the actual memories and associations of the characters." See *Odyssey of Style,* 151–52.

Bloom's, or any other character's, sensibility plunges the reader headlong into an opaque realm of language governed by the unanchored drift of association, a world in which the words of the text form a depersonalizing, one-dimensional screen onto which all repressed fantasies are projected and a distorting filter through which any literal actions, such as Bloom's movements through Nighttown, are relayed. The resulting sensation is that of a hallucinating text either totally out of control or operating according to its own mysterious rules. This disorienting effect, as Joyceans since David Hayman have pointed out, has been anticipated throughout by the novel's gradual evolution toward "autonomy" or arbitrariness: from at least "Aeolus," and certainly "Sirens," on, each successive episode, more daringly experimental than its predecessor, has increasingly given the written word precedence over action, so that by "Circe" any "narrator" (Hayman's formulation), or "the authoritative narrative voice" (Lawrence's), seems to have disappeared altogether.[10] This eclipse of a stable narrating center helps create an illusion of textual autonomy that is in turn strategically abetted by "Circe's" dramatic format: drama, after all, is the one genre that exists for its audience without direct authorial meditation, *appearing* to "happen" of its own volition. At the same time, because this drama is necessarily read as a script rather than witnessed as performance, the illusion of immediacy characteristic of theater is replaced by a sense of distance, an alienation effect enhanced by the hallucinatory, indeed *nonperformable* nature of much of the scripted "action." Thus exploiting his dramatic medium, Joyce creates a textual universe in "Circe" that approximates the workings of the unconscious, appearing to run on its own libidinal energies (although, like the libido, it too is part of a larger operation) and governed by a dreamlike drift of association, in which obsessive, repressed fantasies find expression by indiscriminately attaching themselves to whatever external stimuli are available.[11]

So radically unanchored a textual universe sets the stage for the explosion of the polymorphous perverse that accompanies Bloom's

10. See David Hayman, *"Ulysses," The Mechanics of Meaning* (Englewood Cliffs, N.J.: Prentice-Hall, 1970), 76–77, and Lawrence, *Odyssey of Style*, 8.

11. Or, as Caroline Cowie nicely put it in a paper for a seminar I taught in April 1985: "It is surely more valid to say that fantasies are not prompted by external phenomena but latch on to them, as does the 'dreamwork' of the subconscious, selecting details from waking experience to express the patterns of pre-existing mental currents. 'My girl's a Yorkshire girl' does not prompt an access of guilt, but it allows a loophole for the pre-existing guilt to find its own release" ("Interpreting Circe," 3).

movement through Nighttown. All his sexual sins of the past, all his repressed erotic fantasies (to say nothing of his oedipal and marital nightmares), rise to the surface of "Circe" as comic actors[12]— often with speaking roles—to accuse him of divergence from a hypothetical sexual norm: even within Bloom's "private" psychic terrain, sexuality assumes a series of ever-shifting *public* masks, attesting to its essentially performative nature as one enormous Circean spectacle. On a thematic level this revolt of the psyche, played out as a psychodrama of simultaneous guilt and desire, is largely precipitated by Bloom's internalization of a cultural ethos of manhood which exists at odds with a personal sense of well-being that is predicated, as I have written elsewhere, on his often feminine identifications, passive preferences, and general empathy (a value hardly exclusive to one sex but associated with women in Bloom's Dublin).[13] Given the disastrous public and personal events of Bloom's day, the sources of this unwelcome insurgence of the repressed are not hard to fathom. Made to doubt his adequacy as a man on multiple counts (by Molly's impending affair with Blazes Boylan, by his sensed difference from the hypermasculine and unfeeling world of his Dublin counterparts, by his failure to father a son), denigrated because of his Jewish Otherness and his Christian idealism, torn in his allegiance to nation or empire ("Stage Irishman!" will be one of the accusations leveled against him in the judgment sequence),[14] the already marginalized Bloom undergoes a further process of cultural alienation on June 16 that results in the psychic state of self-division to which the expressionistic format of "Circe" gives articulation. Appropriately, then, Bloom's first appearance in the episode is literally marginalized: his walk-on occurs in a bracketed stage direction (one kind of textual margin), where it is reported that the "concave mirror" (another mode of marginalizing representation) in Gillen's hairdresser's window "presents to him lovelorn longlost lugubru Booloohoom" (*U*, 15.145–46), an image of alterity caught in the process of linguistic fragmentation.

---

12. The importance of theater in shaping "Circe"—a topos to which I will be returning—is the subject of Cheryl Herr's "'One Good Turn Deserves Another': Theatrical Cross-Dressing in Joyce's 'Circe' Episode," *Journal of Modern Literature* 11 (1984): 262–76, which conclusively shows how Joyce's familiarity with the transvestite tradition of popular pantomime influences the depiction of Bloom's sexual disguises in "Circe."

13. Joseph A. Boone, "A New Approach to Bloom as 'Womanly Man': The Mixed Middling's Progress in *Ulysses*," *James Joyce Quarterly* 20 (1982): 67–85; see esp. 71–74.

14. *Ulysses*, ed. Hans Walter Gabler (New York: Vintage Books, 1986), 15.1729; hereafter cited in the text as *U*.

It is psychologically appropriate that Bloom, unsure of himself as acting subject, almost immediately fantasizes about himself as passive object. Likewise, fearing that by Dublin standards he is not enough of a man, Bloom subconsciously punishes himself for his inadequacies by imagining himself transformed into his culture's icon of abject submission: the dominated, cowering, but delighted female. In the fantasy of sex reversal that ensues in Bella Cohen's whorehouse, in particular, Bloom's internalization of his society's sexual values is at its greatest. Summoning up the nightmarish fantasy of Bella-as-Bello, his subconscious exacts its revenge, masochistically whipping him for his supposed failures: "What else are you good for, an impotent thing like you," Bella/o torments Bloom. "Can you do a man's job?" (U, 15.3127, 3132).[15]

These manifestations of guilt and humiliation, however, are only one sign of the repressed content to which "Circe" gives expression. For several of the personal revelations surfacing while Bloom subliminally imagines himself a woman and a sexual misfit attest to quite real, only barely suppressed desires to explore avenues of sexual experience commonly denied men in his culture: among others, passivity, homosexuality, autoeroticism, masochism, fetishism, coprophilia, anality, transvestism. Through the representation of Bloom's subconscious fantasies, then, Joyce valorizes a kind of libidinous fluidity, a play of sexual variation and unending capacities of erotic stimulation, that would seem to confirm Freud's hypothesis, in *Three Essays on the Theory of Sexuality* (1905), that the sexual instinct is multiple in direction, lacking a fixed or "correct"

15. Controversial as the seemingly offensive, negative caricature of Bella-as-Bello is, I would suggest that, as an emanation of Bloom's subconscious, it says more about his destructive feelings toward himself as a "womanly" man than about his (or Joyce's) attitude toward Bella as a "manlike" or destructive woman. Having incorporated his male culture's derision of his behavior as effeminate, unmanly, and servile, he subconsciously fantasizes in this moment that a masculine-appearing woman such as Bella must be his opposite: domineering, castrating, shrewish. Bloom's conceptions of both "feminine" men and "masculine" women are forged out of polarized extremes, culturally inflected distortions of gender identities that ironically imitate the black-and-white, hegemonic stereotyping by which society distinguishes its "manly men" from its "womanly women." I am not suggesting that Bloom's conscious attitudes toward women are not often sexist (his interior monologues offer abundant testimony otherwise), but rather his subconscious projections should not necessarily be taken as "transparent" evidence of his conscious attitudes toward women, "masculine" or otherwise. I develop this reading further in "A New Approach," 715–16. For more negative readings of the Bella/o sequence, see Elaine Unkeless, "Leopold Bloom as Womanly Man," *Modernist Studies: Literature and Culture* 2 (1976): 35–38, and Sandra M. Gilbert, "Costumes of the Mind: Transvestism as Metaphor in Modern Literature" (1980), rpt. in *Gender Studies: New Directions in Feminist Criticism*, ed. Judith Spector (Bowling Green, Ohio: Popular Press, 1986), 73–74.

object or aim.[16] That Joyce finds this radically destabilizing *sexual* free play a matter for celebration rather than condemnation is, I think, evident in the much-touted *discursive* free play or linguistic promiscuity that characterizes "Circe" as text and indeed *Ulysses* as a whole. Not only Bloom's but the narrative's "erotogenous zones" are allusive, associative, amorphous, objectless, as Caroline Cowie has astutely noted.[17]

Here the thematics of "the return of the repressed" resonate most profoundly on the textual level. For in its verbal texture "Circe" can be seen as a mass of random associations and concentrated zones of erotic fantasy which, once stimulated into activity, trigger a series of multiplying intertextual references and allusions whose excitations ripple across the surface of the entire artifact in multiple directions; through such a deployment of the polymorphous perverse on levels of content and technique at once, "Circe" challenges its readers' belief in identity, sexuality, or narrativity as fixed categories. Even the most incidental details of "Circe" convey something of this challenge. The humor of Bella/o's injunction to the onlooking spectators, as she/he prepares to auction the "female" Bloom to the highest bidder—"examine shis points. Handle hrim" (*U*, 15.3103)—underlines the complicity of language, for instance, in the gender stratifications that in this fantasy are being exposed as cultural fabrications. A more significant example involves the disintegration of the unitary "I" along both linguistic and gendered lines as Bloom defends himself to the "Gentlemen of the jury" in the judgment sequence: "Let me explain . . . *I am a man* misunderstood . . . *I am* a respectable married *man* . . . *I* live in Eccles street. *My wife, I am the daughter of . .* " (*U*, 15.775–78; emphasis added). Before the phallic "Law" that should uphold discrete masculine identity, the juridical subject crumbles, cultural "misunderstanding" serving as the trigger for a far more profound psychosexual "gender confusion." By so overloading his system of signifiers throughout "Circe," Joyce explodes, as Frances Restuccia has put

16. Sigmund Freud, *Three Essays on the Theory of Sexuality*, trans. James Strachey (New York: Basic Books, 1962), 13–14, 37–38. Joyce's more specific debt is to Richard von Krafft-Ebing, from whose *Psychopathia Sexualis* he culled much of his technical knowledge of male fetishism and masochism, as documented in Don Gifford and Robert J. Seideman, *Notes for Joyce: An Annotation of James Joyce's "Ulysses"* (New York: Dutton, 1974), 410–15.

17. Cowie, "Interpreting Circe," 7.

it, the "phallogocentrism" that would have been inherent in "manfully . . . thinking up a signifier for every signified in Dublin."[18]

And yet, I would argue, the achievement of such free play is only part of the story of "Circe." First, on the level of content, the episode's affirmation of Bloom's sexual fluidity is qualified by its unwitting valorization of the male arena that provides its overarching context. Because Nighttown's primary reason for existing is to foster and satisfy male fantasies, it in essence forms an extended men's club where men meet, compete, and bond in various oedipal patterns. Houses of prostitution, Jane Pinchin pithily notes, "are places men go to play with one another."[19] This homosocial substratum of "Circe's" narrative clarifies the significance of Bloom's fantasized confrontations with his overbearingly misogynistic grandfather Virag (who taunts Bloom for his lack of virility) and with the overbearingly virile Blazes Boylan (who relegates Bloom to the position of unsatisfied voyeur). It also underlines the fact that the one thread of "plot" winding its way throughout "Circe's" otherwise spontaneous drift of associations is Bloom's quest for a son in Stephen Dedalus. Indeed, Bloom's is the paternal quest for phallic succession, as the final vision of the long-dead Rudy, "slim ivory cane" (U, 15.4966) in hand, rather poignantly, if also ironically, suggests. For all its fantastical content, relations between men shape the waking and dreaming world of "Circe."

Second, on the level where form and content meet, I would suggest that the free play of "Circe" is complicated by the fact that "sex" in Nighttown occurs almost exclusively as a textual-narratological experience. An evocative emblem of this continual displacement of the sexual onto the level of language can be found in the stage direction where Bloom, walking in Nighttown, comes across some "obscene" graffiti: *"He gazes ahead, reading on the wall a scrawled chalk legend* Wet Dream *and a phallic design"* (U, 15.649–50). Not only does sexual release here "occur" only in language (a *scribbled* "wet dream")—where it is relegated, moreover, to the fictive status of a *dream*—but the "phallus," instrument of men's wet dreams, also turns out to be pure text: a representational phantasm, a chalk outline without substance. Within the drama

18. Frances Restuccia, "Molly in Furs: Deleuzian/Masochian Masochism in the Writing of James Joyce," *Novel* 18 (1985): 109.

19. Jane L. Pinchin, "Durrell's Fatal Cleopatra," *Modern Fiction Studies* 28 (Summer 1982): 231.

proper of "Circe," one of the most perverse examples of this substitution of the sexual by the linguistic occurs when the disembodied "Voices" of Boylan and Molly make their stage appearance, mimicking the sounds of "male" and "female" orgasm, respectively (the former signified by its gutteral consonants, the latter by its throaty vowels):

BOYLAN'S VOICE

(sweetly, hoarsely, in the pit of his stomach) Ah! Godblazegrukbru-karchkhrasht!

MARION'S VOICE

(hoarsely, sweetly, rising to her throat) O! Weeshwashtkissina-pooisthnapoohuck!

(*U*, 15.3808–13)

The way in which the section's relentless textualizing of sexuality empties out any "real" sexual content also characterizes the innuendos that cluster around the floating signifier "teapot" in the flirtatious but inconclusive dialogue of Bloom and Mrs. Breen: "BLOOM 'I'm teapot with curiosity . . .'; MRS. BREEN '(gushingly) Tremendously teapot! London's teapot and I'm simply teapot all over me'" (*U*, 15.457–61). Later, Bella/o will identify the "teapot" with Bloom's male signifier—"Where's your curly teapot gone . . . cockyolly?" (*U*, 15.3129–30)—which, linguistically present (cockyolly) but reputedly anatomically absent ("where's [it] gone?"), becomes, like the hollow "phallic design" on the wall, another textual displacement of the sexual.

In addition to this element of linguistic displacement, both literal and fantasized planes of physical action are robbed of any "climax," sexual or otherwise. Not only is there no orgasmic experience, as far as I can tell, for anyone in Bella's bordello, but Bloom's fantasies generally fade before they reach any kind of fulfillment. Thus, just as Bloom's "low, secretly, ever more rapidly" whispered words to Mrs. Breen incite her sevenfold "Yes, yes, yes, yes, yes, yes, yes" (foreshadowing Molly's *attained* climax at the end of "Penelope"), the scenario teasingly fades, replaced by an image of coital impotence as *"armless"* loiterers *"flop wrestling, growling, in maimed sodden playfight"* (*U*, 15.581–83) in the street. Similarly, just as Bloom's fantasy of being birched by Mrs. Talboys nears a climax, with our hero trembling in submissive anticipation of fulfillment, the scene abruptly shifts, depriving Bloom of achieved pleasure (*U*, 15.1114).

Now, on the thematic level these processes of displacement and endless deferral can be explained as an analogue to Bloom's frustrations throughout the day; on a psychoanalytic level they might be explained, in Lacanian parlance, as the inevitable slippage along a chain of signifiers that constitutes desire in language; on a third level they might be read as the workings of a feminine *jouissance*, deilberately frustrating traditionally figured trajectories of male desire. But what disturbs me is the fact that, in any case, the Bloom-persona of "Circe" becomes a mere pretext for *Joyce's* linguistic erotics in these instances. And this points to a further complication in "Circe's" affirmation of sexual-textual free play: the simple fact that, despite the illusion of textual autonomy or authorial erasure effected by the episode's dramatic format, Joyce's fascination with the mechanisms of narrative control and of textual authority inscribe within "Circe" a narrative erotics that runs counter to its proclamations of polymorphous fluidity.

Such authorial pressure is perhaps most obvious in those frequent stage directions (the one dimension of a script, after all, in which the playwright's presence is palpable) where Joyce indulges in his signature punning and verbal bravado—as, for example, when he has "Marion Molly" saunter away "plump as a pampered pouter pigeon" (*U*, 15.353). Such showmanship spills over into the sheer extravagance of many of the speeches assigned the dramatis personae, such as that in which the Papal Nuncio unfolds an incredible genealogy of "begats" stretching from the biblical Moses through twenty-nine generations to our own Bloom (*U*, 15.1855–69). Even more pointedly, the section's many self-reflexive moments call attention to the authorial function. Not only does the litany delivered by the suddenly appearing mythic Daughters of Erin ("Kidney of Bloom, pray for us / Flower of the Bath, pray for us") recapitulate the entire novel to date in encoded form; but the stage direction that follows, announcing "*a choir of six hundred voices . . . sing[ing] the chorus from Handel's Messiah* Alleluia for the Lord God Omnipotent reigneth" (*U*, 15.1953–55), typographically highlights for us the imprint of that other "Omnipotent" creator, Joyce himself, without whose talents this tour de force could never happen. Such textual moments, I would thus argue, function as sites for a kind of extreme authorial exhibitionism, a pyrotechnical flexing of muscle that becomes equivalent to an act of masturbatory display. Indeed, an apt metaphor for Joyce's authorial practice here might be the fireworks that go off *"with symbolical phallopyrotechnic designs"* during the fulfillment fantasy (*U,* 15.1495–96). The irony, then, is that as much as Joyce decries the masculine ethos that oppresses Bloom with its emphasis on male prowess, the author is more than willing to put his own literary prowess on display for all takers.

Before proceeding further, however, I should add that "prowess" or "potency" is not in and of itself a necessarily negative literary quality, nor one necessarily devoid of any progressive sexual politics. In this regard it is necessary to distinguish the authorial derring-do weaving its way through the whole of *Ulysses* from the particular mode of authorial "exhibitionististicicity" (*U* 15.2325)— to borrow Virag's term for Bloom's voyeurism—at work in "Circe." Sandra Gilbert and Susan Gubar have taken Joyce to task for participating in a unilaterally patriarchal rhetoric of mastery—in their words, for "inaugurat[ing] a new patrilinguistic epoch"—through a show of linguistic "puissance" that "sentences" women to the material realm.[20] In contrast, as Karen Lawrence has more recently argued, and as a careful analysis of the narrative erotics inscribed in many of the novel's other "exhibitionistic" tour de forces demonstrates, Joyce often uses style to deconstruct "the symbolic, encoded forms of his own representations," including those of women, and in the process he exposes "the workings of male desire" in producing such representations.[21] For example, "Oxen of the Sun," with its masterly simulation of the history of English literary styles imposed over the story of Mina Purefoy's lying-in, might seem a flagrantly attention-grabbing, misogynistic display of authorial "puissance" (hence Gilbert and Gubar argue that the episode "presents us with a wresting of patriarchal power from the mother tongue").[22] But Joyce's use of stylistic rhetoric in "Oxen" may also be interpreted as critiquing the manner in which male discourse has historically attempted to use the fiat of the word, the patronym,

20. Sandra Gilbert and Susan Gubar, "Sexual Linguistics: Gender, Language, and Sexuality," *New Literary History* 16 (1985): esp. 518–19, 534–35.

21. Karen Lawrence, "Compromising Letters: Joyce and Women," *Western Humanities Review* 42 (1988): 4.

22. Gilbert and Gubar, "Sexual Linguistics," 535. See also Susan Stanford Friedman, "Creativity and the Childbirth Metaphor: Gender Difference in Literary Discourse," in *Speaking of Gender,* ed. Elaine Showalter (New York: Routledge, 1989), who focuses on Joyce's womb envy in distinguishing between male and female modes of (pro)creation but also notes the irony of his presentation of the medical students' attitudes (79–80, 97).

to cover over its *anxieties* about female productivity: hence the relegation of Mina's delivery to offstage action during the parodically inflated argument of the male medical students (which Joyce shows to be empty of content or meaning); hence the dizzying succession of literary styles that, as Lawrence argues, in their very errancy "subvert the integrity of the *pater* texts expropriated."[23] A similar gap between stylistic "prowess" and content characterizes that other scene of literalized exhibitionism and voyeurism in the novel, "Nausicaa"; Joyce's masterly simulation of sentimental prose works precisely to deconstruct the hold that the clichés of contemporary advertising and popular culture exert on the sexual imaginations of Bloom and Gerty.

What makes "Circe" so problematic, in contrast, is the way in which its mechanisms of narrative control work against its simultaneous proclamations of sexual free play. Let me cite one example. If, as I have argued, "Circe's" narrative thwarts sexual release on the level of both action and fantasy, I would nonetheless suggest that in the penultimate moments of "Circe," Joyce manages to have *his own* textual-narratological orgasm—and when Joyce comes, he indeed comes big. I am thinking of the frenzied chase scene that follows Stephen's phallic shattering of Bella's chandelier with his ashplant. In the episode's longest stage direction, which spills across two pages, the text virtually explodes as Bloom, chasing after Stephen, is in turn pursued by what turns out to be a cast of ninety-nine characters, culminating in "Mrs Miriam Dandrade and all her lovers" (*U*, 15.4360–61); this gargantuan release of textual energy, collecting together its dispersive parts into one continuous verbal ejaculation, in effect reassembles the entire text and even manages to foreshadow its ending.[24] One could hardly imagine a more audacious example of authorial fiat. If Clive Hart is correct in suggesting that "Circe" charts Bloom's inner acceptance of the fact that he does not *need* genitally oriented sexuality to be happy,[25] Joyce's maneuvers here suggest otherwise as regards the authorial function: the come-hither call of the prostitutes to their prospective clients

23. Lawrence, "Compromising Letters," 11.

24. The "climactic" explosiveness of this particular passage was brought to my attention by Caroline Cowie, "Interpreting Circe," 7.

25. Clive Hart, "The Sexual Perversions of Leopold Bloom," in *"Ulysses" Cinquante ans après: Temoignages franco-anglais sur le chef-d'oeuvre de James Joyce*, ed. Louis Bonnerot (Paris: Didier, 1974), 131.

which so intimidates Bloom—"Big comebig!" (*U*, 15.1273)—has become the authorial voice's self-assumed badge of honor.

This exhibitionism, in turn, further complicates the playfulness, the polymorphous perversity, of "Circe" by subjecting the reader to a coercive dynamics of textual mastery and control. The fact is that as the audience of such "phallopyrotechnical" displays, we become, like Bloom, the quintessential voyeur, participating in an erotic enactment which necessarily depends on a relation of inequality rather than reciprocity, even if we have willingly consented to be mastered. In so wielding his power as the ultimate authority of our pleasure, Joyce recapitulates on a narrative level the very dynamics of domination against which his representation of Bloom's subconscious guilt and desire is meant to work. Freeing the polymorphous perverse, in this Circean nightworld, occasionally becomes another name for regulating somebody else's desire.

Patrick McGee has argued that the sexual transformations of "Circe" illustrate "the ideology of the patriarch in a state of breakdown,"[26] a sentiment qualified, as we have just seen, by the degree to which Joyce's fascination with the mechanisms of textual mastery begins to overwrite the episode's free play. This does not mean, however, that authorial fiat unequivocally has the last word, or that the polymorphous perverse is incapable of staging its own devious returns. For McGee's statement still holds true on the level at which patriarchal ideology contains its own unconsciously deconstructive seeds. A case in point is the already cited chase scene (*U*, 15.4314–61), which not only proves that Joyce can "come big" when he wants to, but also exposes the anxieties of masculinity that propel such phallic expenditures of sexual-textual energy. I have already mentioned that the ejaculatory prose of this stage direction, summoning forth the entire novel in its breathless list of ninety-nine names, ends with "Mrs Miriam Dandrade and all her lovers." Given the principles of association and substitution governing "Circe," this reference might logically seem an anticipation of the novel's finale, with the name "Miriam" standing in for "Marion" (Molly's proper name), especially since Molly's erotic reverie about "all her lovers" real and fantasized indeed brings *Ulysses* to an end.

But is Mrs. Dandrade really, or only, a "mask" for Molly? It turns out that this obscure character is none other than the person at

---

26. McGee, *Paperspace*, 131.

the Shelbourne Hotel, mentioned in "Lestrygonians," who has sold Bloom her castoff old wraps and black undergarments (*U*, 8.349–51). These "short trunkleg naughties," it turns out, Bloom does not give to Molly but secretly dons himself, in order to practice "various poses of surrrender" (*U*, 15.299–94) in front of the mirror. "You were a nicelooking *Miriam*," Bella/o taunts Bloom in "Circe," "when you clipped off your backgate hairs and lay swooning in the thing across the bed *as Mrs Dandrade* about to be violated by lieutenant Smythe-Smythe," whereupon a list of eleven more names follows (*U*, 15.3000–3007; emphasis added). In light of this revelation we might well recast the phrase "Mrs Miriam Dandrade and all her lovers" to read "Mr. 'Miriam' Bloom and all his violators." Mrs. Dandrade is at once a "mask" or "cover" for Bloom *and* the vehicle of the cross-dressing masquerade ("swooning . . . as Mrs Dandrade") in which he is privately engaging. Moreover, as one of the most overtly *homosexual* of "Circe's" fantasies—Bloom imagining himself anally penetrated by men—it effects by its climactic positioning in the sequence (*U*,15.4314–61) an unsettling displacement not only of the text's *actual*, "heterosexual" climax in "Penelope" (with its marital implications), but also of the heterosexually charged "masculine" bravado characterizing the textual erotics of the passage itself.

Bloom in drag thus becomes the agency whereby the text's polymorphous perverse makes a most playful return indeed, unsettling the "ideology of the patriarch" this time around in the role of the nonheterosexual, repressed Other of Joyce's "phallopyrotechnic" designs. At the same time, Bloom's masquerade illuminates the crucial fact—already implicit in the (psycho)dramatic format of "Circe"—that *all* sexual identification is a kind of masquerade, a donning and divestiture of roles and masks and words. Even within the most interiorized spaces of psychosexual fantasy, the mind remains a *theater*, its sexual guilts and desires and polymorphous pleasures imbricated in a performative play of surfaces and exteriors whose status is never a given but always in the process of being constructed.

Performing (As) "Penelope"

To turn from the way in which "Mrs Miriam Dandrade," aka Bloom, foreshadows the ending of *Ulysses* to the masquerade of

"Penelope" which is the ending itself raises the question of Joyce's representational and formal goals in creating the latter chapter. As in "Circe," the attempt to represent those "hidden tides" and "ascending fumes of sex" expressive of libidinal activity, I would suggest, fuels Joyce's narrative experimentation in "Penelope," where the "uncensored"—now of Molly's rather than Bloom's psyche—is spectacularly put on display. Rather than repeating "Circe's" psychodramatic staging of desire, however, Joyce evokes Molly's psyche by attempting to create, in what is perhaps the modernist example par excellence of uninterrupted stream-of-consciousness, a convincing mimesis of the thoughts and erotic reveries coursing though her mind as she drifts toward sleep. Not only is the gulf between "Circe's" techniques of surreal expressionism and "Penelope's" autonomous interior monologue immense; but, because this *modal* difference is mapped over the axis of *sexual* difference, Joyce's narrative strategies also raise the question of how gender-marked his choices may be. In other words, what assumptions about differences in male and female modes of consciousness and repression may be encoded in the very formulation and deployment of either technique?

Just as the surreal expressionism of "Circe" throws up a screen of opaque language that automatically situates the reader at a remove from its record of psychic "events," so it would seem that the waking Bloom exists at a certain distance from the feverish activity that seethes in his subconscious: repression seems to work more thoroughly, if destructively, to maintain the ego boundaries and psychological differentiation that much recent feminist psychoanalysis has shown to be constitutive of male identity in modern Western culture.[27] A sensation of immediacy, in contrast, is the inevitable effect of interior monologue. By simulating the associative drift of Molly's (literally unpunctuated) libidinal and mental processes, the text of "Penelope" generates an illusion of transparency not only for the reader but for Molly herself, implying that she, as a woman, has more immediate access to her libido than, say, Bloom to his own; her ego boundaries appear more permeable, more capable of admitting to consciousness the desires and dissatisfactions of the subconscious. In Molly's monologue, indeed, "con-

27. See, for example, Jessica Benjamin, "Master and Slave: The Fantasy of Erotic Domination," in *Powers of Desire: The Politics of Sexuality*, ed. Ann Snitow, Christine Stansell, and Sharon Thompson (New York: Monthly Review Press, 1983), esp. 281–82.

sciousness" proves a very relative term, describing a state that, however verbal in its presentation, exists in close proximity to and in communication with the less conscious aspects of mental and psychosexual life. At its most positive, such a representation could be taken to mean that women's access to the unconscious makes them less repressed, hence more healthy, individuals; at its most negative, it risks implying that women, lacking men's more highly developed egos or sophisticated strategies of repression, *are* their libidos, *are* the unconscious.

If these modal distinctions highlight questions of gender, so too does the manner in which each chapter thematizes the "return of the repressed." In "Circe" what is repressed and seeks a return is definitionally psychological—Bloom's fears, doubts, anxieties, desires. In "Penelope," however, the repressed to which Joyce gives expression is frequently culture's—that is, all that has previously been repressed or censored in cultural and literary representations of female sexuality. To put it another way, if "Circe" gives expression to the repressed *in* Bloom, "Penelope" gives expression to Molly *as* the repressed in culture. This subtle difference sheds light on the sexual politics marking Joyce's narrative experimentations. For, whereas "Circe" works to deconstruct the global category of sexuality in the name of a polymorphous free play that is supposedly universal (but assigned to the male subject), the task of "Penelope" is more narrow: to deconstruct the moral category of gender in the name of "woman," specifically as its prohibitive laws forbid the forthright expression of what Joyce views as "true," "feminine" sexuality (even if those prohibitions have "universal" implications for both sexes).

A corollary of these distinctions is that Joyce seems to accord his female protagonist a much more self-conscious—indeed, a culturally mandated—understanding of gender as a construction, a masquerade, that she must continually enact. To the extent that Molly's monologue thematizes and foregrounds gender as a performance, moreover, an unexpected congruence emerges between "Penelope" and the overtly dramatic format of "Circe." Both episodes have roots in the contemporary theater of Joyce's day, as Cheryl Herr has persuasively shown: if "Circe" draws on the pantomime tradition of sexual impersonation to reveal all sexuality and identity as an ensemble of constructed roles and discourses, "Penelope" emulates the music hall tradition of saving the headline performer, the diva, for the star turn or "topper" at the end of the bill.[28] Not only does the narrative positioning of "Penelope" as a kind of novelistic "topper" thus draw on theatrical precedent, but the episode's method also has dramatic affinities. Precisely because Molly's interior monologue is uninterrupted and self-contained, it can also literally be read as a dramatic monologue or dramatic soliloquy—a scripted address directed to a hypothetical audience that observes the dramatic unities of time, place, and action (hence making it more easily adaptable to the stage than "Circe," as Fionnula Flanagan's one-woman show has illustrated). We have already seen how the mental theater of "Circe" becomes a strategic mode of elaborating its psychosexual concerns. Just how the theatrical components of performance subtend the representation of (en)gendered subjectivity in "Penelope" will emerge as one line of inquiry in the discussion that follows. The ramifications of this topos for modernist explorations of sexuality and narrative will become clearer once we have taken a more specific look at the sexual-textual dynamics of Molly's monologue and the controversies to which it has given rise.

Not only is Molly a consummate actress, but her first-person monologue provides the vehicle for what many critics have called Joyce's masquerade of femininity. And indeed, it is the very *intimacy* of Joyce's simulation of a "woman's" voice that has spawned endless debate about the relative success or failure of his method for representing Molly's psychosexual complexities. Among feminist critics there is a widespread, although not unanimous, suspicion that Joyce in effect "violates" Molly, first by penetrating her thoughts and then by appropriating her voice through his ventriloquism.[29] Whatever one's view of Joyce's characterization, the question also often becomes, as one of my students once wisely put it, whether we feminists have to apologize for liking Molly, and whether in reading Molly we are able to avoid collaborating in (what

28. Cheryl Herr, "'Penelope' as Period Piece," *Novel* (Winter 1989): 130–42. Herr notes that it was not unusual for a theatrical bill to include "selected scenes from classics" or favorite arias, which "were valued quite apart from their function in the works from which they were drawn—as tours de force that provided opportunities for an actor's talents to be measured and savored" (131). "Penelope" likewise "shows us a singer doing her most famous aria, a performer delivering the somewhat scandalous speech that made her notorious" (131).

29. For various readings of Molly—as archetypal earth mother, as "real" or essential woman, as stereotypical "bitch," as sexist creation, as the voice of antiphallocentrism—and feminist reactions to them, see Bonnie Kime Scott, *Joyce and Feminism* (Bloomington: Indiana University Press, 1984), 151–61, and Suzette Henke and Elaine Unkeless, eds., *Women in Joyce* (Urbana: University of Illinois Press, 1982).

might well be) her author's reading of her. [30] I will suggest two ways in which the phenomenon of Molly-as-fictional-creation gives us an "out," as her figural presence dodges some of the less desirable impositions of her maker, but first I will review some of those elements which seem problematic in Molly's articulation of her sexual identity and desires; for the moment I will bracket the question of whether these thematized viewpoints attest more to Molly's limitations, Joyce's impositions, or some combination of the two.

Like Bloom, Molly harbors an often negative self-image ("I suppose Im nothing any more" [U, 18.1244]) which is directly related to the state of her marriage and her fears of sexual rejection. As her monologue obsessively reveals, the anxieties engendered by her cultural position as woman and wife mark her perception of sexuality and in particular of female pleasure in profound, and profoundly contradictory, ways. For instance, of her own capacity for erotic fulfillment, she fantasizes procuring sex with "some nicelooking boy . . . since *I cant* do it myself," only to reveal a few lines later that she indeed *can* and *must* "finish it off myself anyway," at least in the case of sex with Bloom, where there is "no satisfaction in it pretending to like it till he comes" (U, 18.84–85, 98–99; emphasis added). Heterosexual intercourse both is (with a "nicelooking boy") and is not (with Bloom) the answer, just as autoerotic satisfaction both is ("finish it off myself") and is not ("cant do it myself") an option to intercourse.

This double-speak of both/neither also characterizes Molly's contradictory relation to her body as a specifically female body. If she at times voices what appears a classically Freudian definition of female anatomy as lack ("whats the idea of making us like that with a big hole in the middle" [U, 18.151]), she also evinces a pride in her breasts ("they excite myself sometimes" [U, 18.1379]) that hovers ambiguously between genuine appreciation, narcissistic self-love, and a male-identified view of women's bodies. Molly's references to oral sex provide another telling indication of her mixed sexual self-image. For whereas she imagines fellatio with Stephen's "lovely young cock there so simple . . . so clean and white" (U, 18.1352, 1354) as entirely pleasurable, she fantasizes that she will punish Bloom by making him

---

30. I am thinking of Moira Wallace's superb (and untitled) paper, written for a seminar I taught in April 1985, which has had a significant influence on my interpretation of "Penelope." Suzette Henke opens her book *James Joyce and the Politics of Desire* (New York: Routledge, 1990), with a similar question: "How can a feminist begin to approach the writings of James Joyce?" (1).

practice cunnilingus on her ("Ill make him do it again if he doesnt mind himself and lock him down to sleep in the coalcellar with the blackbeetles" [*U*, 18.1251–52]). The metonymic process of association that links female genitalia to beetle-infested cellars is, of course, part of the same cultural anxiety that Molly internalizes in the "upward" displacement informing her valorization of "bubs" over "holes."

The simple fact is that the objectifying terms provided by male heterosexual discourse provide Molly with the only *sanctioned* language she knows for expressing the sensuality of her material presence. To appreciate her voluptuousness, much less another woman's, Molly automatically slips into a male viewpoint. Hence her expression of pleasure in the smoothness of her thighs immediately becomes the thought, "God I wouldnt mind being a man and get up on a lovely woman" [*U*, 18.1146–47], and her admiration of her breasts leads her to imagine having a penis in order to conceptualize "the amount of pleasure they [men] get off a womans body" [*U*, 18.1380–84].[31] Although some critics have seen these statements as signs of latent lesbianism, and others as proof of Freudian theories of penis envy, they more crucially index Molly's entrapment within a sociolinguistic order that simply does not provide her with a vocabulary adequate to an articulation of her specific bodily pleasures.

From conceiving of her body in terms of male paradigms of desire, it is a small step to Molly's tendency to measure her self-worth in terms of men's responsiveness to her sexuality. Thus, whatever personal release she finds in sex with Boylan is overshadowed by her preoccupation with whether she has "satisfied" him [*U*, 18.121–22], and, with regard to Bloom, she decides "the only way" to solve their marital problems is to "make him want me" [*U*, 18.1539]. Molly's personal metaphysics of being hence reduces to one thing, her sexual essence as woman: "I suppose thats what a woman is supposed to be there for or He wouldnt have made us the way He did so attractive to men" [*U*, 18.1518–20]. With her position as cultural *and* narrative subject dictated from above by these divine and authorial "He's," Molly in her bedridden immobility has seemed to many readers the embodiment of the archetypal Femi-

31. To emphasize the socially conditioned and gendered pressures that underlie the circuitousness with which Molly here approaches her sensuality, one might hypothetically ask how many heterosexual *men* would express their pride in being well hung by exclaiming to themselves, "God I wouldn't mind being a woman to be mounted by that brute of a thing!"

nine, condemned to play the role of the willing and (im)passive female flesh that always says yes, through a Joycean sleight of hand that transforms her bodily specificity into pure essence.

And yet, simultaneous with this narratively overdetermined acquiescence to biology, Molly reveals much more than she overtly says about her capacity for sexual self-pleasure. If her standard complaint is that sexual enjoyment is a male privilege—"nice invention they made for women for him to get all the pleasure" (*U*,18.157)— she also subtly modifies this judgment when she inadvertently reveals *why* men have "all the pleasure": "they want to do everything too quick take all the pleasure out of it" (*U*, 18.315–16). Pleasure, it turns out, is not exclusively male; the problem is that female pleasure is subjected to male demand within the patriarchal frame of heterosexual coupling. Moreover, for all Molly's psychological reliance on heterosexual paradigms, her discourse positively reverberates with desire and the potential for self-enjoyment as well as self-fulfillment: it is clear that she *knows* what it feels like "to let myself go," to "come again," and to "feel all fire inside me" (*U*,18.584–85), and she *knows*, as the final pages of her monologue reveal, how to give herself satisfaction. However lackluster Molly's love life may be, however inadequate or limited her vocabulary for expressing her eroticism, she nonetheless exercises a sexuality, a sensate eroticism, that often proves sufficient unto itself. It is precisely this unconscious knowledge of the body, this autoerotic sufficiency, that forms the "repressed" of "Penelope."

What Molly's monologue also makes clear is that she is perfectly comfortable with contradiction; any viewpoint she offers at one moment is likely to be reversed the next. Bonnie Kime Scott has written of Molly that "even in the things she dislikes, there are momentary pleasures," as if to apologize for Molly's capitulation to male standards or her stereotypical life.[32] I think one should press the implications of Scott's statement further: to say that Molly's contradictions are evidence of her feminine illogic *or* of Joyce's stereotypical representation of female consciousness finally is not sufficient.[33] In fact, it is precisely this capacity to contain and

32. Scott, *Joyce and Feminism*, 161.
33. Indeed, as Moira Wallace has argued (see n. 30), the pervasiveness of Molly's contradictory stances makes it impossible to categorize her as simply one thing or the other, realistic womanhood or male fantasy, symbolic Eternal Feminine or archetypal Gea Tellus, laudable heroine or despicable whore. The critical endeavor to polarize Molly as only one side of the equation is already contradicted by the contradictions that exist in the flow of

withstand contradiction, along with what I have just called Molly's unacknowledged potential for autoerotic sufficiency, that begins to illuminate at least two routes by which her textually constituted subjectivity eludes not only her maker but her readers. I take as my signposts to these escape routes two phrases Joyce used in writing Frank Budgen on separate occasions to explain the relation of "Penelope" to the rest of *Ulysses*. The first appears in a letter of August 16, 1921, where he calls "Penelope" the *clou* of the book.[34] In its literal meaning of "nail," "spike," or "stud," this French term would seem to summon forth a worst-case scenario of the authorial mastery involved in "pinning" down (a) woman's consciousness, precisely by affixing Molly to her bed. Taken in its aural sense as a "clue" to *Ulysses*, the term hardly serves Molly any better, ascribing to her monologue a superhuman explanatory power that, in effect, makes woman's voice the existential truth or key underlying Everyman's quest—an only slightly less pernicious way of pinning Molly to a traditional literary function.

But *clou* can also mean the "star turn" or "chief attraction" of a theatrical event, and to see Molly, as Cheryl Herr suggests, as the headline performer, the so-called "topper," in *Ulysses*'s novelistic show provides an illuminating context within which to reinterpret the gendered implications of her star performance.[35] Following Herr's cues, Kimberly Devlin has brilliantly argued that "Penelope" not only "foregrounds theatricality," but that "theatricality mediates Molly's visions of self and other." That is, cognizant of the role-playing element in all behavior, of the self-dramatizations underlying any "identity," Molly "dons multiple recognizable masks of womanliness" throughout her monologue, as her thoughts sift through the various props, costumes, gestures, appellations, and signifiers at her disposal in constructing whatever "feminine" image she wishes to project in a given social or personal encounter. The past perfect tense of Molly's wistful claim—"I could have been a prima donna only I married him" (*U*, 18.896)—is at least in part belied by the multiple performances she *continues* to enact, both

---

her associations—contradictions intrinsic, as I shall attempt to show, to the psychosexual spaces of representation opened by her erotic reveries.

34. James Joyce to Frank Budgen, August 16, 1921, in *Selected Letters of James Joyce*, ed. Richard Ellmann (New York: Viking, 1975), 285; hereafter cited in the text as *SL*. The various meanings of *clou* are glossed by Herr, "Period Piece," 131, and McGee, *Paperspace*, 171.

35. Herr, "Period Piece," 130–31.

in her everyday negotiations with others and in the roles she "does" or "pretends" in imagination and memory, for example (to list only a few of the illustrations culled by Devlin), "*Ill do* the indifferent [spouse]"; "*I could do* the criada"; "when I came *on the scene . . . I pretended* I had a coolness on with her over him"; "I pulled him off into my handkerchief *pretending* not to be excited"; "of course I had to say no for form sake dont understand you I said" (*U*, 18.1529, 1482–83, 171–83, 809–10, 324–25; emphasis added).[36]

In the light of this ability to conjure up roles at a moment's notice, the contradictions in Molly's monologue that have caused such debate among critics can more usefully be seen as a function of her awareness that femaleness in her world is always an enactment, a series of sometimes mutually contradictory performances. Hence Devlin, returning to Joyce's description of "Penelope" as "the *clou* of the book," defines Molly's monologue as "a concatenation of roles, an elaborate series of 'star turns' that undermines the notion of womanliness as it displays it."[37] On the one hand, to the extent that Molly submits to cultural norms, she participates in the female masquerade in order to "become" woman through, in Mary Anne Doane's terms, a "hyperbolisation of the accoutrements of femininity,"[38] a phrase that well describes Molly's narcissistic flaunting of her figure, obsession with female dress, exaggerated reliance on male prowess, and the like. But, on the other hand, Molly's consciousness that she is always playing a role, a recognition heightened with every repetition, simultaneously turns female masquerade into a *parody* of the signifiers of gender, and this mimicry constitutes a very different mode of power: "Miming the feminine, playfully 'repeating' it," Carol-Anne Tyler writes, "produces knowledge about it."[39] Experiencing her subjectivity as an enactment, Molly not only performs "femininity" but plays on that very act of role playing, thus becoming, in Devlin's engaging analogy, a modern-day "gender performance artist."[40]

---

36. Kimberly J. Devlin, "Pretending in 'Penelope': Masquerade, Mimicry, and Molly Bloom," forthcoming in *Molly Blooms: A Polylogue on "Penelope,"* ed. Richard Pearce (Madison: University of Wisconsin Press, 1993). Quotations are from ms. 2, 3, 4, respectively. I am grateful to the author for permission to quote from the unpublished essay.
37. Ibid., 5.
38. Mary Anne Doane, "Film and the Masquerade: Theorizing the Female Spectator," *Screen* 23 (1982): 82; quoted in Devlin, "Pretending in 'Penelope.'"
39. Carol-Anne Tyler, "Female Impersonation" (Ph.D. diss., Brown University, 1982, 21–22; quoted in Devlin, "Pretending in 'Penelope.'"
40. Devlin, "Pretending in 'Penelope,'" 8.

The farthest extension of viewing Molly as an actress is to read "Penelope" as a *literal script*, a tack that leads Cheryl Herr to argue that the speaking voice in "Penelope" has no mimetic value or fictive existence at all, that "Molly" is *only* a "role" to be filled by any competent actress—or actor.[41] If such an extreme reading risks stating the obvious about any fictional text's "characters"—who are always verbal artifacts, nothing more nor less—the conceit of "Penelope" as an actor's script serves the useful function of pointing out the degree to which Molly's *words* (whether envisioned as literal theatrical vehicle or internalized dramatic monologue) form a screen, a mask, behind which the character can hide and, in hiding, elude both reader's and author's impositions. Similarly, Patrick McGee argues that "Molly's word . . . is a masquerade, a play of conventions. . . . But this does not mean that [her word] has no relation to something *like* a woman, to something like the feminine, to something that resists Molly's word and Joyce's writing. . . . To read Molly is to half-create her but never to possess her."[42]

Molly's theatrical self-presentation, moreover, holds significant resonances with recent constructionist theories of gender. Judith Butler, for example, hypothesizes that gender's "substantive *effect*," its appearance of a fixed essence or substance, is always "performatively *produced*," inscribing itself through various cultural codes *on* the body rather than rising from *within* the subject. Indeed, Molly's use of masquerade, her gender role playing, is, to use Butler's terms, a "repeated stylization of the body" which reveals gender to be an *act* "that performatively constitutes the appearance of its interior fixity."[43] This formulation sheds a crucial light on the theatricality that pervades Joyce's representation of the psychosexual complexities of Molly's "interior" life. For what promises to be a privileged glimpse into Molly's feminine "essence" or "core" turns out instead to reveal a series of masks, of performative *sur*-

41. As Herr puts it: "I can no longer find it in myself to grant the Molly of 'Penelope' any reality-value whatsoever. . . . For me, 'Penelope' projects simply an actor reading a script. . . . To say this is, for me at least, to argue that Molly does not occupy the level of narrative reality that we have normally granted her" ("Period Piece," 134). As a role that conceivably any actor can assume, the monologue lives up to the letter of its Homeric namesake, since one etymological meaning of "Penelope," as Herr notes, is "'countenance of webs' or mask" (130).

42. McGee, *Paperspace*, 172, 181.

43. Judith Butler, *Gender Trouble: Feminism and the Subversion of Identity* (New York: Routledge, 1990); quotations are from 42, 33, and 70, respectively (emphasis added). A good summary of Butler's thesis appears on 128–41, in chap. 4, section 4, "Bodily Inscriptions, Performative Subversions."

faces, upon which are inscribed those gender prescriptions that culture produces while it pretends they originate in some "interior fixity." Thus, however disparately weighted the deconstructive "tasks" undertaken in "Circe" (with regard to sexuality) and "Penelope" (with regard to gender), the representation of Molly's "inner" consciousness ultimately works to unsettle the assumed boundaries of "interior" versus "exterior," "surface" versus "depth," every bit as much as does "Circe's" flaunting of the unconscious as a theater of unending sexual masquerade.

If theatricality constitutes one path whereby Molly's representation evades authorial and readerly mastery, a second avenue of escape exists in the *formal* attributes of the technique Joyce employs in "Penelope." Critics have often noted the anomalous position Molly's monologue occupies as *Ulysses*'s final word or, as Joyce put it in a second letter to Frank Budgen, the text's "indispensible countersign" (*SL*, 278). In a narrative whose structure has been dictated by the crisscrossing trajectories of its male heroes—which finally meet in "Ithaca," the immediately preceding section—it may come as a surprise to find oneself lodged, at text's end, in a consciousness and a chapter that stands so completely apart from the interests of the rest of the narrative. At first glance this positioning of "Penelope" might seem either a deliberate or a subconscious means of circumscribing Molly's power, adding to her objectification by stripping her consciousness bare and making its excavation the basis for a demonstration of Joyce's virtuoso pyrotechnics. Molly is kept in her bed, as it were, framed by the larger narrative of which she forms only a small part. In the function of "Penelope" as a "countersign" to the entire narrative, however, one of the effects is to establish its *separateness* by virtue of its formulation as, in Dorrit Cohn's words, "a self-generated, self-supported, and self-enclosed text." Rather than an effect of constriction, the autonomous status of Molly's self-enclosed interior monologue thus becomes a vital sign of its formal independence. For, technically speaking, this episode, beginning and ending within a single consciousness, forms, as Cohn also argues, "the only moment of the novel where a figural voice totally obliterates the authorial voice throughout an entire chapter."[44] The point is crucial because it implies that however much Joyce may (or may not) desire to impose

44. Cohn, *Transparent Minds,* 218. I am grateful to Moira Wallace for directing me to Cohn's argument.

his viewpoints on Molly, there is a sense in which her voice, by virtue of its figural constitution as a self-sufficient "I," removes the author, and with him his authority, from the picture: her "I" demands neither audience nor reply.[45]

The few times Molly engages in the language of personal address, directing her thoughts to an imaginary audience, only serve to confirm the degree to which her position as speaking subject grants her a certain independence from the controlling powers in her life. It is no coincidence that all the interlocutors Molly imagines are *male* figures, whose authority, tellingly, is successively desacralized by the contexts of her statements. Thus, to her divine creator she complains, "Give us room even to let a fart God" (*U*, 18.906); to her domestic lord she grumbles, "O move over your big carcass out of that for the love of Mike" (*U*, 18.1426); to her earthly creator she demands, "O Jamesy let me up out of this pooh" (*U*, 18.1128–29). Even what certainly is, on one level, the epitome of "Jamesy's" effort to assert control over Molly by making *her* articulate or voice her subjection to *his* whims ("O . . . let me up") simultaneously ends up unmasking the anxieties that subtend the desire for authorial mastery. For Joyce's name, his self-conscious signature, is left irretrievably stranded among references to menstrual blood (sign of Molly's creative fiat), thoughts about women's capacities to simulate virginity (and hence rob fatherhood of its certitude—the nightmare haunting Stephen's interpretation of Shakespeare in the library episode), and signs of incipient domestic rebellion ("whoever suggested that business for women what between clothes and cooking and children" [*U*, 18.1129–30]). "Jamesy" is fairly outnumbered, his authorial intrusion overwhelmed by the "countersigns" of insurgent female authority most calculated to whet his masculine anxieties. This series of mental addresses appropriately culminates in a prophetic statement of insurrection—putatively directed at Bloom but vague enough to include all men—that augurs a different, more empowering story for female characters such as Molly: "Oh wait now sonny my turn is coming" (*U*, 18.1533). And "coming" Molly indeed is, by text's end.

The way in which the term "sonny" potentially includes more

---

45. As Cohn also notes, this self-sufficiency is reflected in the fact that Molly's thoughts are primarily *exclamatory* in syntax, which is "the self-sufficient, self-involved language gesture par excellence" (*Transparent Minds*, 225).

men than Bloom alone also calls to mind the psychologically enabling use to which Molly puts the pronoun "he" throughout her reveries. One could select any number of instances in which the reference of the third-person singular masculine pronoun is ambiguous; likewise, Molly's memories of the men in her life repeatedly collapse into one syncretic image: "what was his name Jack Joe Harry Mulvey was it . . . no he hadnt a moustache that was Gardner" (U, 18.818, 872–73). As this interchangeability suggests, Molly's thoughts attach no special privilege to any one man, not even Poldy; she receives continual pleasure, rather, from imagining, desiring, manipulating an infinitude of men—or "he"-men, as Cohn jokingly but aptly puts it[46]—ranging from those she has known to those she has glimpsed on the street. Early in her monologue Molly mentions her fancy to have a "new fellow" every spring (U, 18.782), and, at least within her imagination, she fulfills her desire.

Thus interchanging fantasies about men for her private erotic gain, Molly becomes, within the realm of her imagination, an acting subject, not merely a passive object whose existence is entirely dependent on male approval. Amidst the referential instability of the pronouns "he" and "him," her first-person "I" remains the one constant, the single fixity the reader can always depend on to be identical to itself—even if and as that self is divided, contradictory, and multiply positioned. Moreover, just as Molly's figural "I" strips Joyce of a direct authorial voice in her monologue, Moira Wallace suggests that what Molly means by her famous "yes" may not be identical to her author's infamous extratextual assertions, to friends such as Louis Gillet, that her final word denotes "acquiescence, self-abandon, relaxation, the end of all resistance"—that is, feminine passivity in its most archetypal representation. First, to the extent that Molly's "yes" intimates "self-abandon," she only abandons herself to herself, retreating to a private world of her own making as she fades into sleep during orgasm.[47] Second, the very fact that

46. Ibid., 230.
47. Wallace, untitled paper, 14; Gillet is quoted in Richard Ellmann, James Joyce (New York: Oxford University Press, 1982), 712. Wallace's deconstruction of Joyce's reading of Molly's "yes" takes as its starting point a letter to Frank Budgen in which Joyce transforms the Faustian formula "I am the spirit that always denies" into a Penelopean analogue, "Ich bin der [sic] Fleisch der stets bejaht" (I am the flesh that always says yes) (Letters of James Joyce, ed. Gilbert Stuart [New York: Viking, 1965], 1:170); but the text's Molly, Wallace argues, is "far closer to being the acting subject of Faust than she is to being the object of that subjectivity. Molly questions, denies, exploits and interchanges men in a

she *is* bringing herself to orgasm, as the final series of lyrical "yeses" signals, makes it clear that this sexual act of *auto*eroticism is one which, by its very nature, excludes us *even as* we voyeuristically look on. As such, Molly's "yes" also becomes an assertion of what *she* feels; its affirmation is her self-affirmation. Simultaneously, Molly's "yes" is thus also a resistant "no," the refusal of an acting subject to submit her thoughts to others' desires and demands; it is another way of saying, as Molly already has, "I suppose he thinks Im finished and laid out on the shelf well Im not no" (*U*, 18.1022–23), or, "O wait now sonny my turn is coming."

This self-affirmation is not without its problems or ambiguities, of course. If Molly emerges as an acting subject in her reveries, it is also true that her subjectivity may not necessarily or always be congruent with a *female* subjectivity, particularly as defined by feminist psychoanalytic theory following in the wake of Nancy Chodorow and Carol Gilligan. That is, Molly's sense of identity does not seem particularly "relational"; her relations with other women are almost uniformly competitive and denigrating, reflecting a more masculine fantasy of women as "naturally" jealous of one another. And however freeing Molly's grammatical conflation of all male objects to a metonymic series of interchangeable "he's," she still remains dependent on her reflection in male eyes to assure her of her worth. Even in the twist whereby Joyce's boastful "Jamesy" is submerged in references to female menstruation and the like, the ambiguities linger, to the extent that Molly's counterauthority resides in an appeal to the body—again, perhaps more of a male's fantasy of female subjectivity than a woman's evocation of her power.

Literally, of course, Molly, like any fictional character, cannot exist alone. It takes a Joyce to write a Molly into being, just as it takes the reader to give her textual life. Nonetheless, the very act of writing and reading Molly, *because of* her representation within a self-contained and self-generated interior monologue, also frees her figural presence—not of all male markings, as we have just seen, but of any absolute authorial attempt to "make" or "speak for" woman. For the very *grammar* of Joyce's representation of female

---

way that is definitely Faustian. . . . She can be seen as the constructor of an eternal masculine" (12). If Molly thus also says *no*, Wallace proceeds to show, along lines similar to Cohn's and my arguments, how Molly's "yes" is less a sign of female acquiescence than of a self-sufficiency implicit in the structure of autonomous monologue.

consciousness ironically undoes his authority to make his language signify what he might want it to mean: *his* promiscuous "he's" become *her* access to erotic pleasure; *his* inscription of "female" contradiction through Molly's continual self-interrogation becomes *her* means of keeping the question open; *his* "yes" of feminine surrender becomes *her* affirmation of a private space and a public mask that, finally, resist appropriation.

As Molly lies beside Bloom in bed, thinking back on her encounter with Boylan, another of those ambiguous third-person masculine pronouns crosses her mind: "I wonder is he awake thinking of me or dreaming am I in it" (*U*, 18.124–25). Whether "he" refers to Bloom or Boylan, this wistful thought would, at first glance, seem yet another confirmation of Molly's incapacity to imagine herself apart from men: unless they "think" of or "dream" her, she feels she has no real identity or existence. But when Molly's words are applied to the authorial presence who has figuratively dreamed her into novelistic existence—Joyce himself—they take on a tantalizingly different valence. For, in fact, Joyce literally *did* dream about Molly, and his recounting of this dream on two separate occasions quite stunningly attests to what Karen Lawrence has called the authorial anxieties engendered by the possible "presumptuousness" of his attempt "to lend voice to female desire."[48] Simultaneously, his dream attests to his uneasy intuition that Molly's "power" is precisely the power to "escape" his text's boundaries. In the dream Molly comes calling on Joyce to reprimand him for meddling in *her* "business"—that is, for taking over her story—and in response to Joyce's passionate defense of his intentions in writing "Penelope," Molly flings a miniature coffin at him, announcing, "And I have done with you, too, Mr. Joyce."[49] In other words, refusing to be coerced by "Mr. Joyce's" insinuating explanations, she establishes her independence from his authorial control by finishing with him, symbolically killing him off, instead of vice versa. Not coincidentally, Molly also appears in masquerade in the dream: she is wearing a black opera cloak "that looked like *La Duse.*" Having dismissed her creator, she is free to exist beyond his text in a realm to which his representational powers can only gesture. On some profound level that is not merely a critic's dream, Molly La Duse has indeed

48. Lawrence, "Compromising Letters," 3.
49. Joyce's versions of the dream are recounted in Ellmann, *James Joyce,* 549, and in Herbert Gorman, *James Joyce* (New York: Rinehart, 1948), 283.

escaped the bedsteadfastness of *Ulysses*,[50] moving outside the constraints of her fictional context and making an appearance, a kind
of curtain call, as a consummate actress with the uncanny ability
to return without notice to haunt her creator's subconscious. What
is "interior" and what is "exterior" are hopelessly blurred as Joyce's
attempt to represent Molly's "interiority" in external form becomes
a manifestation of his own interior anxieties. In yet another ironic
twist, *Ulysses*'s repressed has made a return, and this time the space
of representation is not the dream-text of "Circe" but the theater
of Joyce's unconscious.

As I hope this overview of the highly charged textual erotics of
"Circe" and "Penelope" has begun to suggest, when it comes to
the modernist endeavor to represent states of interiority, issues of
sexuality and narrative impinge on each other in highly complex,
often unpredicable ways. In this regard I find Joyce's statement to
Djuna Barnes, cited in my opening paragraph, suggestive: "I have
recorded," Joyce says, "simultaneously, what a man says, sees,
thinks, and what such seeing, thinking, saying does, to what you
Freudians call the subconscious." Perhaps Joyce could have at-
tended more closely to his own subconscious operations in making
such a neat summary statement, for not only has he captured the
"Freudian subconscious" in choosing different modes of representing the psychosexual forces driving Bloom's and Molly's inner
worlds; he has also made available throughout *Ulysses* a "textual
unconscious"—his own repressed—in which issues of narrative authority and autonomy, acts of textual elision and expression, continually summon their counterparts into operation. Perhaps it is
this textual unconscious, for instance, that is responsible for his
repressing the question of gender in speaking to Barnes of *Ulysses*'s
achievement in generically male terms ("I have recorded . . . what
a man says, sees, thinks"), when, as we have seen, it is precisely
what Bloom does *not* get to say in "Circe" (given its expressionistic
format) and what a woman *does* get to say in "Penelope" (given its
status as interior monologue) that calls into question the relation
between Joyce's narrative authority and the putative free play of his
characters' psychosexual desires. Likewise, perhaps it is this textual
unconscious that paradoxically allows Molly her orgasm while rob-

50. I borrow the phrase from Phillip Herring, "The Bedsteadfastness of Molly Bloom,"
Modern Fiction Studies 15 (1969): 49–61.

bing Bloom of the satisfaction of his own polymorphous sexuality. And perhaps, finally, it is this operation of *Ulysses*'s "repressed" that allows Joyce to assume Molly's contradictory logic as his own and, as Karen Lawrence has suggested, at once long to recapture woman as origin and simultaneously acknowledge her existence elsewhere, beyond himself,[51] on a textual stage his epic has created for her, finally, to appropriate from him.

51. Lawrence, "Compromising Letters," 6, 15.

PART IV

Incest, Narcissism,
and the Scene of Writing:
Ulysses and *Finnegans Wake*

8

The Preservation of Tenderness: A Confusion of Tongues in *Ulysses* and *Finnegans Wake*

Marilyn L. Brownstein

In an address to the Twelfth International Psycho-Analytical Congress in Wiesbaden in September 1932, Sandor Ferenczi remarked on "too facile explanations" of neuroses "in terms of 'disposition' and 'constitution.'"[1] With the tact and care of a son staging something more sophisticated, more respectful, and infinitely more subtle than an oedipal revolt, he proceeded to offer a radical critique of psychoanalytic theory.[2] He urged that psychoanalysis, instead of focusing on the self-generating causes of hysteria, examine the "traumatic factors in the pathogenesis of the neuroses." Specifically, he insisted that attention be paid to the appalling frequency of "sexual mistreatment of children by parents, persons thought to be trustworthy such as relatives (uncles, aunts, grandparents), governesses or servants, who misuse the ignorance and the innocence of the child."[3] By discussing "the exogenous factor" in neuroses, "unjustly neglected in recent years" (Ferenczi,

---

1. Sandor Ferenczi, "Confusion of Tongues between Adults and the Child: The Language of Tenderness and of Passion," in *Final Contributions to the Problems and Methods of Psychoanalysis* (New York: Brunner Mazel, 1980), chap. 8, 156; hereafter cited in the text as Ferenczi. I am grateful to my dear friend Marcella Bohn, who discovered the Ferenczi paper in the course of her own analytic practice and several years ago sent a copy to me. Without it much of what follows could not have been written.
2. Ferenczi presented his initial introduction of this topic in an "address given to the Viennese Psycho-Analytic Society on the occasion of Professor Freud's seventy-fifth birthday" (ibid., 156).
3. "Even children of very respectable, sincerely puritanical families, fall victim to real violence or rape much more often than one had dared to suppose" (ibid., 161).

156), Ferenczi offered a basic challenge to the long-standing preference of psychoanalysis for theories of infantile sexuality over theories of trauma, a preference that still dominates the field.

In his address, "Confusion of Tongues between Adults and the
Child," Ferenczi attempted a revision of theory and practice by investigating the functions of a doubled language on which the analyst
must base his or her treatment of childhood sexual trauma. This
"language of tenderness and of passion" consists of a dualistic linguistic register that operates distinctively for the analyst, the incest
victim, and the perpetrator. In demonstrating possible variations in
the dialectical arrangements of tenderness and passion, Ferenczi's
work provides linguistic paradigms for the resistances of victim and
perpetrator and for the therapeutic reversals essential to successful
treatment.

His work also offers an intriguing basis for investigating analogous resistances and reversals in the discursive dialectics of *Ulysses*
and *Finnegans Wake*.[4] Initially my reading focuses on the distinctive operations of the language of passion and tenderness within the
father-daughter incest motif that seems to dominate the narrative
modes of each of the Joycean texts. In addition, by disclosing the
dialectical nature of the incest themes operating across both works,
I hope to demonstrate how such a reading produces significant commentary on the political unconscious of the Joycean oeuvre; that
is, a paradigmatic investigation based on Ferenczi's design uncovers
the tropes of a monstrosity-breeding ideology of forgetfulness, the
overriding strategy for dealing with family sex crimes in our culture.[5] The appearance of Ferenczi's paper in *Final Contributions to
Psychoanalysis* presents, moreover, yet another sort of reflection

4. All citations are from James Joyce, *Ulysses*, ed. Hans Walter Gabler et al. (New
York: Random House, 1986), and James Joyce, *Finnegans Wake* (New York: Viking Press,
1955); hereafter cited in the text as *U* with episode and line numbers, and *FW* with page
and line numbers.

5. Although we often lose our way among the digressively various entertainments, it
is in this very (digressive) sense that the kindergarten sprawl of *Finnegans Wake* evokes a
compendium of monstrous forgetfulness, fancy although transparently disingenuous ob-
fuscations of HCE's sin in the park, an ironizing of the moment "when they were yung
and easily freudened" (*FW*, 115.22, 23). In this text primal obscenity and its rationalizations
walk on their hands, freely exhibiting Joyce's penchant for the gritty, girlish ruffles of an
irrational sensationalism: the latter—in a panty raid, if we dare to so name it—would
seem to be a set of anti-ideological underpinnings. There is evidence that Joyce was bitterly
aware of childhood sexual abuse (see notes 28 and 30). I would even venture to guess that
his antipathy toward psychoanalytic practice arose not only from the disappointments of
Carl Jung's brief and unsuccessful encounter with Joyce's daughter Lucia but also out of
what Joyce saw as the intrinsic failing in an overrationalizing science.

on Joyce's method. Even as Ferenczi's insistence on family history and the "exogenous factor" reproaches an ideological resistance within psychoanalysis, a resistance materializes, ironically enough, in the publication history of Ferenczi's revolutionary paper.[6]

This suppression of incest narratives within psychoanalysis—a distinctive feature of the invention of psychoanalysis—establishes the outermost margins of an ideology of taboo linked to forgetfulness or repression.[7] An altogether similar and not surprising suppression has operated over the years with respect to father-daughter incest themes in Joyce's work. Both Margaret MacBride and Jane Ford have marked a path toward this apparently eminently dismissable issue of paternity in *Ulysses*. Both cite narrative lapses at the sites of Bloom's sexual repression, and both note, in strikingly similar fashion, concomitant critical repressions as well. MacBride writes: "What may be the most important element in the story of Bloom has gone virtually unnoticed for over fifty years"; and Ford argues: "The theme of sin . . . is so overlayered . . . that his [Bloom's] repression . . . has largely escaped critical recognition for over fifty years."[8] Thus, each introduces aspects of what I find to be the touchy central issue largely avoided in Joyce studies.[9] In two articles, "At Four She Said" and "At Four She Said: II," MacBride ana-

6. A footnote to the article reports an initial presentation in 1932 and publication in German the following year (Ferenczi, "Confusion," 156n1). Despite Ferenczi's reputation within his profession, "Confusion of Tongues" was not published in English until 1949.

7. It would seem unfortunate, from the perspective of frequent reports of incest across all populations, that family sex crimes are historically linked at all with Freud's formulation of the oedipal relation as part of psychosexual development. For one thing, a number of accounts—including Marie Balmary, *Psychoanalyzing Psychoanalysis: Freud and the Hidden Fault of the Father*, trans. Ned Lukacher (Baltimore: Johns Hopkins University Press, 1982)—posit Freud's own neurosis as an explanation for his abandoning ten years of research pointing to childhood sexual abuse among his patients and his subsequent creation of the oedipal complex as an alternative explanation for certain hysterical symptoms. But even as Freud's theories undergo revision, their longevity and flexibility confirm a cultural predisposition toward normative descriptions of the individual in her or his culture. Abandoning the facticity of the seduction of children would seem to mark, moreover, a most egregious example of an epistemological failure within psychoanalytic theory, an error of linear (developmental norms) and binary (childhood sexual abuse or oedipal trouble) thinking that only begins with Freud.

8. Margaret MacBride, "At Four She Said: II," *James Joyce Quarterly* 18 (Summer 1981): 417; Jane Ford, "Why Is Milly in Mullingar?" *James Joyce Quarterly* 14 (Summer 1977): 436. See also MacBride, "At Four She Said," *James Joyce Quarterly* 17 (Fall 1979): 21–40.

9. In my paper "Who Is He When She's at Home?: The Debased Feminine Symptom in *Ulysses*," read at the James Joyce Conference, Milwaukee, June 1987, I indicated my debt to Jane Ford, who finds father-daughter incest central to the novel. Her article "Why Is Milly in Mullingar" is the basis (and inspiration) for my own reading. I am grateful to Ford and to Christine Froula for their helpful discussions and support during the Copenhagen International Joyce Symposium.

lyzes Bloom's role in abetting Molly's adultery, and in "Why Is Milly in Mullingar?" Ford uncovers the subterranean theme of Bloom's incestuous relationship with Milly. While these essays richly expand my own reading of the text, I believe there is yet more to the story, concerning both Bloom's sexual repression and (at the very least) a lack of critical enthusiasm for these matters.

Forgetfulness is the key for analyst and novelist. Just as the analysand's neurotic repetitions disfigure the narrative of a near-fatal attraction, so the Joycean narrative is pocked and pitted by symptoms. Taking its cues from the illness itself, Ferenczi's treatment effectively deemphasizes guilt by decentering the narrative of seduction. The analytic task is fulfilled in a recuperative remembering. This rescue of the narrative of a traumatic memory from among the repetitive symptoms that obscure and distort it operates in the faith that the narrative, in fact, resting amidst the rubble of neurosis, awaits its (hitherto resisting) subject. Although the actual remembering of the incest narrative is crucial for the subject, we find, most significantly, at the core of the analyst's work an emphasis on recuperation rather than on the narrative itself. Neither a monster myth of the parent-deviant nor litanies of the ruined child are central. Instead, Ferenczi privileges ruminations on the monstrosity-breeding forgetfulness of both parent and child. Analogously, within Joyce's work a foundational irony inheres in the revelation that these deeply historical and historiographic[10] texts have as their originary dynamic the "silence, exile, and cunning" of the artist. Serial traces of forgetfulness in *Ulysses* and *Finnegans Wake*, manifest as a distinctive and formal roominess, offering space for rumination, generate the negative space that, for the most part, determines the shape of each novel. Just as the conspiracy of silence in the suppression of incest shapes a community, the repression of incest, as a central matter in Joyce, organizes the formal aspects of both works. In each case the reader as resisting subject is differently implicated.

Thus, I want to show, at least in a preliminary way, that discursive configurations of father-daughter incest are obliquely and peculiarly secured to major plot functions throughout. That is, linguistic fore-

10. I refer to the influence of Henri LeFebvre's use of *Ulysses* as a methodological paradigm in *Everyday Life in the Modern World*, trans. Sacha Rabinowitz, intro. Philip Wander (New Brunswick, N.J.: Transaction Books, 1971), a work I initially encountered in Jules David Law, "Simulation, Pluralism, and the Politics of Everyday Life," in *Coping with Joyce: Essays from the Copenhagen Symposium*, ed. Morris Beja and Shari Benstock (Columbus: Ohio State University Press, 1989).

grounding, which serves as the key demonstration of Bloom's repression in *Ulysses*, is the key agent of the plot; while in *Finnegans Wake* the major plot function is the concealment of incest. The discourse of Ulysses dialectically mimes the liturgies of repression. Repetitious linguistic symptoms that forestall remembering generate gaps in the plot. To the reader falls the task of lifting the layered and foregrounded veils of language in *Ulysses*. In particular Bloom's polyglot, polysemous idiolect, to the extent that it consists of a dialectic of his own and Molly's confusions of tenderness and passion, serves as an opaque wrapper for the parental fault. In this sense *Ulysses* is a paternal or seductive text, one that elicits the anxiety which is one version of our desire—"the hate impregnated love of adult mating," as Ferenczi writes (Ferenczi, 167).

Throughout *Finnegans Wake* a subterranean code tantalizes with glimpses and hints of a sin or crime in the park; even when the father, HCE, is placed on trial, his crime is not named, at least not until the sixteenth chapter, the last chapter before Part IV, the novel's final section. Moreover, it is not until the final page of Part IV that we discover just how important both the mystery and its resolution have always been. The particular confusion of tongues that marks the long-delayed eruption of the incest narrative, along with the violence, passion, and tenderness of the incest passage, are indexes of the universal power of repression and the complicated struggle toward remembering that is both Joyce's theme and his method. In contrast to the dynamic of desire in *Ulysses*, *Finnegans Wake* is a text that desires the reader, a maternal or oceanic discourse that draws us in to "the guilt feelings that make the love-object of both loving and hating, i.e., of ambivalent emotions" (Ferenczi, 167).

An intertextual analysis of the mirror-image relation of the doubled discourses in *Ulysses* and *Finnegans Wake*—paralleling Ferenczi's formulation of the dialectical arrangement of the languages of tenderness and passion between victim and parent and between analysand and analyst—specifies the madness of incest in relation to language and to culture, a madness constitutive of Joyce's world-making vision. Ferenczi's astute distinctions, applied with some care to the Joycean text, yield a dialectical model which I have used to interrogate form for value in Joyce's work. The analyst's unorthodox treatment substitutes a maternal and lovingly attentive therapy for the more orthodox paternal detachment. Memory is restored within a maternal ambiance. The basis for treatment (which Ferenczi notes is, naturally and practically, regressive) originates in a study of the languages of tenderness and passion that differently constitute the experience of the adultlike child (the incest victim) and the childish adult (the perpetrator). In treatment such a "confusion of tongues" operates in relation to the analyst's maternal language, designed to initiate a healing reformulation of the dialectic of tenderness and passion, a dialectic of "maternal" and "paternal" languages.[11] This is one principle on which the Joycean corpus depends.

Ferenczi's descriptions of the language of tenderness and passion as it operates between victim and perpetrator, and between analyst and victim or perpetrator,[12] provide a model for investigating the effects of debilitating repression and facilitating recuperation. In recognizing just how neatly the repression of the perpetrator and the repression of the victim reflect each other, Ferenczi also realizes that such mirror-image repressions are destined to be repeated during orthodox psychoanalytic treatment. It is, of course, through the mechanism of transference *and* an incidental (and perhaps not entirely gratuitous) matching of behavioral strategies that typical analytic detachment comes to represent to the analysand the position of the careless parent.[13] Within this highly sensitive and altogether

11. "Maternal" and "paternal" in Ferenczi's discussion are terms of gender. The analyst acknowledges that "the real rape of girls who have hardly grown out of the age of infants, similar sexual acts of mature women with boys, and also enforced homosexual acts, are more frequent . . . than has hitherto been assumed" ("Confusion," 162). Maternal language refers to an empathic discourse, to a "maternal friendliness," which, Ferenczi argues, must replace the detached discourse of orthodox treatment. Ferenczi thus makes the distinction to reinforce his observation of the inadvertent and disadvantageous matching of the analyst's detachment with the perpetrator's—a point I will develop more clearly in this essay. Here I simply wish to note that this vocabulary neither indicts fathers nor characterizes mothers but only distinguishes between the discourse of primary nurture (or a subject-object confusion, or empathy, rooted in bodily experience and sensory memory) and the discourse of incest (or an inappropriately sensory invasion of the symbolic). "Paternal" language here then is a doubly mediating form, constituted, as all language presumably is, as a mediation of the real and remediated by the coldness of the perpetrator's repression, matched by "professional hypocrisy," Ferenczi's term for analytic detachment, no matter what the analyst in fact may be feeling with respect to the analysand (ibid., 159). This diction ("maternal" and "paternal") in juxtaposition with point of view in Ferenczi's paper reveals a cultural bias already in flux, an ideology of the traditional family reexamined in Ferenczi's questioning of psychoanalytic orthodoxy.

12. The confusion begins here, since it is becoming increasingly clear that perpetrators tend to have been themselves abused as children.

13. An implication that may be drawn from Balmary's work on Freud's "neurotic" turn from the study of incestuous seduction among his hysterical patients to his favoring of the oedipal theory is how Freud's relation to his own father formulated the paternalistic

familiar alignment of the role of the parent and the role of the analyst, Ferenczi is able to interrogate the psychoanalytic problematic of childhood seduction and childhood desire. This work provides in its diction a gentle rebuke ("a maternal friendliness") for what otherwise might be construed as a stern ("paternal") commentary on Freud's preference for the theory of oedipal attraction over the reality of sexual trauma as the pathogenic factor in certain stubborn neuroses.

We might further conjecture that what naturally follows from Ferenczi's recognition of these dual registers of language is a useful insight into the operation of Joyce's modernist styles. The movement from the seductive discourse of *Ulysses* to the discursive sprawl of *Finnegans Wake* provides distinctions. Subject-object fluidity (reflected in Ferenczi's understanding of problems in the transference relation and his preference for a maternal analyst) is the condition of the engenderment of language. An empathic or maternal dynamic in the language of a paternal figure doubles point of view without the concomitant irony that is thought to be, in the study of modernist discourse, the ordinary consequence of such doubling. It is my own sense that Joyce distinctively balances (*juggles* would perhaps be a better term) these registers in the two works. In a Joycean *ricorso* we can begin (again) to sort out the confusion; with the end in sight, on the final page of *Finnegans Wake*, the Joycean text inevitably rewinds. The organizing situation of *Finnegans Wake*, which includes the reader's awareness of the cyclic possibilities, occurs as the discursive site and circumstance of the father's crime and the daughter's ambivalence. A therapeutic remembering takes place in the dream of the father when ALP, in her death-in-life monologue, reembodies her younger self—a sexually abused daughter.[14] *Ulysses*, by contrast, in this mirror-image,

---

praxes of orthodox treatment. Freud's rejection of his own documentation of the abuse of hysterical patients occurred during the period in which he was mourning his father's death. Balmary cites the mysteries surrounding Jakob Freud's second of three marriages, archivally documented but unacknowledged by the family, and a two-month difference between the date on which the family celebrated Sigmund's birth and his birthdate as given in the city registers as evidence of the "fault of the father"—the fault that Freud's reformulation of the reality of family sexual scandal was designed to hide (Balmary, *Psychoanalyzing Psychoanalysis*).

14. I agree with Kimberly Devlin, who finds HCE's to be the voice of the episode, the narrator of the dream of mother and daughter (Kimberly Devlin, "ALP's Final Monologue in *Finnegans Wake:* The Dialectical Logic of Joyce's Dream Text," in *Coping with Joyce: Essays from the Copenhagen Symposium* [Columbus: Ohio State University Press, 1989],

upside-down world of Joycean narrative, opens with a parodic introduction to ultimate patriarchal authority. "Stately plump Buck
Mulligan" invites us to the penultimate mediation, the symbolic
solace of the ultimate father *("Introibo ad altare Dei") (U,* 1.1, 5).
Bloom's symptoms, of course, represent a weakening of this stability of subject position.

We might say, then, that over the course of the two works Joyce
moved from the initially overly determined symbolic design of
Ulysses (silence and exile) to the overly determined sensory register
of *Finnegans Wake,* a discourse designed around the feminine body
and women's language. Finally, in part IV of *Finnegans Wake* the
neurotic repetition of history's "vicocyclometer" breaks down. Universal "significance" dissolves in the particularity of remembering,
and the passionate father tenderly speaks the daughter's defilement
in the neologism "herword." Thus, in a masculine-feminine turn
he names the real act whose mimesis in the sixteenth chapter
marks the return of the repressed.[15] What is more, Ferenczi's sum-
mation of the effects of incest on the victim so perfectly reflects
the nature and function of language in ALP's monologue within
HCE's dream at the close of the *Wake* that it seems to respond
directly not only to Joyce himself but to the body of feminist criticism that has focused on these final lines as the place to assess
Joyce's sexual politics.[16]

232–47). I also locate an antihegemonic effect in the dream's embrace of feminine history.
That is, as the victim's language is reproduced in the dream of the father, we are afflicted
with the pain of the narrative as well as the confusion that has generated disagreement
over the identification of the speaking subject in this part of the dream. If the dream
belongs to the father, then he speaks the language of the victim here. But he is only her
agent inasmuch as he is *his* own. Agency and authority are joined by way of a certain
logic: it was Freud's observation that the dreamer in the dream "knew and remembered
something which was beyond the reach of . . . waking memory" and that "one of the
sources from which dreams derive material for reproduction—material which is part neither remembered nor used in the activities of waking thought—is childhood experience"
(Sigmund Freud, *The Interpretation of Dreams,* trans. James Strachey [New York: Avon
Books, 1967], 45, 49). Also, according to neuroscientific research on memory, this inacces-
sibility of certain memory—not necessarily forgotten but inarticulable—is especially typical of materials recorded from sensory rather than linguistic input. Since perpetrators of
sexual abuse tend to have been victims themselves, one could account for HCE's male
and female voices within the doubled context of HCE's masculinity (in paternity) and
femininity (in victimization, in himself having been abused).

  15. The development in Joyce's work from the language of the church to the feminized
Wakean discourse is interestingly handled in Frances L. Restuccia, *Joyce and the Law of
the Father* (New Haven: Yale University Press, 1989).

  16. I refer to Joyce's ingenuity in working variations between passion and tenderness
in the distinctive discourses of *Ulysses* and *Finnegans Wake.* These variations provide the
basis for discriminating modernist from postmodernist Joyce, or, in feminist criticism,
masculinist from feminist Joyce. In the present it would seem that there are as many

Tenderness and Passion

In Ferenczi's birthday tribute to Freud, in all liklihood written over a succession of the very same days on which Joyce toiled over his "Work in Progress," Ferenczi, the maternal son, distinguishes the pathogeny of the adult's response to incest from the child's. He explains the disorders thus: "An adult and child love each other, the child nursing the playful fantasy of taking the role of the mother to the adult. This play may assume erotic forms but remains, never-theless, on the level of tenderness. It is not so, however, with patho-logical adults. . . . They mistake the play of children for the desires of a sexually mature person or even allow themselves—irrespective of any consequences—to be carried away" (Ferenczi, 161). He elabo-rates the paired ambivalences: "If *more love* or *love of a different kind from that which they need* is forced upon children in the stage of tenderness [as opposed to the stage of passion, a stage of love between adults that involves conflict and violence], it may lead to pathological consequences in the same way as the *frustration or withdrawal of love . . ."* (Ferenczi, 164). The confusion of tongues refers, initially, to the superimposition of passionate and guilt-laden love on an immature and guiltless child. This confusion belongs in strikingly similar ways to adult and child.[17] Parental pathology breeds its mirror image, usually a child with precociously adult predilections.

According to Ferenczi, then, the confusion of tongues, in a devel-opmental view, is the result of a dangerous conflation of registers

feminist positions on the nature of Joycean discourse as there are feminist commentators on Joyce, although most agree that the close of *Finnegans Wake* is a special instance of a late move toward the feminine. For a range of interpretation, see, for example, Sandra Gilbert and Susan Gubar, who find a phallocentric Joyce ("Sexual Linguistics: Gender, Language, Sexuality," *New Literary History* 16 [Spring 1985]: 515–43); Frances Restuccia, who describes a femininized sadomasochism (*Joyce and the Law of the Father*); Margot Norris, who notes Joyce's "nonverbal semiologies" ("Anna Livia Plurabelle: The Dream Woman," in *Women in Joyce* [Urbana: University of Illinois Press, 1982], 197–213); and Kimberly Devlin, who hears the speaker of ALP's monologue as the "female voice imag-ined yet again, the fantasized voice of the fantasized other" ("ALP's Final Monologue," 233). Using *The Interpretation of Dreams* as lexical authority, one might prefer "remem-bered" to "fantasized," as I do here in distinguishing my own position.

17. The adult, in assuming the child is operating out of passion, is employing the sub-ject-object confusion of early life organization (a rationalization of tenderness) as a means of ordering the seduction, while the child is forced into the maternal-subject or caretaking role, a role reversal within the realm of tenderness rather than passion.

of experience. The father, whose register for the child is all and only symbolic (that is, the paternal relation operates through nomination), has intruded on the child's register of the real (the register of body memory and maternal tenderness). For the child, incest becomes the agent of precocious development. The traumatized child internalizes rape and violence in an attempted normalization of passion. Tenderness for such a child is a facade; it is the unsupported activity of a self divided between premature passion and maternal instincts for preserving the family relation. Thus the affect of these divisions, of this self-fulfilling need for reparation which is also a self-effacing mechanism, exists in opposition to the rage, guilt, and violence which also occur among the violated innocent's repertory of responses. In other words, the psychic fractures are compound. Strategies for managing the trauma of incestuous assault include the magical incorporation of both parents: the child, in dealing with the failure of good parental attention, hovers between self-parenting instincts consisting of both mothering (self-preservation, reparation) and fathering (self-annihilation). At the same time, the child must endure the excess (the violence of emotions accompanying the reality of victimization) which cannot be transformed by splitting or by projective identifications (the coping mechanisms of earliest development, the self-mothering and self-fathering which I have mentioned, engaged, in these circumstances, to manage disturbance within the register of the real).

For the incest victim the disorder of tenderness and passion erupts discursively. A failure in the transformation of organismic panic to signal anxiety (a breakdown between the registers of the real and the imaginary) results in eruptions of the real through rents in the symbolic. The violent objects of the real surface at the symbolic level unmediated by condensations and displacements, the mollifying tropes of the unconscious (or the register of the imaginary). Loss and vulnerability thus operate as active principles in the symbolic register of these subjects. Such a formulation only begins to account for the distinctively fluctuating registers of sensory and symbolic in the languages of *Ulysses* and *Finnegans Wake*.

Within the realm of confusions that exists between the passionate parent and tender child, Ferenczi, in the role of analyst, creates another layer of complexity. In what is perhaps the paper's most radical demonstration, he observes that traditional analytic treatment exacerbates hysterical anxiety in incest victims. He finds that the cool and polite analyst recapitulates, in the method of the treatment, the transgressing father: "Almost always the perpetrator behaves as though nothing has happened, and consoles himself with the thought—Oh it is only a child, he does not know anything, he will forget it all. Not infrequently after such events, the seducer becomes overmoralistic or religious and endeavors to save the soul of the child by severity" (Ferenczi, 163). Ferenczi resourcefully notes that in stubborn cases of hysteria the analyst must abandon the detached position of the "insincere father"—the position, I would add, in which paternal discourse reproduces for the victim not paternal discourse but the body of the father. This is the failure of the imaginary, or what Jacques Lacan would call a *point de capiton*, a piercing of the symbolic by the real. Ferenczi's solution is to offer the child a paternal admission of guilt within a maternal ambience. Such an acknowledgment makes possible the abatement of hysteria, the transformation of an organismic panic (the real) to a signal anxiety (a movement between imaginary and symbolic, that is, a mediation—a remembering within the analysis). What is essential to the regressive treatment is that the memory of the paternal body is converted to language at the *site of a maternal holding*, a willed and healing confusion of subject and object that is enabling since the victim is safely ensconced upon a maternal screen. The victim, safe within a maternal holding, can thus be vulnerable and at the same time empathetic, can be once again both child and parent, but in a distinctively reorganized relation.[18] In this way the incest victim can recognize the guilt, pain, and desire of the intrusive body as congruent with her own. Such an occurrence is the key to sorting out the confusion of tongues, the languages of tenderness and passion.

Bloom/Zerlina, or Symbolic Passion

In discussing *Ulysses* I will not rehearse the evidence in the MacBride and Ford articles except to fill in the narrative. In "At

18. This therapeutic remembering of the victim as both child and parent is a reordering of the pathogenic doubling I have discussed. In the incestuous relationship the child (in denial and divided within herself) behaves maternally toward (identifies with) the abusive parent. In the therapeutic relationship the child as subject (identified in her pain and victimization, and recognizing her prior self-objectification) can also (ideally) forgive rather than identify with the abuser. In this sense she is granted her vulnerability in exchange for her guilt. Reparation includes a transformation of guilt and shame into the "capacity

Four She Said," MacBride establishes Bloom's repression of the appointed hour of Molly's assignation by documenting the variety of
narrative techniques which convey, in part by concealment and delay, this information. The second MacBride essay computes the peculiarly manipulative valence of Bloom's repression by reminding
us that Bloom introduced Molly to Boylan, ignored their flirtation,
and announced his absence from home not merely at the appointed
hour of Boylan's visit but for most of the evening. MacBride stops
short, however, of speculating on Bloom's motives.

Jane Ford documents the incest narrative: Milly's initiation of the
relation in her "gluey," somnambulistic kisses and Bloom's ambivalence, his fascination and his guilt. Ford, in this manner, provides
a motive for Milly's exile, a motive that serves as well, in my view,
Bloom's clumsy attempt at reparation in arranging Molly's adultery.
Bloom, in his prolonged dance of the hours, his wending of the
longest way home, acts out the winding of the clockworks, the
priming of the machine of the plot. As the main character of *Ulysses*, Bloom, in his roles of husband and father, quite naturally is an
agent of the plot, but Bloom also, and very specifically in the narrative innovation that MacBride cites, gives birth to the plot. Hence,
Bloom *authorizes* the plot, and he does so by enacting a feminine
version of Stephen's Shakespeare theory. Joyce's main character is
both self-born and parent to the plot of *Ulysses*.[19] A Lacanian analy-

---

for concern" (D. W. Winnicott, "The Development of the Capacity for Concern," in *The
Maturational Processes and the Facilitating Environment: Studies in the Theory of Emotional Development* [New York: International Universities Press, 1982], chap. 6)—in this
case self-concern, which breeds empathy for the other.

19. Bloom's relationship to Shakespeare and to Joyce's project, the creation of the arche-
type "linguafied" (Joyce's purpose in *Ulysses*, according to Hugh Kenner in *Joyce's Voices*
[Berkeley: University of California Press, 1979]) is spelled out in the "Orthographical"
section of the "Aeolus" episode. Bloom is father to himself as he is literally born out of a
languaged version of his inner life, in this instance a spelling conundrum in which the
proper spelling of his unparalleled embarrassment, "the unpar one ar alleled embarra two
ars is it? double ess ment" (*U*, 7.167), would seem to present a physicalized or barely
undecoded version of Bloom's hidden feelings. In the spelling exercise Bloom's vulnerability and his specific concerns are represented. The bare arse—or "double ess," ass—of the
"harassed [or shaken] pedlar" (*U*, 7.168) is unparalleled, that is, like no other. Bloom's
inner state becomes statement, and unparalleled meaning, meanings unique to the text,
proliferate under the auspices of the proper spelling. The pedlar is "unpar"ed, which is to
say disconnected from the text's proliferating "pears" or pairs, "pars," and "parrs." In this
turn, moreover, universal meaning is reborn. For Bloom is also parent to the plot as the
shaken sexual will and a shaken pairing system are graphically, orthographically, and
phonetically melded whether they occur as the problematic of translation, that is, the
question of "will" in *Ulysses* in English, Latin, and Italian; the problematic of reference,
the relation of words and things; or the sexual problematic, the worrying of married and
adulterous pairs with which the text teems. Adeline Glasheen, of course, has speculated
on Shakespeare as the "matrix" of *Ulysses* (*A Third Census of* Finnegans Wake [Berkeley:

sis of the feminine symptom in the text attests to Bloom's feminine self-birth, to his incorporation of Molly's idiolect and its function as the agent of foregrounding, of the shifting of the registers of symbolic and real or form and content which define Joyce's high modern style. Such a reading accounts, moreover, for the seemingly unheroic and incestuous Bloom, while also presenting thematic coherences in *Ulysses* and *Finnegans Wake*, coherences that disclose in the failure of conspiracies of silence the core of the sexual politics informing the Joycean oeuvre.[20]

Like the play of Stephen's adopted linguistic paternity contained in his Shakespeare theory, Bloom's symbolic paternity operates variously out of "will." Bloom's predominantly Italian "will" is most revealing. For Bloom's symptom, repeated throughout the day, is his substitution of the present tense of "will" in Italian, *voglio*, for the conditional, *vorrei*. His neurotic repetition is a mistaken remembering of Molly's portion of the duet "Là ci darem la mano" from *Don Giovanni*. The subjectless Italian *voglio* barely conceals his parental helplessness, his vulnerability, and his guilt—his parental fault reiterated in his characteristically subjectless phrases in English. Bloom's abrogation of certain responsibilities, represented in this rejection of subject position, reveals his anguish and his ambivalence. But most telling is Bloom's "confusion of tongues," his error in Molly's portion of the duet from *Don Giovanni*. The *voglio-vorrei* confusion in Bloom's rendering of Molly's part, the song of the peasant girl Zerlina, literally exposes a sad and ineffectually sadomasochistic Bloom failing in the symbolic transformation of his guilt. From within his ordinary adult (symbolic) situation— that is, as father, Bloom quite unexpectedly speaks the daughter's part. In the neurotic repetition of *voglio*, he mimes the function of the incest victim, who, according to Ferenczi's formulation, appears to be "willing" in her attempts to normalize incest. In Bloom's

University of California Press, 1977]). I quite agree, so long as we see the shaky wills of Bloom leading us to the book's central statements, the answers to what is in the name: Will Shakes-peare (or "pairs" or "pars") or in Bloom's lack, the problematic of his sexual will worked out as woman's sway: "While others have their will, Ann-hath-a-way."

20. Although I agree with Gubar and Gilbert's analysis of the status of the feminine in *Ulysses* ("Sexual Linguistics," 523, 524), my reading of *jouissance* in *Finnegans Wake* identifies the operation of a feminine and even feminist politics in the later work (see Marilyn L. Brownstein, "The Rule of the Postmodern in the *Phaedrus* and *Finnegans Wake*," in *European Joyce Studies Annual*, vol. 1, *Joyce, Modernity, and Its Mediation*, ed. Christine van Boheemen [Amsterdam: Rodopi, 1989], 79–96).

symbolic and real failures we discover his humanity and the potential for family tragedy.

A Lacanian linguistics explains the transformations of Bloom's will. Lacan, in valuing the signified over the signifier[21] (a Bloomian "metampsychosis" or an inversion of the Saussurean formula), creates a particular re-membering of a system of reference in which the signified, the individual concept of a thing, is privileged. Language becomes interesting not at the level of the phoneme, where, according to Lacan, the arbitrary nonsense of communal meaning reigns, but at the level of the "patheme," the symptom of the "passion of the body," the effect of language. The patheme is generated, moreover, in "père-version." Language is, in fact, ineluctably marked by perversion, defined in the "21 January Seminar" as the father's role, "the sole guarantee of his function as father." Since children of both sexes desire the maternal body, the role that falls "père-versement," or toward the father, is the prevention of mother-child incest. The father attempts to fulfill his role in the demand for a substitution of the symbolic for the real, an attempt at the foreclosure of the real by which the "passion of the signifier then becomes a new dimension of the human condition."[22]

The father's role is also perverse in that it is an impossible one. Finally, as Lacan explains, since no father can be perfect (or in my view flawed—which is to say, *human*—in exactly the same way that other fathers may be) the range of perversions and pathematic manifestations (symptoms of the father's imperfections, his lack) is equally and idiosyncratically various. In *Ulysses* the relation of two pathemes—Bloom's repetitious mistakes of will, based on Zerlina's coy reply to Don Giovanni (the operatic waverings of the nearly seduced daughter) and Bloom's repetitions of Molly's repetitious "O's" (the sexualized exclamations of the the adulterous mother)—represent his perversion. Bloom debases the feminine symptom, the symptom of the daughter as well as that of the mother. We may discover the root of such debasement in considering the Freudian notion that, for the male, heterosexual relations depend on a prior

21. "Lacan has reformulated Saussure's concept of the sign in which the signified (concept) is superior to the signifier (sound or form) in determining meaning" (Ellie Ragland-Sullivan, "Jacques Lacan: Feminism and the Problem of Gender Identity," *SubStance* 11 [1982]: 19.

22. Jacques Lacan, *Feminine Sexuality: Jacques Lacan and the Ecole Freudianne*, trans. Jacqueline Rose, ed. Juliet Mitchell and Jacqueline Rose (New York: W. W. Norton, 1985), 165, 167, 78, hereafter cited in the text as *FS*.

disfiguring of the maternal or sororal.[23] For Lacan, of course, there can be no sexual relation; instead there seems to be a sexual ideal which is either transcendent or located in the *jouissance* of the woman.

This version is Bloom's, for Bloom's femininity is fundamental to his père-version. Its source, his "abnegation," is a sort of doubled self-denial resting in a rejection of his own father's version (and perhaps rooted for Joyce in a rejection of his father's behavior, a case variously made by Ruth Bauerle, Hélène Cixous, and Lacan).[24] The confirmation of the sin of the father visited upon the son is the aberration of Rudy, Bloom's son: "Mistake of nature. If it's healthy it's from the mother. If not from the man" (*U*, 6.329). An already guilty Bloom, by force of family circumstance, then, must find his reflection in his daughter's mirror ("O, Milly Bloom, you are my darling. You are my lookingglass from night to morning" [*U*, 13.287, 288]) rather than in the son who does not survive to mirror him ("If little Rudy had lived. . . . My son. Me in his eyes" [*U*, 6.76]).

Bloom as a father himself, and in defiance of his own father's père-version (suicide), distorts the mirror most peculiarly, taking his cue from the reflection he finds in his own daughter's mirror. Bloom's perversion, his made-up version of the paternal act he refuses to follow, surfaces as desire for his daughter, a hardly original but nonetheless perverse means of blocking oedipal desire.[25] Bloom's relation to Milly, in fact, has affected the marriage tie as well as the tie between mother and daughter.[26] In the sequence "Young student. Yes, yes: a woman too: Life, life" (*U*, 6.89, 90), Bloom defies his father's suicide, the ultimate abrogation of paternal function, in an affirmation of life which he finds in his daugh-

23. "It sounds not only disagreeable but also paradoxical, yet it must nevertheless be said that anyone who is to be really free and happy in love must have surmounted his respect for women and have come to terms with the idea of incest with his mother or sister" (Sigmund Freud, "On the Universal Tendency to Debasement in the Sphere of Love," in *On Sexuality* [New York: Viking Penguin, 1977], 254, 255).

24. Ruth Bauerle, "Date Rape, Mate Rape: A Liturgical Interpretation of 'The Dead,'" in *New Alliances in Joyce Studies: "When It's Aped to Foul a Delfian,"* ed. Bonnie Kime Scott (Newark: University of Delaware Press, 1988); Hélène Cixous, *The Exile of James Joyce*, trans. Sally A. J. Purcell (New York: David Lewis, 1972); Jacques Lacan, "Joyce le symptome," in *Joyce and Paris: Actes du Cinquième Symposium International James Joyce*, ed. Jacques Aubert and Maria Jolas (Paris: Publications de l'Université de Lille, 1979), 13–17.

25. In Lacan, oedipal desire refers to a desire to return to the maternal, a regression to the nondifferentiated state of mother and infant. Thus Bloom, in desiring Milly, makes possible her separation from the maternal.

26. See Ford, "Why Is Milly in Mullingar?"

ter's sexuality. Ironically, then, Bloom rediscovers in "Hades," in the land of the dead, a life principle in a womanly version.

It is worth noting here that for Lacan as well as for Joyce, the life principle resides in perversion. The father's affirmation of life as model for his children is his duty toward his desire for the maternal (*FS*, 167). Thus the sexual bond of matrimony and the incest taboo, which preserves the paternl prerogative, represent the father's basic function. In Bloom's case, however, the perversion must somehow be a disavowal of his father's choice. Bloom struggles, it would seem, to maintain paternal function despite the hardships of the past—his father's suicide and Rudy's death. In his paternal role as incestuous desirer, moreover, Bloom, in yet another turn, comes to a femininity of his own creation, an ambivalence in which he acts out, pathematically, the role of the seduced as well as that of the seducer. He thus suffers the inevitable pains as well as perverse pleasures of incestuous confusions.

Bloom's distress is focused in his longing for Milly. Jane Ford provides good evidence that Bloom has sent Milly to Mullingar to keep her safe from his desire. Milly's absence situates Bloom's ambivalence and his symptom. Bloom's paternal role is that of "*le juste mi-dieu*," creator of not the perfect solution but a happy "*medeum*" (*FS*, 167). In *Ulysses* the wrong word (*voglio*), the repetitious symptom of paternal "justice," becomes the creating word (in translation, "I will" is also "I lust," an archaic form in English) and in that very sense *le mot juste*.

The wrong-word-that-gets-things-right becomes the sign of Bloom's incestuous desire. In "Calypso" Bloom begins his abuse of the libretto of *Don Giovanni* (V, 4.327, 328). One might even say that Bloom debases Zerlina, pathematically, as he confuses Zerlina's answer to Don Giovanni's sexual demands, substituting the present, *voglio*, for the conditional, *vorrei*, in nearly every one of the book's episodes in which he appears. On the day of Molly's seduction, Bloom becomes his own version of a seduction in a mirror, a perversion of the innocent Zerlina, a phantasm of the nearly seduced daughter. So we might speculate, then, that he is Molly's understudy, her stand-in, playing out a wish that Molly not succumb to Boylan.[27] This does not necessarily explain, however, why Bloom

27. In "Calypso" the *voglio* symptom is introduced in the context of Molly's adultery. Bloom searches the bed for Molly's book, and his thoughts leap from her song to his

plays the role of daughter, Zerlina, rather than that of seducer, Don Giovanni, who is after all disappointed by Zerlina. (Just once—in "Lotus Eaters"—Bloom attempts to sing the seducer's part but reverts to worldless lalation, to infants' noises, after the initial "Là ci darem la mano" [U, 5.227, 228].) More to the point, Bloom preserves Milly's presence (daughter-as-seducer in his memory of her kisses) by thinking, throughout the day, of the events leading to Milly's exile, and, similarly, he acts out Zerlina's choice by repeating, throughout the day, her answer to Don Giovanni, by remembering his own versions of Zerlina's duet.

Bloom's lack—Milly's absence—has become his symptom. Bloom has introjected Milly/Zerlina; he entertains her in his thoughts rather than entering her. By colluding in Molly's assignation, Bloom abuses himself-as-daughter rather than abusing his daughter. Bloom's faulty memory, his mistake in Zerlina's part, is the symptom of his missing his daughter—and of the near miss in a sexual encounter with her. Bloom sings "Voglio e non vorrei": I wish or I will yet I wouldn't—or I lust and I couldn't—as opposed to the true Zerlina's playfully ambivalent "vorrei e non vorrei."

Bloom's *voglio* mistake, which persists even after its correction in "Hades," persists as a confusion in planes of experience, registers of being. Bloom's impotence, his inability to respond completely to Milly's sticky kisses, remands him to his infantile body—to the register of the real which invades his adult life. Bloom, then, is quite appropriately one who takes it lying down, and it is from this position that his perspective as a regarder of rears—"his pale Galilean eyes were upon her mesial groove" (U, 9.615)—makes both comic and good practical sense.[28] In the lexicon of the *Wake*, Bloom's "prixcockcity" is his impotence, his paternal genius as symptom, reflected in his linguistic symptom, a neurotic repetition of his painful desire. "Voglio e non vorrei," Bloom sings, true to his père-version.

Bloom's copy of the hitherto maidenly ambivalence of Zerlina's

---

purpose: he says, "Voglio. Not in the bed" (U, 4.328). His symptom contains a wish, then, that Molly not say *voglio* to Boylan in that bed later in the day. The book Bloom seeks, moreover, a tired piece of pornography, has prophetically fallen to rest (as Molly will later in the day) "sprawled beside the orange-keyed chamberpot."

28. If we consider Bloom's position to be an echo of Stephen "rere regardant" on the strand (U, 3.502), then we get a sense of the upside-down arrangements of the masculine relation, of father to son, in this discourse.

role is also played out with respect to Molly's liason with Boylan. Bloom dreads the encounter which he has helped to arrange and also feels guilty about his need to arrange it. Thus, ruled by the genius of his symptom on June 16, Bloom suffers, enjoys his fantasies, and shops for Molly; even in this instance we observe his ambivalence as he forages for concrete reparation for his sin. He buys soap and (not insignificantly) washes with it, orders and then forgets Molly's lotion, plans the purchase of a silk petticoat, and acquires *Sweets of Sin*. The gifts of the guilty lover work two ways, indicating Bloom's guilt in both its pleasurable and its painful aspects. And like the gifts of the guilty lover, the guilty Bloom's sexual impulses, throughout the day, are equally unconsummated, generous and undeliverable, onanistic. The notable exception is the pornographic text, *Sweets of Sin*, the symbolic in substitution for the real. Or is it? For "everything speaks in its own way" we are reminded in "Aeolus," where the language of machines and a spelling conundrum only begin to suggest the range of semiosis in the Joycean text. Nearly consistently for Bloom, the "sweets of sin" speak double-talk. By contrast, in Mozart's (far less narratologically complicated) version of dangerous love between lass and lord, the unblemished but guilt-ridden bride returns to the arms of her true love, lyrically inviting her straightforward punishment, "Batti, batti, O bel massetto" (Beat me, beat me, my handsome Massetto).

In accordance, moreover, with the accretive laws of this Joycean epistemo-illogic or disembodied double-talk, Bloom's tortured and lost "I" not only yields to Zerlina's aria but also to Molly's sign, the *O*. If the *O* is the feminine water sign, it is no less Bloom's symptom than Molly's. Bloom's *O* is the symptom of his desire.[29] In Lacan "desire" is the excess, the unfulfillable residue, the sensational memory of undifferentiated maternal and infantile part objects. The patheme which Lacan defines as "the passion of the body," for Bloom, the *O*, is bound, as it is in Lacan, to first desire, to the formation of the "moi," and to the body's orifices and their margins, initially the anus and the mouth; to his list Lacan adds the voice and the urinary flow, and later the eye and the ear—agents of what Lacan calls spherical or spheroidal modes of perception.

29. While the *O* is notably the sign of Molly's idiolect and her connection to water as female principle, it also becomes Bloom's sign in that he frequently speaks Molly's idiolect; his speech is punctuated with her "O's," particularly in passages in which his vulnerability prevails (see, for example, *U*, 5.8, 15; 5.208; 5.468; 5.471).

Bloom's symptoms and habits are constituted in these modes. In "Molly. Milly. Same thing watered down," the water theme emerges (*U*, 6.87). Here it is a debased *O*, a urination symptom, and one which would seem to be pathemogenic: "She mightn't like me to come that way without letting her know. Must be careful about women. Catch them once with their pants down. Never forgive you after that. Fifteen" (*U*, 6.493–85). This sequence suggests an altogether likely yet disturbing occasion for the awakening of paternal lust and one, of course, repeated in *Finnegans Wake* as a version of HCE's crime in Phoenix Park.

This allusion to Bloom's voyeurism, or perhaps his innocent error of walking in on a micturating Milly, follows closely after the passage in "Hades" where Bloom-Zerlina first translated the *voglio-vorrei* confusion, a moment in which he contemplates a visit to Milly. "Perhaps I will without writing," muses Bloom during Dignam's funeral (*U*, 6.449). This translated *voglio* in "Hades" is the correct version, the conditional that Bloom briefly speaks. It is Bloom's stronger version. Here the "I" is reinstated and the verb is in the present form, "I will," modified by "perhaps." In a burst of clarity about his affiliations, Bloom speaks, however, a debased form of the *O*. "Watered down" Milly suggests not merely a dilution of the mother's sexuality in the figure of the daughter but a père-version, too, a debasement of the daughter in this allusion to urination.

Because Bloom compulsively repeats his Zerlina symptom as the sign of his père-version, the symptom would seem to reveal an unconsummated incest. Bloom is like Zerlina in his ambivalence. He has been approached, and he would if he could. So a guilty Bloom wends his way, making reparation to Molly for what almost occurred. Alternately Bloom relishes and despises his responses to Milly's kisses, and he even reenacts them at tolerable distances with Martha and with Gerty. Hence, the père-version works: it preserves the family. In repeating Zerlina, another nearly seduced daughter, Bloom introjects Milly. Molly's adultery is, then, only a small measure of Bloom's torment. In Lacanian terms, Bloom has already faced his own castration. In embracing Milly, he has embraced *jouissance* beyond the phallus. As a result, Bloom's sexuality is *nostalgic*, that is, feminine, and his and Molly's sleeping position evokes the consummation of this nostalgia. Such displacement, then, does not betray a lack of sexual contact between them but rather conveys the nature of Bloom's not exclusively genital organization. Bloom's sexuality, it would seem, is more diffuse, feminine, polymorphously perverse. *Nostos*, in the end, becomes a sexual pun on Bloom's (anally organized) return (to the body from which he was born) and Milly's exile, part of Bloom's poignant character, his sign of parental ability and disability. One might say that Bloom does the best he can do. We read his lack, the feminine symptom in the text.

Incest in *Ulysses* operates in Ferenczi's terms in the detachment, the coolness of the paternal tongue. In Lacanian or Freudian terms, much of the language of *Ulysses* functions through an overdetermined symbolic, a register of triangulated desire. Bloom's incestuous slide moreover uncovers the nature of the marriage tie as it displays Bloom's body as an infantile body. His symptoms locate him in a maternal real. Bloom straddles the registers of the symbolic and the real. In the failure of the incestuous union and in Bloom's complicity in the success of the adulterous union, the pain and guilt and heroism of the devoted husband and father emerge. In his bodily symptoms, as they break through into the symbolic, we come to know the jewgreek Bloom in thrall to loss, to history, to memory, and finally to the maternal body. Most significant for my argument, father-daughter incest as a discursive theme in *Ulysses* reveals the subject-object confusion of earliest life, the infantile tendencies at the base of Bloom's desire. That is, the linguistic foregrounding is the symptom of narrative repression, of forgetting. Form nearly concels content, which in this case would be the narrative of the genius of the father's body. Given his history, Bloom is a survivor and a genius at living. His impotence is his *recovery of the father*, his body remembering the *will* (once more, that *voglio*) as if it were the deed (or the dead).

Also, Bloom's debasement of the daughter, *à la lettre*, is clearly his own version of sexuality rather than Molly's; for Molly knows the proper song as well as the satisfying impropriety of the correct verb. Additional evidence of his life role, Bloom's fragmented speech, his subjectless phrases, his *voglio's*, his repetitions of Molly's "O's," are linguistically metonymic. These language habits are not the products of unconscious (or, in Lacan, imaginary) tropes (condensations and displacements which typically govern linguistic mediations), but rather they represent unmediated infantile objects and part-objects inappropriately occurring in the symbolic register.

Bloom's symptoms (his love objects)—his assumption of Zerlina's role, his fascination with body function and body parts, his appetite for organ meats and the "fine tang of faintly scented urine" (*U*, 4.4,5)—emerge as childlike and narcissistic, emanating from the core constituents of self. Like the language of Ferenczi's incest perpetrator, Bloom's language is cool, paternal. Yet he is most unlike the punitive and passionate perpetrator because his symptoms are those of tenderness.

Bloom's primal yearning, for which—as primal yearning goes, according to Lacan—there is no satisfaction, produces a gap between self and environment. This painful lack is disguised, ordinarily, by covering it with an ideal figure. If in Bloom's case it is Milly, Molly, and Rudy who are missing, his desire for his daughter barely contains or conceals all of his loss. A missing or incomplete part of himself is the true and unattainable object of his desire.[30] Bloom's losses are unmollifiable—*unmillifillable*. They cannot be mediated. Ultimately it is the politics as well as the poignancy of such loss that interests us. In the context of the former, Bloom's femininity, his impotence, would seem to be features of the nonviability of the conventional paternal function and a concomitant disfigurement of the marriage tie, at least as it is defined by the discourse of *Ulysses*.[31]

HCE and Formalist Tenderness

In *Finnegans Wake* the relation of language to narrative seems to be the reverse of that which we find in *Ulysses*. There are several ways to view this shift. Lacan's analysis of Joyce's life and work posits his doubled discourses as linked to a father-child disturbance. As Ellie Ragland-Sullivan has noted, Lacan, in studying *Finnegans Wake*, indicates that Joyce's dissociation within the oedipal relation

---

30. For the incest victim an incomplete identification with the aggressor results in castration anxiety. This would be Joyce's bind (and Bloom's) in a Lacanian reading. Such unresolved father conflict would produce, quite predictably, a female (castrated) ideal. That it would be the most helpless female figure, the daughter, rather than the mother is equally predictable.

31. Joyce's aversion to the marriage tie is, of course, well known. No speculation on the topic can ignore the apparent misery of May Joyce's marriage and her eldest son's carefully documented guilt ("self-penned") as well as his sympathy for his mother's suffering; evidence exists, of course, in Joyce's long-standing resistance to the marriage ceremony despite his allegiance to his bond with Nora.

is the basis of "passages of *Finnegans Wake* [that] signify nothing to anybody (including Joyce) beyond the signifying function itself."[32] Lacan locates problems such as Joyce's eye condition, his increasingly arcane prose, and Lucia Joyce's illness along the axis of a disturbed father-son relationship.[33] Lacan thus would seem to view the Wakean discourse as a further disintegration, a failure without therapeutic potential.

Ferenczi's analysis of the language of disturbance in incestuous families provides another explanation. Just as I argue that Bloom's impotence is the physical gesture of his genius at parenting, in Ferenczi precocious intelligence is also a symptom, part of the victim's drive to normalize abuse (a precocious parenting of the perpetrator, a striving to secure the family tie). The confusion of tongues, initially a symptom of abuse, becomes for perpetrator and victim an accommodation, a survival strategy—in some cases a strikingly ingenious symbolic reparation for deeply buried sorrow and terror.

Although the Lacanian analysis is helpful, Ferenzci's work raises questions about a "language signifying nothing . . . beyond the signifying function." The Lacanian reading makes sense to the extent that it sees a disturbance in the symbolic as symptomatic of a disturbance with the father, but such a formulation does not necessarily mean that the resulting language does not mean. Such a formulation merely privileges a paternal symbolic. Alternatively, Ferenczi's "confusion of tongues" distinguishes among arrangements of the maternal and the paternal in language. In this context one could profitably speculate on the distinctiveness of the dialectics of the maternal and the paternal in *Ulysses* and *Finnegans*

---

32. The source of this comment is a personal communication, March 1987. Much of Lacan's work on Joyce, as Ellie Rayland-Sullivan pointed out in her talk at the Joyce Conference, Milwaukee, June 1987, is unpublished and untranslated. In his Introduction to *Joyce between Genders: Lacanian Views*, a recent *James Joyce Quarterly* 29 (Fall 1991): 13–19, which he edited with Ragland-Sullivan, Sheldon Brivic observes that Lacan's seminars on Joyce, "given weekly from 18 November 1975 . . . to at least 11 May 1976," will, "once they are assembled by Jacques-Alain Miller, make up Lacan's twenty-third volume of seminars" (18). Brivic lists souces for French publications of several seminars and some English translation "by E. Tito Cohen on audio tapes."

33. Discussions of John Joyce's alcoholism, indebtedness, and verbal and physical abuse of family members may be found in Bauerle, "Date Rape, Mate Rape"; Cixous, *The Exile of James Joyce*; George H. Healey, *The Complete Dublin Diary of Stanislaus Joyce* (Ithaca: Cornell University Press, 1962); and Colbert Kearney, "The Joycead," in *Coping with Joyce: Essays from the Copenhagen Symposium*. John Joyce's excesses and brutality produced in Stanislaus a hatred for his father and in James a bind between an overwhelming need to reject his father and an overriding inability to do so. In that language acquisition is tied to the oedipal relation, Joyce's bind, from a Lacanian view, would be Joyce's genius.

Wake. Such an analysis is constitutive of a linguistic dramatization of the movement from the repression of a personal sorrow in *Ulysses* to a politically motivated focus on a communal repression and the re- or dismembering of a sexist ideology in the maternally discursive antics of *Finnegans Wake.*

I refer here specifically to the representations of the act of father-daughter incest and subsequent (and eventually simultaneous) textual commentary on the act in *Finnegans Wake.* A consideration of key episodes indicates that the productions of the precocious intellect of the abused child would seem to be the model for a paternal narrative in a maternal register. Content is a rationalized attempt to normalize passion and form the sensory manifestation of a physical dialectic of tenderness and passion. Although the drive toward reparation or survival for the incest victim becomes apparent, as Lacan suggests, in symptomatic disturbances of the symbolic, such disturbances would be, in Ferenczian analysis, symptomatic of a greater disturbance, a failure of the mediating impulses of the imaginary. It is this failure that reproduces the reified forms of the maternal field. Since in the *Wake* the maternal is not field but river, we find evidence of the reified emotional forms in the watery field of tears with which or in which Anna Livia Plurabelle remembers and reproduces herself in her cyclic wash to the sea at the end of the text.

Such an invasion of the symbolic by a discourse of the real, this failure of mediations of the imaginary, results in a language organized by so-called regressive or primary process tropes. Accordingly, the movement from *Ulysses* to *Finnegans Wake* may be viewed as a shift not so much from an overdeterminedly modernist discourse to a language that "signifies nothing" as from an overdeterminedly symbolic or overrationalized discourse in *Ulysses,* a brilliantly detached paternal discourse, to an overwhelmingly maternal discourse in *Finnegans Wake.* A discourse designed to mediate paternal violence in *Ulysses* reverts to the mother tongue, a giving over to a maternal ethic, in the physicialized narrative of *Finnegans Wake.* Joyce's "arcane prose," then, means a great deal; it operates idiosyncratically, resurrecting the vulnerable and abused body, the specifically victimized or marginalized body altogether dependent on an empathetic observer for re-membering, for re-cognizing its abuse. (Remember, in Ferenczi the victim's self-denial is a mode of processing incest; the victim's return to self must originate in the discoverable empathy of the abuser—or a surrogate, who, as Ferenczi reminds us, must substitute for orthodox "paternal coolness" a "maternal friendliness.")

While the plot of *Finnegans Wake* operates playfully to conceal incest, the discursive register remembers incest. The persistence of a "maternal friendliness" at the level of expression, this feminine (double)-engendering of the discourse of the *Wake*, eventually leads to a therapeutic remembering. The sensory resurrection of the father's body is preparation for the empathic recovery of the daughter's body. Joyce's "arcane prose," making possible a symbolic return to the mother coinciding with an embrace of the paternal, contains the possibility of the therapeutic remembering. Ferenczi's work, in its designation of the potential for a balance of the maternal and paternal in language, quite specifically supports such a reading.

Throughout Joyce's writing we can discover a dialectic of the languages of tenderness and passion, replications of the confusions of incest victim and perpetrator. In *Finnegans Wake* the language system is maternal or real (a language of formalist tenderness), while the narrative of desire itself is one not of tenderness but of passion. This is the arrangement of the dialectic of remembering. In *Ulysses* the language system is overdetermined, symbolic (that is, paternal, detached). Even as it deeply encodes the wisdom of Bloom's body, this discourse resonates with the real (of tenderness and vulnerability), a representation of the impotent father in his childlike body. This is the arrangement of a dialectic of a failing repression. All of the preceding suggests, then, not that the Joycean discourses are constituted by the complementarities of a dialectic in a mirror but that in the variations of the dialectical confusions of tongues, we come to our relations with discursive possibilities.

"Herword in Flesh"

In *Finnegans Wake* the father takes the daughter in acts alternately violent, passionate, and tender. Even before the re-membering of the paternal body in the sixteenth chapter and the paternal empathy on the last page, if we "havelook, we seequeerscenes" (*FW*, 556.24). Although Roland McHugh annotates the word "Havelook" or "Havelock," as an allusion to the fourteenth-century Dane, we can safely assume that a modern Havelock, surnamed Ellis, who studied the eros of micturition in adult sexuality, is also suggested.[34] (Turnabout is fair play, or perhaps the only act in town; here is evidence of the irruption of tenderness in adult passion as opposed to the irruption of passion into the childhood sphere of tenderness in the case of incest.) Queer scenes in the *Wake* often involve, of course, the crimes in the park; urination and voyeurism throughout are familiar transformations of the scene of father-daughter incest. In the psychoanalytic case history, and, similarly, in HCE's attraction to Issy, the love object, here the language of the text, projects a tender or infantile sexual orientation, while the act itself, a voluptuously adult union, demonstrates the confusion of tongues in its therapeutic aspect. Thus, a narrative romance occurs in the *Wake*. The father mistakes "the play of children for the desires of a sexually mature person" (Ferenczi, 161). It is, however, upon this paternal, and in this case poetic, narrative that the crude physical realities of the passionate body of the father are superimposed. The writing of the paternal body in the physicality of sexual engagement violently contradicts the lyric intensities of the incest passage. In other words, this maternal text invites us to entertain, in the père-version, the romantic pleasures and contingent revulsions of father-daughter incest. The consummation scene, couched in a bucolic and typically Wakean musical and passionate discourse, unveils the paternal genitals in a childishly physicalized language.

The ideal love object of the *Wake*, psychoanalytically viewed, is the delusion covering the inevitable rupture between self and environment. The choice of such an object forecloses on further development. The many repetitions of Issy and the manifestation of ALP at the cycle's end as daughter rather than mother or wife confirm the *Wake's* love object, the paternal repetition, as incestuous. Just as Milly is to Bloom, Issy is to HCE: yet another patch job, a "ms Butys Pott," a cover for the text's hole, a repetitious marker for unassuageable lack. She is also "saintette," martyred, a little saint, or *sans tête*—irrational, all body. In the movement from *Ulysses* to *Finnegans Wake*, there is an apparent slip in registers of experience. In the gap we may discover what the figure of the daughter barely conceals. For desire's symptoms in *Ulysses* produce the symptoms of repression in the girlish Bloom and the guilty Bloom, while inces-

---

34. Roland McHugh, *Annotations to Finnegans Wake* (Baltimore: The Johns Hopkins University Press, 1980). I am grateful to Susan Stanford Friedman, who offered me this connection.

tuous desire in *Finnegans Wake* reproduces blissful consumma-
tions, paternal anguish, and, most strikingly, filial terror and
resignation.

The *Wake* works, then, as Ferenczi contends a regressive therapy
would: the maternal atmosphere makes possible a therapeutic return to tenderness. In *Finnegans Wake*, in fact, a maternal language
prevails. It is established in a proliferation of preverbal tropes: disruptions of categories, binarisms, and the text's linearity and in the
multispatial and shifting registers of the text. Within this infantile
linguistic field there remains, however, a confusion of tongues, for
the incest narrative is one of passion (a mode of violence and conflict as Ferenczi defines it). Such speech contains, then, a significant
remembering without reparation. But it is in this sense that the
open form of *Finnegans Wake*, the gap before we begin again, holds
potential for reparation as well as repetition.[35]

The situation in the sixteenth chapter of *Finnegans Wake* is
analogous to Ferenczi's thereapeutic situation. The paternal embrace and the paternal admission of wrongdoing are contained
within a maternal field (and quite distinct from Bloom's symbolic
displacements and infantile embrace). The chapter moves in epi-
sodic fits and jerks from the symbolic register and paternal passion
toward a tender conclusion in the maternal real. The shift occurs
in the dialectical arrangement of discursive strategies in the father-
daughter narrative. For example, at first Issy's presentation operates

---

35. One might, for example, reread this nightmare (of history's nightmare) as a narrative
of the decline of patriarchy. In the beginning there is the fall—of Adam, Napoleon, Welling-
ton, or "Willingdone," as he is known in the *Wake*, the last a transformation that repeats
on a grander scale the *voglio* theme of *Ulysses* while at the same time it functions as
commentary on the roles of mastery and power in conventional historical narratives,
especially as we come to recognize that "each harmonical has a point of its own" (*FW*,
12.31). At the end of a linear reading we find, moreover, that the fall of a daughter eclipses
or perhaps summarizes the fall of *the* fathers. The ethical-epistemological-historical axis of
Joyce's radical rewriting of history's nightmare would seem to resonate with the negative
dialectics of a contemporaneous radical social theory—a "coincidence" of the sort Joyce
might have cherished. The Critical Theory of the Frankfurt School, for instance, is dominated by the construction of a negative (and unsynthesizable) dialectic, a reading of individual suffering against the concept of history. Theodor Adorno, in formalizing the praxis,
refers to it as a cognitive concept constitutive of the "speculative moment" (Theodor W.
Adorno, *Negative Dialectics*, trans. E. B. Ashton [New York: Continuum, 1973], 15–18).
Finnegans Wake specifically formulates such an anti-ideological critique as cognitive strategy in the dialectical arrangements of the daughter's suffering and the ideology of patriarchy (a concept of history as paternal power and sexual mastery). The potential for
reparation thus occurs, initially, in the recognition that canonization, another version of
the hegemony of patriarchy, in the case of Joyce's last work, has been maintained by a
silence that repeats the silence of patriarchal control: these, then, are the interludes that
reparation seeks.

from an ambivalent paternal perspective. Initially she is made of literary allusion and language games: as "infantina" she is everybody's love but also "queenly pearl," prized object of her father's lust. But she is also poetry turned real: not only is "Isobel . . . so pretty truth to tell," but she is so sad, "like some losthappy leaf, like blowing flower stilled, as fain would she anon, for soon again 'twill be, win me, woo me, wed me, ah weary me! deeply now . . ." (*FW*, 556.20–22). HCE's Isobel, closely related here to Bloom's daughter ("Milly. Molly, same thing watered down"), occurs as some combination of herself and her mother. She is leafy as the Liffey and flowery as herself. Of greatest significance is that in this passage her name (Issy, Isabelle, and so on) is spelled with an *o*. The passage floats on *o*'s: "Isobel . . . so pretty . . . wildwood's eyes . . . primarose hair . . . woods so wild . . . in mauves of moss . . . how all so still. . . ." This river of sound demarcates a shift from the symbolic to the real. Here the sign of the mother, Molly's "O," the water sign, is transformed. This time *l'eaux de lust*, however, are tears—perhaps deep waters of lamentations. The symbolic—the linguistic foregrounding with its historically allusive "infantina" and literary "queenly pearl"—has turned to the maternal (word has become substance) as the passage's *o*'s overtake us. The symbolic is transformed to the maternal or real, as *o*'s (already mostly *eaux* in *Ulysses*) become tears in *Finnegans Wake*. The physical real, the text's sensory memory, is foregrounded in what only *appears to be* linguistic foregrounding.

Yet we cannot be quite certain where all this watery sadness leads. We do find, however, that love's charm, a coup de grace (in its ambivalence also a "grace cup") to theories of language as symbolic substitution for the mother, has a name: "What an excessively lovecharming missyname to forsake, now that I have come to drink of it filtred, a grace cup fulled of bitterness . . ." (*FW*, 561.14–16). Incest and the name of the father are one. In this rite of passage the father "comes" to drink "filtred"—not sacramental wine but virgin's blood. Thus he destroys the "maiden" in "maidenname." In a confusion of tongues and fluids, which becomes an ambivalent conflation of loss of virginity and "grace," his deepest sorrow is concomitant with profoundest gain. In replacing the "maiden" with "missyname," he has, moreover, recreated her out of his destruction of her earlier identity. His determination is clear: "I *will* to show herword in flesh" (*FW*, 561.27; emphasis added). "Herword," yet another neologism, synonymous with or replacing the already obsolete "missyname," is a mystery yet, while the *voglio* has been retranslated once more: the name of the father now functions as an archaic verb. To will is to lust. "Herword in flesh" is a transgression of the symbolic, an affirmation of the father's desire for the subject-object confusion of maternal intimacy, an intrusion of the real into the symbolic.

Such drunken transgression would seem to invoke a defensive enchantment. In fact, the unnameable, sleep-inducing act ensues, while the word, its name, is forbidden, repressed; word and act evaporate like dreams: "It is dormition! She may think, what though little doth she realize, as morning fresheth, it leath happened her, you know what, as *they too* dare not utter" (*FW,* 561.28–30; emphasis added). This passage, leading toward the lyric union of father and daughter, shifts to a plural pronoun and direct address. Out of the (neurotic) repetitions of Issy's many manifestations, a narrative remembering of the multiple sins of the fathers occurs at the site of this daughter's repression. Like all her sisters, Issy will repress the love whose name she "dare not utter," while her father recalls her sisters are legion.

As the narrative voice speculates—perhaps hopefully, one might wonder—on Issy's repression, there is a confusion of subject and object, typical of the infantile or maternal field. Here maternal language (and empathy) is managed from the paternal position or situation. And yet sorrow still speaks elliptically. And in the meantime, in a somewhat evasive interlude, sleep brings about the seemingly digressive disturbance of the twin's nightmare which lasts until the family appears, veiled in what I would call a reassertion of the symbolic, a linguistic digression, a costume drama: "Here The infant Isabella from her coign to do obeisance toward the duffgerent, as furst furtherer with drawn brand. Then the court to come in to full morning" (*FW,* 566.23, 24). The subject (doubled, in the sense of syntactic position as well as in the narrative sense of *subject to* her "furst furtherer") is the "infantina" once more. But is the court-to-come-in, the paternal courtship and consummation, already doomed? Could it be in full *mourning* as Isabella bows before her sire's drawn sword? Thus, the language of detachment, of "dormition," persists.

Toward the section's end, passion's moment (*FW,* 570–71)—doubly disturbing in the explicitness of the incest narrative and the lyric beauty of its expression—is introduced with Finnegan's stammer and Finnegan's leer, the symbolic stamp of literary homage and literary paternity. The *Hamlet* themes, the passivity and hesitation themes of *Ulysses*, shift into the active, tragic *Lear* themes in *Finnegans Wake* in the name, of course, of Will: "She, she, she! But on what do you again leer? I am not leering, I pink you pardons. I am highly sheshe sherious" (*FW*, 570.24, 25). The Celtic Lir, a Neptune figure, had two sons and a daughter, like HCE. The feminine trilogy is Will Shakespeare's version.

And just as in *Ulysses*, where sexual willing, Bloom's lust in its symbolic formulation, transforms to Molly's "O's" at the appropriate instance, so the same sexual symptom recurs in the maternal language of the *Wake*. Loss and sexual excitement, the return of the maternal, is announced metonymically in O's. And as I noted earlier, the O which signifies maternal lust in *Ulysses* also embodies regret in the *Wake*—and an increasingly precarious vertigo. In a text so pocked with O's it seems there is nowhere left to go but down and "on": "Do you not must want to go somewhere on the present. Yes, O pity! That prickly heat feeling! Forthink not me spill it's always so guey. Here we shall do a far walk (O pity) anygo Khaibits till the number one of sairey's place. Is, is" (*FW*, 570.25–30). The cognitive dissonance generated by "*on* the present" leads compellingly to explicit paternal passion (omnipresent, besides) and an intricately deteriorating symbolic and almost incomprehensibly demanding line: "(O pity) anygo Khaibits till the number one. . . ." McHugh's annotation supplies the Egyptian: *khaibits* is shadow. The line then reads: *Annie go shadow or ALP in HCE's arms becomes a shadow until the number one of Sarah's place* (beside, astride, beneath her master), *the best choice in the first monotheist's place, in Abraham's first wife's place, is (his daughter) Isabelle.*

The passage continues: "I want you to admire her sceneries illustrationing our national first rout, one ought ought one." If "her sceneries" are related to "queerscenes," I would not be surprised if micturition were once more the topic. The "national first rout" is riveting and explicit. In apposition to the "first rout," the thousand-and-one-nights formula is a statistic (and a stream of droplets as well, a stream of O's). It could also be the Irish father's version of the Dane's indecision, and *ought*, or zero, functions both as a verb and a discrimination of moral responsibility. In all cases, the sexual and sad O has been transformed. The sexual sign, a quite literal sign of the father's lack, the sign of castration anxiety, the hole in the text, generates a moral design.

The sin in the park, we learn as the passage proceeds, forecloses on the afterlife. This warning leads to a clearing in the park which is also a clearing of the mind of HCE (since, according to the topographical logic of the *Wake*, the park is also the landscape of the paternal body and the "fungopark" [*FW*, 51.20], his beard). Thus his responsibility would seem to increase in direct proportion to an increase in his detachment; here the narrative has shifted from the third-person singular, in which the narrator speculated on what was on Issy's mind, to third-person plural, in which we are joined to him in the voyeuristic escapade. This shift in narrative voice is also, of course, a sign of HCE's doubling, of his paternal and maternal manifestations, of his desire and his empathy. And the confusion of tongues is managed in this passage in the equilibrium of maternal and paternal discourses:

> They arise from a clear springwell in the near of our park which makes the daft to hear all blend. The place of endearment! How it is clear! And how they cast their spells upon, the frond that thereup float, the bookstaff branchings! The druggeted stems, the leaves incut on trees! Do you can their tantrist spellings? I can lese, skillmistress aiding. . . . Yes they shall have brought us to the water trysting, by hedjes of maiden ferm, then here in another place is their chapelofeases, sold for song, of which you have thought my praise too much my price. O ma ma! Yes, sad one of Ziod? Sell me, my soul dear! Ah, my sorrowful, his cloister dreeping of his monkshood, how it is triste to deth, all his dark ivytod! Where cold in dearth. Yet see, my blanching kissabelle, in the under close she is allso gay, her kirtles green, her curtisies white, her peony pear, her nistlingsloes! I, pipette, I must also quicklingly to tryst myself softly into this littleeasechapel. I would rather than Ireland! But I pray, make! Do your easiness! O, peace, this is heaven! O, Mr Prince of Pouringtoher, whatever I hear from you, with limmenings, lemantitions, after that swollen one? I am not sighing, I assure, but only I am soso sorry about all in my saarsplace. (*FW* 571.2–24)

The father acts out his inevitable role[36] and *also* reacts maternally, that is, therapeutically, in his tripled apology: he has been

---

36. The father's role in repressing for his children their versions of his desire, their oedipal longing, is always problematic. "Rarely," Lacan comments, "does this . . . succeed" (*Feminine Sexuality*, 167).

disastrously "sheshe sherious." Now he is "so so sorry." (At least as Lear, he has exhausted his possibilities; he has cried "O" three times.) Thus the word of the father (remade in part from the moral letter of the mother's sexuality, her O) attempts reparation simultaneous with his passion.

Accordingly the confusion of tongues persists, only to be resolved at the last possible moment out of the incredible momentum of the entire text. Ferenczi's assessment of the incest victim's situation can serve as an assessment of Wakean discourse:

> It is difficult to imagine the behavior and the emotions of children after such violence. One would expect the first impulse to be that of reaction, hatred, disgust, and energetic refusal. "No, no, I do not want it, it is much too violent for me, it hurts, leave me alone," this or something similar would be the immediate reaction if it had not been paralysed by enormous anxiety. These children feel physically and morally helpless, their personalities are not sufficiently consolidated in order to be able to protest, even if only in thought, for the overpowering force and authority of the adult makes them dumb and can rob them of their senses. *The same anxiety, however, if it reaches a certain maximum, compels them to subordinate themselves like automata to the will of the aggressor, to divine each one of his desires and to gratify these; completely oblivious of themselves they identify themselves with the aggressor.* Through the identification, or let us say, introjection of the aggressor, he disappears as part of the external reality, and becomes intra- instead of extra-psychic; the intrapsychic is then subjected, in a dream-like state as is the traumatic trance, to the primary process, i.e. according to the pleasure principle it can be modified or changed by the use of positive or negative hallucinations. In any case the attack as a rigid external reality ceases to exist and in the traumatic trance the child succeeds in maintaining the previous situation of tenderness. (Ferenczi, 162)

On the last page of *Finnegans Wake* the Celtic Lir resurfaces and remembers ALP as the daughter who draws the world round in her weary return "to my cold mad feary father, till the near sight of the *mere* size of him, the moyles and moyles of it, moananoaning, makes me seasilt saltsick and I rush, my only, into your army. I see them rising! Save me from those horrible prongs! . . . Yes carry me along taddy, like you done throgh the toy fair" (*FW*, 628.1–5; emphasis added). The father, at this late point in the narrative and with His Complete Empathy for the victim's position, remembers incest as an inevitable part of the feminine cycle—a place of return related to a place of origin.

She has cried a river, it would seem. (And paternal speech affirms the origin; "moananoaning" rings not only with a lament for the mother—*o an, an, o, an*—but also recalls her to this infinitely sadder version of the father's tale of the "m*oo* cow" on the first page of *Portrait*. Here, in a wish fulfillment *vers le père,* a reversal occurs in which paternity is not only known through nomination. In the daughter's last words his desire is real-ized. ALP's watery transformation contains the paternal gain which is her loss, but the mother watered down is hardly washed out; ALP does not revert to Issy nor to her younger self.

She is all daughters. In Joyce's oceanic world the inevitability of "herword," *incest*—"our national first rout"—is as clearly and poignantly presented as the nature of love and of life itself. Only the point of view has changed. The père-version yields the source of the daughter's subversion, her subordination remembered in the protean unreliability of the name of "love." An ideology of concealment, failure, and transformation in *Ulysses* thus finds release through acknowledgment and potential for reparation in the feminine consciousness of Joyce's late work. Here the maternal father opens the symbolic by re-*o*-penning the feminine wound at the site of his lack. "Herword" is "allflesh" remembering. "Herword" is our legacy.

9

Textual Mater:
Writing the Mother in Joyce

Ellen Carol Jones

> . . . (the mother of the book with a dustwhisk
> tabularasing his obliteration done upon her
> involucrum). . . .
>
> JAMES JOYCE, *Finnegans Wake*

Tabularasing the Mother

The erasure of and by the mother of the book, the textual mater, is double in this parenthesis from James Joyce's *Finnegans Wake:* the male has already blotted out the letter of her involucrum, her vulva.[1] But that obliteration itself leaves a trace, a spoor, that she must then "tabularase" in order to disappear "entirely spoorlessly"[2]: a double movement of tabulating and scraping the tablet or slate. That a book has a mother suggests a certain origin for the act of writing. But that writing is obliterated, its letter blotted out in a first, incomplete erasure. The male, signaled by the possessive pronoun *his,* obliterates the mother's involucrum: her vulva and perhaps, to extend the Latin root of "covering," her hymen, the folded, never single space in which the pen writes its dissemination. The letter blotted out is that of the woman's genitalia penetrated, penned, and torn in the sexual act, the trace of the pen's inscription still legible.

---

1. The text plays upon the Latin *oblitterare,* "to blot out," from *ob,* "over," and *littera,* "letter," and upon the Latin *involvere,* "to wrap," "to cover," and *vulva,* "covering."
2. James Joyce, *Finnegans Wake* (New York: Viking Press, 1939), 50.11; hereafter cited in the text as *FW* with page and line number. The epigraph is from 50.12–13.

The double erasure of the mother's involucrum prepares a tabula rasa for the annunciating male word. Origin is thus not in the flesh but in the word. The male production of the logos usurps the reproductive power of the mother, the "power of the beginning(s)," by seizing the "monopoly of the origin."[3] In the economy and ideology of (re)production, the resorption of femininity within the maternal represents, according to Julia Kristeva in "Stabat Mater," a masculine appropriation of the maternal, a "fantasy masking primary narcissism," a masculine sublimation of the maternal considered necessary for the creation of art.[4] Kristeva describes the maternal as a fantasy for a lost territory, an idealization of primary narcissism: the maternal is the "ambivalent principle that is bound to the species, on the one hand, and on the other stems from an identity catastrophe that causes the Name to topple over into the unnamable that one imagines as femininity, nonlanguage, or body" (*Tales*, 234–35). Writing causes the subject to confront an archaic authority, a maternal authority that resides on the nether side of the proper Name. For Joyce, according to Kristeva, the feminine body, the maternal body, "in its most un-signifiable, un-symbolizable aspect, shores up, in the individual, the fantasy of the loss in which he is engulfed or becomes inebriated, for want of the ability to name an object of desire." The feminine is an Other without a name—an unnamable Otherness that is *jouissance* and writing as well.[5]

The text of male discourse gains its coherence through a double displacement of woman: the coupling or augmenting of woman with man in a hierarchized equation and the subtracting or cutting out of what the male considers the representational excess of the female sexual organs, for example, the effacement of the clitoris as

3. Luce Irigaray, *This Sex Which Is Not One*, trans. Catherine Porter with Carolyn Burke (Ithaca: Cornell University Press, 1985), 102; hereafter cited in the text as *This Sex*.
4. Julia Kristeva, *Tales of Love*, trans. Leon S. Roudiez (New York: Columbia University Press, 1987), 236; hereafter cited in the text as *Tales*. "Stabat Mater," a text split between an exposition of the Catholic church's iconography of the Virgin Mother Mary and the lyric portrayal of Kristeva's own experience of motherhood, represents formally the division of flesh and language for which the maternal body is the site. Compare Jacques Lacan's claim that analytic discourse proves woman's nonexistence by subsuming woman into the maternal: "If any discourse proves it to you, it is surely analytic discourse, by putting into play this notion, that woman will be taken only *quoad matrem*. Woman comes into play in the sexual relation only as mother" (quoted in Irigaray, *This Sex*, 102).
5. Julia Kristeva, *Powers of Horror: An Essay on Abjection*, trans. Leon S. Roudiez (New York: Columbia University Press, 1982), 75, 20, 58–59; hereafter cited in the text as *Powers*.

the signifier of the sexed subject.[6] Joyce's writing, transgressive of philosophical, political, social, and sexual laws, enjoys what could be termed an "incestuous relationship with language," where language is treated as a metaphor for the maternal body.[7] In the children's game in *Finnegans Wake*, the double movement of "tabularasing" the mater entails tabulating her by the augmentation of the annunciating word, but erasing her by the subtraction of desire: "Think of a maiden, Presentacion. Double her, Annupciacion. Take your first thoughts away from her, Immacolacion" (*FW*, 528.19–21). A double movement of "tabularasing" characterizes Joyce's "writing the mother": an annunciatory augmentation of the material-maternal matrix by privileging (male) word over (female) flesh—a privileging that would deny or erase the very materiality of that matrix by making the (m)other serve as matrix/womb for the male subject's signifiers—and a simultaneous undermining of such a phallogocentrism by calling attention to what is oppressed by and repressed in a patriarchal law of Being-same. Through this double movement of "tabularasing" the mother, Joyce attempts to reach the threshold of repression, to reach that which is beyond figuration for the (male) artist: the ineffable *jouissance* of the mother, the body rejoicing of the maternal experience.

The Wake of the Other

The (male) artist's attempt to reach the threshold of repression both upholds and negates the censorship of text and (female) sex within an economy in which writing itself is unthinkable without repression. Indeed, Jacques Derrida argues that the symptomatic form of the return of the repressed is the metaphor of writing and the systematic contradictions of the ontotheological exclusion of the trace.[8] Writing enacts the loss of a self-presence never actualized

6. Gayatri Chakravorty Spivak, "Displacement and the Discourse of Woman," in *Displacement: Derrida and After*, ed. Mark Krupnick (Bloomington: Indiana University Press, 1983), 191; hereafter cited in the text as "Displacement." See also Gayatri Chakravorty Spivak, "French Feminism in an International Frame," *Yale French Studies* 62 (1981): 154–84.

7. Leslie Hill, "Julia Kristeva: Theorizing the Avant-Garde?" in *Abjection, Melancholia, and Love: The Work of Julia Kristeva*, ed. John Fletcher and Andrew Benjamin (London: Routledge, 1990), 150.

8. Jacques Derrida, *Writing and Difference*, trans. Alan Bass (Chicago: University of Chicago Press, 1978), 197; hereafter cited in the text as *Writing*.

but nevertheless "always already split, repeated, incapable of appearing to itself except in its own disappearance."[9] Systematic and systemic contradictions inhere in a series of metaphors marking the relation of the self to the Other: the trace as the mark of difference, repeating itself infinitely as the same by referring to the Other, revealing origin as a myth of annulled supplementarity and a myth of erasure; writing as the simultaneous production and erasure of the transcendental distinction between the origin of the world and Being-in-the-world; memory as the permanence of the trace and simultaneous virginity of the matrix; the semiotic chora as the place where the subject is both generated and negated; abjection as requisite for the reconciliation, in the mind, between flesh and the law; the repression of the maternal as abjected in order to ensure the subject's entry into language. Tabularasing itself has as its end the return to an impossible, irretrievable, unknowable origin, to the repressed body of the mother as Other of the self. Inasmuch as Joyce's texts play out these contradictions, they unravel the masculine appropriation of the maternal yet, as representations, remain inevitably caught within their net.

In the act of tabularasing, the spoor, the "trace, the wake of the letter is never finally eradicated."[10] For example, in *Ulysses* Leopold Bloom recognizes the impossibility of a spoorless "obliteration" when he blots his clandestine letter of desire to Martha Clifford and realizes it could still be read off the blotting pad. That he should decide the blotted letter could constitute the origin of a story, a "prize titbit" in which a detective reads a letter off a blotting pad, is a reaction dependent, as Colin MacCabe notes, "on the written trace left by his earlier reading of Matcham's masterstroke," the prize story of *Titbits*.[11]

Bloom tries to efface the letters of the message he writes in the sand to his Nausicaa: "I." "AM." "A."—a message that, incomplete and hence indeterminate, seems to confer no identity, a message of nothing: I am a thing, a thing of nothing. But Sandymount Strand teems with traces of messages: "All these rocks with lines and scars

9. Jacques Derrida, *Of Grammatology*, trans. Gayatri Chakravorty Spivak (Baltimore: Johns Hopkins University Press, 1976), 112; hereafter cited in the text as *Grammatology*.

10. Colin MacCabe connects the trace with the wake of the letter in *James Joyce and the Revolution of the Word* (London: Macmillan, 1979), 127.

11. James Joyce, *Ulysses*, ed. Hans Walter Gabler with Wolfhard Steppe and Claus Melchior (New York: Garland, 1984), 11:901; hereafter cited in the text as *U*, with episode and line numbers. MacCabe, *James Joyce*, 127.

and letters," Bloom reflects as he surveys the strand. He thus comprehends what Stephen had also noted earlier that day: these "heavy sands are language tide and wind have silted here," a language Stephen is determined to decipher: "Signatures of all things I am here to read, seaspawn and seawrack, the nearing tide, that rusty boot" (U, 13.1261; 3.288–89; 3.2–3). Paradoxically, the one trace Bloom might read, he cannot, the message rendered as unreadable by the elements as the letter/litter the hen Biddy Doran in *Finnegans Wake* scratches—that is, both inscribes and effaces—out of the dump: "Mr Bloom stooped and turned over a piece of paper on the strand. He brought it near his eyes and peered. Letter? No. Can't read. . . . Page of an old copybook. All those holes and pebbles" (U, 13.1246–49). If the sands are language, they also blot (out) the letter. Stephen's question that morning as he writes his poem—"Who ever anywhere will read these written words?"—has as its answer everyone . . . and no one (U, 3.414–15).

The trace, or the spoor, is the wake of the Other within the sign and the intimation of an origin forever deferred. As Derrida claims, the sign as a structure of difference is the place where "the completely other is announced as such—without . . . any identity, any resemblance or continuity—within what is not it" (*Grammatology*, 47).[12] Word and thing or word and thought are never "at one." For Derrida, the trace is "the part played by the radically other within the structure of difference that is the sign." That is, difference cannot be thought without the trace: the "structure of the sign is determined by the trace or track of that other which is forever absent" (*Grammatology*, 57, xvii).

As *différance*, the reopening of ontic-ontological difference, the trace retains "the other as other in the same." The trace would

12. Jane Flax, calling for excluded or repressed material and voices to be heard, faults "postmodern" philosophers for not being "free from a will to power whose effects they trace elsewhere." Succumbing to the will to power coopts "the others" and effaces the traces of such a cooptation: "This double erasing may account for some of the obscurity in the writing of postmodernism; tracks have to be erased or effaced as they are made" (Jane Flax, *Thinking Fragments: Psychoanalysis, Feminism, and Postmodernism in the Contemporary West* [Berkeley: University of California Press, 1991], 192). The metaphors deliberately echo Derrida on the trace and erasure in order to call into question his work on the problems of origin and difference. "Without intermediary and without communion, neither mediate nor immediate, such is the truth of our relation to the other," claims Derrida in discussing the work of Emmanuel Levinas, "the truth to which the traditional logos is forever inhospitable. This unthinkable truth of living experience, to which Levinas returns ceaselessly, cannot possibly be encompassed by philosophical speech without immediately revealing, by philosophy's own light, that philosophy's surface is severely cracked, and that what was taken for its solidity is its rigidity" (*Writing*, 90).

seem to mark an anterior presence, an origin, but instead it marks the absence of a presence, of being as full presence; it calls the possibility of origin into question by revealing that origin itself "was never constituted except reciprocally by a nonorigin, the trace" (Grammatology, 62, 61).[13] The present is not primal but, rather, reconstituted. To say that différance is originary is "simultaneously to erase the myth of a present origin. Which is why 'originary' must be understood as having been crossed out, without which différance would be derived from an original plenitude. It is a non-origin which is originary" (Writing, 203). The concept of origin is nothing but the myth of addition, "of supplementarity annulled by being purely additive." And it is simultaneously the myth of erasure: "the myth of the effacement of the trace," of an originary différance that is neither absence nor presence (Grammatology, 167).

For Derrida, the text of metaphysics and the language we speak signal their own transgressions if one considers presence not as the signification of the sign or as the referent of the trace but as "the trace of the trace, the trace of the erasure of the trace." Thus, there is no contradiction between an originary tracing and effacement, "the absolute erasure of the 'early trace' of difference and that which maintains it as trace, sheltered and visible in presence."[14] Because the trace can only "imprint itself by referring to the other," its force of production stands in necessary relation to its erasure.[15] Always deferring, the trace presents itself only in its erasure: "Tracing and effacing are not simply in a relation of exteriority; what constitutes the trace in depth is precisely the relation to Otherness by which the trace's self-identity and self-presence are marked, and thus effaced, by the detour through the Other." The originary trace is thus "the constituting impurity or alterity, the constituting nonpresence," that allows the phenomenologically primordial to come into its own by providing it with "the mark of a minimal difference within which it can repeat itself infinitely as the same by referring to an Other and to (an Other of) itself within itself." The archetrace

13. Derrida reiterates in Positions "that the trace is neither a ground, nor a foundation, nor an origin, and that in no case can it provide for a manifest or disguised ontotheology" (Jacques Derrida, Positions, trans. Alan Bass [Chicago: University of Chicago Press, 1981], 52).

14. Jacques Derrida, Margins of Philosophy, trans. Alan Bass (Chicago: University of Chicago Press, 1982), 66; hereafter cited in the text as Margins.

15. Jacques Derrida, Dissemination, trans. Barbara Johnson (Chicago: University of Chicago Press, 1981), 331.

must be understood, like the hymen, as "the fold of an irreducible 'bending-back,' as a minimal (self-)difference within (self-)identity, which secures selfhood and self-presence through the detour of oneself (as Other) to oneself."[16] The hymen is the self's alliance in the language of the Other.[17]

Writing as one of the representatives of the trace entails the loss of a "self-presence which has never been given but only dreamed of and always already split, repeated, incapable of appearing to itself except in its own disappearance" (*Grammatology*, 112). The scene of writing reveals not the myth of an "originary or modified form of presence" but the trace, Other, difference, change. Derrida defines the "*symptomatic* form of the return of the repressed" as "the metaphor of writing which haunts European discourse, and the systematic contradictions of the onto-theological exclusion of the trace. The repression of writing as the repression of that which threatens presence and the mastering of absence." The history of metaphysics is that system of logocentric repression organized in order "to exclude or to lower (to put outside or below), the body of the written trace as a didactic and technical metaphor, as servile matter . . . " (*Writing*, 197). Writing is the space of the Other, the space of the repressed.

The labor of writing erases the transcendental distinction between the origin of the world and Being-in-the-world—"erases it while producing it" in a double movement of tabularasing, as Freud recognizes. An unerasable trace is not a trace but a full and incorruptible presence. The trace is the erasure of selfhood, of one's own presence, and is constituted, as Derrida notes, by "the threat or anguish of its irremediable disappearance, of the disappearance of its disappearance." This erasure is death itself, and Derrida reminds us that "it is within its horizon that we must conceive not only the 'present,' but also what Freud doubtless believed to be the indelibility of certain traces in the unconscious, where 'nothing ends, nothing happens, nothing is forgotten.'" This erasure of the trace is "the very structure which makes possible, as the movement of temporalization and pure *auto-affection*, something that can be called re-

16. Rodolphe Gasché, *The Tain of the Mirror: Derrida and the Philosophy of Reflection* (Cambridge: Harvard University Press, 1986), 189, 192.

17. Jacques Derrida, "Living On: Border Lines," in *Deconstruction and Criticism*, ed. Harold Bloom et al. (New York: Continuum, 1984), 77.

pression in general, the original synthesis of original repression and secondary repression, repression 'itself'" (*Writing*, 212, 230).

Tympanum

The word of the annunciation penetrates the tympanum of the ear of the virginal body, its reverberation suggesting the trace of the letter, its echo revealing male narcissism as the force underlying the construct of virgin birth. Father Cowley, that false priest of "Sirens" (the episode of *Ulysses* whose organ is the ear), draws the medieval Catholic analogy between tympanum and hymen by hinting that the "base barreltone" bass of Ben Dollard, the singer of the tight trousers with "all his belongings on show," could pierce more than the *oreille* of his female listener:

> —Sure, you'd burst the tympanum of her ear, man, Mr Dedalus said through smoke aroma, with an organ like yours. . . .
> —Not to mention another membrane, Father Cowley added. (*U*, 11.559, 557, 536–40)

Indeed, the female virginal body is necessary for this vocal conception: within a male homosexual economy, as Stephen reflects in "Scylla and Charybdis," the love that dares not speak its name falls on "singular uneared wombs" (*U*, 9.664). Bursting the tympanum is connected in "Circe" with male anxiety about the origin of the annunciatory word when Philip Drunk asks the question Joseph posed to Mary: "*Qui vous a mis dans cette fichue position, Philippe?*" and Philip Sober answers: "*C'était le sacré pigeon, Philippe.*" The mirroring names point to the male narcissism configuring the virgin birth, whereas the sacred pigeon alerts us to its improbability. When he sees Ben Dollard enter, Bloom's grandfather Virag allays male anxiety of origin and affirms the priority of the Son over the Virgin Mother: "Messiah! He burst her tympanum," whereupon the virgins mob Dollard (*U*, 15.2582–85; 2601–2; see 3.161–62 for Stephen's first reference to the sacred pigeon).

For the Messiah/son to burst her tympanum is to commit incest with the mother: as Stephen argues the doctrine of the virgin birth in "Oxen of the Sun," "she knew him, that second I say, and was but creature of her creature, *vergine madre, figlia di tuo figlio*" (*U*,

14.302–3).[18] Saint Bernard of Clairvaux glorifies Mary as beloved and wife of Christ in his allegorical reading of the Song of Songs. The opening line of Saint Bernard's prayer to Mary on behalf of Dante in *Paradiso* 33, "Vergine Madre, figlia di tuo Figlio" (Virgin Mother, daughter of thy Son), erases the materiality, the specific corporeality of the three feminine functions of mother, daughter, wife and establishes in that space a bond of "unchanging and time-less spirituality"—"*Termine fisso d'eterno consiglio*," as Dante claims, "the set time limit of an eternal design" (quoted in Kristeva, *Tales*, 243–44).

Stephen posits two readings of the problematic doctrine of the virgin birth: either the Virgin Mother knew her son,

> or she knew him not and then stands she in the one denial or igno-rancy with Peter Piscator who lives in the house that Jack built and with Joseph the joiner patron of the happy demise of all unhappy marriages, *parceque M. Léo Taxil nous a dit que qui l'avait mise dans cette fichue position c'était le sacré pigeon, ventre de Dieu! Entweder* transubstantiality *oder* consubstantiality but in no case subsubstantiality. And all cried out upon it for a very scurvy word. A pregnancy without joy, he said, a birth without pangs, a body without blemish, a belly without bigness. (*U,* 14.303–11)

Knowledge entails either incest and subordination to the priority of the son or betrayal. If the Virgin Mother "knew" her god and son in the biblical sense of coitus, then the doctrine of the virgin birth does indeed sublimate but also celebrate incest: "*Ma mère m'a mariée*" (*U,* 14.1453). If she does not "know" him, she either has not been impregnated by the Holy Spirit or, as vessel of flesh, is unaware she has carried the Word of God made flesh. If, like Peter, she denies her knowledge of him, she reenacts his betrayal. Ste-phen's quibble derives from Saint Bernard's *Divine Office* for the October 11 Feast of the Motherhood of the Blessed Virgin Mary: "But Mary knew herself to be His mother and she trustfully calls Him her Son, whose majesty the Angels serve with awe. . . . God, I

18. Karl Marx relates *Aufhebung* (sublation, the negation of the negation, at once deny-ing a thing and preserving it on a higher level) to supporting the Christian desire for maternity in virginity (see Jacques Derrida, *Glas*, trans. John P. Leavey, Jr., and Richard Rand [Lincoln: University of Nebraska Press, 1986]). In "Freud and the Scene of Writing" (*Writing and Difference*) and in "The Double Session" (*Dissemination*), Derrida points out that in Freud and in Mallarmé the desire is to find a surface both marked and virgin. In *Of Grammatology* Derrida reveals Rousseau's desire for a category that was both tran-scendental (virgin) and supplementary (marked). See Spivak, "Displacement."

say, to whom the Angels are subject . . . He was subject to Mary. . . .
That God should obey a woman is humility without precedent;
that a woman should command God, exaltation without parallel."[19]
Christ as subject to Mary raises the question of precedence and
equality: Is Mary consubstantial with Christ as Christ is with God?
The shifting prefixes expose the insubstantiality of a dogma that
denies the substantiality of the maternal experience.

In "Tympan," Derrida playfully suggests that all of philosophy
could be considered "conception through the ear," speech being
"the sperm indispensable for insemination." He links that auricular
conception with *homoousios*, the mastery that the concept of Being-same, or Being-proper, assures philosophy, and also with its heretical denial: the Arian heresy proclaiming that Christ the Son is
not consubstantial with God the Father—"Arius, warring his life
long upon the consubstantiality of the Son with the Father," Stephen Dedalus recalls (*U*, 1.657–58).[20] The ear, Derrida notes, is by
its oblique structure "the distinct, differentiated, articulated organ
that produces the effect of proximity, of absolute properness, the
idealizing erasure of organic difference." Such an erasure, in claiming to obliterate difference, leaves the trace of an *in*difference, an
economy of the same. The multivalences of the word *tympanum*
as drum, as triangular architectural space, and as mediating and
equalizing membrane and printing device present the tympanum as
unmarked, "virgin, homogenous, and negative space" which is
ready, "like matter, the matrix, the *khōra* [maternal receptacle], to
receive and repercuss type" in the printing operation. In printing,
the matrix, from the Latin word for womb, is the metal plate used
for casting typefaces. But the tympanum is also that which "punc-
tures itself or grafts itself" and thus operates parthenogenetically as
both (female) hymen and (male) penis, surface and tool of writing
(*Margins*, xvii, xxvii–xxviii).

The ideal virginity of the present *(maintenant)* is constituted by
the work of memory. Derrida points out how Freud, in "Note on
the Mystic Writing-Pad" (1925), realizes that to explain memory he
must account simultaneously "for the permanence of the trace and

19. Quoted in Don Gifford with Robert J. Seidman, *Ulysses Annotated: Notes for James Joyce's Ulysses* (Berkeley: University of California Press, 1988), 416.
20. The Nicene Council's refutation of the Arian heresy in A.D. 325 claims that Christ is "begotten, not made, of one essence consubstantial with the Father," but Stephen recognizes that he, like the Christ of the heretic Arius, is "made not begotten" (*U*, 3.45). Derrida mentions the Nicene Council's refutation of the heresy (*Margins*, xivn6).

for the virginity of the receiving substance, for the engraving of furrows and for the perennially intact bareness of the perceptive surface," a kind of tabularasing. Freud discovers such a double system contained in a single differentiated apparatus: "a perpetually available innocence and an infinite reserve of traces" are reconciled in a contrivance on the market known as the Mystic Writing-Pad. Such a market item accords with his hypothetical structure of the human perceptual apparatus: "an ever-ready receptive surface and permanent traces of the inscriptions that have been made on it" (Writing, 200, 223).[21] Two hands are necessary to the maintenance of this writing machine, a system of gestures, an organized multiplicity of origins: "If we imagine one hand writing upon the surface of the Mystic Writing-Pad while another periodically raises its covering sheet from the wax slab, we shall have a concrete representation of the way in which I tried to picture the functioning of the perceptual apparatus of our mind" (SE, 19.232). Derrida notes that the depth of the Mystic Writing-Pad is "simultaneously a depth without bottom, an infinite allusion, and a perfectly superficial exteriority: a stratification of surfaces each of whose relation to itself, each of whose interior, is but the implication of another similarly exposed surface." In this doubleness it joins "the two empirical certainties by which we are constituted: infinite depth in the implication of meaning, in the unlimited envelopment of the present, and, simultaneously, the pellicular essence of being, the absolute absence of any foundation" (Writing, 224).

Trace as memory is not a pure breaching (Bahnung, breaking of a path, tracing of a trail) which might be appropriated at any time as simple presence. Traces are rather the ungraspable and invisible differences between breaches that enact the double movement of tabularasation (Writing, 201). The contradictory requirements fulfilled by the Mystic Writing-Pad are formulated in terms that align breaching and writing: "an unlimited receptive capacity and a retention of permanent traces" (SE, 19.227). Trace becomes gramme, in Freud's thought, and the region of breaching a ciphered spacing, as Derrida notes: "Traces thus produce the space of their inscription only by acceding to the period of their erasure. From the beginning, in the 'present' of their first impression, they are constituted by the

---

21. Sigmund Freud, *The Standard Edition of the Complete Psychological Works of Sigmund Freud,* ed. and trans. James Strachey (London: Hogarth, 1957), 19:228; hereafter cited in the text as *SE.*

double force of repetition and erasure, legibility and illegibility."
Derrida posits Freud's "two-handed machine, a multiplicity of agen-
cies or origins," as "the original relation to the other and the original temporality of writing, its 'primary' complication: an originary
spacing, deferring, and erasure of the simple origin. . . ." The Other
is necessary to writing: "We must be several in order to write, and
even to 'perceive.' The *simple* structure of maintenance and manu-
scription, like every intuition of an origin, is a myth, a 'fiction' as
'theoretical' as the idea of the primary process." For that idea is
contradicted by the theme of primal repression. Writing itself is
unthinkable without repression: "The condition for writing is that
there be neither a permanent contact nor an absolute break between
strata: the vigilance and failure of censorship" (*Writing,* 226). For
Freud, the maternal body is the origin of what is censored.

Lithography before Words

The originarily displaced scene of writing is the scene of
woman. Her hymen remains forever (in)violate. Derrida envisions
the question of the representation of woman as "at once too old and
as yet to be born: a kind of old parchment crossed every which way,
overloaded with hieroglyphs and still as virgin as the origin, like
the early morning in the East from whence it comes."[22] According
to Kristeva, if we "are entitled only to the ear of the virginal body,"
then its taut eardrum may well tear "sound out of muted silence"
(*Tales,* 248, 240). Figured as receptacle of the word but instead receptacle of the nonverbal, of the semiotic—a lithography before words:
metaphonetic, nonlinguistic, alogical—the "Virginal Maternal" represents the "return of the repressed" in monotheism. Kristeva
traces its trajectory: "Starting with the high Christly sublimation
for which it yearns and occasionally exceeds, and extending to the
extra-linguistic regions of the unnameable, the Virgin Mother occupied the tremendous territory hither and yon of the parenthesis
of language."[23] Obliterated and tabularased, the mother of the logos
in *Finnegans Wake* exists, literally, in the parenthesis of language.

22. Jacques Derrida and Christie V. McDonald, "Choreographies," *Diacritics* 12 (Summer 1982): 75.
23. Julia Kristeva, *The Kristeva Reader,* ed. Toril Moi (New York: Columbia University
Press, 1986), 174–75. See also Kristeva, *Tales,* 250.

"Stabat Mater" parallels Kristeva's analysis of Mariolatry with her own "post-virginal" discourse of the mother, stressing the impotence of a phallogocentric language to reveal the experience of motherhood:

> Words that are always too distant, too abstract for this underground swarming of seconds, folding in unimaginable spaces. Writing them down is an ordeal of discourse, like love. What is loving, for a woman, the same thing as writing. Laugh. Impossible. Flash on the unnamable, weavings of abstractions to be torn. Let a body venture at last out of its shelter, take a chance with meaning under a veil of words. WORD FLESH. From one to the other, eternally, broken up visions, metaphors of the invisible. (*Tales,* 235)

The laugh is not only, like Stephen's laugh in "Scylla and Charybdis" (*U,* 9.1016), to free the mind from the mind's bondage—a laugh that acknowledges the impossibility of measuring word against world—but also to free the (female) body from the (male) subject's language.[24] In highlighting "word" and "flesh" by typographically demarcating them from the other words of the passage, Kristeva emphasizes the conjunction of word and flesh within a discursive economy in which words are always too distant and too abstract. The flash on the unnameable—here, in the mother's discourse, the embryo, and in the main body of the text, the maternal, the feminine—epiphanizes what is still exiled from language: "FLASH—instant of time or of dream without time; inordinately swollen atoms of a bond, a vision, a shiver, a yet formless, unnamable embryo. Epiphanies. Photos of what is not yet visible and that language necessarily skims over from afar, allusively" (*Tales,* 234–35). Derrida, reading Emmanuel Levinas, asserts: "To express oneself is to be *behind* the sign. . . . To be behind the sign which is in the world is *afterward* to remain invisible to the world within epiphany." The Other is that which does not reveal itself, which cannot be made thematic. The Other can only be invoked, called in the vocative, "the bursting forth, the very raising up of speech." The Other is the inaccessible, the invisible, the intangible (*Writing,*

24. Colin MacCabe argues that Stephen, caught in the contradiction that his theory of Shakespeare must hold good for all of the plays, including those he has not read, laughs to free himself from the constrictions of characterizing Shakespeare's work as a representation of his life. His laugh acknowledges the impossibility of total knowledge and "the ridiculous claims of language to place us in a position of knowledge" (*James Joyce,* 120–21).

101, 103).[25] The epiphany of Kristeva's "Stabat Mater" comes as an annunciation, as does the epiphanic, mystic—and ejaculatory—"morning inspiration" to which the artist Stephen awakens in *A Portrait of the Artist as a Young Man*: "The instant flashed forth like a point of light and now from cloud on cloud of vague circumstance confused form was veiling softly its afterglow. O! In the virgin womb of the imagination the word was made flesh. Gabriel the seraph had come to the virgin's chamber."[26] The male artist receives the impregnating word in the virgin womb of the imagination, the imagination a *khora*, a maternal receptacle, for the logos, the seraph Gabriel the fecundator. The need to masturbate to return to the ecstatic moment of annunciation suggests the male narcissism at the heart of a conceit that figures a wet dream as an annunciation.

In Stephen's envisioning of the postcreation in *Ulysses*, the corruptible flesh born of the mother is transformed by the (male) artist into the incorruptible logos: "In woman's womb word is made flesh but in the spirit of the maker all flesh that passes becomes the word that shall not pass away" (*U*, 14.292–94). The spirit of the maker echoes woman's womb, but the artist requires no annunciation to transform flesh to word. Indeed, the word of the artist revivifies the dead: "You have spoken of the past and its phantoms," Stephen remarks to Costello, echoing Hotspur. "Why think of them? If I call them into life across the waters of Lethe will not the poor ghosts troop to my call? Who supposes it? I, Bous Stephanoumenos, bullockbefriending bard, am lord and giver of their life." *Amor matris* may be the only true thing in life, but Stephen's proclamations about creation, whether of art or of life, either ignore or incorporate into paternity itself the necessary maternal matrix. Yet the namegiver's empowering paternity is undermined when Vincent/Lynch remonstrates Stephen as the artist encircles his hair with a poet's coronal of vine leaves: "That answer and those leaves, Vincent said to him, will adorn you more fitly when something more, and greatly

25. For Levinas the feminine is that which disrupts and transforms what he terms "the virility of the force of being"; yet the feminine also facilitates its continuance, "since the exterior realm, the public realm where signification takes place, would be a closure without the undecidable or equivocal feminine 'interiority.'" To deploy the feminine is to adopt a strategy of oppositional structuring in which women are encoded "as other, or as the excess which escapes, and yet also provide the boundary to that excess" (Alison Ainley, "The Ethics of Sexual Difference," in Fletcher and Benjamin, *Abjection, Melancholia, and Love*, 56).

26. James Joyce, *A Portrait of the Artist as a Young Man: Text, Criticism, and Notes*, ed. Chester G. Anderson (New York: Viking, 1968), 217.

more, than a capful of light odes can call your genius father" (*U*, 14.1112–19). Lenehan's reassurance to Lynch, "Have no fear. He could not leave his mother an orphan," seems a non sequitur, but follows the logic of the mother as *figlia di tuo figlio*, the son/artist as both logos and father. *Amor matris* is thus indeed a sublimated celebration of incest: *"Ma mère m'a mariée"* (*U*,14.1123, 1453).

Trading Flesh against Word

In portraying his characters as composed of traces of written language they have appropriated, Joyce reveals how we all "are composed in and by the text." To read any novel, Colin MacCabe asserts, is "to trade flesh against word," a transaction *Ulysses* specifically enacts in "Oxen of the Sun," where the history of English literature parallels and usurps the history of the gestation and birth of a child.[27] As Susan Stanford Friedman points out: "The fact that Joyce partly envies the fecundity of female flesh and despairs at the sterility of male minds does not alter the fundamental sexual dualism of his complex birth metaphors: Joyce's women produce infants through the channel of flesh, while his men produce a brainchild through the agency of language."[28] In the parade of literary languages, each new style incorporates and displaces the old, signaling a progression that is itself usurped by the disintegration of meaning in the final style, as Joyce explained to Frank Budgen:

> Technique: a nineparted episode without divisions introduced by a Sallustian-Tacitean prelude (the unfertilized ovum), then by way of earliest English alliterative and monosyllabic and Anglo-Saxon ("Before born the babe had bliss. Within the womb he won worship." "Bloom dull dreamy heard: in held hat stony staring") then by way of Mandeville ("there came forth a scholar of medicine that men clepen etc") then Malory's *Morte d'Arthur* ("But that franklin Lenehan was prompt ever to pour them so that at the least way mirth should not lack"), then the Elizabethan chronicle style ("about that

27. MacCabe, *James Joyce*, 127. For source analyses of "Oxen of the Sun" in relation to gestation, see Phillip F. Herring, *Joyce's Ulysses Notesheets in the British Museum* (Charlottesville: University of Virginia Press, 1972), and Robert Janusko, *The Sources and Structures of James Joyce's "Oxen"* (Ann Arbor: UMI Research Press, 1983).

28. Susan Stanford Friedman, "Creativity and the Childbirth Metaphor: Gender Difference in Literary Discourse," in *Speaking of Gender*, ed. Elaine Showalter (New York: Routledge, 1989), 79–80.

present time young Stephen filled all cups"), then a passage solemn, as of Milton, Taylor, Hooker, followed by a choppy Latin-gossipy bit, style of Burton-Browne, then a passage Bunyanesque ("the reason was that in the way he fell in with a certain whore whose name she said is Bird in the hand") after a diarystyle bit Pepys-Evelyn ("Bloom sitting snug with a party of wags, among them Dixon jun., Ja. Lynch, Doc. Madden and Stephen D. for a languor he had before and was now better, he having dreamed tonight a strange fancy and Mistress Purefoy there to be delivered, poor body, two days past her time and the midwives hard put to it, God send her quick issue") and so on through Defoe-Swift and Steele-Addison-Sterne and Landor-Pater-Newman until it ends in a frightful jumble of Pidgin English, nigger English, Cockney, Irish, Bowery slang and broken doggerel.[29]

Even in this early description of the technique for the episode, the embryonic development, the gestation and birth of the child, and the mother are submerged in the welter of styles. The language of the literary forefathers in "Oxen of the Sun" is played out on the body of the mother, its linguistic virtuosity sounded out of her silence. Although the "frightful jumble" of styles in the episode's finale presents the language of the dispossessed, of the colonized and racial Other to the imperialist subject, these nonetheless powerful styles also are played out on, take possession of, the maternal body. The woman is the womb, the "unconscious womb of man's language." She has no relation to her own unconscious except one, as Luce Irigaray writes, "marked by an essential dispossession," a dispossession manifested in absence of self and articulated only by silence (*This Sex*, 94). No parallel mater text in "Oxen," no voicing of the mother's experience, exists to rival the textual parade of literary history. Her double erasure leaves no spoor to be read.

In erasing while producing the transcendental distinction between the origin of the world and Being-in-the-world, writing tabularases the material matrix. To be written while simultaneously erased is to be metaphorized. The origin posited for the linguistic phylogeny of "Oxen of the Sun" is a tripartite heliotropic gesture—"In the beginning was the gest" (*FW*, 468.5)—a turning toward the sun god Helios (in Joyce's schema, the doctor Horne, master of the National Maternity Hospital, Holles Street, Dublin, the scene of the episode) to entreat him to send forth life and the fruit of the womb:

29. James Joyce to Frank Budgen, March 20, 1920, *Letters of James Joyce*, vol. 1, ed. Stuart Gilbert (New York: Viking, 1966), 139–40.

Deshil Holles Eamus. Deshil Holles Eamus. Deshil Holles Eamus.
Send us bright one, light one, Horhorn, quickening and wombfruit.
Send us bright one, light one, Horhorn, quickening and wombfruit.
Send us bright one, light one, Horhorn, quickening and wombfruit.
Hoopsa boyaboy hoopsa! Hoopsa boyaboy hoopsa! Hoopsa boyaboy
hoopsa! (*U*, 14.1–6)[30]

What is the significance of this heliotropic gesture of origin, this
incantation to the sun god as the one who brings forth life—even
though his sacred cattle, symbols of fertility in Joyce's schema, are
castrated—in an episode whose organ, according to that schema,
is the womb, whose symbol is mothers, and whose technique is
embryonic development? Metaphor retraces within the unconscious the path of paternal myth. For Aristotle, as Derrida notes in
"White Mythology: Metaphor in the Text of Philosophy," the sun
is the proper name, the "nonmetaphorical prime mover of metaphor, the father of all figures." Its "referent has the originality of
always being original, unique, and irreplaceable." "Everything turns
around it, everything turns toward it." But in the Aristotelian problematic of metaphor, no clear opposition necessarily adheres between proper, literal meaning and figurative meaning. Thus, in
querying what is proper to the sun, Derrida asks of metaphor: "Is
not this flower of rhetoric (like) a sunflower?" Metaphor itself, he
argues, "means heliotrope, both a movement turned toward the sun
and the turning movement of the sun"; it is itself always already
the sun, a re-turn to itself (*Margins*, 243, 250, 251). This return to
itself is the property of metaphor in the text of philosophy, the
heliotropic gesture calling attention to the law of the same that
constitutes that text:

Does not such a metaphorology, transported into the philosophical
field, always, by destination, rediscover the same? The same *physis*,
the same meaning (meaning of Being as presence or, *amounting to
the same*, as presence/absence), the same circle, the same fire of the
same light revealing/concealing itself, the same turn of the sun? What
other than this return of the same is to be found when one seeks
metaphor? that is, resemblance? and when one seeks to determine
the dominant metaphor of a group, which is interesting by virtue of

30. *Deshil* is Irish for "turning to the right" and "turning toward the sun"; *eamus* is
Latin for "let us go."

its power to assemble? What other is to be found if not the metaphor of *domination*, heightened by its power of dissimulation which permits it to escape mastery: God or the Sun? . . . The tenor of the dominant metaphor will return always to this major signified of ontotheology: the circle of the heliotrope. (*Margins*, 266)

The circle of heliotrope is a specular circle, "a return to itself without loss of meaning, without irreversible expenditure," an interiorizing turn that is the philosophical desire to master the division between origin and self. Such a de-tour is "a re-turn guided by the function of resemblance (*mimēsis* or *homoiōsis*), under the law of the same." The opposition of the metaphoric and the proper, then, explodes when it is revealed to be a specular opposition in which the one and the other reflect and refer to each other (*Margins*, 268–71).[31]

In beginning the history of English literature with a heliotropic gesture, Joyce reveals how the specularity of the literary canon itself reflects the specularity of philosophy and a politics of power and domination: as Hélène Cixous asserts: "Literary history has been homogeneous with phallocentric tradition, to the point of being phallocentrism-looking-at-itself, taking pleasure in repeating itself."[32] The thrice-repeated invocation to Helios to send "quickening and wombfruit," the invocation that *precedes* the prelude symbolized by the unfertilized ovum, calls upon the god/sun/father to bring forth life, denying the necessity of the maternal body. As Derrida points out in comparing the metaphor of the sun in the thought of Levinas and of Plato: "Creation is but creation *of* the other; it can be only as paternity, and the relations of the father to son escape all the logical, ontological, and phenomenological categories in which the absoluteness of the other is necessarily the same. (But did not the Platonic sun already enlighten the visible sun, and did not excendence play upon the meta-phor of these two suns?)"(*Writing*, 86).[33] In usurping the reproductive function of the

31. Margot Norris analyzes heliotrope as a figure for heterosexual desire and as a model for deciphering nonverbal semiologies in "Joyce's Heliotrope," in *Coping with Joyce: Essays from the Copenhagen Symposium*, ed. Morris Beja and Shari Benstock (Columbus: Ohio State University Press, 1989), 3–24.

32. Hélène Cixous and Catherine Clément, *The Newly Born Woman*, trans. Betsy Wing (Minneapolis: University of Minnesota Press, 1986), 97.

33. Levinas employs the term *excendence* to denote a "departure from being and from the categories which describe it." Incapable of respecting "the Being and meaning of the other," phenomenology and ontology, Derrida points out in "Violence and Metaphysics: An Essay on the Thought of Emmanuel Levinas," would be philosophies of violence. "Through them, the entire philosophical tradition, in its meaning and at bottom, would

mother and appropriating the monopoly of origin, the logos forces the potency and potentiality of the maternal back into the circular logic of the same: "to Sameness—in itself and for itself."[34] The heliotropic gesture, "Deshil," written in the *materna lingua* of Irish, begins the parade of styles of the *English* literary tradition, a tradition of male authors and a cooptation of Irish-born writers into the dominant English canon: Swift, Sterne, Goldsmith, Burke, Sheridan. The heliotropics of style reflect the heliopolitics of imperialism.

Amor Matris

Patriarchal history dispossesses woman of her return upon herself. As Luce Irigaray notes: "She remains outside the circularity of a thought that, in its telos, turns to [man's] ends the cause of his desire: she is the unconscious basis of that attempt to find metaphor for an originary matrix in the sphere of intimacy with self, of nearness to self, of a 'soul' or a mind" (*Speculum*, 240). The interiorizing, heliotropic circle—figured by Joyce in the threefold heliotropic invocations that open "Oxen of the Sun"—is the philosophical desire to master the division between origin and self. But what the mother unveils is, as Kristeva writes, "a continuous separation, a division of the very flesh. And consequently a division of language . . . " (*Tales*, 254). Christian theology posits the maternal body as "a sort of subject at the point where the subject and its speech split apart, fragment, and vanish," the maternal body as the place of that splitting.[35] In that split the mother disappears "spoorlessly." Comprehending this maternal split entails what Kristeva calls a "vertigo of language weakness," a vertigo for which art's oversaturation of sign

make common cause with oppression and with the totalitarianism of the same. The ancient clandestine friendship between light and power, the ancient complicity between theoretical objectivity and technico-political possession. . . . Henceforward, the heliological *metaphor* only turns away our glance, providing an alibi for the historical violence of light: a displacement of technico-political oppression in the direction of philosophical discourse. . . . If there is no history, except through language, and if language (except when it names Being *itself* or nothing: almost never) is elementally metaphorical, Borges is correct: 'Perhaps universal history is but the history of several metaphors'" (*Writing*, 91–92).

34. Luce Irigaray, *Speculum of the Other Woman*, trans. Gillian C. Gill (Ithaca: Cornell University Press, 1985), 229; hereafter cited in the text as *Speculum*.

35. Julia Kristeva, *Desire in Language: A Semiotic Approach to Literature and Art*, ed. Leon S. Roudiez, trans. Thomas Gora, Alice Jardine, and Leon S. Roudiez (New York: Columbia University Press, 1980), 237; hereafter cited in the text as *Desire*.

systems attempts to compensate, an oversaturation that Joyce's texts both reflect and parody (*Tales*, 252–53). Woman is then the matrix for masculine specularity, the origin for the male's representations, her body his text, as Leopold Bloom considers the blank page on which he will inscribe his veiled desire to Martha Clifford: "Blank face. Virgin should say: or fingered only. Write something on it: page" (*U*, 11.1086–87).

To define *matrix* only as origin and to ignore its concomitant function as frame is a fallacy Joyce exposes not in the content but in the structure of "Oxen of the Sun," in the framing of the language of his literary forefathers by the offstage and thus silent travail of the mother. Patrick McGee argues that the woman's body, in particular the mother's womb, envelops the languages of the patriarchy in "Oxen," but the very act of framing, of enveloping their discursivity, subverts their claims to power:

> Joyce's writing now displaces the patriarchal interpretation of the human body as the body of man by framing man's body with woman's body, the body that frames and transgresses the law of the father. Woman's body demystifies the body of man by exposing the illusion of its completeness, its self-idealization (even when that idealization takes the form of castration); it insists on the representation of what has been foreclosed by the symbolic construction of the body of man: the frame, the groundless ground of becoming, the organ that folds and expands in the production of that which is of itself and not of itself. The fold in woman's body that frames the production of sexual difference signifies itself in the exclusion of what remains at (as) the end of its labor; the human body is the remainder of woman's body, itself the remainder of itself, the frame framing itself. Woman's body is the unfinalized frame of the body of man and woman, of the unfinalized human body.[36]

The split between self and not-self, the production of another who, once born, opens the abyss between the body and what had been its inside, exposes the mother as frame: "I remain henceforth like a framework. Still life," the mother's voice of "Stabat Mater" confirms (*Tales*, 243). This still life, this *nature morte*, is the frame for the "herethics" Kristeva calls for: *amor matris*, maternal love,

---

36. Patrick McGee, *Paperspace: Style as Ideology in Joyce's Ulysses* (Lincoln: University of Nebraska Press, 1988), 101. For a discussion of the frame in the discourses of aesthetics and philosophy, see Jacques Derrida, *The Truth in Painting*, trans. Geoff Bennington and Ian McLeod (Chicago: University of Chicago Press, 1987).

a-mort or un-death—a heretical ethics, separated from the conventions of morality, that makes the thought of mortality bearable.

Stephen Dedalus aligns the mother with both love and death. "*Amor matris*, subjective and objective genitive, may be the only true thing in life" to redeem the uncertainty of paternity (*U*, 9.842–43). That the love is subjective and objective genitive reveals its reciprocity: the love of the mother *for* the child, the love of the mother *by* the child. And as (m)other, as the infinitely Other, she is death. Returned from the grave and arrayed for the bridal, the ghoulish May Dedalus in "Circe" speaks to Stephen of a *jouissance* both maternal and marital, the giving of birth as an inverse incest: "Years and years I loved you, O, my son, my firstborn, when you lay in my womb" (*U*, 15.4204–5). Her giving birth to her firstborn, her maternal passion, replicates the passion and death of Christ, as the syntax of her prayer for mercy also elides the anguish of the grieving Virgin Mother with that her dying Son: "Have mercy on Stephen, Lord, for my sake! Inexpressible was my anguish when expiring with love, grief and agony on Mount Calvary" (*U*, 15.4238–40). Such a love may be eternal, but her torn bridal veil suggests that where there is sexual copulation, there is also death.[37] As corpse she reveals what Stephen must thrust aside in order to live: "Let me be and let me live" (*U*, 1.279)—and what he cannot fully reject: the utmost of abjection, the border become object, an elsewhere imagined beyond the present, hallucinated in the present as an object who speaks. All abjection acknowledges the *want*, the inaugural loss, on which any being, meaning, language, or desire is founded: the loss of the mother. Abjection is the violence of mourning for an "object" that has always already been lost. The (male) writer approaches the hysterical, hystericized body of the woman—of the

37. Impregnation without sexuality triumphs over death: "For where there is death there is also sexual copulation, and where there is no death there is no sexual copulation either," Saint John Chrysostomos argues in his fourth-century treatise *On Virginity*. Saint Jerome opposes Eve and Mary, death and life: "Death came through Eve but life came through Mary." The patriarch Irenaeus adds the opposition of snake and dove, confirming the interpretation that the temptation of Eve is a sexual temptation, the Fall of Man a fall into (female) sexuality and death: "Through Mary the snake becomes a dove and we are freed from the chains of death" (quoted in Kristeva, *Tales*, 239). Sexuality, specifically female sexuality evidenced in maternity, betrays Man to sin and death: expounding the church doctrine of the Annunciation to the medical students in "Oxen of the Sun"—the episode that unmasks the "crime committed against fecundity by sterilizing the act of coition" (Joyce, *Letters*, 1:139)—Stephen affirms that Mary is "the second Eve and she won us, saith Augustine too, whereas that other, our grandam, which we are linked up with by successive anastomosis of navelcords sold us all, seed, breed and generation, for a penny pippin" (*U*, 14.298–301).

mother—so that he might speak of what eludes speech, as Kristeva writes, "of the excluded, the outside-of-meaning, the abject" (*Powers*, 5, 15, 22).[38]

Both dead and resurrected, virginal and maternal, May Dedalus may in her womb make the word become flesh, but she does not reveal to Stephen the "pregnant word" when he asks her to voice it: "Tell me the word, mother, if you know now. The word known to all men" (*U*, 15.4192–93). The word may be the word her toothless mouth utters when she first appears to Stephen, but the word she utters is silent (*U*, 15.4161). Even death fails to give a woman knowledge of the word known to all men. Stephen cannot hear her word; he can see only her death. As is true of the doubter in the *Wake*, "His hearing is indoubting just as [his] seeing is onbelieving" (*FW*, 468.15–16). Her death betrays the very love her maternal *jouissance* has unveiled. Her ethics are not heretical but are those of the church, her language that of the Virgin Mother, the only discourse on motherhood the patriarchy sanctions—an ethics and a language Stephen will not serve: "*Ah non, par exemple!* The intellectual imagination! With me all or not at all. *Non serviam!*" (*U*, 15.4226–27). The language he will serve is the language of the devil, the *non serviam* of the ultimate heretic. Yet Stephen has heard the word of the mother before, although she does not voice it, and that word is, indeed, love: "Do you know what you are talking about?" he asks himself as he expounds his theory on Shakespeare. "Love, yes. Word known to all men" (*U*, 9.429–30).[39] The Word discloses the abject, for Joyce, but at the same time, the Word alone purifies from the abject. Art, for him, Kristeva writes, is rooted in the abject it utters and through that utterance purifies (*Powers*, 23, 17).

38. Patrick McGee argues that the mother is the body of the woman whom Joyce cannot identify and cannot elude: "[I]n facing this woman it is the woman in himself—the woman he devours and by whom he is devoured, the mother—that speaks." He rightly points out that what gives form to Joyce's abjection, "channeling its negative power into the deconstruction of the styles of Western literature, involves more than the ambivalence that survives in each of us as the trace of our fall into language. *Ulysses* also gives form to the abject horror of history's nightmare and illustrates Adorno's assertion that 'The unresolved antagonisms of reality reappear in art in the guise of immanent problems of artistic form,'" a textual symptom of a political unconscious (*Paperspace*, 188–89).

39. The restoration in the 1984 Critical and Synoptic Edition of *Ulysses* of this manuscript passage has been controversially received. The full passage from the Rosenbach manuscript is several lines long and as such restores the longest passage omitted from the published text: "Do you know what you are talking about? Love, yes. Word known to all men. *Amor vero aliquid alicui bonum vult unde et ea quae concupiscimus. . . .*" That the *patrius sermo* of Latin is garbled as it attempts to define the word known to all men suggests that *amor matris* constitutes the eruption of the semiotic into the symbolic.

Having had a child, could a woman, asks Kristeva, speak another love, a love unknown to all men? Love may be an object "banished from paternal Death"; but *amor matris* may indeed be subjective and objective genitive, a "shattering of the object across and through what is seen and heard within rhythm: a polymorphic, polyphonic, serene, eternal, unchangeable jouissance that has nothing to do with death and its object, banished from love" (*Desire*, 157).

Maternal *Jouissance*

Unfolding patriarchal English literary history as embryonic development, Joyce reveals the split symbolization—the "threshold of language and instinctual drive, of the 'symbolic' and the 'semiotic'"—which constitutes both art and, Kristeva argues, the giving of birth (*Desire*, 240). Of these two signifying processes, the symbolic is the instituting of sign and syntax, paternal power, the law as the name of the father. The term *semiotic* Kristeva derives from the Greek for "distinctive mark, trace, index, precursory sign, proof, engraved or written sign, imprint . . . figuration."[40] She relates the semiotic process to the *chora*, a term Plato describes in his *Timaeus* as a maternal "receptacle": "an invisible and formless being which receives all things and in some mysterious way partakes of the intelligible, and is most incomprehensible" (quoted in *Desire*, 6). The *chora*, as Kristeva defines it, is an economy of primary processes articulated by the instinctual drives through condensation and displacement. It is not a position, a model, or a copy. Rather, it "precedes and underlies figuration and thus specularization," a rhythmic space in which can be read "the process by which significance is constituted," the work of language that enables a text to signify what representative and communicative speech cannot say. It is "the place where the subject is both generated and negated, the place where his unity succumbs before the process of charges and stases that produce him" (*Revolution*, 26, 28).

The semiotic *chora* appears within the signifying process "as the trace of the *jouissance* that the subject gives himself with the other,

---

40. Julie Kristeva, *Revolution in Poetic Language*, trans. Margaret Waller (New York: Columbia University Press, 1984), 25; hereafter cited in the text as *Revolution*.

with or through language itself."[41] The mother's body as ordering
principle of the semiotic *chora* is what mediates the symbolic law.
The maternal body is the site of the semiotic and the precondition
of the symbolic. Maternity constitutes a breach or rupture in the
symbolic, an unspoken residual site of *jouissance*, "whose pleasure
is reduced to but never exhausted by the symbolic—except perhaps
in art."[42] For Kristeva, the language of art follows the maternal
jouissance that is "the sublimation taking place at the very moment
of primal repression within the mother's body" (*Desire*, 242), a sublimation that arises perhaps unwittingly out of her marginal position in a social-symbolic order empowered by the phallus.
Literature, written as the language "of that impossible constituted
either by a-subjectivity or by non-objectivity," propounds a sublimation of abjection. The aesthetic task is to descend into the founda-
tions of the symbolic construct, retracing "the fragile limits of the
speaking being, closest to its dawn, to the bottomless 'primacy'
constituted by primal repression" (*Powers*, 26, 18). Through and
across the founding of signs, the aesthetic practice touches on primal repression: "At the intersection of sign and rhythm, of representation and light, of the symbolic and the semiotic, the artist
speaks from a place where [the mother] is not, where she knows
not. He delineates what, in her, is a body rejoicing [*jouissant*]." Her
"translibidinal jouissance," her mediation between semiotic and
symbolic, enables the artist to incorporate the eroticism of her maternal body into the language of his art (*Desire*, 242, 243). Subject
and object stand at the boundary of what is thinkable: the abject.
The woman's body may function as a fetish, a graspable object
within representation, as Molly Bloom's body functions for the men
of *Ulysses*.[43] Or there may exist a maternal function that eludes

41. Julia Kristeva, "Within the Microcosm of 'The Talking Cure,'" in *Interpreting Lacan*, ed. Joseph H. Smith and William Kerrigan (New Haven: Yale University Press, 1983),
38.

42. Elizabeth Gross, "The Body of Signification," in Fletcher and Benjamin, *Abjection,
Melancholia, and Love*, 96.

43. Frances Restuccia argues that it is the fetishized image of the Mother/Virgin that
"assists Joyce in getting beyond the referential, beyond the Father." Such a fetishistic
disavowal of the reality of women "allows textuality or free play even as it provides the
security of a dominant position—only the son's (disguised as the mother's) rather than
the father's." Substituting the law of the Mother/Virgin—determined by the son—for the
law of the Father enables Joyce to achieve his own artistic freedom, Restuccia claims
(Frances L. Restuccia, *Joyce and the Law of the Father* [New Haven: Yale University
Press, 1989], 176). But is such a substitution possible? And is artistic freedom that cleanly
achieved?

representation: an "ineffable jouissance" that is "beyond discourse, beyond narrative, beyond psychology, beyond lived experience and biography—in short, beyond figuration" (*Desire*, 247). If representation is death, if a proposition that may be transformed to death is (only) representation, writes Derrida, it is nonetheless bound "to life and to the living present which it repeats originarily" (*Writing*, 227). The eroticization of abjection—and abjection itself, given its status as already eroticized—acts as a threshold before death (*Powers*, 55).

Stephen, that "embryo philosopher," argues in "Scylla and Charybdis" that the Catholic church is founded on the mystery of fatherhood and "not on the madonna which the cunning Italian intellect flung to the mob of Europe" (*U*, 9.839–40). But, as Kristeva perceives, such a construct of the mystical estate and apostolic succession of paternity responds to the threat to male narcissism posed by the maternal body:

> It is as if *paternity* were necessary in order to relive the archaic impact of the maternal body on man; in order to complete the investigation of a ravishing maternal jouissance but also of its terrorizing aggressivity; in order somehow to admit the threat that the male feels as much from the possessive maternal body as from his separation from it—a threat that he immediately returns to that body; and finally, in order, not to demystify the mother, but to find her an increasingly appropriate language, capable of capturing her specific imaginary jouissance, the jouissance on the border of primal repression. . . . (*Desire*, 263)

Enveloping the discourse of the fathers by the womb of the mother, Joyce, as Giovanni Bellini accomplishes in his madonnas, "penetrates through the being and language of the father to position himself in the place where the mother could have been reached." This penetration by the artist/son is an incest, a possession of the mother, which "provides motherhood, that mute border, with a language." Bellini's madonnas testify to what in the feminine and the maternal is repressed in the religion of the patriarchs: "the joyous serenity of incest with the mother." As Kristeva points out, it was not until the end of the nineteenth century "and Joyce, even more than Freud, that this repression of motherhood and incest was affirmed as risky and unsettling in one's very flesh and sex. Not until then did it, by means of a language that 'musicates through letters,' resume within discourse the rhythms, intonations, and echolalias of the mother-infant symbiosis—intense, pre-Oedipal, predating the father—and this in the third person" (*Desire*, 249, 156, 157). In *Finnegans Wake* Joyce posits the relation between (male) artist and woman as incest between the "Godpossibled" son and the mother: "In the beginning was the gest he jousstly says, for the end is with woman, flesh-without-word, while the man to be is in a worse case after than before since she on the supine satisfies the verg to him!" (*FW*, 468.5–8). The artist/son penetrates through the frame, the parenthesis of language, to give what is silenced a voice. But in presenting motherhood with a language, he nonetheless deprives it of "any right to a real existence," according it only a symbolic status. That is, mother as speaking subject—indeed, woman-as-subject—does not return. The point of this consummation, Kristeva states, is "to reach the threshold of repression by means of the identification with motherhood (be it as heterosexuality or symbolic incest), to reach this threshold where maternal jouissance, alone impassable, is arrayed" (*Desire*, 249). Like the children of *Finnegans Wake*, the artist would re-turn to the repressed, only to see "figuratleavely," as figure, as symbol, the "whome"—womb, home, the (impossible) origin—of the "eternal geomater" (*FW*, 296.31–297.1).

10

Mothers of Invention/ Doaters of Inversion: Narcissan Scenes in *Finnegans Wake*

Christine Froula

Necessity is the mother of invention.

PROVERB

Nircississies are as the doaters of inversion. Secilas through their laughing classes becoming poolermates in laker life.

JAMES JOYCE, Finnegans Wake

[W]e know it to be characteristic of the libido that it refuses to subordinate itself to reality in life, to necessity.

SIGMUND FREUD, "The Theory of the Libido: Narcissism"

Every self-portrait presupposes what we might call a Narcissan scene: the artist gazing at his or her reflection in an attitude of desire—the sort of desire that impels representation. Often the mirror falls outside the picture's frame, its implied place coinciding with that of the viewer before the finished portrait. When, however, the artist renders not just the reflected image but the mirror and the act of looking as well, the Narcissan scene becomes explicit and the act of self-portraiture self-reflexively analytic. To analyze such scenes of the self depicting itself in the very act of depicting itself is to discover something of the motives and dynamics that issue in its own creation, or, one might say, of the necessity that underlies its invention.

Joyce's gallery of self-portraits holds up to our gaze a number of Narcissan scenes. In "The Dead," the failed artist Gabriel Conroy catches a puzzling glimpse of his own face in the mirror after Gretta surprises him with her grief for Michael Furey[1]; in *A Portrait of the Artist as a Young Man*, the fledgling artist Stephen Dedalus looks in his mother's mirror after he writes his first poem; in *Ulysses*, Bloom's and Stephen's gazes converge parallactically in Bella Cohen's mirror, which reflects back Shakespeare's face. In *Finnegans Wake*'s fuller rendering, the dreaming artist/hero answers necessity with "nircississies," creating virtual images that mirror back his own desire by transforming necessity into "doaters of inversion."[2] Read in light of the earlier Narcissan scenes, this last rendering not only recapitulates them but exposes a dynamic that accounts for them all as narcissistic moments born of a certain necessity and issuing, by "inversion," in "doaters," or daughters. The transformation of necessity into self-gratifying "nircississies" and the self-mirroring desire that this inversion mediates involve an imaginary crossing of the boundary of sexual difference. This essay explores the dynamics of desire visible in Joyce's Narcissan scenes, using his self-reflexive depictions of his own art of self-portraiture to account both for the fluid, dissolving, merging dream-selves of *Finnegans Wake* and for the dreamer's pervasive crossings between, as he puts it, "[t]he form masculine. The gender feminine" (*FW*, 505.25).[3]

As early as *Stephen Hero*, Stephen/Joyce implicitly projects his own future art as a radical kind of self-portraiture, a self-vivisection

---

1. For an illuminating analysis of Gabriel Conroy as an autobiographical projection of a failed artist figure, see Adrienne Auslander Munich, "Form and Subtext in Joyce's 'The Dead,'" *Modern Philology* 82 (1984): 173–84.

2. James Joyce, *Finnegans Wake* (New York: Viking Press, 1939) 526.33–35; hereafter cited in the text as *FW* with page and line numbers. "Secilas" inverts and multiplies "Alices," performing at the level of the letter the *Wake*'s thematic play on narcissism, mirroring, and inversion.

3. See also Claudine Raynaud's exploration of the narcissistic theme in the *Wake*, "Woman, the Letter Writer/Man the Writing Master," *James Joyce Quarterly* 23 (Spring 1986): 299–324. Arguing that the female writers in the *Wake* are always overmastered by male authorial desire, Raynaud asks whether language will "ever speak woman's desire? Is she condemned to be the end of the wor(l)d, the 'flesh-without-word' [*FW*, 468.06]? Will she ever write letters that have not been taught to her by a writing master?" (319). In the view that we are mistaken to seek "woman's" voice or desire in Joyce's texts, I take the female voices/writers in the *Wake* as representing Joyce's own ventriloquised *male* desire, that is, as figures of the male dreamer/writer's desire to be female; hence, as driven by a narcissistic writing economy that has nothing to do with representing "women" as such.

that, in the very act of exposing his own inner workings, lays bare the workings of the culture that he inherits and reembodies. "The modern spirit is vivisective," Stephen informs Cranly. "Vivisection itself is the most modern process one can conceive."[4] I take the self-vivisection that Stephen claims to perform as a master metaphor for his autobiographical art from *Dubliners* through the *Wake*, a trope that crosses self-portraiture with cultural history. Joyce, through his autobiographical artist figures, first represents himself engorging his culture and embodying it in and as himself, and then vivisects that culture in its reincarnation *as* himself. Studied in this light, Joyce's self-portraits reveal themselves as a series of self-vivisections that probe progressively deeper, each performing a more radical and penetrating exposure of the artist and his culture than the last. Anatomizing the "body" of Western culture since Genesis in the act of exposing the artist's metaphysical body, *Finnegans Wake* is Joyce's ultimate and most elaborate fulfillment of Stephen's early prophecy of his own "modernity," his furthest realization of his promise to reveal "the esthetic instinct in action" (*SH,* 186).

Although the face of the dreamer in Joyce's last self-portrait is familiar, the *Wake*'s self-vivisection cuts more deeply into the artistic process, laying bare structures and functions only glimpsed in the earlier works. The *Wake*'s narcissistic economy bridges the apparent gap between the book-as-self and the book-as-world. When, a few months after *Ulysses* appeared, Harriet Shaw Weaver asked Joyce what he would write next, he replied, "I think I will write a history of the world."[5] *Finnegans Wake* is a history of the world predicated on absolute subjectivity: on a simulated return to the state of originary narcissism, a vantage point from which the as yet unbounded self perceives no discontinuity between itself and the world. In late Joyce, the book-as-world containing discrete (if still autobiographical) characters mutates into the book-as-self-as-world. As intralinguistic boundaries dissolve, merging, condensing, and mutating the signs that mediate between one mind and another, so also discrete characters dissolve and merge until there are no boundaries and no characters, only virtual representations of the artist's psyche—a simulacrum of regressive, originary boundariless-

---

4. James Joyce, *Stephen Hero,* ed. John J. Slocum and Herbert Cahoon (New York: New Directions, 1944, 1963), 186; hereafter cited in the text as *SH.*

5. Richard Ellmann, *James Joyce* (New York: Oxford University Press, 1982), 536–37; hereafter cited in the text and notes as *JJ.*

ness. From the perspective of its artist-hero, lost in the sleep and dreams that Freud views as everyday versions of the narcissistic return, the book-as-self is indistinguishable from the book-as-world. Creating a language of dissolving boundaries to represent this originary, oceanic subjectivity, Joyce inflates narcissistic self-portraiture to epic dimensions and, by this crossing of genres, recreates the world in his own image.

If necessity is the mother of invention, what might it mean that nircississies are as the doaters of inversion? Necessity—limitation, constraint, lack—leads to improvisation, to inventing something that will do the trick in lieu of the thing that is wanted but missing; something that substitutes for, or even surpasses, that missing thing. From necessity arise creativity, inventions, art—in Joyce's case, the art of self-portraiture. As necessity is the mother of Stephen's "old father" Daedalus' wax-and-feather wings, a body-extending invention to free the earthbound man from his Cretan prison, no less is necessity the mother of Joyce's own art. No less, too, are his playful inventions and inversions designed to extend his being beyond his body—to free him, that is, from what his art represents as the prison of his *male* body. Joyce's punning reinscription of the proverb illuminates the interrelations among self-portraiture, narcissistic desire, and the obsessive sex and gender crossings found in the *Wake* and throughout his works.

What does it mean, then, for necessity to "mother" inventions that are also inversions, themselves mothers of some sort, whose daughters or "doaters" in some way resemble those "nircississies" which necessity has at once given birth to and become? Both Joyce and Freud invoke Narcissus as exemplar not simply of a pathological and doomed self-love but of an originary phase of human development that is never entirely abandoned or outgrown.[6] Freud describes narcissism—the "universal original condition" of every human life—as continuing long past infancy to play a part in a whole range of normal activities, including sleeping, dreaming, illness, a "happy love," and creativity, or what one might call, with

6. See Sigmund Freud, "On Narcissism: An Introduction" (1914), in *The Standard Edition of the Complete Psychological Works of Sigmund Freud*, ed. and trans. James Strachey (London: Hogarth, 1957), 14:73–102; hereafter cited in the text and notes as "ON"; and "Twenty-Sixth Lecture: The Theory of the Libido: Narcissism" (1916–17), in *A General Introduction to Psychoanalysis*, trans. Joan Riviere, ed. Ernest Jones and G. Stanley Hall (New York: Washington Square Press, 1952), 419–37; hereafter cited in the text as "TLN."

the *Wake* in mind, a happy art ("TLN," 423; "ON," 83, 100). Joyce, for his part, demonstrated the *Wake's* narcissistic ontology in ways that show he shared Freud's view that this narcissism is entirely natural, normal, and universal. During the book's composition Joyce struggled with despair when his friends reported that they could make nothing of his "universal history," the *Wake*-in-progress; he professed amazement that they could find it incomprehensible. In an astonishing gesture—as Richard Ellmann says, "one of the strangest ideas in literary history"—Joyce dramatized his assumption that the narcissistic psychic economy that underlies the *Wake* is universal by suggesting that someone else finish it for him (*JJ*, 591). In 1927, between bouts of eye trouble, he proposed to Harriet Shaw Weaver that the Dublin-born poet James Stephens (whose name, date and place of birth, and vocation set him up for Joyce's narcissistic self-mirroring) might take over and complete the composition of his book-as-self-as-world: "Of course he would never take a fraction of the time or pains I take but so much the better for him and me and possibly for the book itself. If he consented to maintain three or four points which I consider essential and I showed him the threads he could finish the design. JJ and S (the colloquial Irish for John Jameson and Son's Dublin whiskey) would be a nice lettering under the title. It would be a great load off my mind"[7] (*JJ*, 591–92).

Within the *Wake* and throughout his work, however, Joyce's representations of narcissistic desire bring out a point that Freud more

---

7. Joyce remarked on the coincidence that he had for some years been carrying in his pocket photographs of Patrick Tuohy's portraits of his father, himself, and James Stephens; when he discovered that the poet Stephens was born in Dublin on February 2, 1882, his own birthdate, he regarded him as his "twin" (*JJ*, 593).

Stephens, for his part, resisted Joyce's narcissistic attempt to assimilate him with ironic good humor; in "The James Joyce I Knew," he describes how Joyce called him in Paris and "revealed to me that his name was James and mine was James, that my name was Stephens, and the name he had taken for himself in his best book was Stephen: that he and I were born in the same country, in the same city, in the same year, in the same month, on the same day, at the same hour, six o'clock in the morning of the second of February. . . .

"Well, I was astonished. I was admired at last. Joyce admired me. I was beloved at last: Joyce loved me. Or did he? Or did he only love his birthday, and was I merely coincident to that? When I spoke about my verse, which was every waking minute of my time, Joyce listened heartily and said 'Ah.' He approved of it as second of February verse, but I'm not certain that he really considered it to be better than the verse of Shakespeare and Racine and Dante. And yet he knew the verse of those three exhaustively!

". . . If I were Joyce's twin, which he held, then I had to celebrate this astonishing fact in my own way. So upon our next birthday I sent him a small poem. . . . Joyce reported back to me that he was much obliged. He practically said 'Ah' to my poem, and I could almost see him rubbing his chin at it" (*JJ*, 593).

or less glosses over:[8] that sexual difference makes a difference in the narcissistic return. Portraying himself in the *Wake* as a very young man, Joyce—the self-consciously "modern" artist—vivisects the Narcissan scene to reveal a regression to an earlier self that is also a transgression: a crossing of the boundary between male and female. For the male subject, the narcissistic return crosses the barrier between the masculine self (the father-identified ego) and a primordial self that, since it as yet perceives no boundary between self and m/other, is de facto female-identified. The early self that the narcissistic return recovers contains also the early mother; the return recovers the primal mother-identified dimension of the self that the son represses upon his cultural initiation into masculine identity.

Through art, as through fantasies, dreams, a "happy love," the culturally initiated son can return or regress to an early, unbounded, undifferentiated self—a self that, since it precedes both ontological and sexual differentiation from the m/other, might retrospectively be experienced as daughter. Such a return would explain how the *Wake*'s dreamer dreams out "[a] tale told of Shaun or Shem? All Livia's daughtersons"; it would account for the dreamer's query, "Who were Shem and Shaun the living sons or daughters of?" (*FW*, 215.35, 216.1–2). Joyce's invented nircississies, living sons become daughters by inversion, vivisect the "daughtersons" Shem and

8. "On Narcissism" betrays Freud's anxiety about acknowledging the crucial role that early maternal identification plays in male no less than female development in his elaborate deflection of the issue of a possible primordial identity of sexual and ego instincts by means of an analogy that opposes the bodily mother-child relation ("primal kinship") to the "legal fiction" (James Joyce, *Ulysses* [New York: Random House, 1961], 207; hereafter cited in the text as *U* with page number) of an explicitly proprietary paternity, identifying the "science" of psychoanalysis with the latter: "It may turn out that, most basically and on the longest view, sexual energy—libido—is only the product of a differentiation in the energy at work generally in the mind. But such an assertion has no relevance. It relates to matters which are so remote from the problems of our observation, and of which we have so little cognizance, that it is as idle to dispute as to affirm it; this primal identity may well have as little to do with our analytic interests as the primal kinship of all the races of mankind has to do with the proof of kinship required in order to establish a legal right of inheritance. All these speculations take us nowhere. Since we cannot wait for another science to present us with the final conclusions on the theory of the instincts, it is far more to the purpose that we should try to see what light may be thrown on this basic problem of biology by a synthesis of the *psychological* phenomena" ("ON," 79). Although Freud does not here explicitly identify the "primal identity" that precedes the "differentiation in the energy at work generally in the mind" with the early mother/self, his kinship analogy—which superimposes the name and law of the father upon what Freud, like Joyce, imagines more or less as the maternally produced "strandentwining cable of all flesh" (*U*, 38)—suggests that at stake in this question Freud does not wish to pursue may be the prestige of the oedipal complex, and so of the father's name and law as the origin of social identity.

Shaun. These daughtersons, generated through Joyce's art of the narcissistic return, are in fact "as" the daughters or "doaters" of an imaginary sexual inversion by which the son self-gratifyingly becomes daughter/doater as well, thereby recovering a primordial self undifferentiated from the mother.

But what motivates the narcissistic return? Wherein exactly does its pleasure lie? As necessity is the mother of invention, Joyce's necessity is the mother of his inventions. Moreover, one of Joyce's necessities is precisely to *mother* his inventions: his imaginary inversions of sons into daughtersons are transactions within a symbolic economy in which artistic creativity models itself on and substitutes for maternal creativity. Joyce's play on mothers, doaters, and daughtersons carries forward his appropriative "inversion" of the Annunciation to describe his own art in *Portrait:* the "virgin womb of the imagination" in which he imagines his villanelle gestating vividly dramatizes the necessity, for Joyce, not merely to invent but to become a mother by inventing.[9] Insofar as Joyce's is an art of self-portraiture, furthermore—insofar as what he invents is himself—the "nircississies" that are (as) daughters/doaters of his inventive inversion gratify his longing to return to an early, female-identified state even as they reveal it. In Joyce's art, the energy that fuels the narcissistic return expresses itself as a longing to cross not merely ontological boundaries but specifically the boundary of sexual difference, thereby at once to "mother" himself and to reinvent himself as daughter-by-inversion.

Throughout his works, Joyce's Narcissan scenes dramatize sexual difference as the driving force of the son's narcissistic return. In *Portrait,* Joyce's first self-portrait of the young artist at work explicitly stages the scene of writing as just such a Narcissan scene, one in which the artist-son, by mothering his invention, symbolically crosses the boundary of sexual difference to become "doater" or "nircississie" as well, gazing at his own reflection in a glass or pool. Stephen writes his first successful poem the day after he rides the tram home from the party with E— C— and finds that something keeps him from kissing her, as he feels she would like him to do. The poem that he writes about this experience is not a realistic depiction of the failed kiss but a transformation of the failed literal kiss into a successful symbolic one. In the poem,

9. James Joyce, *A Portrait of the Artist as a Young Man,* ed. Chester G. Anderson and Richard Ellmann (New York: Viking Press, 1968), 217; hereafter cited in the text as *P.*

all the elements which he deemed common and insignificant fell out of the scene. There remained no trace of the tram itself nor of the trammen nor of the horses: nor did he and she appear vividly. The verses told only of the night and the balmy breeze and the maiden lustre of the moon. Some undefined sorrow was hidden in the hearts of the protagonists as they stood in silence beneath the leafless trees and when the moment of farewell had come the kiss, which had been withheld by one, was given by both. After this the letters L. D. S. were written at the foot of the page and, having hidden the book, he went into his mother's bedroom and gazed at his face for a long time in the mirror of her dressingtable. (P, 70–71)

Although this poem originates in "real life," as it were, Stephen does not draw from life mimetically. Rather, falling "into a day-dream," he rewrites history and in doing so makes good his loss or lack. The poem symbolically heals the wound that the artist sustains in real time and so transmutes "life," or what *Finnegans Wake* will call "beogrifright," into a self-gratifying work of art. The poem fulfills the unacted wish that the beogrifrightened Stephen censors in "life," first by failing to kiss Emma and again by hiding his manuscript book.

But what exactly is the nature of Stephen's self-gratification here? Or, in the lingo of the *Wake*, "what goes on when love walks in besides the solicitous bussness by kissing and looking into a mirror?" (*FW*, 618.18–19). Why does an unacted kiss inspire Stephen's first poem, and what does it mean that he cannot kiss in "life," only in art? Joyce does not give us the text of Stephen's poem but rather places a narrative about its inspiration and composition at the center of his canvas, inviting us to explore the artistic economy that produces it. While this creative economy might at first glance seem oedipal in nature (with E— C— cast as desired object in lieu of the mother his Clongowes experience has taught him to renounce, and the imaginary kiss signaling Stephen's successful negotiation of the father's law conceived as the incest taboo), the scene's concluding psychodrama points to a deeper substrate. When, having completed his poem, Stephen goes into his mother's bedroom and gazes at his own face in her mirror, he acts out a desire not merely to kiss E— C— but, by doing so, to recover an archaic, forbidden, woman- and mother-identified self through his creation of a work of art: that is, to mother his inventions and so recover himself as daughterson or "doater" by "inversion." Gazing on his own face in the mirror that usually frames his mother's, Stephen acts out the fantasy that artistic creation frees him from his imprisonment in late-born and partial masculinity and restores him to that primordial identity originating in the bodily union of mother and child. Framing his own face in his mother's mirror—and implicitly aligning his symbolic creative powers with her material creativity— the young artist expresses a wish to recover, through his symbolic creativity, something more than the kiss as such, more even than the mother as desired object: the mother as desired self, the early mother/self renounced and repressed upon his initiation into masculine identity.

Together with others in *Portrait*, this scene suggests that what is at stake for Stephen/Joyce in the "solicitous bussness" of kissing is not simply sexual desire but identificatory desire. The artist Stephen's deepest necessity or "nircississie" is not to kiss Emma but symbolically to become her through his act of creation. Later in *Portrait*, he acts out this identification explicitly: when he tries to recall what she looks like, he remembers only "that she had worn a shawl about her head like a cowl" (*P*, 82); and in the villanelle scene, in which Stephen becomes an inverted Virgin Mary, giving birth to flesh made word, he again remembers that Emma had "worn her shawl cowlwise about her head" and he "mak[es] a cowl of the blanket" he has wrapped around himself (*P* 221–22). For Stephen, the fledgling male artist, becoming Emma through fetishistic imitation of her habiliments is, more profoundly, becoming once more the woman-self originally mirrored in the mother. As virtual woman, he makes the divine Word flesh in his "virgin womb" even as he transfigures Emma into a godlike inseminator, "enfold[ing] him like water with a liquid life: . . . like a cloud of vapour or like waters circumfluent in space the liquid letters of speech, symbols of the element of mystery, flowed forth over his brain" (*P*, 223).

Joyce uses similarly inverted figures of sexual transaction in *Ulysses*, in Molly's and Leopold's memories of her tonguing chewed seedcake into his mouth on Howth Hill, and in the *Wake's* allusions to Dion Boucicault's *Arrah-na-Pogue* (Arrah of the Kiss), whose heroine has enabled her foster brother to escape from prison by secretly passing him the rescue plan by way of a kiss: "Lps. The keys to. Given!" (*FW*, 628.15). In all these moments the Joycean kiss inverts male and female procreative roles, figuring an act of female seeding or insemination the fruit of which is the male's imaginary s/exchange of barren necessity for liberating fecundity.. For the Stephen of *Portrait*, writing is the proof of this exchange: the kiss transfers symbolic "seed" which originates in female fluid, mouth, or lips to the receptive male body/brain, working a transformation that frees what Joyce regularly represents as the artist's "female" soul from his male body through artistic creativity.

The "solicitous bussness" of kissing becomes, in other words, a figure for desire's escape from necessity—construed as the strictures both of the male or unfemale body and of the masculine ego culturally imposed upon that body—through a narcissistic return to a lost, originary female "body" recovered through and as symbol making. When Stephen, having written his poem, goes to his mother's bedroom to gaze at his face in her mirror, he acts out the desire implicit in likening himself to Emma and his mother in this scene of writing. His gesture makes visible the quite specific nature of the gratification writing affords this artist-son by expressing— subliming—his repressed desire to remember an archaic, forbidden (since it transgresses the father's law of masculine identification), female-identified self. Superimposing his own face over the site of his mirroring mother's, Stephen symbolically returns to that primordial "place" in which he again perceives himself as virtually coextensive with her, no boundary between.

The symbolic economy of the narcissistic return explains why not least among the elements of the actual scene that Stephen "deem[s] common and insignificant" and so suppresses from his poem is sexual difference: "There remained no trace of the tram itself nor of the trammen nor of the horses: *nor did he and she appear vividly*" (*P*, 70). In Stephen's poem, as in Joyce's *Portrait*, "woman" does not exist in and for herself but rather represents his own originary state to which his own sense of loss compels him to return.[10] The perceived "necessity" that compels his narcissistic return originates in the artist-son's perception of his own male (or unfemale) body. The shape of Stephen's symbolic quest and the Narcissan figure that almost ceremoniously completes it point to

10. Cf. Sarah Kofman's observation that men's fascination with the narcissistic woman "is nothing other than the fascination exerted by their own double, and the uncanny feeling [*Unheimlichkeit*] which men experience is the same as that which one feels before any double or any ghost [*revenant*], before the abrupt reappearance [*reapparition*] of what one thought had been forever overcome or lost" ("The Narcissistic Woman: Freud and Girard," *Diacritics* 10 [September 1980]: 39; cited also by Raynaud, "Woman," 314).

the nature of the lack that his narcissistic return symbolically compensates. Necessity is indeed the "mother" of Stephen/Joyce's inventions; of the inversions that, transforming necessity into "nircississie," are the parodically self-doating daughtersons to which his art gives birth.

As I noted earlier, Freud's thinking about narcissism led him to speculate on a primordial identity prior to sexual desire: "It may turn out that, most basically and on the longest view, sexual energy —libido—is only the product of a differentiation in the energy at work generally in the mind."[11] This primordial identity, he suggests, preexists the differentiation between self and m/other and gives rise to (sexual) desire when that differentiation occurs. Thus, we may suppose, it belongs to and characterizes the "blissful isolation of the intrauterine existence, . . . the primal state . . . of absolute narcissism, in which libido and ego-interests dwell together still, united and indistinguishable in the self-sufficient self" ("TLN," 424). If "absolute narcissism" is the blissful illusion of perfect wholeness and self-sufficiency prior to birth and self-differentiation, then narcissistic desire pursues the impossible dream of perfect identity between self and other, self and mother, self and world; it acts out a love of seeming sameness, a denial of actual difference, in an effort to restore the world to the self, if only in imagination.

Ovid's narcissistic prototype pursues this desire to the point of no return. As Julia Kristeva points out, Narcissus gazes at his own image in a pool whose maternal waters, previously untouched by so much as a falling leaf, recall the mother-child oneness, before any cut, mark, or sign has intervened.[12] Falling in love with his own image, Narcissus unwittingly acts out a hopeless and paradoxical wish for that early oneness. In striving to overcome the illusory difference between himself and the loved object, he simultaneously denies the real difference between himself and the watery element that mediates his illusory love. Desiring to become one with what is only apparently other, he overlooks the real difference between himself and his mere watery reflection—and between that reflection and an actual other who could be desired—insisting to the face

11. See note 8.
12. Julia Kristeva, *Tales of Love*, trans. Leon S. Roudiez (New York: Columbia University Press, 1987), 42, 113. Milton's adaptation of Ovid's Narcissan scene to Eve's nativity in *Paradise Lost* (4.451ff.) brings into high relief the opposition between the father's law or word and a watery maternal origin.

in the pool that "almost nothing / Keeps us apart."[13] As Kristeva reads the fable, Narcissus finally "gathers that he is actually in a world of 'signs'" and so gains "self-knowledge: 'He is myself! I feel it, I know my image now.'"[14] Yet, since even so he pines away, we might also say that Narcissus' error, his failure to mark the difference between self and m/other, is ultimately a fatal failure to embrace a world of signs—a failure, by extension, to comprehend the dependence of desire, language, and representation upon difference: "If I could only / Escape from my own body! if I could only— / How curious a prayer from any lover— / Be parted from my love!"[15] Instead of finding in the watery mirror the matrix for his recognition of identity and difference, Narcissus drowns, so to speak, in the m/other that he mistakes for himself; in a shadow that he mistakes for substance; in a primal scene of identity, or self-recognition, that he mistakes for one of love.

But whereas Narcissus pines away, metamorphosing into a flower on the grassy bank, Joyce sits and writes. Whereas Ovid's Narcissus confuses the real with the reflection, the mere image—betraying what *Finnegans Wake* deplores as "a poor trait of the artless"— Joyce knows that he inhabits a world of signs (*FW*, 114.32). His symbolic art, with its power of differing from "life" or "beogrifright," preserves him from Narcissus' error. His not strictly mimetic writing re-creates the primal Narcissan scene by means of symbolic forms, thereby containing narcissistic desire and gratification safely within the psychopathology of everyday life—as geniuses do, according to Stephen Dedalus, who narcissistically and autobiographically explains to his audience in the library scene of *Ulysses* how "[h]is own image to a man with that queer thing genius is the standard of all experience, material and moral" (*U*, 195).

Not coincidentally, this remark also occurs in a context of daughters, doaters, and inversion, as Stephen speculates that the birth of Shakespeare's granddaughter healed the poet's narcissistic wound, softened his heart, lifted the shadow from the late plays: "Marina, Stephen said, a child of storm, Miranda, a wonder, Perdita, that which was lost. What was lost is given back to him: his daughter's child" (*U*, 195). In the autobiographical artistic economy that the

---

13. Ovid, *Metamorphoses*, trans. Rolfe Humphries (Bloomington: Indiana University Press, 1983), 71.

14. Kristeva, *Tales*, 104.

15. Ovid, *Metamorphoses*, 72.

Stephen of *Ulysses* projects upon Shakespeare, the women in his family—Ann Hathaway, Judith, and Judith's daughter—are, like E—— C—— in *Portrait*, only figures for the loss of a daughter-self, the repressed early female self that the work of art "give[s] back to him." This joyous recovery explains why, as Stephen says, the (grand)daughter's "appeal will touch the artist," while the "images of other males of his blood will repel him. He will see in them grotesque attempts of nature to foretell or repeat himself" (*U*, 195–96). Or, in Leopold Bloom's rendition of this idea, "*O Milly Bloom, you are my darling. / You are my looking glass from night to morning*" (*U*, 63). The daughter/mother/wife is a funhouse mirror in whose image the Joycean artist seeks a reflection of his female soul, against the fathers, brothers, and sons who reflect clearly and unforgivingly the "grotesque" masculinity he artfully contrives to evade.

Mirroring the writing self as the mother, Joyce's self-vivisection of his own masculine "esthetic instinct" not only renders Stephen's art through a Narcissan scene but writes the early mother into that scene as indistinguishable from the early self revived through the creative act. Joyce's excavation of the narcissistic artistic economy underlying the ostensibly oedipal motive of the kiss casts light on the nature of the transgression he commits by writing the poem no less than by the kiss itself (evidenced by Stephen's hiding his copybook). In Freudian and Lacanian psychoanalytic theory, the oedipal crisis instigates and resolves itself in the institution of the father's law (construed as the incest taboo, derived from the preeminence of the father's desire) in the individual psyche. Kissing Emma would seem simultaneously to evoke that law and the transgression it forbids and to honor it, inasmuch as this kiss would displace oedipal desire, substituting a different object of desire for the mother. But Stephen does not kiss Emma, and Joyce's vivisection of Stephen's creative process uncovers a deeper stratum of desire which entails a different sort of transgression. If, in the oedipal model, male desire is a sexual drive to possess the woman as, or instead of, the mother, in the narcissistic model it is the male subject's drive to possess her as himself—that is, the desire to return to, or to recover, the early mother/self. If, as I am arguing, Stephen's secret, imaginary kiss is moved less by desire to possess Emma sexually than by desire to become her symbolically, this narcissistic desire transgresses against the very condition of the father's law: the demand that he identify with the father and the father's culture against woman, including the early mother with whom he was once merged. The kiss is taboo not because it transgresses the oedipal law but because it transgresses the law of paternal identification which forbids narcissistic desire, that is, desire for the self in the "place" (or symbolic "body") of the mother.

Joyce's dissection of Stephen's (and his own) artistic economy articulates and clarifies some implications of Freud's writings on narcissism as to the difference sexual difference makes in the structure of the narcissistic return and the nature of the gratification thereby attained. As we saw, Freud views narcissism as the primordial human condition prior to the differentiation of the self from the world and posits a narcissistic energy that makes no distinction between self and world, or self and m/other. As Freud describes it, even as the ego develops by departure from this primary narcissism, the narcissisism itself is never entirely abandoned; moreover, by virtue of its anteriority, narcissistic desire remains essentially independent of the (relatively late-born) ego's demands. The regressive narcissistic states of everyday life (sleeping, dreaming, illness, happy love, happy art) recover, Freud writes, this primordial "absolute narcissism, in which libido and ego-interests dwell together still, united and indistinguishable in the self-sufficient self" ("TLN," 424).

But herein lies a special problem for the son, one that Joyce's Narcissan scenes explicate. The narcissistic return, in recovering this primordial state of being, recovers also the early mother from which the self is not yet differentiated. That is, the narcissistic return is a return to an early mother/self against which—indeed, on the burial site of which—the male-identified ego erects itself in patriarchal culture.[16] The first law of the father dictates that the son repress his early female identification in favor of a masculine identity constructed dialectically against woman/the mother; it requires, in other words, that the son construct not just a differentiated ego or self but a specifically male-identified one. The narcissistic return thus entails a double transgression, a double crossing, not only of the boundary of sexual difference on which the male-identified ego posits itself but also of this law: the law that prescribes male identification and in the very act of doing so

16. I am elaborating here some implications of object relations psychology, with its emphasis on the developmental importance of early maternal identification. See, for example, Nancy Chodorow, *The Reproduction of Mothering* (Berkeley: University of California Press, 1978).

charges that boundary, like a metaphysical electric fence, with the status of a taboo, forbidding the son's return to that originary state. If, as Freud writes, narcissistic desire seeks to recover the primordial mother-child union, "the blissful isolation of the intrauterine existence" that is everyone's "original condition," Joyce's self-vivisection uncovers the fact that, in the son's case, the narcissistic return involves an outlawed desire, a forbidden archaic self, a primordial identification with femaleness the repression of which is the very condition of the relatively fragile male-identified self, as of masculinist culture as such. The son's narcissistic return as Joyce depicts it entails not only a crossing of the ontological boundary between self and other but the crossing of the boundary of sexual difference between self and mother, which is to say, a breaking of the father's law. From the perspective of the culturally instituted masculine ego (or father-identified self), then, the narcissistic return would appear to be intrinsically transgressive, flouting the cultural "law" that makes the mother-identified child over to the father and to masculine culture.

Joyce's narcissistic writing economy thus acts out a strategic evasion of the (culturally constructed) masculine ego's demand that the threatening, archaic, female-identified self be repressed. Carrying further the self-vivisection of *Portrait*'s "To E—— C——" scene, *Finnegans Wake* capitalizes on the criminality of the male artist's narcissistic writing economy, playing with and parodying the joys of transgression through exhibitionistic gender crossings that repeatedly insist upon "[t]he form masculine. The gender feminine" (*FW*, 505.25). Freud writes that we do not outgrow our primary narcissism in maturity but only partly renounce it, never entirely willingly, completely, or securely. Consequently, he says, we remain fascinated by the transgressive antics of such free spirits as children, criminals, humorists, artists, and cats, who—appealing to this repressed desire—"compel our interest by the narcissistic self-importance with which they manage to keep at arm's length everything which would diminish the importance of their ego. It is as if we envied them their power of retaining a blissful state of mind—an unassailable libido-position which we ourselves have since abandoned."[17] *Finnegans Wake* exploits all these embodiments of narcissistic desire, including the cats. "Children may just as well play as

17. I cite here Joan Riviere's revised version of the *Standard Edition*'s Cecil M. Baines translation of "On Narcissism," in *A General Selection of the Works of Sigmund Freud*, ed. John Rickman (New York: Doubleday, 1957), 113.

not. The ogre will come in any case," Joyce wrote Harriet Shaw Weaver in defense of his dream-book, pursuing in face of nearly all his friends' incomprehension his project of "retaling" in a dreamer's language of puns, errors, and baby talk the world-shaping crimes of HCE, mirrored in the word-shaping crimes of Shem/Jim the Penman (*JJ*, 582).

The autobiographical artist figure Shem is at once Joyce's most playful representation of his art's transgressiveness and his most revealing.[18] Shem/James is defined, or better produced, by his "low" crime, which his "biografiend" deplores as "beneath all up to that sunk to" (*FW*, 55.06, 171.13). It is not only social laws that Shem's crimes deliberately flout but quite specifically the law of the father that dictates gender identity, as "the first riddle of the universe" that he poses to his "little brothron and sweestureens" spells out: "when is a man not a man? . . . when he is a . . . Sham!" (*FW*, 170.5, 170.23–24). Shem is so bad that his "back life will not stand being written about" (*FW*, 169.7–8), and that "back life" is precisely what Joyce the autobiografiend does write about in the *Wake*, purloined-letter style, in a language that hides its meanings from the sharp, logical, censoring eye/I even as it gleefully and gratifyingly parades them before the secret, criminal, humorous, feline eye/I, the play-fully regressive reader who finds in Shem, and in the symbolic re-turn to his inadmissible "back life," a flagrant recognition of forbidden desire.

The *Wake* glosses one aspect of Shem's ostentatiously scandalous "back life" as that early time when sons were "doaters" or "daugh-tersons." Writing mediates this secret, subversive return to little-boy/girlhood in *Finnegans Wake* as it does in *Portrait:* "[t]hat . . . is what papyr is meed of, made of, hides and hints and misses in prints" (*FW*, 20.10–11). Shem's "papyr" is his own skin—in both senses, his own "hide"—which, covered with signs in the special ink this "alshe-mist" fashions out of his own excrement, at once hides and hints at the status he gains through writing of being symbolically female, a "miss" in print (*FW*, 185.35). The litter that "literature[s]" Shem's study floor includes "neverworn breeches"—signifying as a mere dis-carded costume the culturally constructed masculine identity that he refuses to inhabit—along with an enormous garter collection (*not*

18. For a fuller treatment of the Shem/James figure, see my "Past Eve and Adam's: Revolution and Return in *Finnegans Wake*," in *Joyce and Woolf: Gender, Authority, Modernity* (New York: Columbia University Press, 1993).

described as "neverworn") (*FW*, 183.10–18). As Shem's means of transgressing the (masculine) ego's barricades, writing is the very essence of his crime. It is "stolentelling"—language stolen from the female/self whose repression masculinist culture decrees (*FW*, 424.35). It is "patent henesy," a foray into forbidden gender identity, a crime compounded by Shem's shameless "scribicide" of hen and author Biddy Doran—his murder of the female mother/author in order to appropriate all symbolic creativity to himself (*FW*, 463.18, 14.21). Shem's writing is, therefore, not just plagiarism but, worse, heretical "pelagiaris[m]," a pun that invokes the fourth-century Christian heretic Pelagius, who denied the doctrine of original sin, holding that children are born innocent (*FW*, 182.3). With respect to orthodox accounts of a male-authored Creation, Shem's "pelagiaris[m]" is heretical in its very positing of the "original hen" (as in Biddy Doran, the maternal chicken/mother-god, who, by virtue of her authorship of the "litter" that runs from alpha to omega, appears to have preceded the patriarch-egg HCE/Humpty); and he adds injury to the mother to his insult of the father by his plagiarizing, pelagiarizing, female-impersonating, scribicidal usurpation of her authority (*FW*, 110.22, 93.24).

Shem/Jymes makes "litteringture" not only out of his crimes but out of his guilt (*FW*, 570.18). His biografiend depicts him condemned for his sins to life in his own filthy, haunted inkbottle, at moments transmuted into the foul fowlhouse that shelters his shamming female creativity, where he is terrorized and tormented perpetually by the ghost of the repressed and appropriated mother, ever threatening return: "Mother of moth! I will to show herword in flesh. Approach not for ghost sake" (*FW*, 561.27–28). As in *Ulysses*, the buried mother's ghost threatens the fragile and illusory stability of the narcissistic self who defends against her perceived powers by symbolically incorporating them. In the *Wake*'s dream-world Joyce parodies Stephen's art, transmutting the high-flown "virgin womb" of his imagination into the shamming art of egg laying that Shem copies from the "original hen," in defiance of the "Uncontrollable Birth Preservativation (Game and Poultry) Act" (*FW*, 184.15–16). As his transgressive, transvestite "ABORTISEMENT" makes clear, Shem's symbolic mothering adorns itself in raiment borrowed from theology even as it exhibitionistically parades itself as comic, self-conscious shamming: "Jymes wishes to hear from wearers of abandoned female costumes, gratefully received. . . . His jymes is out of job, would sit and write. He has lately committed one of the then commandments but she will now assist. Superior built, domestic, regular layer" (FW, 181.27–32). Arraying himself in the habiliments of femininity, Shem becomes a sham-man, subject of "the farst wriggle from the ubivence, whereom is man, that old offender, nother man, wheile he is asame" (FW, 356.12–14). Joyce may be incorporating in this passage an error in the telegram he received from his father to summon him home from Paris to his mother's deathbed: NOTHER [Mother] DYING COME HOME FATHER."[19] The question of identity, in any case, reduces for this artist-son to a question of origins, implicitly rendered in the *Wake* in the form of the question: Who came first, the chicken or the egg? More specifically, the artist-son of the *Wake*, the artist-son as Shem/sham, finds the question of his identity inseparable from the fact of the mother as origin, the mother in respect to whom he was once "asame"—that is, "nother man," not a man, in other words, a mother/man—in the early world of narcissistic desire to which his shamming and playing return him. His crimes, his offending art, the inversions born of purported necessity attest to his experience of his own difference from the mother *and from himself:* his sexual difference, the open-ended riddle through which his shamming words seek sameness through their very difference.

In the *Wake,;* then, Shem/Jymes writes not as a woman but "as" a "woman." That is, he writes not as though he were a woman—not as he writes in Molly Bloom's monologue—but as a man parodying his own desire to write like a woman (although this is arguably a difference more of degree than of kind). He writes, in other words, like a man vivisecting the vicissitudes of his own gender identity, his own relation to sexual difference, by means of symbolic terms that allow him to "borrow" feminine clothes, feminine positions, which become meaningful precisely and only through their appropriation by a desire that represents itself as not merely accidental to but determined by a male body. Expelled from the "Dustbin's United Scullerymaid's and Househelp's Sorority," Shem/Jymes can still insist on his identification with his "inverted" self,

---

19. The Rosenbach manuscript, in Joyce's hand, reads "Nother"; Gabler's 1984 text adopts this reading. Herbert Gorman, *James Joyce* (New York: Rinehart and Co., 1939, 1948) writes that the telegram read: "MOTHER DYING COME HOME FATHER" (108). This is also the reading of the 1922 *Ulysses* (U, 42) and of Ellmann's rendering (JJ, 128), which capitalizes all the letters but cites only Gorman and the 1922 *Ulysses*, not the actual telegram.

that female self, constituted by "borrowed" symbols, which he represents as the daughter/doater born of—and necessitated by—his
male body: "[L]etters be blowed! I is a femaline person. O, of provocative gender. U unisingular case" (*FW*, 181.17–18, 251.31–32).
This Shem/Jymes, this writing I—criminal, provocative, wishfully
"female," feline—flaunts his borrowings and stealings in the very
act of claiming an identity *not self-evidently his:* an I that "is"
instead of "am," its reconstructed status betrayed in its inability to
utter itself in the first person. The I that "is" in *Finnegans Wake*
can exist only by predicating itself on "capital" borrowed from
women and cats: it cannot simply assume the attributes it flaunts
but must explicitly underwrite itself through naming them. The
narcissistic, "femaline" I of the *Wake* is an I self-reflexively (and
inextricably) in debt to the letters that constitute it, as its very
effort to utter itself acknowledges: I.O.U.

By the same token, this cross-gendered I demonstrates the accidental relation of sex to the gender play of its letters. The I's of the
Wake—fluently merging, emerging, remerging—dramatize identity
as a kind of fluid dynamics, unbounded by body or essence, as virtual and free as the forming and dissolving symbols that momentarily constitute it. All the dream-selves of the *Wake* interpenetrate:
all the men are women, one might say, all the women men, a situation that undresses gender down to a matter of mere letters, carved
neither in stone nor in flesh. The dreamer, echoing Mr. Deasy, can
be Eve, "no better than he would have been before he could have
been better than what he warrant after" (*Fw*, 359.7–9). He can sham
a womb, "crying out something vile about him being molested after
him having triplets, by offers of vacancies from females in the city"
(*FM*, 530.5–7). He can confound gender boundaries, as in "[t]his
missy, my taughters, and these man, my son," the slipping demon-
stratives again doubling and crossing "taughters" and "son" (*FW*,
543.15–16). He can recall, in doing so, the daughterson James Au-
gusta, the author as daughterson, imaginatively resurrected in the
Wake as Kevin Mary (his mother now become his middle name),
the hydrophobe now transformed into the hydrocomic Hydrophilos
of his obscene "back life": who, having exercised/exorcised the
daughter within, his "holy sister water," that she might fill his tub,
and meditating on "the regeneration of all men by affusion of
water," solipsistically achieves that "feminiairity which breathes

content" (FW, 605.36–606.01, 606.11–12, 22–23).[20] Whereas, then, the artless Narcissus succumbs to his own "poor trait" and falls for his "poolermate," Joyce with his happy art does not sink but swims, buoyed up by fluid letters, his imaginary "salvocean" (FW, 114.32, 526.38, 623.29). At home in a world of endlessly dissolving signs, the *Wake*'s playful narcissist sees in the face in the mirror ("meme mearest!") "Crystal elation!" (*Christe eleison*, "Christ, have mercy"), a merciful escape from the necessity of his own body (FW, 527.3, 528.9).

In their structures no less than in their highly self-conscious functions, Joyce's inversions gesture toward their own necessity: not, by any means, the male body as such, but, unmistakably, the male body as represented by the masculinist culture that Joyce reincarnates in himself and vivisects in the dream-self of *Finnegans Wake*. The spirit of Joyce's letters can (and must, if we are to read the fluid dynamics of gender identity in his work with any accuracy) be traced back to the flesh to which they insistently refer, precisely in their function as compensatory "inversions," born of necessity, bearing "nircississies." The mind that inhabits that flesh constructs its sexual difference as a wound or lack that obsessively generates compensatory myths of quasi-female generativity. It would, of course, be absurd to claim that Joyce's inversions issue necessarily from his male flesh, or that only such invented inversions are as it were conceivable by him or by male artists more generally. At the same time, Joyce's self-vivisection reveals, in his own particular yet culturally recognizable case, a compensatory erection of a symbolic

20. For a different perspective on the *Wake*'s transsexual aspirations, see Margot Norris's reading of the Saint Kevin episode, "The Last Chapter of *Finnegans Wake*: Stephen Finds His Mother," *James Joyce Quarterly* 25 (Fall 1987): 11–30. Norris sees in Saint Kevin in his tub a regressive recapitulation of the Stephen who sits in his bath being scrubbed by his mother in *Portrait*; she views the merging of son into mother as a "bridg[ing of] all the great ontological chasms: between time and space, between life and death, between male and female": "Stephen, by imaginatively enacting his intellectual musings in dream, is reconciled with his mother, immersing himself and disappearing mystically into the lake that is her figure, only to become part of her own regression into childhood. . . . By the end of the *Wake* it has all become reconciled; dying has become being born and gestation, male has become female, who in turn becomes male, for every son was once his mother, and every mother was once her father, and space has become time as the present retrieves all the past it embodies" (11, 28–29). Whereas Norris views sexual difference as one among many "ontological chasms," I read Joyce's self-vivisection as revealing a psychic economy of narcissistic "bridging" fantasies that belongs not to a universal subject but to one constructed as specifically masculine, a subject for whom such bridging and merging serves not merely as disinterested transcendence of "ontological chasms" but as a means to his invention/inversion of himself as "daughterson," which is to say, a symbolic reconstitution of his early mother/self.

economy upon a male body represented as disadvantaged in comparison to the mother's, a body symbolically made whole through a regressive reincorporation of a fetishized maternal body by means of his happy art.

Even as Joyce's inversions demonstrate the unnecessariness of essence to accident, of the sexed body to the signs of gender, then, they necessarily (or nircissistically) presuppose an essentialist position. Before one can transgress a barrier, one must first posit it; and in positing the barrier Joyce's dreamer-artists implicitly posit gender as reality, accident as essence. Agreeing with Kristeva that it is a mistake to look for "female" subject positions in Joyce's works, I want also to suggest that the essentialism of Joyce's texts originates in and continues, even as it deconstructs, a masculine subjectivity that defines itself by its very reification (or essentializing) of masculinity, femininity, and the boundary between them. Joyce's myth of a "vaulting feminine libido . . . controlled and easily repersuaded by the uniform matteroffactness of a meandering male fist" gratifies a desire that his self-vivisections represent not only as not specific to female subjects but as quite specific to this particular masculine subject: one who inhabits a male body and interprets himself in respect to sexual difference as does the *Wake*'s dream-subject, his pen-wielding male fist meandering through and re-creating his culture's mythologies of the feminine (*FW*, 123.8–10). In the *Wake*'s parodic dream-world, Joyce self-consciously generates "feminine fiction[s] stranger than the facts," much stranger: daughters, doaters, daughtersons that—like Marina, Miranda, and Perdita in Stephen's Shakespeare theory—make up the male artist's self-professed loss or lack (*FW*, 109.32). Orchestrating all these "doaters of inversion," these female shadows of a substanceless early self, is finally a substantial artist-son who, unlike Ovid's Narcissus, turns necessity ("If only I could escape my own body!") into invention, casting himself imaginatively into reflecting pools of language; remembering and recovering his drowned early self while never forgetting that "here's nobody here only me" (*FW*, 624.30).

Notes on Contributors

JOSEPH A. BOONE is Associate Professor of English at the University of Southern California. He is the author of *Tradition Counter Tradition: Love and the Form of Fiction* (1987) and co-editor, with Michael Cadden, of *Engendering Men: The Question of Male Feminist Criticism* (1990). He is at work on two books, one on issues of sexuality and narrative in modern fiction (of which this essay is a part) and the other on the homoerotics of Orientalism in narratives of the Near East.

MARILYN L. BROWNSTEIN is Assistant Professor of English at the University of Georgia. She has published articles on postmodern theory, neuroscience and gender, Marianne Moore, Plato's *Phaedrus*, and Joyce's *Finnegans Wake*. She is completing a book, *Postmodern Strategies: Cognitive Dialectics and the Dimensions of Difference*, and is co-editing a volume of essays on politics and cognitive linguistics.

JAY CLAYTON is Associate Professor of English at Vanderbilt University. He is the author of *Romantic Vision and the Novel* (1987), *Narrative and Power: Writing in a Multicultural Society* (1993), and co-editor of *Influence and Intertextuality in Literary History* (1991). He has published on nineteenth-century poetry and fiction and on literary theory and the contemporary novel. He is at work on a book titled *The Genealogy of Postmodernism*.

LAURA DOYLE is Assistant Professor of English at Harvard University. She is completing a book titled *Bordering on the Body: Racial Patriarchy, the Mother Figure, and Modern Fiction*, which combines anthropology, history, and philosophy to explain the narrative innovations and the sexuo-racial matrix of modern experimental fiction. She has also written about Jean Toomer, Virginia Woolf, and Toni Morrison.

SUSAN STANFORD FRIEDMAN is the Virginia Woolf Professor of English and Women's Studies at the University of Wisconsin-Madison. She is the author of *Psyche Reborn: The Emergence of H.D.* (1981), *Penelope's Web: Gender, Modernity, H.D.'s Fiction* (1990), co-author of *A Woman's Guide to Therapy* (1979), and co-editor of *Signets: Reading H.D.* (1990). She has published articles on narrative theory, feminist criticism, women's poetry, autobiography, modernism, psychoanalysis, childbirth metaphors, gender and genre, and women's studies. She is at work on *Portrait of an Analysis with Freud: The Letters of H.D., Bryher, and Their Circle, 1933–1934* and *Return of the Repressed in Modernist Narratives.*

CHRISTINE FROULA, Professor of English at Northwestern University, is the author of *A Guide to Ezra Pound's Selected Poems* (1983), *To Write Paradise: Style and Error in Pound's Cantos* (1984), and *Joyce and Woolf: Gender, Culture, and Modernity* (1993). She has published numerous articles on feminist theory and modern literature, and is working on a book, *Women and Western Literature: Tradition and Transformation.*

ELLEN CAROL JONES is Assistant Professor of English at Purdue University and Managing Editor of *Modern Fiction Studies*, for which she has edited the special issues *Feminist Readings of Joyce* (1989), *Virginia Woolf* (1992), and *The Politics of Modernism* (1992) and co-edited the special issue *Feminism and Modern Fiction* (1988). She has published essays on Joyce and Woolf and is completing *Writing the Other: Joyce's Ulysses*, a book on *Ulysses* read through feminist, poststructuralist, and postcolonial theories. She is also editing a collection, *Joyce: Feminist Studies.*

ALBERTO MOREIRAS is Assistant Professor of Spanish at the University of Wisconsin-Madison. He is the author of *La escritura política de José Hierro* (1987) and *Interpretación y diferencia* (1992). He has also published articles on contemporary Latin American fiction and literary theory. He is currently at work on a book on aesthetics and mourning in Hispanic fiction.

RICHARD PEARCE is Professor of English at Wheaton College in Massachusetts. He is the author of *The Politics of Narration: James Joyce, William Faulkner, and Virginia Woolf* (1991), *The Novel in Motion: An Approach to Modern Fiction* (1983), and *Stages of the Clown: Perspectives on Modern Fiction from Dostoyevsky to Beckett* (1971). He has published essays on modern fiction, modern drama, science and literature, film and literature, and teaching *Ulysses*. He is the editor of *Critical Essays on Thomas Pynchon* (1981) and *Molly Blooms: A Polylogue on "Penelope" and Cultural Studies* (1994).

ROBERT SPOO is Assistant Professor of English at the University of Tulsa, where he is also editor of the *James Joyce Quarterly*. He edited the first publication of H.D.'s *Asphodel* (1992) and co-edited *Ezra Pound and Margaret Cravens: A Tragic Friendship*, 1910–1912 (1988). He has published articles on Joyce, Pound, H.D., and other modern writers and is completing a book-length study of historiographic narrative in Joyce's *Ulysses*.

Index

Abrams, M. H., 118
Adam, 250n
Adams, Hazard, 118n
Adorno, Theodor, 250n, 278
Aeschylus, 45, 45n
African Americans, 133–34, 136, 139–40, 140n
Africans, 14–15, 171, 188; western mythologies of, 169
Ainley, Alison, 270
Aldington, Richard, 44
Almeida, Hermione de, 118n
Androgyny, 153, 173, 197n. *See also* Transvestism
Annunciation, the, 258–59, 264–66, 269–70, 277
Aquinas, Thomas, 32, 43
Archer, William, 100
Aristotle, 273
Artist, representations of the, 8, 12, 13, 15, 22, 33, 35, 39, 42, 43, 53, 63, 79, 81, 97, 100–101, 103–4, 117, 164–65, 171–73, 257–61, 270–71, 276, 280–82, 282–303
Attridge, Derek, 2
Aubert, Jacques, 62n
Autobiography, 12, 13, 26, 28, 47, 48, 55, 282–303

Baker, James R., 100n
Bakhtin, Mikhail, 128
Balmary, Marie, 227n, 230n
Barnacle, Nora. *See* Joyce, Nora
Barnes, Djuna, 156, 191, 192n, 220
Bauerle, Ruth, 93n, 132, 239n, 246n
Beja, Morris, 117–18
Bellini, Giovanni, 281
Benjamin, Jessica, 206n
Benstock, Bernard, 2, 59–60
Benveniste, Emile, 68n
Bernard of Clairvaux, Saint, 265

Bible, 162–63, 165, 169
Bishop, John, 76n
Bismarck, Otto von, 152
Blake, William, 118
Blasingame, John, 134
Boheemen, Christine van, 21n
Bömer, Franz, 76n
Boone, Joseph A., 11, 14, 15, 190–221, 196n
Bosinelli, Rosa Maria Bollettieri, 21n
Boucicault, Dion, 291
Brandabur, Edward, 98n
Bratton, J. S., 138, 139
Brewer, Wilmon, 75
Brivic, Sheldon, 2, 32, 24, 51n, 61, 246n
Brooks, Peter, 1, 10, 112, 114–16, 120–21, 126
Brownstein, Marilyn L., 11, 15, 225–56, 237n
Brunazzi, Elizabeth, 92n
Budgen, Frank, 212, 215, 217n, 271
Butler, Judith, 214
Byrne, John Francis, 45
Byron, George Gordon, 118

Chambers, Ross, 93n
Chatman, Seymour, 116
Cheng, Vincent, 161n
Chodorow, Nancy, 218, 296n
Chora, the, 260, 266, 270, 279–80
Christianity, 124, 158, 163, 171, 173, 196; Roman Catholicism, 35, 38, 41, 45–48, 50, 53, 143–46, 164–66, 168–69, 181, 251, 258n, 264–65, 269–70, 275–79, 280n, 281; Jesuits, 36, 38, 40, 164
Chrysostomos, Saint John, 277
Cixous, Hélène, 38, 110, 193, 239, 246n, 274
Clayton, Jay, 9, 13, 114–27

309

Library of Congress Cataloging-in-Publication Data

Joyce: the return of the repressed / edited by Susan Stanford
   Friedman.
        p.   cm.
   Includes bibliographical references and index.
   ISBN 0-8014-2799-1 (alk. paper). —ISBN 0-8014-8073-6 (pbk.:
alk. paper)
    1. Joyce, James, 1882–1941—Criticism and interpretation.
I. Friedman, Susan Stanford.
PR6019.O9Z6693   1993
823'.912—dc20   92-54966